THREE GERMANIES

From Partition to Unification and Beyond

SECOND EXPANDED EDITON

MICHAEL GEHLER

translated by Anthony Mathews

REAKTION BOOKS

Published by Reaktion Books Ltd
Unit 32, Waterside
44–48 Wharf Road
London N1 7UX, UK
www.reaktionbooks.co.uk

First published 2011
Second expanded edition published 2021

Printed and bound in Great Britain
by TJ Books Ltd, Padstow, Cornwall

A catalogue record for this book is available from the British Library

ISBN 978 1 78914 335 5

Contents

Foreword 7

1 Occupation and the Road to Two Different German States *11*

2 Partial Integration of the Federal Republic and the GDR
Externally and Internally, 1949–55 *54*

3 The Two German States: Bloc Building in
Central Europe, 1949/55–61 *73*

4 Germany as Two States, 1961–72 *119*

5 'Change Through Rapprochement': Détente and
Normalization, 1972–9 *150*

6 New Confrontation, Disarmament and Erosion of the
Defence Blocs, 1979–89 *175*

7 Return of the 'German Question' and the
Unification of Germany, 1989–90 *195*

8 The Consequences and Burdens of Unity: Transformation,
Stagnation and the End of the Kohl Era, 1990–98 *233*

9 The 'Red-Green' Coalition as a Half-way Experiment,
1998–2005 *260*

10 New Beginnings and Tradition: The Grand Coalition under Angela Merkel, 2005–9 *288*

11 From Europe's Troubleshooter to the Continent's Lame Duck: The Merkel Era and the Berlin Republic at a Crossroads *302*

12 Three Different Republics: Bonn – Pankow – Berlin, Attempt at a Summary *346*

Abbreviations 366
Bibliography 370
Acknowledgements 381
Index 383

Foreword

This book is about three German republics: the Federal Republic of Germany (FRG) from 1949 to 1990; the German Democratic Republic (GDR) over the same period; and the Berlin Republic since the unification of Germany. It will deal with aspects of domestic, foreign, social, cultural and economic politics.

However, there are a series of problems that need to be addressed: for a long time the events of the 1980s and '90s were hardly the object of systematic research. The key official source material for those decades is still classified, so there is a lack of work on the basic facts relating to West Germany. After the end of the GDR, the relevant files on the whole of the 40-year period became available and have been the object of research for the last three decades. The challenge as regards the subject matter and methodology consists in dealing with the FRG and the GDR simultaneously and taking them both into equal consideration. This leads to a further problem in that there are very few equally weighted accounts of the history of the two German states. Exceptions prove the rule: as a trained historian, outstanding journalist, publicist and writer, Peter Bender has published impressive analyses, as has the team of researchers led by Clemens Burrichter, Detlef Nakath and Gerd-Rüdiger Stephan, the editors of a comprehensive encyclopaedic textbook.

Younger colleagues like Stefan Creuzberger, Dominik Geppert and Dierk Hoffmann wonder how the history of a divided nation between 1945 and 1990 should be written. The discussion is still in full swing and shows the gaps and omissions left by the historiography of the respective divided nations and partial states.

A further problem arises from the fact that selective historical writing on each of the German partial states has been carried out without regard to the other state and therefore has been one-sided. The FRG and the GDR, in spite of their alienation and growth apart from each other, remained related to one another, above all as regards competition between the two systems. Each one wanted to outdo the other and to be proven the better of the two. This has had its effect on the writing of history on each side and is still the case today. The history of the GDR presented by East German historians before 1990 – as directed by the Socialist Unity Party or SED – was ideologically loaded and politically blown up into a socialist success story. The history of the FRG, on the other hand, was also largely represented by West German historians as the story of the better Germany, a Germany that emerged as the winner and champion from the inter-German confrontation. This dichotomy of success and failure, as well as the binary opposition of winner and loser, however, will not take us far in dealing with the deficiencies and weaknesses that existed in both states. In viewing the position overall, it is also not enough just to compare the two Germanies, since Germany was more than the sum of its individual parts (as Bender puts it). What needed to be done was to judge both states based on the same criteria and standards; not from either a Western or an Eastern viewpoint, but from one in between.

A decade has passed between the first and the second edition. As a central power in Europe, the new Berlin Republic had to live up to its responsibilities in the face of new challenges (the euro, refugee, Ukraine and Brexit crises, and recently coronavirus), but it was also increasingly criticized in the course of its EU crisis management and the role of Chancellor Merkel was strongly questioned. The changes in the domestic political landscape due to the entry of the right-wing Alternative für Deutschland (AfD) party into the Bundestag had to be fathomed and the last years of the Merkel era assessed.

The years in Germany from 2015 onwards are characterized by radicalized political development. The still young self-image of Germany as an 'immigration country' was subject to strong tensions and cracks. New political movements and a communication society without inhibitions have eroded the classic political system with its popular parties (the CDU/CSU and SPD). The various coalition governments were and are confronted with an abundance of hardly manageable challenges and numerous unresolved tasks for the future (digitization, climate change, migration, transport infrastructure and housing), which have brought them to the limits of their capacity to act and solve problems. Yet Germany's society and politics are more divided than they have been since the state was united. The Grand Coalition is in an existential crisis. This has already led to weakened German leadership of the EU. Without including the continuing history of the three German states – the

GDR is still very much present in the minds of the middle and older generation of East Germans – Germany can hardly be understood 30 years after 'reunification', as is explored in a new chapter of this updated edition.

1

Occupation and the Road to Two Different German States

'Germany First': The European Advisory Commission (EAC) of 1943–5

The attempts by Hitler to gain 'Lebensraum' (living space) for the German people through war against Poland in 1939 to create a Greater German Reich and the attack on the Soviet Union in 1941 had failed due to the common efforts of the Allies. Up until 1943 there was neither agreement nor coordination between the three main Allies of the coalition against Hitler as to the question of what should happen after the victory. With the defeat of Nazi Germany in sight, the post-war planning of the Allies became more clearly engaged from the autumn and winter of 1943. The Moscow Foreign Ministers conference from 19 October to 1 November decided on the formation of the European Advisory Commission (EAC). From 15 December 1943 up to the conclusion of its activity on 2 August 1945 – its roles were then taken over by the Allied Control Council as well as by the Council of Foreign Ministers of the Four Powers – the EAC drafted four key documents: first, the draft of a declaration of surrender (25 July 1944); second, an agreement by the Three Powers on the zones of occupation and the administration of 'Greater Berlin' (12 September 1944); third, the control mechanism (14 November 1944); and fourth, the declaration of the Four Powers in relation to the defeat and the assumption of the power of governing Germany (5 June 1945). Apart from Germany, the EAC was only concerned with Bulgaria and Austria. It was the British who were thinking most along European lines in the context of the EAC and who also were the most interested in its continued existence. The Allied Consultation Committee (ACC), which only had its first session on 18 December 1944, dealt with summaries of the proposals put forward by the 'minor allies' but these were hardly taken into account by the EAC. The British government kept its dominions informed in confidence about the consultations and gave privileged treatment to the Committee for French Liberation (CFLN). The other European exiled governments in London were generally only kept informed superficially and given short notice before the publication of the results. The treatment of the other partners as 'minor allies' demonstrated that for the USA and the USSR Europe was only a marginal factor. Although the work of the EAC made only slow progress, its output was considerable. In the shape of the agreements on the control procedures and the establishment of the occupation zones in Germany and Austria (including Berlin and Vienna) it had done decisive preliminary work for the future Four Power presence in the two countries. There was no consensus for a dismemberment of Germany arising from the various deliberations of the 'Big Three'. The EAC therefore aimed at only minimum compromises while a lot was left open as regards the fundamental questions over which the Allied Control Council in Berlin also failed. The great expectations that the British Foreign Office had had for the EAC were not to be fulfilled, particularly since it never discussed the shape of Europe in the post-war period. Quite apart from the fact that the EAC was sufficiently preoccupied with the agreements on the surrender and the occupation systems of Germany, the other members lacked the political will. Washington and Moscow were not prepared to make the EAC into a forum for the planning and restructuring of Europe after the end of the Second World War.

The Contradictory Liberation of 1945: Unconditional Surrender, 'Collapse' and 'Zero Hour'

Following the demand of the coalition against Hitler at the Casablanca Conference of 14–26 January 1943, the German Wehrmacht surrendered unconditionally on 8/9 May 1945. It is significant that two surrender documents were signed: in Reims for the Western military and in Berlin-Karlshorst for the Soviet military. The end of the Nazi regime proceeded with the military occupation of the Reich by Allied troops. The victors and those suppressed and persecuted by the Nazis in the concentration camps saw the overcoming of Hitler's Reich as a liberation from Nazi terror and referred to it as such. The majority of Germans did not necessarily see it as a liberation. In the wake of the complete collapse of the nation, the prevailing atmosphere was one of depression, but also one of relief at the end of a war that the Germans had experienced as a catastrophe due to the British, American and Canadian carpet bombing of the cities, a time of extreme privation and great suffering. Over 500,000 civilians had been killed. Many German towns were

War damage in German towns.

reduced to rubble and ashes in the last weeks of the war. Nearly 90 per cent of
the beautiful medieval district of Hildesheim, with its many churches, was destroyed
by British and Canadian bombs on 22 March 1945. This kind of liberation was
ambivalent and contradictory, particularly since it was associated with the loss of
family members as well as belongings and property. Not just large towns but even
medium-sized and small towns were badly affected by bombing. Around five
million homes were totally or considerably destroyed. The Germans lived in base-
ments under the ruins, in huts or emergency dwellings. The supply of electricity
and gas had largely broken down. Water was in short supply. The word *Zusammen-
bruch* ('Collapse') can be explained not only in relation to the collapse of the

German Reich and the defeat of the Nazi regime. Buildings, institutions, traffic and transport infrastructure had collapsed and been destroyed; the railway and the postal service no longer functioned; the authorities and official services had disintegrated. The 'liberators' had not been summoned by the majority of the *Volksgenossen* (citizens of the Nazi state), nor had they desired the occupation. There were bans on fraternization. In 1945 one could still not speak of friendship and partnership or an alliance on a general level. For many people that year was a deep personal turning point: National Socialism had proved to be a criminal and destructive movement. Occasionally, one had shared the responsibility and the guilt. Traditions were severed and values shaken. Values like leadership, hard work, the nation, law and order had originally provided direction. Now they seemed worthless; in any case, they had been used as tools and corrupted by Hitler and his regime. For many Germans the occupation of the country meant insecurity and fear of the future. There were a number of suicides on the part of authority figures and civil servants along with those who supported and sympathized with National Socialism.

The military occupation and the different occupation policy in the Soviet occupation zone and in the Western zones meant in practice the setting-up of different social, economic and organizational systems that brought about an internal split within Germany. It was not Hitler and his war that many Germans saw as a kind of punishment from God, but the different occupation practices and the diverging Allied ideas about a future resolution of the German question that led to the division of Germany.

For many refugees and people forced out of the former German territories in the East who ended up in what was to become the Federal Republic, the term 'liberation' came over as cynical. The people in the Soviet Occupation Zone did not feel liberated at all. Rapes, arrests and deportations were commonplace in the first months after the end of the war. A new dictatorship was set up, associated with repression and terror. At first, for many Germans, it was a matter of getting by from day to day. Together with the military authorities, transport problems had to be solved and the population supplied with food, fuel and clothing. The *Trümmerfrauen* ('women of the ruins') carried out valuable work clearing the rubble left over from the bombing and rebuilding the towns. The catastrophic situation as regards supplies was worsened by the refugees and people forced out of the former German territories in the East. The need for a political new start was seen as a zero hour, and referred to as such. In fact there were many ideological and personal continuities as regards the economy, politics and administration. The room for manoeuvre was limited by the fact that Germany was becoming the theatre of the East–West conflict in Europe that was taking on a global dimension. The occupation powers were the key factors in the political development, yet it would be wrong to think that the Germans were not able to take their fate into their own hands and join in the process of decision-making, as we shall see. At first, however, the Allies had all the say.

Yalta, Potsdam and the Forced Removal of Germans from the Eastern Territories in 1945

At the conference in Yalta from 4 to 11 February 1945 the 'Big Three' – Joseph Stalin, Franklin D. Roosevelt and Winston Churchill – decided to divide Germany into zones. For Berlin, the capital of the Reich, there was to be a settlement as to the sectors. France was later recognized as an occupying power and was allocated its own zone in the southwest, made up from the American and the British zones, along with a sector in northwest Berlin. The British zone consisted of the northwest of Germany, while the Americans occupied Bavaria along with Bremen and Bremerhaven. The USSR in its occupation zone in central and eastern Germany had put the north of East Prussia under its administration and the rest of Eastern Germany beyond the Oder-Neisse Line under Polish administration, without consulting the Western Allies. Germans living there were expelled and forced to flee. Stalin thus created a *fait accompli* and the Western powers looked on helplessly and without any power to act. The situation in the West was worsened by millions of refugees and people driven out of the former German territories in the East.

At the Potsdam conference from 17 July to 2 August 1945 far-reaching decisions about the future treatment of Germany were made. The aims of the Big Three were the abolition of the Nazi Party and its associations; decentralization of the German economy; removal of Nazis from official and semi-official positions as well as from positions of responsibility in private businesses; democratic renewal of education and the legal system; the reinstatement of local autonomy and permission for the formation of democratic parties. 'German militarism' and Nazism were to be 'eradicated' and all measures undertaken to prevent Germany from threatening its neighbours or the peace ever again. Part of this goal was the destruction and dissolution of 'Prussia', which was held to be the actual root of 'German militarism', and by a decision of the Allied Control Council in 1947 it was abolished. This decision was largely Winston Churchill's; against this background he had agreed to the western shift of Poland carried out by Stalin in 1945 that had been allotted by him to the Soviet sphere of influence in the last years of the war.

The German population was to be given the opportunity to 'reconstruct their life on a democratic and peaceful basis'. Clearly diverging concepts of 'democracy' still remained. The decision made in Potsdam to treat Germany as an economic unity was rejected and sabotaged by France, the fourth occupying power. The French rejection of a centralized administration covering the whole of Germany was to prejudice things in the direction of the division that took place in the following years. Furthermore, Potsdam established that the occupiers could demand reparations in their zones following their own imagination. Thus, the principle of economic unity was already damaged below the waterline. Germany's foreign assets were taken over by the Allied Control Council and divided between the navy and the merchant marine.

A pie chart, 'Census of 13.9.1950', shows the proportion of refugees and people forced to leave the former German Eastern territories. 56.9 per cent were from the Eastern territories, 24 per cent from Czechoslovakia and 8.2 per cent from the former republic of Poland and the Free City of Danzig (Gdansk), from Eastern and South Eastern Europe 8 per cent and from Western countries or from overseas 2.9 per cent.

In Potsdam, the Western powers were represented by new politicians who were partly inexperienced regarding foreign policy. The place of Franklin D. Roosevelt, who died on 12 April 1945 and who had been responsible for bringing the USA into the war, was taken over by Harry S. Truman. The British Prime Minister, Winston Churchill had been voted out of office and replaced by the Labour leader, Clement Attlee. Stalin exploited the weakness and indecisiveness of his Western negotiating partners. The communist-led Polish government was to be given the Eastern German territories up to the Oder-Neisse Line in compensation for the Eastern Polish territories handed over to the USSR. This question led to conflicts in Potsdam, but in the agreement of 2 August 1945 the Western powers finally accepted the Oder-Neisse Line as the Western border of Poland, subject to a definitive resolution by the peace treaty with Germany. At the same time they agreed to the 'transfer' of Germans from these territories as well as from Poland, Hungary and Czechoslovakia, which should be carried out 'in an orderly and humane manner'. The reality looked completely different, however: forced removal had started months before the conference. The first waves of fleeing Germans got underway against the threatening background of the advancing Red Army. Further waves, which one could call an organized forced removal but which were officially termed 'emigration', were carried out in a disorderly and inhumane manner. Most of the people had to leave all their belongings behind. Approximately 12 to 14 million Germans were forced to flee from the former German Eastern territories and the neighbouring states (Poland, Czechoslovakia and Hungary). The number of dead and missing cannot be calculated exactly due to the chaotic circumstances. They are usually estimated at more than two million. Enormous numbers of people sought refuge in the 'Free West'. The reception and integration of these masses of refugees into a land largely destroyed by the victorious powers, in which the indigenous population, themselves bombed out of their homes, found it difficult to gain shelter and in which the situation as regards supplies was extremely poor, presented an enormous additional challenge for the occupying powers and the German authorities. The overall integration of those forced to flee from the former German Eastern territories within what was to become the Federal Republic counts as one of the most considerable successes of post-war German society.

Allied Control of the Reorganization of Party and 'Länder' Politics, 1945–7

The Allied Control Council met in the building of the former Berlin Supreme Court and consisted of the commanders-in-chief of the four victorious powers who, as military governors, formed the supreme governing body in each of their occupation zones. The Control Council was concerned with the abolition of Nazi laws and regulations and with denazification, demilitarization and dismantling in accordance with the Potsdam Agreement. It had no executive power, however, but had to rely on its decisions in the form of orders, directives, laws and proclamations being carried out by the respective military governors in the different zones. The Allied occupation was seen as an obstacle on the part of nationalistically and patriotically minded Germans in their attempts to overcome the division. The Allied Control Council did not agree on a common procedure for the creation of economic unity, as the Four Power agreement provided for. The individual commanders-in-chief of the Allied military forces were able to act on their own authority in their zones. As the supreme body the Allied Control Council had to make decisions on the basis of unanimity, i.e. it was unable to act in the event of a single veto.

The four military commanders-in-chief of the American, British, French and Soviet forces in Germany announced in their Berlin declaration of 5 July 1945 the setting up of the Allied Control Council, proclaimed on 30 August 1945. The USSR, USA, UK and France as the victorious powers had the supreme authority in

The German Länder under the Occupation Powers up to 1949.

Germany, divided into four occupation zones. Berlin was given four sectors and Four Power status. The occupying powers formed Länder based on the old territorial borders within their zones. Prussia, however, was divided up into several parts by the borders of the occupation zones. The administration was filled with Germans. As early as July 1945 the Länder of Sachsen (Saxony), Sachsen-Anhalt (Saxony-Anhalt), Thüringen (Thuringia), Brandenburg and Mecklenburg were established in the Soviet occupation zone. The Office of the Military Government of the United States (OMGUS) made Bavaria, Hessen (Hesse) and Württemberg-Baden Länder in September 1945 and Bremen in January 1947. From the middle of 1946 Nordrhein-Westfalen (North Rhine-Westphalia), Niedersachsen (Lower

Saxony), Schleswig-Holstein and Hamburg were formed in the British zone, Baden, Württemberg-Hohenzollern and Rheinland-Pfalz (Rhineland-Palatinate) in the French zone. The Saarland was given a special status and included within the French customs zone. Despite the occupation political life immediately sprang up amongst the Germans. The Allies tried to appoint politically untainted people as mayors and representatives of the Länder. In Summer 1945 political parties were permitted, often harking back to the Weimar Republic as regards their membership and organizational structure.

On 10 June 1945 Moscow issued the order for the foundation of 'democratic parties' in the Soviet occupation zone. Germany as a whole was at no time involved to any extent. One day later the Central Committee of the German Communist Party (KPD) sent out a call also directed at the middle class. It was the first party to call in Berlin on 11 July 1945 for Germany to be shown 'the way to the setting up of an anti-Fascist, democratic regime, a parliamentary democratic republic with all the democratic rights and freedoms for the people'. A union with the German Social Democratic Party (Sozialdemokratische Partei Deutschlands, SPD) was still rejected. Walter Ulbricht, who shortly before the end of the war had flown from Moscow to Berlin as the leader of the exiled German communists, was one of the signatories who launched himself with great commitment into the new political activity. Ulbricht was born the son of a tailor in Leipzig in 1893. In the course of his wanderings as an apprentice carpenter to Dresden, Nuremberg, Venice, Amsterdam and Brussels, he joined the SPD in 1912. During the First World War he saw action in Poland, Serbia and on the Western Front. In 1918 as a member of the Workers' and Soldiers' Council of the XIxth army corps, after returning to Leipzig, he joined the Spartakist League. In 1919 Ulbricht became a member of the newly formed KPD and as early as 1923 a member of the Central Committee. For a short time in 1925 he worked on the Executive Committee of the Communist International at the Lenin School in Moscow and was active as a party instructor in Vienna and Prague, as a member of the 'Landtag' of Saxony, the state parliament, from 1926 to 1928, and as a communist member of the Reichstag from 1928 to 1933. After the seizure of power by the Nazis, Ulbricht went into exile working for the KPD in France and finally in 1938 in the Soviet Union where he was a representative of the KPD at the Communist International. In 1943 he was one of the founders of the resistance group the Nationalkomitee Freies Deutschland ('National Committee of Free Germany'). In April 1945 he left Moscow along with trained party officials, named the Ulbricht Group, for Berlin where he implemented the refounding of the KPD.

On 15 June 1945 in Berlin the Central Committee of the SPD put forward ambitious demands for nationalization and, in contrast to the KPD, called for the unification of the two workers' parties 'as a moral reparation for political mistakes of the past'. The former SPD Reichstag member Kurt Schumacher had started on the reorganization of the SPD in Hanover and was elected as their chairman in May 1946. Despite serious body injuries caused by the war and internment in a concentration camp, suffering the loss of one leg, he committed himself to the work of building up a political party and went on to become one of the most outspoken political opponents of Adenauer.

The division of Germany into Allied zones of interest had a debilitating effect on the development of democracy and the formation of parties, both at the level of the whole state and at the level of the Länder. The division immediately manifested itself at the party-political level.

In June 1945 the Central Committee of the SPD in Berlin under Soviet supervision had called for the 'unity of organization of the German working class', but this was categorically rejected by Schumacher. The intensification of the differences led to a separation on the organizational level as early as the Reich conference of the SPD at Wennigsen near Hanover on 5–6 October 1945: the Central Committee was to be responsible for the Soviet Occupation Zone, Schumacher for the Western zones. Amongst other things, it was Schumacher's rigid anti-communism, his inflexible attitude and his desire to keep the KPD separate from the SPD. When the communists realized that they would have fewer supporters than the SPD, from autumn 1945, with the support of the Soviet Military Administration in Germany (SMAD), they pressed for a merger with the SPD of the Soviet Occupation Zone. Schumacher rejected both the claim of the Berlin SPD to represent the whole of Germany and the merger with the KPD. The split in the German labour movement culminated in the merging of the KPD and SPD into the Socialist Unity Party of Germany (Sozialistische Einheitspartei Deutschlands, SED) in the Soviet Occupation Zone. This had a peculiar prehistory.

The KPD initially rejected the wish for the unification of the two left-wing parties that had been expressed by a number of social democrats and by the SPD Central Committee. For the time being, each of the parties was to be consolidated and the Soviet Occupation Zone structured according to the communist model by cooperation with the SMAD. When it became clear that the KPD could expect to gain less approval than the SPD and the 'bourgeois' parties, from October 1945 the KPD called for unification with the SPD. This party and its Central Committee in Berlin, led by Otto Grotewohl who laid down conditions for the unification, came under increasing pressure from the SMAD. Arrests of SPD politicians began. A ballot on the merger was stopped by the SMAD. The ballot of SPD members which took place in the Western sectors of Berlin on 31 March 1946 with 73 per cent of the votes cast resulted in over 82 per cent of the votes against a unification with the KPD. Nevertheless, the Central Committee of the SPD gave in to political pressure. On 19 and 20 April 1946 the 15the KPD Party Conference and the 40th SPD Party Conference decided in favour of unification with the SED. The Communist Wilhelm Pieck and the Social Democrat Otto Grotewohl cooperated as chairmen of the new amalgam. The official positions within the Party were at first occupied on equal basis. After Tito's break with Stalin in 1948, which started Yugoslavia on its own socialist path, the SED was transformed into a rigid party of cadres, a 'party of a new type' as it was called, following the course of the Communist Office of Information (KOMINFORM) and submitting to Moscow's way of seeing things. Ideas about a particular German way to socialism were shelved. In 1949 the SED came out against 'social democracy'. The unification of the KPD and the SPD into the SED, finally carried out under Soviet Communist pressure, confirmed Schumacher in his stand, particularly since the social democrats' area for manoeuvre in the Eastern Zone had been reduced to zero. Critics amongst them, as well as 'old communists' who had opposed the merger, were interned in a newly erected camp in Buchenwald within the area of the former Nazi concentration camp. Thousands of opposition figures died in this way. Not until the *Wende*, the 'change' in 1989–90, did the crimes and misdeeds carried out there come to light.

After the shock of the opening up of the concentration camps the occupation powers at first lacked a belief in the moral integrity and political reliability of the Germans. The USA and Great Britain did not give permission for the formation of political parties in their occupation zones until August and September 1945. The newly formed Christian Democratic Union (CDU) and its Bavarian sister party, the Christian Social Union (CSU) were no longer comparable with the Centre Party, or the Bavarian People's Party, of the Weimar Period. This was particularly because as new Christian, bourgeois collective movements, they arose from the resistance to National Socialism; they developed a profile going beyond religious denomination and thus were able to win over Protestant voters who in the 1930s had voted for the German nationalist or liberal parties. The CDU and the CSU became influential People's Parties of the centre right which were to shape the history of the Federal Republic and Bavaria for decades.

The CDU was founded in Berlin, Cologne and Frankfurt am Main. At the head in Berlin and the Soviet Occupation Zone was Jakob Kaiser, who propagated a

'Christian socialism' and therefore was also acceptable in the Western zones. This programme was propagated in the Rhineland by Karl Arnold, influencing the Ahlen Programme of 1947. In the Soviet Occupation Zone the CDU joined the anti-fascist bloc and so lost its independence. All Christian democrat groupings in the West united at the 'Reich conference' in Bonn-Bad Godesberg from 14 to 16 December 1945, under the common name CDU, without forming an overall organization. On 13 October 1945 in Bavaria the CSU was founded as an autonomous party going beyond religious denomination. It was more conservative and at the same time more Federalist than the CDU.

The central figure in the founding of the CDU was Konrad Adenauer. Born in Cologne in 1876 as the son of a master baker and later civil servant, after studying law, Adenauer became a junior judge and from 1906 was a member of the local council in Cologne. He aligned himself with the Catholic political party 'Zentrum'. The Rhineland Catholic quality, an automatic religious tendency and the rejection of the Prussian Protestant world of the Wilhelminian Period put social limits on his success. This gave rise to one of his lifetime principles, 'to become something' by his own efforts. From 1917 to 1933 he held the office of Oberbürgermeister (Chief Mayor) of Cologne, and was a member and president of the Prussian State Council. During the Franco-German conflict over the occupation of the Ruhr in 1923 he was in favour of a Republic of the Rhineland separated from Prussia within the German Reich and under French influence, in order to contribute to the reduction of the potential for confrontation. Dismissed from all his official positions by the Nazis in 1933, he defended himself in court against all allegations made against him, succeeded in gaining an additional payment of his royal pension and used the period of his political exile to build a big house near Bonn. As a result of the enthusiasm and opportunism of many Germans about National Socialism Adenauer had considerable doubts as to their political maturity. This basic mistrust that he had towards his own people was to remain with him when he later became Federal Chancellor. Following the attempt on Hitler's life on 20 July 1944 Adenauer was arrested in August and imprisoned for some months, but he managed to escape and survive. In 1945 the US military government appointed him Chief Mayor ('Oberbürgermeister') of Cologne; however, the British General John A. Barraclough dismissed him after a few months for 'incompetence' over the organization of food supply and the clearance of rubble. The British banned him from involvement in party activities from 6 October to 4 December 1945. Adenauer still retained his party political ambitions and in 1946 he took over the chairmanship of the CDU both in the Rhineland and in the British zone. In 1950 he became its first Federal chairman.

The strongly socially oriented Ahlen Programme was issued by the CDU in the British zone in February 1947. While the British military government was open to socialist ideas, the US occupation authorities rejected them. US General Lucius D. Clay, who was in favour of a liberal economic system in his zone, supported the commitment to US credits for the reconstruction of Germany. These could only be obtained from the US Congress for a non-socialist national economy.

The CDU was very soon in accordance with the occupation policy of the USA. The influence of the trade unions within the party, however, soon decreased in favour of the bourgeois-capitalist and industrial wing. The CDU departed from the Ahlen Programme. It was never declared invalid, however. In the 'Düsseldorf Principles' of 15 July 1949 the CDU declared itself to be in favour of a 'social market economy', which Ludwig Erhard propagated under the slogan 'Prosperity for all'.

The founding of the liberal parties after 1945 helped to overcome the separation that had existed since the nineteenth century between right-wing and left-wing liberalism. Primary men of action were the former supporters of the German Democratic Party (Deutsche Demokratische Partei, DDP) and the German People's Party (Deutsche Volkspartei, DVP). On 5 July 1945 the Liberal Democratic Party of Germany (Liberal-Demokratische Partei Deutschlands, LDPD) was set up under the former 'Oberbürgermeister' of Zittau and an earlier Minister of the Interior in the Weimar Republic, Wilhelm Külz. The party stood for the whole of Germany, its influence, however, was restricted to the Soviet Occupation Zone. The strongest area of involvement on the part of the liberal parties in the Western zones was in Baden and Württemberg. Theodor Heuss and Reinhold Maier were the leading figures here. In Hamburg the Party of Free Democrats was founded in September 1945 which later, as a Federal Party, was to be known as the Free Democratic Party (FDP). In both the British and American zones liberal parties were set up in 1946, and later formed in the French zone. Their aims were oppositional to the influence of the churches and support for private enterprise.

After taking part in the German People's Congress in the Soviet Occupation Zone and coming under the influence of the SED, the LPDP, which had been formed in 1947 with a Germany-wide party organization, quickly broke up. The regional parties in the Western zones merged with the FDP in Heppenheim an der Bergstrasse on 11 December 1948. Its first Federal chairman was Theodor Heuss.

Different Perspectives on Remembering the Past

When one considers the concentration camps such as Buchenwald on the later GDR territory or Bergen-Belsen in the British occupation zone, later the Federal Land of Lower Saxony, significant differences arise in the development of perspectives on remembrance of the past in the two emerging German states. In the case of Bergen-Belsen the first move towards the setting up of a memorial was made by the prisoners themselves, when they erected a temporary wooden memorial amidst the mass graves on 25 September 1945 on the occasion of the Congress of the Liberated Jews. As the barracks at the Bergen-Hohne parade ground, which had at first been used as an emergency hospital for the survivors of Bergen-Belsen, were turned into a camp for Jewish displaced persons in the course of summer 1945, the Jewish survivors of the concentration camp were actively involved in setting up the memorial site. Already on the first anniversary of the liberation, 15 April 1946, the Belsen Jewish Committee unveiled a memorial to the Jewish victims of the Holocaust. This was positioned on a flat-topped pedestal with three steps leading up to it; it consisted of a tall squared stone and carried an inscription in both Hebrew and English recalling the approximately 30,000 Jews murdered at Bergen-Belsen. Following the decision by the British military government to turn the area into a fitting burial and memorial site, work was started in early 1947 on the construction of a large memorial consisting of a 24-metre-high obelisk and a wall of inscriptions 50 metres long on which the victims of Nazi persecution who died on this spot were remembered in various languages.

Along with the big extermination camps such as Auschwitz, Belzec, Treblinka and Sobibor, which were not situated within Germany, the concentration camps on German soil were also to be included as memorial sites. In the concentration camp of Buchenwald near Weimar the first memorial act had already taken place a few days after liberation: on 19 April 1945 the prisoners who had just been liberated set up a provisional memorial on the roll call square. A black wooden column on the front of which was written 'K.L.B.' for the concentration camp of Buchenwald and the number 51,000 calculated at the time as the total dead, stood in memory of all of those who had died. In their national groups, the concentration camp prisoners paraded past the memorial and paid their last respects to their dead fellow prisoners. The 'Buchenwald oath' was spoken in four languages:

We of Buchenwald . . . here do swear before the whole world, on this site of Fascist atrocities. We will not cease the struggle until the last guilty person has been sentenced by the court of all the nations. The destruction once and for all of Nazism is our watchword. To build a new world of peace and freedom is our ideal. This we swear to our murdered comrades and their families. As a symbol of our readiness for this struggle raise your hand and make the oath: 'We swear!'

Even at the first memorial commemorating the victims of Buchenwald not all of the victimized groups felt that they were being addressed, as particularly the persecution policy of the National Socialists motivated by racial biological theory had been edited out. As early as 1945 the first suggestions were made for a permanent memorial site. Because of the takeover of the area by the Soviet People's Commissariat of Internal Affairs (NKVD) and its use as a Special Camp, however, this wish could not be fulfilled. The local KPD leadership of Thuringia and other former concentration camp prisoners who took over leading positions in the KPD gave the new director of the University of Architecture and Creative Arts, Hermann Henselmann, the task of developing a plan dedicated to the motto 'In the suffering of terror solidarity of the new Europe is forged amongst the prisoners from 36 nations'. Nevertheless this proposal could not be turned into reality. From 1947 a temporary memorial was erected in Weimar on the anniversary of the liberation of the camp by the Allies. It displayed a red stripe that pointed towards a biased representation of the society of the prisoners as 'anti-fascist resistance fighters' and leading to the disappearance of the victims of the Nazi racial policy. The prisoners' cemetery, in which the people who died after liberation had been buried by the Americans near the mass graves of spring 1945, was overlooked during the debates about building a permanent memorial.

In 1949 the SED became directly involved in the planning of a memorial site when Walter Ulbricht gave to the Buchenwald Committee of the Association of People Persecuted by the Nazi Regime (VVN), set up in 1947, the task of preparing a design for a memorial, or monument of admonition. The development of the earlier planned memorial had been overtaken because the information department of the Soviet Military Administration (SMAD) had proposed to turn the camp, in which there were still people interned at this time, into a memorial site. After the Central Committee of the SED had also agreed to this project, emphasis was laid on the development of the prison camp that had still not been vacated. Through the recognition of the anti-fascist resistance fighters, the GDR was to be legitimized as a new, better Germany. The name 'Thälmann Memorial Site' referred to the former chairman of the KPD, Ernst Thälmann, who represented the anti-fascist resistance and was a symbol for the communists and their fight for freedom. After the site of the camp had been handed over to the GDR, in May 1952 the implementation of the decision of the Central Committee of the SED of 9 October 1950 began (i.e. the dismantling of the majority of the prison camp along with the former SS quarters). Only the crematorium in which Thälmann had been shot on 18 August 1944, the gateway with its watchtowers and parts of the barbed wire were to be kept; the former prisoners' area was to be wooded over. The first permanent exhibition was set up in the former canteen of the prison camp by the Museum of German History in Berlin in 1954. With the setting up of a memorial tablet to Thälmann the foundation was laid for remembrance in the GDR, particularly highlighting the communist resistance, about which silence was maintained for a long time in West Germany. Not only the official emphasis on the communist prisoners but also the architectural development of the memorial site – which displayed an interweaving of erasure and preservation of what remained of the camp – was directed towards a particular model of interpretation in which, however, the erasure and memorializing of the Special Camp was not at issue. The camp itself represented an equivocal and ambivalent history; it stood too much for vulnerability, impotence and suffering for it to be capable of being integrated into a decidedly heroic history of political resistance led by the communists without minimizing what remained. In face of this fact, the playing down of what remained was the basis of the playing up of the signification in a heroically communist manner.

The inauguration of the Buchenwald National Memorial Site took place on 14 September 1958. It was laid out in such a way that the visitor entered the gate by walking down steps bordered by embossed columns towards the mass graves ringed by walled enclosures, intended to symbolize the 'night of fascism'. Next, one came to the 'avenue of nations', symbolizing the common international fighting spirit, and the 'freedom steps' up to the statue representing the liberated prisoners along with the 'freedom tower'. The visitor was supposed to understand and appreciate that the victory of communism was inevitable. One was to visualize the autonomous liberation of the prisoners and the release at the hands of the antifascists, i.e. by the GDR. In addition, one should understand that the struggle for the achievement of communism had to continue. The identification with the GDR was to be equated with the rejection of West Germany and the Western alliance as potential successors to the SS state. These ideas of commemoration dominated by communist propaganda were largely adhered to until the end of the GDR.

During the GDR period the Special Camp No. 2 was not discussed. The fact that a camp of the Soviet Occupation Zone had existed on the site of the former concentration camp was not denied, but it was portrayed as a typical internment camp in the context of denazification by the Allies. The large number of deaths at the Special Camp as well as the existence of mass graves in the area was suppressed. Up until the end of the GDR a silence was imposed on the history of the Special Camp in the Soviet Occupation Zone.

The taboo was only broken against the background of the events of 1989/90. The comprehensive contrast in the different perspectives on remembrance of the past in East and West Germany, taking Bergen-Belsen as an example, shows that the end of the Second World War was a caesura (cutting off a historical process). The Germans now had to come to terms with the crimes of the Nazis. The full extent of the atrocities of the Nazi extermination policy towards the Jews was not at first known to the population; the pictures and films of the conditions in the concentration camps liberated by the Allies, however, caused shock and horror amongst the public. It was not only the guilt of the Nazi regime that was at issue but also one's own individual responsibility. Against the background of denazification, many Germans attempted to distance themselves from National Socialism by portraying themselves simply as fellow travellers or even as being persecuted or oppressed by the Hitler regime. The direct attribution of guilt by the Allied powers in addition contributed to the denial of one's own involvement and to fend off any accusation of personal guilt. The Germans largely rejected any collective attribution of guilt and repressed what had happened. This made the task of remembrance more difficult in both parts of Germany, strengthed by the new confrontation of the Cold War in Europe and the East-West tensions as a global conflict. Only since the 1970s, which not by chance marked a period of détente in the history of the Cold War, has there been an increase in coming to terms with the Nazi past (at least in the Federal Republic). Along with this went the task of setting up memorials in general relating to the Nazi crimes. Still, the 1960s had served to raise people's consciousness of the enormous scale of the Nazi crimes in light of the debate about those responsible and the statute of limitations for murder. Noteworthy here is the trial against Adolf Eichmann in Israel in 1961, attracting worldwide attention, but also the Auschwitz trials (1963–5, 1967–8) and before that the Treblinka trials (1950–51, 1964–5) in the Federal Republic. There were eyewitness accounts to all aspects of Nazi crime like euthanasia, the historic sites were often transformed into memorial sites or extended as such. Unlike in East Germany there was an earlier coming to terms with the task of remembrance, admittedly not in the sense of remembering all the victims of Nazi rule. Above all the purpose was to legitimate communism. In the Soviet Occupation Zone or later, in the GDR, one did not remember the total range of victims but above all the anti-fascist fighters (i.e. mainly the communists) as the development at the Buchenwald memorial site demonstrated. Commemorating the Nazi period was generally given a higher priority in the GDR than in the Federal Republic, though it served less to promote knowledge about the history of National Socialism than to legitimate the developing socialist SED system as a haven of 'anti-fascism', and at the same time to discredit the political system of the capitalist Federal Republic as a refuge for former fascists, Nazis and imperialists. Commemoration of the anti-fascist struggle played a large role in the education system and in the public arena in the GDR aimed at the portrayal of itself as a better Germany.

At first there was agreement in both parts of Germany about wiping away the stains of the Nazi system. In Bergen-Belsen in the British occupied zone all the wooden huts were burned down, not just in order to eradicate disease, but also to signify the definitive victory over the Nazi regime. The buildings were seen as 'stigmata of history' and were consigned to oblivion, particularly since the larger and main extermination sites, such as Auschwitz, Belzec, Sobibor or Treblinka, were behind the Iron Curtain, where they had, however, already been partly destroyed by the Nazis in order to make them unrecognizable.

As a result of the end of the GDR and German unity, the way memorial sites in East Germany were presented had to be changed so as to overcome the bias of GDR anti-fascism and to dedicate them to a second phase of history (i.e. to come to terms with the existence of the Special Camps). The year 1989 saw the launch of a new perspective on remembrance in both parts of Germany, characterized by a critical coming to terms with the past and a reorganization of the remembrance sites of the Nazi crimes as places of information and commemoration. In the 1990s the Buchenwald memorial site was transformed following the proposals of a commission of experts in such a way that the history of the Soviet Special Camp No. 2 is accessible to the public. The perspective on remembrance was linked to a more open society and transformed by the change of the governmental and political system.

Examples Without Consequences: The IMT in Nuremberg in 1945–6 and the Subsequent Trials, Stalling of Denazification and Difficulties with Re-migration

In the Moscow Three Power declaration of 30 October 1943 on the 'German atrocities in Europe', the coalition against Hitler had announced the punishment of war crimes. In the wake of the Potsdam conference they reached an 'Agreement on the charges against the main war criminals' of the Axis powers and passed a 'statute on the International Military Court' that was set up by the victorious powers in Nuremberg, the city where the Nazi Party rallies had taken place. On 20 November 1945 the massive trial against the 22 chief culprits of the Nazi regime began. It concluded on 1 October 1946 with the judgement. Two weeks later ten death sentences were carried out. The policy planned by Hitler to gain 'Lebensraum in the East' could be proved beyond doubt. The evidence filled 42 volumes that were already published in 1947. The huge extent of the atrocities that National Socialism was responsible for, above all the genocide involving the mass murder of millions of Jews organized on an industrial scale, was documented and provoked worldwide condemnation. In the German population feelings of perplexity and shame predominated as those living in the vicinity of the concentration camps were led through the installations of death: for example, the citizens of Weimar were taken to the Ettersberg hill to see the former concentration camp of Buchenwald. Those accused at Nuremberg also included, along with high-ranking Nazi representatives, organizations such as the Nazi Party (Nationalsozialistische Deutsche Arbeiterpartei, NSDAP), the Secret Police (Geheime Staatspolizei, the Gestapo), the Security Service (Sicherheitsdienst, SD), the Stormtroopers (Sturmabteilung, SA), the SS (Schutzstaffel), the Reich government and the supreme command of the armed forces, especially the Wehrmacht (OKW). The indictment consisted of the following points: participation in the planning of a crime against peace and preparation and execution of a war of aggression; infringement of the international conventions on war (war crimes) and crimes against humanity, in particular genocide. Three of the chief people responsible, the Reich Chancellor, Adolf Hitler, and the Reich Propaganda Minister, Joseph Goebbels, along with the head of the SS, Heinrich Himmler, had already committed suicide before the trials. Of the 22 accused, twelve were sentenced to death by hanging, among them the Foreign Minister, Joachim von Ribbentrop, the head of the Wehrmacht, Wilhelm Keitel, the Minister of the Interior, Wilhelm Frick, and the Gauleiter of Franconia and publisher of the anti-Jewish magazine *Der Stürmer*, Julius Streicher. Keitel uttered these remarkable last words: 'I have believed. I have been wrong and have not been able to prevent what should have been prevented. This is my guilt.' Although it was not clear what Keitel had positively believed in, these words, unlike in the case of other Nazi war criminals, testified to a certain degree of insight into his own failure and personal guilt. Hermann Göring committed suicide. The former Reichsleiter, or leader of the Nazi Party, Martin Bormann, was sentenced to death in absentia. Seven of the accused were given prison sentences between ten years and life. There were also controversial acquittals, such as those of the former Reich Chancellor, Franz von Papen, and the former head of the Reichsbank, Hjalmar Schacht. The IMT condemned the NSDAP-Führerkorps, the Gestapo, the SD and the SS as 'criminal organizations'. The SA was not condemned, however, neither were the Reich government, the general staff nor the Wehrmacht. Those sentenced were put in the prison for war criminals at Spandau in Berlin, which was under alternating Four Power supervision. They were kept there until the 1960s. The 'deputy Führer', Rudolf Hess, was given life imprisonment. He had been tricked by the British Secret Service into flying to Scotland on 10 May 1941 with a peace offer for the British, aimed at backing Hitler for his war against Soviet Russia. Moscow had no interest in an early release. Hess served his prison sentence until his mysterious suicide in 1987. After his death the prison was razed to the ground, leaving no place that could be associated with a 'martyr'.

The IMT trials were closely followed by the German population and their results welcomed. For the first time the individual guilt of politicians and the military was investigated and punished. The trial process contributed decisively to the exposure of the Nazi atrocities. However legitimate it was politically and morally, it remained questionable from the legal point of view.

'Corporate crimes' were a matter of debate. The infringement of the legal principles of *nulla poena sine lege* (no punishment without a law) and *tu quoque* (equal fault) was a grave matter. Unjust treatment and crimes on the part of the Allies were not allowed either to be dealt with or punished (the 'secret protocol' of the Hitler–Stalin Pact of 1939 dividing up Poland and the massacre of Polish officers at Katyn by units of the NKVD were denied; the Anglo-American carpet bombing of German cities and the civilian population was not admissible; the dropping of atom bombs on Japan by the US went unpunished, etc.). In the London statute on the IMT it had already been agreed amongst the Big Three not to permit the raising of the question of Allied infringements of international law in the trials. 'Victors' justice' was therefore the objection. An even graver matter was, admittedly, the fact that a legal ruling on wars of aggression binding on all the powers could not be achieved and the IMT was to remain unparalleled as regards the later development of international law in the following decades (except for the war crimes trial against Slobodan Milošević in 2002–6) and thus largely ineffective on the international stage. In the aftermath of the IMT there were another 12 subsequent trials between 1946 and 1949 against 39 doctors and lawyers, 56 members of the SS and the police, 42 industrialists and bankers and 26 military leaders as well as 22 ministers and high-ranking representatives of the government. Five were acquitted, 24 sentenced to death, 20 to life imprisonment and 98 were detained for periods ranging from 18 months to 25 years. In 1951 the US high commissioner John McCloy reduced the sentences. Federal Chancellor Adenauer had also appealed on behalf of those sentenced to death. Twelve of them were executed, eleven had their sentences reduced to imprisonment and one was extradited to Belgium. Not just the big, but also the 'little' Nazis were to be held responsible.

The numbers mentioned seem low given the large-scale involvement of these groups of professions and people in the Nazi system. There never was a thorough and all-encompassing denazification. This stalled in 1948–9 in the wake of the founding of the Western German state taking place against the background of the Cold War breaking out and the rapidly rekindled anti-communism that was part of a strong and little acknowledged tradition in the history of Germany in the twentieth century (according to Josef Foschepoth). Not so much 'old Nazis' as anti-communists were now also welcomed by the USA in the 'new' Federal Republic. Communists were seen as bigger enemies of the state than (former) National Socialists. This consideration also gives the lie to the accusation, often made by German nationalists, about 're-education' being a kind of 'brainwashing' of the Germans. A long-term, thorough, systematic and effective denazification of society, the legal, mass-media and medical establishments and state institutions never actually took place. The aim, after the experiences of 1918, 1933 and 1945, was above all to build a strong and sovereign state. According to Foschepoth, this goal took precedence over democracy, liberty, pluralism and the rule of law. To this extent the 'pursuit of security' (Eckart Conze) and the concept of a 'successful democracy' (Edgar Wolfrum) appear in a rather different light.

The German term *Entnazifizierung* arose within Eisenhower's circle of advisors, coming from the American word 'denazification'. A broad spectrum of measures was meant by this, such as the eradication of the Nazi Party, the overturning of Nazi philosophy, laws and decrees, the abolition of Nazi symbols, street names and monuments, the confiscation of Nazi goods and documents, the internment of Nazi officials, the removal of Nazi authority figures from public life and the prohibition on the spreading of Nazi ideology as well as the banning of Nazi demonstrations. Denazification was an extremely complicated process linked to the official and legal endeavour, following the end of the 'Thousand Year Reich', to exclude National Socialists from leading positions in the administration and economy and to institute expiation measures against them – in proportion to their involvement in the Nazi Party, the Nazi regime and the Nazi state – ranging from fines and prison terms to the death penalty.

The Federal state of Austria, established again after 1945, passed laws on denazification. In Baden, Bavaria and Württemberg-Hohenzollern, the respective Länder decreed specific legal regulations in association with the French and American occupation regimes. Although a unified legal basis existed throughout the country, the individual occupying powers and Land authorities interpreted these in different ways, leading to deviations and differences in their respective denazification policies. A comparison of Austria with Germany points out differences as well as similarities. In relation to the purging of labour force and personnel one can identify different phases, or types of denazification: 'savage' (i.e. spontaneous and disorganized activities such as in France, Italy and the Balkans amounting to the 'settlement of scores' and acts of revenge). In Germany and Austria this hardly ever happened; denazification on the level of bureaucracy and the legal system based on criminal law was followed by denazification on the level of politics and bureaucracy in line with the expressed will of the occupiers and the new political elites, along with the later 'instrumentalized political purging' that one associates with the Soviet Occupation Zone, the later GDR.

Denazification was carried out in different ways in the different occupation zones. In the Soviet Occupation Zone it was a struggle against the 'class enemy' and thus also worked towards the transformation of the social and economic system. Land reform, confiscation and nationalization were legitimated in this way. This, on the whole, produced a contradictory image: on the one hand, the SMAD forced through denazification, particularly in legislation and administration as well as in the case of teachers; on the other, former members of the Nazi Party were soon admitted into the SED. In the French Occupation Zone, denazification was carried out in the area of administration to fit in with political expediency. The British military government for its part proceeded pragmatically, giving priority to the efficiency of the administration being set up. This took precedence over political purging, leading to the reinstatement of a number of former Nazi civil servants. The British retained all decisions on denazification measures for themselves up until the middle of 1947. The greatest number of cases of denazification was recorded in the US zone, where it was put into practice most strictly. In principle, a questionnaire with 131 questions had to be filled in. The OMGUS, working together with the German administration, had introduced so-called sentencing and summonsing courts, which acted like law courts and categorized people under investigation into five groups: the main accused; those who were incriminated; minor accused; fellow travellers; and those cleared of suspicion. Persons belonging to the first three categories faced punishments ranging from several years in a labour camp to a ban on following their profession and a loss of public office or pension, and extended to a denial of the active and passive right to vote. 'Fellow travellers' had to pay a fine. The judgements and the measures associated with them were at times seen as arbitrary and, in some cases, they were counterproductive. Even opponents of National Socialism objected to them. In Bavaria, around 70 per cent of the population were involved in trials in the sentencing and summonsing courts, causing problems for the bureaucracy. This and the fact that the administration dealt with the easier cases first caused discontent; more serious cases were postponed. Sympathy was in increasingly short supply when the US government wound down its purging activities in view of the deepening East–West confrontation. This culminated in widespread disinterest in the continuation of denazification until it was concluded on 31 March 1948; in fact the trials against those accused of serious crimes were never completed! In this climate it was not a straightforward matter for emigrants to envisage returning to Germany.

The fate of one individual might illustrate the conditions as regards social policy in relation to the recent past in West Germany after the war. Later SPD-state representative of Lower Saxony and citizen of honour of Hildesheim, Lore Auerbach, gives a glaring account of the early stages of the return journey with her parents. Born in Amsterdam on 5 August 1933, she went to schools in the Netherlands and in England. Her father was from an Orthodox Jewish family but had left the faith quite a long time before and broken with his religious origins. He had been integrated within German social and political culture, had received a doctorate in social sciences and had been active in the sphere of the employees' representative association, People, Goods and Transport (formerly Services and Transport), based in Berlin. As active social democrats, after Hitler's seizure of power the Auerbach parents had found a suitable refuge in Amsterdam, the location of the International Transport Workers' Federation, through international contacts in the sphere of the German social democrats. They were forced to move for political motives. Auerbach's mother was not of Jewish extraction; nevertheless, if she had remained in Germany, she would have been threatened with persecution because of her husband's Jewish origin. In 1938 Auerbach's father had his German nationality withdrawn. Moreover, he was deprived of the doctorate that he had gained in Germany. After exile in the Netherlands the family emigrated to England in 1940. The 'extremely high expectations' associated with a return to Germany immediately foundered on the realities of the post-war period. The whole family was shocked by the widespread destruction in Osnabrück (an experience that left Auerbach traumatized to such an extent that she did not visit the town again until decades later) and the completely untouched small town of Lemgo, seeming like an idyll and the first place of residence after the return with her parents in October 1946, formed a strong contrast. In Lemgo the family found their first place of shelter. Auerbach's father ran an employment exchange. They were accommodated in a two-room flat belonging to an unwilling landlady. The family had only been able to bring their hand luggage with them – not much for two adults, a thirteen- and a seven-year-old daughter. The winter of 1946/7 was extremely harsh – temperatures were below zero for several months up until the end of March 1947. The shipping container with the most important household goods had got stuck at the port of Hamburg due to the freezing temperatures. They were only able to get through this difficult time thanks to the meagre rations of coal and potatoes that were handed out to them. At the school which Auerbach and her sister attended Auerbach received a daily extra ration of milk on account of malnutrition, which gave rise to discontent on the part of others. Her sister was bullied by other children who were trying to get chocolate that the family did not have. There were still pupils who were keen on the Nazi League of German Girls (Bund Deutscher Mädel, BDM). They had perhaps been spared negative experiences at the hands of the Nazis and had not lived with the fear of bombing raids. Lemgo was completely intact whereas the Auerbach family had lived through the Blitz in London, including the danger from the German 'vengeance weapons', the so-called V1- and V2-bombs in the closing months of the war. After his return their father was looked upon as a 'traitor to the Vaterland' who had had a good time abroad. It is true that the withdrawal of his nationality was legally annulled after 1945, but he continued to be deprived of his doctorate. Only in 2005 was his doctorate posthumously recognized at the University of Cologne or, rather, newly awarded.

Denazification, which was carried out largely on a bureaucratic level and only half-heartedly, and was stalled in its tracks, was not only continually criticized but also obstructed and overshadowed the process of personal and political reconstruction in Germany. Complicated formalities and the obtaining of 'Persil tokens' (certificates of clearance from suspicion) involved in denazification made the idea of the 're-education' of the Germans after 1945 questionable. In the Western zones, denazification as a matter of paying lip service was generally seen as being over by 1948 so that, in the following year, 'laws bringing denazification to an end' were passed in all the Länder of the Federal Republic. Even if an example had been set by the IMT at the highest level (which remained relatively consequence-free internationally), denazification stalled at the lowest level. In the wake of the escalation of the Cold War, denazification was brought to an end. It was not a matter of 're-education' any more. Reliable anti-communists were needed and the former Nazis certainly answered to that description. The immediate construction of a capitalist German state in the West based on the private economy was the priority. The main worry of most Germans was directed towards ensuring their survival. Many hoped they could forget the past and start again 'at zero' by dealing with the tasks presently facing them. Here the term *Stunde Null* ('zero hour') becomes a problematic issue, too. The effects on society and politics were to become all too apparent at the end of the 1960s and the beginning of the 1970s.

The Start of the Cold War and Circumstances Favouring a Division Within Germany, 1947–8

Even during the war the anti-Hitler coalition was subject to friction and division. It totally collapsed two years after the end of the war. The USA and the USSR had emerged from the victory over Nazi Germany as undisputed world powers. Great Britain was already a seriously battered victor, France a latecomer that was tolerated by the other three as an occupying power. The British and the French were, in addition, dependent on American financial and economic aid. The contradictions within their constitutional structure and the different aims on the world political stage led to massive conflicts, and not just in Europe. The USA were the first with the nuclear bomb, being ahead of the USSR in terms of nuclear policy. Germany was on the front-line of the Cold War, with immediate effect on the policy of the occupation powers and their zones. The East–West confrontation influenced the German political culture in both East and West. With the formation of parties the debate on the future organization of German society and economy began, in the course of which worker participation at works' and company level and nationalization were demanded, particularly by the SPD and the trade unions. Similar thoughts informed the ideas of the Christian Democrats around Jakob Kaiser. The Ahlen Programme of the CDU in the British zone in February 1947 maintained 'that the era of the unrestrained domination of private capitalism is over'. Coal and steel were to be nationalized and big firms to be broken up. The demands for nationalization were reflected in the constitutions of the Länder. The Americans were successful in opposing nationalization, to which the British had to give in. Private firms were more easily bought up by the all-powerful US dollar than nationalized industries. The 'social control of the means of production' was thus prevented in the Western zones. Even if there was widespread enthusiasm for nationalization and worker participation in the social and economic organization in the Western zones, reflected in the constitutions and legislation of the Länder, the USA obstructed the implementation of such measures, arguing that the settlement of the economic system was the job of the whole German state alone.

Unlike the SPD, the FDP and CDU were against nationalization from the start. In the CDU in 1948–9 a move towards the policy of the 'social market economy' developed by Ludwig Erhard existed, based on capitalism and private property and giving the state the task of social protection and a politically corrective function. The controversy about the future of German foreign policy likewise soon got swept into the maelstrom of the Cold War. In view of the potential Soviet threat only very few politicians in the West were in favour of an orientation towards the East. The Western orientation, admittedly, was not uncontested. In the CDU supporters of a Western commitment dominated the proponents of a middle ground between East and West. A leading exponent of the Western option was the former 'Oberbürgermeister' of Cologne and later Federal Chancellor Adenauer. Jakob Kaiser, later Minister for German Affairs, was considered to be a 'bridge-builder' for Germany between East and West. From 1949 to 1955 Adenauer was able to decide for himself on the controversial question, especially as he had the Western powers on his side, with their policy after 1949–50 also aiming to create a West German partial state. Maintaining his position and pursuing his policy, which were to decisively mark the fate of the German nation for decades, had been made distinctly favourable by political developments from 1947 to 1949.

There had already been the first signs of a division of Germany on 1 January 1947, when the Americans and British ran their zones jointly against protests from the French and the Soviets concerning the food shortages of the winter of 1945–6. Under Anglo-American supervision the Bi-zone was given a sort of parliament, called the Economic Council, a Länder Council as well as an executive body. The Bi-zone was the predecessor of the FRG and integrated into the Western hemisphere. In its governing bodies the debate of the CDU representatives about political organization changed from demands for nationalization, as laid out in the Ahlen Programme on 3 February 1947, to the idea of a 'social market economy'. Together with the FDP the West German Christian Democrats in the Economic Council chose the independent expert Erhard as director of the administration of the economy. Later on, as Economics Minister he was to be recognized as the founder of the 'German Economic Miracle', particularly since Adenauer had no expertise in the field of economics.

In the Soviet Occupation Zone, as in the Western zones, politicians in the immediate post-war period were keen to keep up connections in order to maintain unity. Kaiser, the CDU chairman in the Soviet Occupation Zone, had succeeded in the interzonal CDU/CSU working group in March 1947 in getting acceptance for representatives from all the zones to be involved in the leading organizing bodies of the parties, so as to form a preparatory platform for a parliamentary representation of the whole of Germany within the framework of a permanent conference. The plan was agreed to in the parties of the Western zones; it failed, however, against the opposition of the chairman of the SPD, Schumacher, who rejected a conference in which the SED would take part as long as the SPD was not permitted to set up shop in the Soviet Occupation Zone. When no consensus was reached among the politicians, the minister-presidents of the Länder initiated the idea of a representation of the whole of Germany.

The Minister-President of Bavaria, Hans Ehard (CSU), issued an invitation on 7 May 1947 to a gathering of the heads of all the Länder governments for 6 and 7 June 1947 in Munich. The purpose and objective of this gathering was the 'discussion of measures . . . which are to be put forward by the responsible minister-presidents to the Allied military governments in draft in order to prevent the further decline of the German people into irredeemable economic and political chaos'. This did not mean the reinstatement of the German national state, but the consideration and organization of a future Federal state structure for Germany. Ehard represented the view that the minister-presidents were to be seen as 'trustees of the German people' as long as there was no authority for the whole of Germany. In addition to the urgent questions of food and the economy, the conference was to deal with the state of development of the Bi-zone, the existence of which was not to be threatened, and with the problem of refugees.

The participation of the minister-presidents of the Eastern zone in Munich was not certain at first. They had to gain permission from the Soviet Marshal, Vasily Danilovich Sokolovsky, for the journey to Munich and they pressed for participation. Once they had arrived in Munich, they criticized the fact that an agenda was already established and that the subject of 'German unity' had been removed from the agenda. As their desires for change were only partly taken into account, they left before the conference began. Ehard opened the conference with a commitment to 'German unity' to persuade the politicians from the Soviet Occupation Zone, who were still in a Munich hotel, to return. The only attempt to maintain German unity in the course of the conference of minister-presidents from the whole of Germany had the opposite effect. Ehard insisted on a clear and full awareness of the departure of the official colleagues from East Germany: 'This event means the division of Germany.' The representatives from the Western zones did not subsequently do anything to turn things around. For the time being they came to terms with the development towards separation. This scenario, for which the Germans themselves were responsible, had wide-ranging consequences for the complete division later on, but the Western Allies were also implicated in the process. Several factors were involved: at Schumacher's initiative, the heads of government in the British zone had agreed that the Munich conference should not deal with political subjects. France had made it a condition for the ministerpresident of its zone to deal only with economic subjects. At Ulbricht's instigation the minister-presidents of the Soviet Occupation Zone were sent with a binding recommendation that the proposal for the formation of a German central administration, through the agreement of the German democratic parties and trade unions on the creation of a German unified state, should be a specific item on the agenda and that they should 'immediately leave the conference in the event of its rejection'. The heads of the German Länder all kept to the guidelines set by the occupiers and were apparently incapable of emancipation and agreement. Added to this was the desire of the Western Allies, particularly the French and British, for the creation of a Western German state detached from the Soviet Occupation Zone. The hopes of the politicians from the Länder of the Western zones in Munich were directed towards an integration of the French zone to the 'bi-zonal economic area'. France was not to be upset by declarations on political unity. Ideas of a 'magnet theory' of the West influenced not only Adenauer but also Schumacher who, at the end of May 1947, maintained: 'The prosperity of the Western zones . . . can turn the West into an economic magnet. From the point of view of German 'Realpolitik', there is no other way to achieve German unity than through this economic magnetizing of the West which will inevitably have such a power of attraction on the East that in the long run the mere control of the apparatus of power will not be able to do anything against it. It is certainly a difficult and in all likelihood a long road.' Schumacher's supposition contained an ominous final sentence anticipating the political problems of the Western zones: for 40 years Germany and the people in the East would have to pay the mortgage on the division and the human, economic, social and political negative effects would be immense. Not just the Allies, but German politicians as well, were responsible for the division of Germany.

We are the natives of Tri-zonia, tarara-bum-di-ay.
Our girls are full of attitude . . .
We're not cannibals, you know,
but we know how to kiss for all that . . .

The good old days are over, mate,

if you don't laugh, you have to cry.

C'est la vie, one, two, three . . .

These were the approximate words of a popular carnival song by the composer, song-writer and singer Karl Berbuer that came out on '11.11.' (the first day of the carnival season) in Cologne in 1948. He had had to change the title as it was originally called the 'Bi-zonial Song'. Before 11 November it had already become apparent that the Bi-zone would be united with the French zone to become the 'Tri-zone'. In spring 1949 the London *Times* ran the headline 'The Germans are Getting Bold Again', and complained about an upsurge in feelings of revenge in Germany. In fact Berbuer was satirizing the ideology of the exaggerated 'German attitude' (i.e. 'deutsches Wesen', calling it 'Wesien', to rhyme with 'Trizonesien', something far removed from Nazi ideology). Worries on the part of foreigners were calmed and the song also caught on with the occupiers. 'Tri-zonia' was more pressing and important for German politicians than German unity, above all for economic and political reasons. Private economic concerns and fear of the Russians had a lot to do with this.

The Victory of the Western Powers in the Cold War over Germany

The Marshall Plan, End of the Allied Control Council –
The Contrasting Programme in Austria

The opposition in world politics between the USSR and the USA had already developed during the Second World War. The military and, above all, the political involvement of the Soviet Union in Central and Eastern Europe, particularly the Polish border resolution and the measures in its zone in Germany, provoked scepticism and produced resentment in the West. On 5 March 1946 the Conservative politician Churchill, at that time Leader of the Opposition, gave a speech in Fulton, Missouri, in which he visualized the image of an 'Iron Curtain' coming down on Europe from Stettin to Triest. The Soviet Union was now able to consolidate its sphere of influence, gained in the war through support from the Anglo-Americans, in Central and Eastern Europe by the promotion of communist one-party systems and the apparatus of state repression, thus prompting a decision by the West in relation to the Cold War. Further American-Soviet differences of interest in Iran, Greece and Turkey marked the start of the confrontation in 1946–7. The administration, under the new President, Harry S. Truman, reacted by establishing a policy of 'containment'. Behind this was the conception of Yalta and the division of the world into spheres of influence. Germany was the first to be affected by this: the Western zones were soon involved in the European Recovery Programme (ERP) announced by US Secretary of State, George C. Marshall, at Harvard on 5 June 1947, which President Truman had already initiated on 12 March by his proclaimed 'containment policy' in Europe. The economically catastrophic conditions in Europe were seen as an impediment to the achievement of containment by the USA. The situation regarding foodstuffs and supplies was critical. The rationing of consumer goods in the war was continued by the occupying powers. Ration cards, however, no longer secured the promised goods. As a result of the Nazi war economy, enormous sums of money were in private hands and were only equivalent to a small quantity of goods. This gave rise to the growth of the black market, where nearly everything was available. Cigarettes from the USA served as the currency. After the freezing winter of 1946/7 there was great need in the cities. Anyone who had 'Ami-Zigaretten' ('Yankee cigarettes') was able to get almost any basic foodstuffs and groceries on the black market. Many Germans were involved in this forbidden barter economy. It was a matter of pure survival. The US aid up to this time had been inadequate and further credits were a matter of controversy among the American public. There had to be a new approach making it possible to strike out in a new direction through the tying in of the European states, the introduction of a liberalization of commerce and the system of payments.

What was termed the 'Marshall Plan' was based on free capital and private economics. At a conference in Paris on 2 July 1947 the large Soviet delegation led by Molotov, on the one hand, rejected participation in the ERP. Its 'fraternal states' had to follow this line. Most of the Western European states, on the other hand, accepted the European policy of the US. The Marshall Plan was passed by the US Congress on 3 April 1948. The aid was distributed by the Organization for European Economic Cooperation (OEEC) in Paris. The ERP involved not only credits but also principally supplies of goods, fertilizer, foodstuffs, machinery and raw materials.

The ERP, amounting to $12 billion, went to Great Britain ($3.6 billion), France ($3.1 billion), the Western zones of Germany, the later West Germany ($3.6 billion), Italy and Austria (approx. $1 billion). Austria was given the aid outright, whereas the Federal Republic had to pay back a large part of the money received. In the countries that received the aid, the 'counterparts' for the aid received were accumulated in local currency in the national issuing banks. Thus in the ERP countries funds were built up with the potential for investment, making possible individual economic activities within the national frameworks – under the control, admittedly, of the USA. Moscow therefore interpreted the Marshall Plan as interference in the internal affairs of sovereign states. Foreign Secretary Molotov rejected the participation of the states in Central and Eastern Europe that were under Soviet control precisely for that reason, particularly since the ERP was linked to the imposition of capitalist and private enterprise. In July 1947 the USSR retaliated with the Molotov Plan, out of which was to emerge, in 1949, the Council for Mutual Economic Aid (CMEA) or COMECON. It was to become the counterpart to the OEEC and the Marshall Plan.

The ERP fund in 'Deutsch Mark' with the Bank of the German Länder was instituted above all for investment in basic industry, agriculture, research and the promotion of exports, as well as in the transport and building sectors. Up until 1957, the three Western zones and West Berlin (i.e. the Federal Republic, which had joined the OEEC agreement on 15 December 1949), received aid which acted as a form of self-help but was not in itself decisive for the later 'Economic Miracle'. There were other substantial factors: the hard work and willingness of Germans to rebuild their country, particularly on the part of the 'Trümmerfrauen' ('women of the ruins' who cleared the rubble left over from the bombing) and of those who returned home from the war; adequate resources being available; the concept of the 'social market economy'; the strength of the German export economy; and the healthy domestic demand and boom at the time of the Korean War. On their own efforts, and with the support of the USA, West Germany saw an unprecedented economic rise in comparison to France and Britain, which became known as the Economic Miracle and made the Federal Republic the most respected player in the Western world and the most feared opponent in the Eastern world. One image of the 'Economic Miracle' was to be the Volkswagen (the VW). On 5 August 1955 the millionth Beetle rolled off the assembly line. This model was golden and was on display in the Autostadt (Car City), the VW Museum in Wolfsburg. The VW was the engine of the economy.

The Marshall Plan was supported by US anti-communist propaganda and was above all psychologically valuable for the growing self-confidence of West Germans. However unstoppable the ERP idea 'Do good and talk about it' seemed, it was ominous for Europe and Germany as a whole: the rejection of the British nationalization policy in relation to the Ruhr was just as much bound up with the ERP as the Americanization of the political organization and economy. Moscow condemned the economic unification of the Western zones instigated by Washington to improve the organization of the supply of people's needs as well as the ERP as

The Volkswagen, part of the Economic Miracle of the Federal Republic.

conscious attempts at 'Dollar Imperialism', particularly since the repeated demands by the USSR to participate in the control of the Ruhr were rejected by London. Occupied Germany was particularly affected by the developing confrontation on the world political stage, in which the failure of mutual perceptions and misunderstandings played a considerable part. The German policy of the Soviets was interpreted by the USA as an attempt to bring the whole of Germany under their control.

Their answer was the doctrine of 'containment'. The measures for the consolidation of power in the Soviet Occupation Zone appeared in this light. What was much more serious, however, was the fact that aid for the reconstruction of Western Europe and West Germany also implied the exclusion of Central and Eastern Europe, combined with a precedent for the division of Germany, particularly since the Soviet Occupation Zone was excluded from US aid. The price paid for the division of Germany and of Europe had to be taken over by the Federal Republic and EU Europe after 1989–90. Forty years of the Cold War between the Federal Republic (from Adenauer to Kohl) and the GDR (from Ulbricht to Honecker) was a heavy price to pay.

The increasing confrontation in 1947/8 and the growing mistrust between the Soviet Union and the USA, as well as the particular ideas of France and the different development in the occupation zones, increasingly brought the work of the Allied Control Council into question. On 20 March 1948 the Soviet representative left the Allied Control Council under protest, admittedly in face of the first London Six Power conference of 23 February to 6 March, where the three Western occupying powers along with the Netherlands, Belgium and Luxembourg, as the immediate neighbours of Germany, had agreed a common state organization for their occupation zones in West Germany. Sokolovsky left the council room for good. The Allied Control Council was now history and with the blockade of 1948–9 Berlin was already a divided city, while the representatives of the occupation powers continued to drive around the international sector in Vienna as the 'Four in a jeep'. This leads us to a short digression.

The programme unfolding in Austria was in remarkable contrast to the one in Germany. Even if both German states soon came to terms with their respective occupying powers as later alliance partners and largely joined in with the East–West confrontation, there was no Cold War in Austria. The two countries followed very different paths for a long time after 1945–9. This had already started with the occupation policy: the main enemy, on the one hand, in the war for the victors was Germany. Austria, on the other, was to be 'liberated'. The occupying powers had different geopolitical aims. The policy of the Allies towards Germany was, in general, much stricter and more restrictive than towards Austria. In Berlin there was the Allied Control Council, in Vienna only an Allied Council. Whereas the Soviets intervened in the election campaign in their German zone, they did not in Austria. In both zones they wanted to create a model for one single state. While they were successful with the recognition of the government under Karl Renner on 20 October 1945, promoted even by the Western occupying powers, the Soviets temporarily failed in 1948/9 with their policy directed towards a unique German single state. Even if the forced merger of the KPD and the SPD into the SED had been successful in the Soviet Occupation Zone in 1946, the idea of a socialist 'Unity Party' in Austria did not come about. The SPÖ (Sozialistische Partei Österreichs) distanced itself from the KPÖ (Kommunistische Partei Österreichs). Moscow insisted on the unity of Austria as a state and rejected proposals by the KPÖ for a separation. The break-up of Germany was not the only option in Soviet policy on Germany. Stalin had neither decided on the founding of the GDR as a model for a communist German state, nor had he initially been in favour of a neutral Austria. Whether the Austrian solution in 1955 (unity plus freedom on condition of neutrality) was a model for Germany was officially strongly contested on the part of West Germany, but this has been interpreted in various ways by historians before and since. The fact is that – quite apart from the practicability of such a policy – Adenauer expected such a Soviet policy and strongly rejected this option right from the beginning. He was proud to have got the better of the 'dragon of neutrality', as he expressed it to Josef Schöner, the Austrian representative in Bonn.

In contrast to the Soviets, American post-war planning and occupation policy in relation to Austria was rather laid-back; although, in relation to Germany, it was very aggressive. In respect to the Marshall Plan, the Soviet Occupation Zone of Austria remained part of the European Recovery Programme (ERP), just as later the USSR tolerated the participation of the GDR in the European Common Market (economic activity within Germany was part of internal trade), forming an interesting parallel.

Another thing in common relates to anti-communism, which in both the Federal Republic and Austria was stirred up on the part of the Americans, in a way reminiscent of Nazi propaganda. It is also worth noting the different practices of denazification in Germany and Austria. While the Soviet Union adopted a moderating role in Austria and handed the task of administration over to the Austrian authorities, it saw the denazification of the GDR as part of its socialist revolutionary transformation. In contrast to the Soviet Occupation Zone in Germany, there were no internment camps for Nazis in their zone in Austria. However, such camps existed in the US zone of Austria, at Glasenbach, and in the British zone, at Wolfsberg.

It is certain that the Cold War affected the Federal Republic more sharply than Austria. Soon there developed a 'spirit of Vienna' and a far more impartial climate in the context of neutrality, whereas in the two Germanies one's orientation was politically biased. Surprisingly, the political elites in West Germany soon came to terms with the developing division, whereas in Austria the desire for the maintenance of unity was predominant and this desire found clear expression in the Grand Coalition of the ÖVP (Österreichische Volkspartei) and the SPÖ. In the case of Germany, since the failed uprising of the people in the East on 17 June 1953 (see further below) it was a matter of 'put candles in the windows and send parcels to the zone' – and this is how it remained for decades. Austria was spared this fate and the burdens accompanying it. The Cold War affected the Austrian writing of history much less than that of West Germany, which had no choice in its position on Western integration and was ready to accept a limited territorial sovereignty and the creation of an identity in terms of a partial state. The four Allies were largely seen as one whole in Austria, whereas in the Federal Republic the principle of 'Three Allies against the fourth' was the order of the day. This road also led from freedom as a part of a state to the division of Germany as a nation.

Currency Reform and Resistance to the
Berlin Blockade of 1948–9

The revaluation of the currency (the change from the Reichsmark to the Deutsche Mark) was an American precondition for the participation of the Western zones of Germany in the ERP. After the foundation of the 'Bank deutscher Länder' (BdL), a currency law issued by the three Western military governors was announced over the radio and in special editions of newspapers on 19 June 1948. The currency reform followed on 20/21 June. The exchange was carried out at the rate of 1:1. The actual reform, admittedly, consisted of a number of special measures. Each private citizen in the Western zones received a one-off per capita allowance of 40 Deutsche Marks (DM) when exchanging 60 of the old Reichsmarks and in August an additional 20 DM. Companies received 60 DM per employee to aid the transition. The assets of public funds and financial institutions were no longer valid – as a reciprocal gesture demands for compensation were made. Wages, salaries, pensions, annuities and rents were converted at a rate of 1:1, most of the other Reichsmark liabilities of private assets in the old currency at 10:1 (i.e. for 10 Reichsmarks one received 1 DM, 50 per cent in private non-bank credit balance, 50 per cent blocked in a fixed deposit account). Later 70 per cent of the monies in blocked accounts were cancelled without compensation. Thus there was a fundamental redistribution of wealth. Whereas it affected savers, since their assets underwent a devaluation at the rate of 100:6.5 as a result of these measures, the owners of real assets (land, property etc.) were advantaged. And, more important, the currency reform in the Western zones was a further step towards the division of Germany. As early as 1945 in the Soviet Occupation Zone a reform of the banking and financial system had been implemented so that two days after the currency reform in the West a similar one took place in the East. The move towards a division in respect to currency policy was thus immediately paralleled in the East. There was no alternative to this. There, banknotes up to 70 Reichsmarks per head were exchanged at the rate of 1:1, the rest at the rate of 10:1 as well as savings between 1,000 and 5,000 Reichsmarks, under 1,000 Reichsmarks at the rate of 5:1 and under 100 of 1:1. With the 'Ostmark' and the DM, there were two German currencies even before the formation of the two German states.

At the same time Erhard, in his position as director of Economics in the administration of the 'Tri-zone', acting independently and without the agreement of the occupying powers, announced the almost complete abolition of exchange controls and price-fixing. By means of these measures and the currency reform the reconstruction of the Western zones was accelerated. There followed a relaxation in the situation in the food sector. The supply of goods was more regulated in the shops and the black market was a thing of the past. The SMAD followed on 23 June 1948 with its own currency reform, which was to be extended to the whole of Berlin. As a result of these events a conflict in the former capital of the Reich was inevitable.

At the end of the war the Red Army had conquered Berlin on its own and, in the process, had suffered more losses (more than 300,000 men) than the USA during the whole of the Second World War. For giving up Thuringia and Saxony, which had initially been occupied by US troops, areas that the Americans handed over to the Soviets, the USA and the other Western powers were also allocated zones in Berlin. Within the framework of the European Advisory Commission (EAC) an administration for Berlin had already been set up on 12 September 1944 by the victorious powers. The subsequent Four Power status led to the division into sectors, but no provisions were made for the transport of troops between the zones. Only in the field of air transport was an agreement achieved at the end of November 1945 to establish three corridors from Hamburg, Hanover and Frankfurt am Main to Berlin as well as an Allied control zone above the city. The Allied Control Council had to come to an end with the departure of the Soviet representative on 20 March 1948. After the withdrawal of the Soviets from the Allied Command of the City on 16 June the Western powers created a Three Power Command in West Berlin in December 1948 and confirmed the election of Ernst Reuter as 'Oberbürgermeister' (Chief Mayor) by the assembly of city delegates elected on 5 December 1948 only in the Western sectors. There were repeated obstructions to troop transports of the Western Allies on the access roads to Berlin on the part of the Soviets. The Americans and British retaliated with a limited air lift.

In reaction to the introduction of the DM currency in the Western zones and the Western sectors of Berlin, Moscow finally declared a total blockage of rail, road and waterway links to Berlin on 24 June 1948. The Western sectors had cut off the electricity supply from the Eastern sector, likewise the delivery of milk and other foodstuffs from the Soviet Occupation Zone. The Soviet Union interpreted the Western zone currency introduced unilaterally in the West as an attempt at division and replied with the cutting off of all access routes to Berlin. For their part, the Americans and the British retaliated with a large air-lift under the overall control of the US military governor, Lucius D. Clay.

The Berlin Blockade lasted from 24 June 1948 up until 12 May 1949. Over a period of eleven months and in approximately 195,000 flights, almost 1.5 million

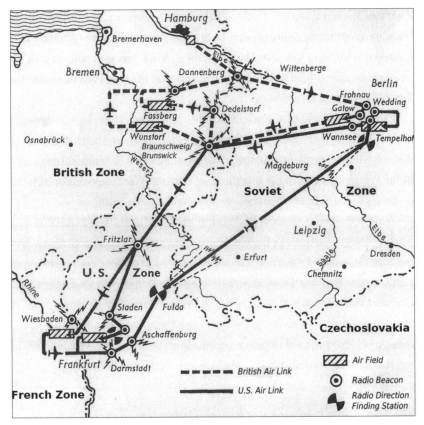

The Berlin Air Lift.

tonnes of food, coal and other goods were flown to West Berlin. The planes landed minutes apart at one of the three Berlin airports after being flown from eight West German airfields via only three air corridors, each 30 kilometres wide. With the blockade Stalin was trying to put pressure on the Western powers in order to prevent them creating a West German state directed against the USSR and to bring them back to the common table of the Four Power administration. This vain attempt failed against the resistance of the West Berlin population and the Anglo-Americans, who guaranteed the supplying of Berlin from the air. The Blockade and the Air Lift were early flash points of the first Cold War over Germany; it forced through the foundation of the West German state and made West Germans and Western Allies partners in the resistance to Soviet threats. For the bulk of the German population there was thus almost a smooth transition from Nazism to capitalist anti-communism. This strengthened cooperation between the USA, the United Kingdom and the German politicians in the Western zones.

47

When Stalin realized that he could not win with his policy, only succeeding in bringing about the opposite of what he actually wanted, he gave the green light for his representative, Jakob A. Malik, to take part in secret negotiations with the US representative, Philip Jessup, for an agreement of the Four Powers, ending the Berlin Blockade on 12 May 1949.

During the Blockade the administrative separation of Berlin was brought about. Friedrich Ebert (SED), son of the earlier President of the Reich, had been in office as 'Oberbürgermeister' in the Soviet sector since 20 November. The victory of the Western powers in the first phase of the Cold War (1947–53) contributed decisively to the foundation of the Federal Republic and the GDR.

What remained a controversial and, in the end, unanswered question was whether Stalin's Germany policy was aimed at the incorporation of Germany into the Soviet-dominated sphere or if he simply wanted to prevent the integration of Germany into the capitalist West, so as to create one united bourgeois and neutral Germany that was not hostile to the Soviet Union. In the West there was a fear of losing the whole of Germany to the USSR, and the start of an acceptance of the division of Germany, so as to form a separate West German state. Whatever Stalin was motivated by, he failed in his policy towards Berlin and Germany.

A Doubly Provisional Situation under Occupation Control

The 'Parliamentary Council' and the 'Grundgesetz' (Constitution)

The Potsdam Agreement, treating the whole of Germany as one economic unit, was not adhered to by any of the occupying powers. This became clear in the face of the difficult supply crisis of the winter of 1945–6. France refused permission for the setting up of German central authorities. The USA initially failed in pressing for a common economic administration for the three Western zones. While the USSR rejected the US proposal and France decided to wait and see, the British agreed to it.

The declaration of intent and the turning point of Anglo-American policy on Germany was the speech by US Secretary of State, James F. Byrnes, on 6 September 1946 in Stuttgart, promoting the rapid setting up of a non-communist German core state. On 1 January 1947 the American-British agreement on the 'Bi-zone' came into force. The British zone had raw materials and the basic industries at its disposal, the American zone the manufacturing industry. Together the two zones encompassed approximately 39 million people. The Americans and the British pointed to the Potsdam Agreement and called upon both the Soviets and the French to add their zones. The USSR refused whereas France played for time. Not until 8 April 1949 did it join the unified economic area, the 'Tri-zone', leading to the formation of a West German state but establishing a precedent for the division of Germany. French opposition to the combination of the three zones was overcome at the Six Power conference between 20 May and 12 June 1948 in London after the Americans and the British had gone on the offensive in London to form a West German partial state with 'quasi-governmental responsibility' out of the fusion of the three Western zones. The minister-presidents of the West German Länder at first rejected this move as well as the offers from the USSR and the SED to force through German unity in line with the People's Congress in the direction of a socialist people's movement. The 'London recommendations' were the basis for the so-called 'Frankfurt documents' that the Western military governors, Lucius D. Clay (USA), Brian Robertson (UK) and Pierre Koenig (France), handed over to the West German minister-presidents on 1 July 1948, and at the same time authorized them to convene a national assembly, creating a constitution to be convened no later than 1 September 1948. A statute was promulgated to regulate the relationship between the German government being formed and the occupying powers. The minister-presidents emphasized their view that there had to be an avoidance of 'a deepening of the split between West and East'; they opposed the characterization as a state of the polity that was being founded and said that they were only in favour of its provisional nature. As a consequence, the word 'constitution' was not agreed to. The 'Bürgermeister' of Hamburg, Max Brauer, suggested 'Grundgesetz' (the constitution of the FRG) as an alternative and this was acceptable to a majority. The minister-presidents rejected a referendum. The parliaments of the Länder would put it into force. This 'Grundgesetz' would not be worked out by a national assembly voted for by the population, but by a Parliamentary Council. Its 65 members would be appointed by the parliaments of the Länder. The minister-presidents then dropped their reservations towards the foundation of a separate West German state after Clay had warned of the consequences for Berlin, boxed in by Stalin, and its governing mayor, Reuter, had argued that the division of Germany was a reality.

The minister-presidents then called a 'constitutional convention' in Herrenchiemsee in Bavaria that sat from 10–23 August and worked out a draft constitution. On 1 September 1948 the 'Parliamentary Council', elected by the parliaments of the Länder of the Western zones, was formed in Bonn, consisting of 27 parliamentary members each from the CDU/CSU and the SPD, five from the FDP, and two each from the KPD, the DP and the Zentrum (Catholic Centre Party), along with five parliamentary members from Berlin, admittedly with only an advisory franchise. Adenauer was elected its president and Carlo Schmid (SPD) its main committee chairman. Points of contention were, above all, material questions such as the distribution of finance and division of responsibility between the Federation and the Länder. Emphasizing the provisional nature, the 'Parliamentary Council' worked out a 'Grundgesetz' for the 'Federal Republic of Germany'. On 8 May it was passed by 53 to twelve votes (the KPD, the DP and the Zentrum, as well as six of the eight CSU parliamentary members). The new organization of the state was too centralized for Bavaria's taste. All the other 'Landtage' of the West German Länder agreed to it. The three military governors then approved it. On 23 May the 'Grundgesetz' was promulagated and on 24 May 1949 it came into force. With its coming into effect, the Federal Republic was founded as a parliamentary democracy. With a conscious reference to the Nazi dictatorship great emphasis was laid on the establishment of basic and human rights. Article 1 of the 'Grundgesetz' is: 'Human dignity shall be inviolable. To respect and protect it shall be the duty of all state authority. The German people therefore acknowledge inviolable and inalienable human rights as the basis of every community, of peace and of justice in the world.' The Weimar Constitution (1919) had not recognized such a definition. In the 'Preamble' to the 'Grundgesetz' the provisional nature of the new partial state was emphasized: one can talk of a 'transition phase' in the life of the state, necessitating 'a new organization'. This should also be the case for the Germans who have been denied participation: 'The whole German people is called upon to achieve, by free self-determination, the unity and freedom of Germany.'

The Parliamentary Council had given the name 'Federal Republic of Germany' (BRD, i.e. 'Bundesrepublik Deutschland') to the new state created out of the fusion of the three Western zones by the declaration of the 'Grundgesetz'. This name expressed the federal nature of the state and the division of labour of the state between the federation as the state as a whole and the Länder. The addition of 'Germany' pointed to the claim of the West German partial state to speak for the whole of Germany, something that was seen as arrogance in the Eastern partial state, even if it was, from their point of view, not inconvenient for the Federal Republic to take over the political and moral responsibility for National Socialism. The West German population would be represented in the Bundestag (Federal Parliament). The Federal Republic was an indirect (i.e. a representative) democracy. The Bundestag, as the supreme body of the legislature, was at the centre of the political debate. The President of the Bundestag was the second highest representative of the Federal Republic after the Federal President.

The Federal Chancellor was appointed by the Federal President after being elected. He was then able to propose to the Federal President the appointment of the ministers and state secretaries chosen by him. The Federal Chancellor and the Federal ministers formed the Federal government, in which the Federal Chancellor had power over the general direction of policy. The Federal government was the supreme executive body and was dependent on the confidence of the Bundestag, and of the Bundesrat (Federal Council), as the representative of the Länder. This acted as a second chamber and participated in the legislation of the Federation in regards to legislation concerning the Länder.

In September 1951 the Constitutional Court was set up in Karlsruhe in order to oversee the legality of the organization of the state. The Federal President was elected by the Federal Assembly. He had the function of the head of state. His term of office was fixed at five years and only one re-election was possible. The Parliamentary Council wished to make up for the deficiencies in the Weimar Constitution of 1919. Thus the direct election of the State President by the people was done away with, something that, in the long run, meant a disenfranchisement of the Germans as regards democratic politics. The Federal President himself had only protocol and representative duties to perform. The chairman of the FDP, Theodor Heuss, became the first Federal President to be elected on 12 September 1949 by the 'Bundesversammlung' (consisting of both parliaments).

The 'Grundgesetz' had the status of a constitutional law and had priority over any other legal norms. It could only be changed by laws that expressly altered the text of the 'Grundgesetz' or completed it, as well as by the agreement of two-thirds of the votes of the Bundestag and two-thirds of the 'Bundesrat'. The Allies emphasized that the central elements of the constitution could not be abolished, such as the inviolable nature of human dignity or the basis of the structure of the state as a 'democratic and social Federal state'. The Western Allies agreed to it with reservations.

On 10 April 1949 the Parliamentary Council was informed of the Occupation Statute worked out at the Foreign Ministers' conference in Washington. It was never officially relinquished and came into force on 21 September 1949. By that the Federation and the Länder were given full legislative, executive and judicial power. There were restrictions in matters of disarmament, demilitarization and the associated industry and in the area of civil aviation. Reserved powers remained in relation to the Ruhr, restitutions, reparations, decartellization, foreign-owned property and claims involving financial law against Germany. The reputation and security of the Allied forces had to be preserved along with control over foreign trade and foreign exchange. This new West German state was not sovereign at all but was still under occupation status. The occupying powers retained the right 'to take over full powers of government once again totally or in part, if they think that it is unavoidable for security reasons or to uphold the democratic form of government in Germany'. They also gave notice of their willingness to revise the statute and to enlarge the area of responsibility of German administration. In 1951 the rights to object were further reduced and on 5 May 1955 the Occupation Statute was brought to an end by the coming into force of the Paris Treaties. The Federal Republic had achieved 'internal sovereignty' after ten years; it had to wait another 35 years for 'external sovereignty'.

From early on Adenauer's efforts were directed towards the revision and reduction of the Occupation Statute. His actual goal was not German unity but (according to Josef Foschepoth) to gain as much sovereignty as possible for the Federal Republic. His visit along with the ministers of the Federal government to the Petersberg outside Bonn, the residence of the High Commissioners of the Western Alliance, was symbolic. A carpet on which the representatives of the occupation stood was supposed to express the distance between them and the representatives of the Federal Republic. Adenauer immediately exploited the opportunity and stepped on the carpet in order to demonstrate that he was on the same level as the victors. His area of manoeuvre during the Occupation Statute was greater than West German historians (e.g. Hermann Graml, Rudolf Morsey) would credit him with.

In the Petersberg agreement of 22 November 1949, two months after the Occupation Statute came into force, Adenauer achieved an initial change to the treaty. The Federal Republic was permitted to establish consular relations with third countries and to join international organizations. Specific restrictions on the construction of ocean-going ships were dropped and the dismantling of numerous factories in the Ruhr, in the Rhineland and in Berlin was stopped. The Federal Republic was able to join the International Ruhr Authority and to achieve approval for joining the Council of Europe. Just as integration into West European institutions and organizations manifested itself early on, the Eastern part of Germany developed in the direction of the Soviet Union.

The People's Congress, People's Council and the GDR Constitution

On 6 and 7 December 1947 the People's Congress for Unity and a Just Peace was founded in Berlin. Its representatives were largely chosen from parties and mass organizations of the Soviet Occupation Zone on the basis of personal information from and the direction of the SED. The aim of the Western Allies of forming a separate West German state was clearly understood in Germany's East. The People's Congress under SED leadership, therefore, in the interest of the Soviet policy on Germany, called for preparatory measures for the completion of a Peace Treaty and the formation of an all-German government that would be made up of 'representatives of all the democratic parties'. The second People's Congress met on 17 and 18 March 1948. It rejected the Marshall Plan, recognized the Oder-Neisse Line, called for a referendum on German unity and elected the German People's Council, consisting of 400 members, including 100 from the Western zones. Its constitutional committee under the leadership of Otto Grotewohl produced a draft for the Constitution of the German Democratic Republic on the basis of an SED proposal. This was approved by the People's Council on 22 October 1948 and passed on 19 March 1949. Up to 1,400 deputies from the Soviet Occupation Zone, who took part in the third German People's Congress from 29 to 30 May 1949, were elected by the population on 15 and 16 May on the basis of a single list ensuring the leadership and control by the SED. The discontent of the citizens was expressed in a negative poll: the SED received only 31.5 per cent with 6.7 per cent invalid votes.

The third Congress adopted the constitution of the GDR and elected the second People's Council, which was to be transformed into the provisional Volks-kammer (People's Chamber) of the GDR on 7 October 1949. It issued a manifesto for a National Front, which was to replace the People's Congress movement and charged the former SPD man, Grotewohl, with forming a government. The foundation of the second German state was thus complete. While Austria was able to balance the Four Power occupation and thus keep its unity, in Germany precedents had already been set from 1945 to 1949 for the division of the country. German politicians also had a share in this coming about.

2

Partial Integration of the Federal Republic and the GDR Externally and Internally, 1949–55

Adenauer's Western State, Erhard's 'Social Market Economy' and the German 'Economic Miracle'

Starting at the end of the 1940s in the Western zones of Germany a 'West Germany made in the USA' came into being, with a definite taking-on of the American way of life: Coca-Cola, jazz, jeans etc. The British and French occupation powers had nothing equivalent in the way of popular culture to compete with US mass cultural influences. In the Soviet Occupation Zone, however, the communist claims of the USSR were so dominant as regards the structure of politics and society that a little 'Soviet Germany' gradually evolved.

At first there was a lot of dismantling in both the East and the Western zone. The British in particular soon felt the burden of the occupation. New ways had to be found. The creation of a Western-oriented German partial state was based on American and British political decisions. The aim was to create an 'occupied alliance partner' (as Hermann-Josef Rupieper puts it). The GDR was exploited by the Soviets, particularly as it was also 'Stalin's unloved child' (as Wilfried Loth puts it). The Soviet dictator had ambitions regarding the whole of Germany. Without the acceptance and approval of German politicians, the policy of the victorious powers towards Germany would not have been achievable. Adenauer's great rival in the second German partial state took on a much less visible and prominent role. As First Secretary of the SED, it took a while before Ulbricht was able to assert and consolidate his political position. He had survived Stalin's purges in Moscow at the end of the 1930s. Stamina, patience, tenacity and tactical finesse were his significant qualities. While Adenauer had his strongest support in the USA, for Ulbricht it was the USSR that made the powerful position of the SED possible in the first place. At first Adenauer's and Ulbricht's politics were contested. The escalation of

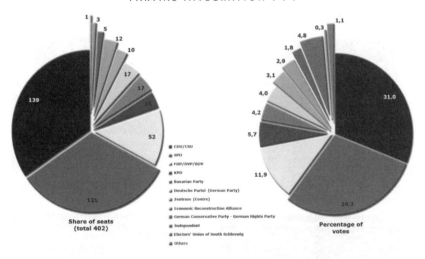

Bundestag elections of 14 August 1949.

the Cold War after 1950, however, strengthened their positions in both parts of Germany as they developed into participants in the Cold War and regular front-line states. The Western Allies had their greatest spokesman and strongest ally in Adenauer, who not only welcomed the invitation to found a Western state but was also ready to put it into practice – even at the cost of German unity. He already played a considerable role in the Parliamentary Council, continuing in the Bundestag. He led the CDU, its grouping within the Bundestag and the Federal governments, in an authoritarian manner, so that the term 'Chancellor's democracy' was often applied to his period in office.

In the 'Grundgesetz' nothing had been decided about the direction of the West German economy, but the participation of the three Western zones in the Marshall Plan had set a precedent in favour of a structure of the economy based on Western capitalist private enterprise. The end of constraints on the economy and the currency reform pointed in this direction and were confirmed by the first Bundestag elections in 1949. It resulted in a legislative majority for the implementation of the 'social market economy'.

Adenauer and Erhard were 'unequal founding fathers' (as Andreas Metz puts it). In 1949 the Rhinelander Adenauer was elected Federal Chancellor by a majority of one vote (his own), and in the same year the Franconian Erhard was elected Federal Economics Minister. In 1949 Adenauer had led the CDU as chairman of the British zone into the first Bundestag election campaign while the independent Erhard had been elected a year earlier on the initiative of the liberals as director for the economic administration in Frankfurt am Main. With

Chancellor Erhard with his predecessor Chancellor Adenauer shown on a First Day Cover commemorating the 25th anniversary of Adenauer's death.

Adenauer's help he joined forces with the CDU before the election. However, there soon developed an antipathy which lasted up until Adenauer's death in 1967. Adenauer and Erhard, the main figures in the politics of the Federal government of this period, formed an unequal duo that was very successful, but also ambivalent. The quarrel was not preceded by any 'great honeymoon' (as Daniel Koerfer puts it). Adenauer did not have many friends. Erhard's legendary concept of the 'social market economy' had different points of reference. The early contact between the economics expert who was bound by no party, a graduate of the Freiburg school and passionate about the German national economy, and the Free Democrats (FDP member of the Bundestag, Thomas Dehler, with the chairman of the FDP grouping in the Economic Council, Franz Blücher) played a decisive role. Without these connections Erhard's rise would have come to a speedy end, particularly in view of his previous failure as Bavarian Economics Minister. In the shape of Viktor Agartz, director of the Administrative Office for the Economy of the Bi-zone, a declared socialist succeeded in gaining a key position. Supporters of the liberal school congregated around Erhard. Liberalization of the economy, currency reform and the Marshall Plan appeared to him as suitable stimuli to ensure an economic upturn. Higher priority was to be given to production and consumption, and competition was to be encouraged as a matter of principle.

The concept of the 'social market economy', after initial obstacles had been overcome, made the upturn in the West German economy possible. The so-called 'Economic Miracle' was to be seen, admittedly, in a European context in which it resulted in growth in nearly all the countries. The 'social market economy' provided for a regulatory function in the delivery of economic freedom and for a means of controlling the state, making economic prosperity and social justice possible. The state should reduce and correct harmful developments for its citizens and free competition should be protected against cartels and monopolies. It should be the job of the state to ensure the stability of the currency.

Adenauer and Erhard were held together by their determination not to let West Germany and its citizens become the object of socialist experiments. Adenauer mainly kept out of the economic debate and Erhard stayed out of the political and party-political discussions. Not remotely a party politician (i.e. an expert dedicated to an academic approach), Erhard was not a member of the CDU until 1963. He maintained good relations with the FDP. Adenauer saw him as a useful tool for the success of the CDU, but nothing more. As the 'electoral engine', in the aftermath of the formation of the government, Erhard was restricted in his sphere of influence by Adenauer, who robbed the Economics Minister of his essential areas of responsibility. The democratic Chancellor and organization man ruthlessly triumphed over the individualist and expert. In this process, without Erhard and the Centre-Right coalition, made up of the CDU/CSU-FDP and the DP, it would have been difficult to imagine Adenauer taking the role of Federal Chancellor.

Kurt Schumacher of the SPD represented a socialist concept of economic policy and opposed the re-establishment of the conditions of capitalist private enterprise. He was certain that the social democrats would be not just influential, but the leaders in post-war politics. The results of the election of 1949, however, saw Schumacher becoming the first leader of the opposition in the Bundestag. He vigorously fought against the policy of integration with the West and, in particular, against Adenauer, whom he referred to in Parliament as a 'Chancellor of the Allies'. Schumacher made it known that: 'We are not the servants of the Western powers and even less are we the servants of the Soviet Union.' Adenauer's overriding goal was not the much quoted 'reunification' with 'our brothers and sisters in the Zone', but 'full sovereignty' for the Federal Republic (which he was admittedly never to achieve). Integration with the West was only possible by alignment with the USA. However, Schumacher started (correctly) from the premise that the unification of Germany would be obstructed by the integration of the Federal Republic with the West. As a result of his gruelling political engagements and his serious physical handicaps he died prematurely on 20 August 1952 in Bonn. Thus, Adenauer was relieved of his greatest opponent. Schumacher's successor, Erich Ollenhauer, lacked his charisma and the little extra it took to be Chancellor.

Societal and social questions in the Federal Republic were fraught with considerable potential for tension. The situation of welfare claimants did not improve with the upturn in the economy. A comprehensive restructuring of social policy was at issue. A key element was the pension reform of 1957, which all political parties were involved in. The CDU under Adenauer was able to take the political credit for itself when he won the Bundestag elections of 1957 with an absolute majority. Another big challenge was dealing with the integration of millions of refugees and people driven out of the former German territories in the East. In addition, there were the prisoners of war returning home. Not only had jobs to be found for these people but their social integration into post-war West Germany had to be facilitated: they had to be compensated for loss of property and means and their pension claims met. Here the Adenauer government achieved a considerable amount, financially and materially, and was considered as making a contribution to the internal integration and socio-political stabilization of the Federal Republic. The 'Law on Returned Soldiers and the Equalization of Burdens' of 1 December 1952 was seen as a guarantee of social peace and the integration into West German society of those Germans who were deprived of their rights and had been forced to flee from their homeland and thus were rootless and impoverished.

However, the myth of an allegedly totally successful integration of German refugees and people forced to leave the former German Eastern territories into post-war (West) German society has been seriously questioned. New research indicates that around 14 million refugees from the former German Eastern territories were not always received with open arms by their compatriots but were often excluded. They experienced a 'cold homecoming', a bitter arrival. There was no trace of national solidarity. The West Germans felt threatened by the 'alien' immigrants 'from the East' they were now supposed to share their territory with. Reservations about a different origin and language ('The Polish are taking over') as well as envy at the growing advantages from the equalization of burdens led to a new German racism on the part of Germans towards German refugees ('Polish trash'), and made living side by side and getting on with one another considerably more difficult. The pain of the people forced to leave the former German Eastern territories was to remain largely unaddressed, only in the Soviet Occupation Zone in the GDR 'a secret four million' of them ended up having to undergo a radical forced assimilation and to 'disappear' as 'resettlers'. They did not always fare much better in the West. On the

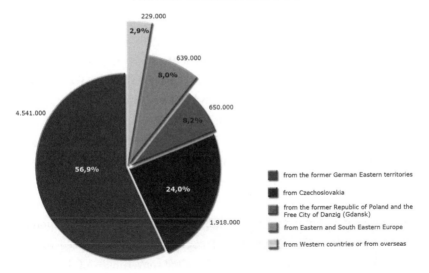

Historical census of 13 September 1950: Demographic overview of refugees and people forced to leave the former German Eastern territories.

one hand, homesickness was often given as the cause of death and, on the other, there were hopes of returning, attempts to start from zero. Over 80 per cent of Germans forced to leave the former German territories in the East went into agriculture. There they were, in some cases, treated like the former forced labour during the Nazi regime. Misunderstandings and prejudices remained. Without the people that were forced to leave the former German territories in the East, who can be regarded as 'tolerated engines of modernization', there would have been neither such a push for innovation, nor the 'Economic Miracle' in the Federal Republic (according to Andreas Kossert amongst others), which is known as the real political achievement of the Adenauer era. The alleged success story of Western integration obscured the tragedies of the German refugees from the East, manifesting itself as an inability to mourn.

Economic development in West Germany after the end of the war had very difficult conditions to start afresh: characterized by bombed-out working and living areas, ruined production plants and destroyed communication networks, transport problems and obstructions in supply, corruption, self-sufficiency and the black market. In place of the Morgenthau Plan of 1944, which provided for the limitation of German economic capacity to half of what it was before the war, the USA launched the Marshall Plan in 1947, which included the Western zones of Germany in 1948. They were represented by the Allied military governors within the framework of the Organization for European Economic Cooperation (OEEC) in Paris, which helped to distribute the means at the disposal of the European Recovery Programme. The currency reform and the introduction of the Deutsche Mark (DM), the gradual abolition of exchange controls and the system of supply, as well as the change to market economic forms of organization with a free system of prices and competition, were all stimuli towards encouraging production that were set in motion. The ERP was more 'aid towards self-help' (as Werner Abelshauser puts it) and was not significant for the German 'Economic Miracle'; decisive stimuli for accelerated growth in the 1950s were provided more by the end of the dismantling of industry, German willingness to rebuild the country and readiness for hard work, increased investment activity and the creation of new jobs. The gross domestic product rose from 145 to 310 billion DM between 1950 and 1960. New investments, above all, created new opportunities for activity. The stream of refugees from the former German territories in the East as well from the GDR added valuable skilled workers. In 1957 full employment was reached, in 1958 the convertibility of the DM was achieved and the German 'Economic Miracle' complete. As early as 1959/60 the pace of economic growth was already slowing and a shortage of workers arose, making the recruitment of 'Gastarbeiter' (migrant labour) necessary.

Ulbricht's Moscow Orientation Towards a State-socialist 'Centrally Planned Economy'

A different social and economic system was introduced in the Eastern partial state. The SED owed its powerful position overwhelmingly to the Soviet occupying power. It was seen as the 'Russians' Party'. Any serious political opposition was eliminated. The party went along with the land reform and expropriations with their effectively imposed 'anti-fascism', leading to a new organization of society in which it proclaimed the 'construction of socialism'; after 1952 this was not only the declared object of the party but also the goal of the state. In 1949 the 'planned economy' was introduced and two years later the first Five Year Plan (1951–5) was put into effect. Considerable reparations paid to the USSR weakened the economic situation of the GDR. Under Ulbricht heavy industry was promoted in order to serve as the basis for the proletariat and the foundation of the economy of the GDR. Through a strict insistence on work norms the SED regime, with the maximum of pressure, attempted to achieve the socialization of the means of production.

In contrast to the Federal Republic, the GDR constructed a centralized state after the pattern of the Soviet Union that would direct the economy according to plans and steer it centrally (i.e. based on a politically motivated objective). State authorities directed and controlled the economic development. The same thing happened as in the other socialist states in Central and Eastern Europe dominated by the USSR, like the GDR belonging to the Council for Mutual Economic Aid (CMEA or Comecon). This *dirigisme* (governmental control on economy) was based on 'perspective plans' that were to be achieved in stages, mostly as Five Year Plans. The content of the Plans was the distribution of raw materials, relief goods and industrial goods to the respective 'nationalized enterprises' (VEB, i.e. 'Volkseigene Betriebe'), combined with the fixing of prices as well as the establishment of nominal amounts of production. The overall plan was divided up into single plans based on investment, production and consumption.

At the highest level the Politburo of the SED, the Council of Ministers and the State Planning Commission had responsibility for the planned economy. At the lower level regional planning commissions that were the organs of the council of each Bezirk (county) were responsible for individual areas. Responsibility for the local planning lay with the planning commissions of each Kreis (district) which worked for the Kreisrat (district council) and were subordinate to it. At the same time they were subordinate to the regional planning commission. The first GDR Five Year Plan was aimed at doubling industrial production from 1951 to 1955 and making up for the war damage, reparations payments and severe dismantling by the Soviet Army. The SED therefore laid great emphasis on energy production and development of heavy industry and the chemical industry, as well as machine production. The area of consumer goods was neglected in the process. Despite enormous burdens and obstacles the targets of the plans were achieved (unlike the later ones). In the GDR the productivity of labour at first rose by 55 per cent. Opponents were faced with police threats and the power of the state and the party. In February 1950 the Ministry of State Security (Staatssicherheitsdienst, to become known as the Stasi) was set up in Berlin in the barely one-year-old GDR. Protests grew against the increased pressure of work and the denial of the right to be consulted in political decision-making and exploded on 17 June 1953 (this will be further discussed later). With the help of Soviet military intervention, the SED managed to suppress the opposition in large areas of the population. An improvement of living conditions was promised and the political pressure was taken off for the time being. The 'de-stalinization' announced by Nikita S. Khrushchev, head of the Communist Party of the Soviet Union, in a secret speech at the 20th Party Congress on 26 February 1956, remained largely without consequences for the GDR. Little of any substance or importance changed in Ulbricht's regime. Against the background of the Hungarian People's Uprising in October and November 1956, reformist Communists (such as Wolfgang Harich) in the GDR, who propagated a specific all-German road to socialism, were severely punished. At the 5th Party Congress of the SED in 1958 Ulbricht, carried away by overestimation of the real capacity of the GDR, announced that the Federal Republic would shortly be matched and overtaken in consumption per capita. With this speech, Ulbricht was admitting to the degree to which the ongoing comparison of the living conditions between the two states was to remain relevant. In this competition, there was a question about the existence, even the survival, of the GDR. Already by the 1960s it had become clear that the SED had announced an impossible goal. The gap between the state and the citizens, and between the party and society, grew bigger and bigger. The citizens who 'voted with their feet' (i.e. by continual escape attempts), showed that the SED regime could only be consolidated by the building of the Wall in Berlin on 13 August 1961.

Internal integration within the GDR had failed very early on. The second Five Year Plan did not come into effect until 1958 and was dropped as a result of its unrealistic notions. It was absorbed one year later into a Seven Year Plan. In 1963 the SED regime agreed upon the New Economic System of Planning and Management of the Economy, combined with the expectation of a more efficient and profitable economic policy, aiming to promote the production of consumer goods. In the same year the Seven Year Plan was replaced by a Perspective Plan leading up to 1970, which would be realized within annual plans. It was only relatively successful.

Reparations (*Wiedergutmachung*) on the Part of the Federal Republic – Refusal on the Part of the GDR

Political and Moral Integration with the West

With the recognition of the moral guilt and the resulting political responsibility for the persecution and mass killings of not only German but also European Jews at the hands of the Nazi regime, and the continued readiness to pay financial reparations, a process without parallel in the history of the world, the Federal Republic succeeded in gaining consideration and recognition. This brought the young Federal Republic respect, even if there remained reservations about the Germans and Germany as a result of the Nazi past, but fears soon surfaced again in light of its recent (economic) power. It was to prove an illusion on the part of the Germans to think that they could reduce this mortgage to history by material means. With the enormous payments the West German policy attempted to lighten the moral burden and calm its bad conscience. Its biased positioning in the Western sphere and the USA sowed new doubts in the East as to the peaceful development and the reliability of the new Germany. The extent to which the process of creating trust might be successful or remained questionable was demonstrated by the denial, the reserve and, in particular, the scepticism on the part of the Western world in relation to Germany's unity in 1989–90.

As early as the Yalta conference in February 1945 it had been fundamentally established that, after the defeat, the German Reich would have to compensate for the destruction wrought during the war and as a result of the Nazi occupation. At Potsdam the USA insisted that each occupying power would make good its claims for reparations from its own zone. The USSR also demanded the payment of reparations from the Western zones for its reconstruction. This intention was foiled by the stop to dismantling ordered by the US military governor, Clay, on 3 May 1946. The forced dismantling, which was all the more intense in the Soviet Occupation Zone, weakened the reconstruction of the GDR more than the Western zones.

The Allied military governments had agreed to the compensation and the cancellation of the expropriations carried out by the Nazi regime. The Federal Republic accepted the demand for reparations on the part of individuals and population groups who had been persecuted in the Nazi period for racial, religious or political reasons. The Israeli government approached the Four Powers in a note of 12 March 1951 and claimed reparation payments to the value of $1.5 billion. $1 billion should be paid by the Federal Republic, $500 million by the GDR. The note was rejected by the Western powers: the GDR and the USSR did not accept it. Adenauer conceded that the size of the sum was like a blank cheque. On 27 September 1951 the Federal government finally declared itself, by a unanimous agreement, to be prepared to pay reparations to the state of Israel. On 10 September 1952 the Luxembourg Agreement was signed between Adenauer and the Israeli Foreign Minister, Moshe Scharet. The negotiations had started at the Castle of Wassenaar in the Hague in March. The Federal Republic agreed to pay 200 million DM to the state of Israel in the first two years, and further supplies of goods and payments to the value of 3.45 billion DM over a period of twelve to fourteen years, as well as 450 million DM to the Jewish Claims Conference (as the overall representative of more than 50 Jewish organizations in Western countries).

The payments were still being made up to the twenty-first century. In 2007 the total amount of compensation paid by the Federal Republic came to over €65 billion. With these reparations a process was completed that was unique in the international history of nation states.

The Israeli opposition under Menachem Begin strongly criticized this, claiming that the dignity of the victims would be slighted if this redeemed the murderers of their guilt by means of 'blood money'. An attempted bomb attack on Adenauer on 27 March 1952 had an uneasy background: this attack had been planned under the auspices of the Israeli underground organization, Irgun Zwai Leumi, around Begin, and it was discovered by chance at Munich Central Station. When the packet, containing a bomb inserted into a book and addressed to the Federal Chancellor, was discharged in the basement of the Munich Police Headquarters, bomb disposal expert, Karl Reichert, was killed. The forensic investigations of a special commission and of a security group of the Federal Bureau of Criminal Investigation at first went into top gear and – when the background became clear – continued in secret. Criminal prosecutions were then dropped after the motives of the suspects were confirmed. There is no telling what might have happened had the attack been successful. On behalf of the relations between the two young states, the matter was hushed up. The German public only found out about it through a publication in 2003 (see Henning Sietz).

The Federal Chancellor had two essential motives for his position on the 'Jewish question', as he called it, and the material payment of reparations: looking back over it in 1965, in an interview for ZDF (the second German television channel), he voiced the opinion that the wrongs and the crimes committed by the Nazi regime demanded atonement and reparations in order to restore the good name of Germany. He also pointed to the 'power of the Jews' in the world and particularly their influence in the USA, which was 'not to be underestimated'. On every opportunity he let it be known that the Federal government must endeavour to reduce the 'resentment of world Jewry'. Adenauer's attitude was based on this mixture of moral responsibility and its use as a political tool in his inflexible policy in pursuit of the interests of the state; he had already belonged to a pro-Palestine Committee in the 1920s as 'Oberbürgermeister' of Cologne and supported the formation of a separate Jewish state.

The Israeli government under Ben Gurion urgently needed German money to ensure the existence of the state and could see no other choice. Israel was totally dependent on the USA and West Germany. The Bundestag agreed to the Luxembourg Treaty on 18 March 1953 with the votes of the CDU and the SPD, although the amount of the payments caused doubts within the ranks of the CDU, as voiced for instance by the Finance Minister, Fritz Schäffer. A Federal Law on Reparations of 29 June 1956 referred to those persecuted by the Nazi regime and established the procedures. Through this the victims of National Socialism were awarded financial compensation: settlements, loans and study grants, allowances for the sick and dependants and pensions.

The policy of paying reparations did not arise from purely altruistic motives. It was part of a larger plan for integration on the part of West German foreign policy. For decades it was characterized by three main goals: integration with the West in tandem with the Franco-German rapprochement within the context of Western European unification; a transatlantic orientation aimed at an alliance with the usa (something that complicated relations with France); and *Wiedergutmachung* (reparations) towards Israel, extending to the supply of weapons (German tanks) to this front-line state in the Middle East. Since that time the army of Israel has also been the best-armed in that region and one of the most powerful in the world. With an ideologically and geographically biased policy, involving a clear departure from a neutral position, Bonn took sides in both the East–West and the Middle East conflicts. It became one of the most reliable partners of the Western world and of the usa. Its policy thus also contributed to the escalation of confrontation between the blocs and to a consolidation of the division of Europe and the world. This foreign policy was fiercely contested between the opposition and the Federal government. It is true that the Social Democrats under Schumacher, and later under Erich Ollenhauer, were just as anti-communist in their views as Adenauer, but they represented the interests of German unity more actively and with more courage than the Christian Democrats. They also tended to accept a neutral Germany. They criticized Adenauer's policy of integration with the West as being premature and, above all, disastrous for Germany, because its division would thus become more entrenched. The spd was to be proved right in this assessment, but it had to recognize the practicality of Adenauer's Realpolitik and the power of circumstances. In order not to be continually out of step with the reality of the division, they came into line at the end of the 1950s and gave up their opposition to Western integration in their German policy.

It is true that Adenauer was a new, but much reduced, 'Iron Chancellor' hailing from Rhöndorf. Unlike Bismarck, he was not a Chancellor of German unity, maintaining close relations with Russia and facing up to the French, but became the Chancellor of a partial state within the framework of a Franco-West European plan of integration and a champion of us policy in the fight against Soviet Communism.

Isolation and Orientation towards the East

The GDR was oriented in a completely different direction in its foreign policy. Totally isolated from the West and completely dependent on Soviet support, it only gained equal status in the Eastern Bloc within the framework of the Warsaw Pact as a result of a treaty with the USSR in 1955. In contrast to the Federal Republic, the GDR did not see any reason to pay reparations to Israel. It argued that – unlike the Federal Republic – it was not the successor to the German Reich and saw itself as a newly founded state: as 'the first German Workers' and Farmers' State', founded on 'anti-fascism'. The Federal Republic, on the contrary, was denounced by the GDR as a bastion of 'Dollar Imperialism', of 'Nazi-fascism' and of 'Monopoly Capitalism', a state that more or less for that reason also had to pay these reparations. Above and beyond that, Israel was also portrayed as a US outpost in the Middle East and a representative of 'Imperialism', which condemned the whole foreign policy of the Federal Republic. Against this background there were not only officially anti-American, anti-capitalist, anti-Israeli and anti-Zionist positions in the GDR but also veiled anti-Semitic attitudes.

Pankow, the seat of the GDR government in East Berlin, recognized the dilemma of the opportunity to present itself within the system of the Eastern states as a 'different' German state, combined with the situation of being dependent on the West for policy concerning trade and finance.

Walter Ulbricht had been keen to promote his idea of two German states since the early 1950s. His subservience towards the USSR had the effect of creating trust on the part of the Soviet Union and gave the GDR rather more freedom to act in the 1960s. The division affected the people in East Germany far more than those in the West. For them it was a far more oppressive situation than for West Germans. In the first two decades after the end of the war many people had the hope for 'unity' around Christmas time in the following year. From the start the economic reconstruction fully occupied the Germans and allowed political concerns to recede into the background. On the one hand, in both states people worked hard and determinedly; on the other, they sought refuge in domestic life after the work was over. The Germans were tired of politics. Set free by the end of the war and from air raids, family and community life gradually started to flourish again. The Nazi period was not a subject of conversation and was repressed. To that extent the situation in both German states was similar. The division of Germany, however, resulted in the economic and social conditions drifting apart.

In the Federal Republic the 40-hour week was introduced in stages, giving rise to shortages of labour. The recruitment of migrant labour was a later consequence. The 1950s was a decade of modernization resulting from the currency reform and the reconstruction. As the war damage was enormous, the infrastructure had to be re-established. All the towns were newly planned. The restoration of old buildings was not seriously considered any more; instead, completely new urban areas sprang up. In 1953 the population of Hildesheim decided in a referendum to reject the reconstruction of the 'Nuremberg of the North', their badly damaged old town quarter. It was necessary to make everything new. Functional flat roof and utility buildings predominated, catering for the immediate needs of life without any atmosphere or appearance of warmth. But there was a lack of strong emotional identification with the new style of architecture. The style of this architecture mirrored a partial return to the Weimar Republic. In the construction of industrial plants and administrative buildings there was a departure from the monumental architecture of the Nazi state. For the Federal Republic this was the way of showing that it was a functional, correct, modern and prosperous state. The growth of prosperity resulted in a society oriented towards consumption and enjoyment, making for stability in social policy but also reflecting a lack of criticism of the prevailing conditions and self-satisfaction.

The unquestionable economic rise of the Federal Republic proved to be attractive to the citizens of the GDR. They did not profit from the upturn, they were not part of the US Recovery Programme for Western Europe and had to live with and put up with the SED dictatorship. This double discontent on the part of the inhabitants of the GDR – on the one hand, with the socio-economic conditions, on the other, with the political conditions – led to a rise in the numbers of refugees. There was the threat of an exodus from the GDR, particularly since those people who were badly needed for the continuing reconstruction had left. With the construction of the inner German border area demarcation line after 1952, and finally with the building of the Berlin Wall in 1961 (see below), the SED regime prevented the premature collapse of the satellite state and its economy in East Germany. Not only was the flood of refugees stopped, it also led to a consolidation and stabilization of the GDR. In the West the self-satisfied and well-fed people talked of 'over there' in the 'Zone'. The Federal Republic and the GDR had to come to terms with one another and had to institutionalize and cultivate distancing and mutual exclusion. This was successful on the road to the integration of the blocs and the militarization that went on apace in both states just one decade after the end of the war.

Limited Western European Policy: The Co-Founding of the Coal and Steel Community, Membership of the Council of Europe, the General Treaty and the Failure of the European Army

On the insistence of the French, an international authority for the Ruhr was set up on 28 April 1949, involving Belgium, France, Great Britain, Luxembourg, the Netherlands and the USA. Demands by the Soviet Union to share in the resources of that region were rejected. The Ruhr remained German territory, though its economic use remained in the hands of the control authority. In the Petersberg Agreement of 22 November 1949 the Federal Republic under Adenauer declared itself ready to join the Ruhr authority, something sharply criticized by Schumacher, the SPD leader of the opposition. The growing pressure of US policy on France to cooperate with the Western zones and the later Federal Republic instead of the continuation of their control led to a turning point in the French policy on Germany after 1947–8; they came into line in 1949–50 in order not to lose the opportunity to be involved in the creation and resolution of the German policy. Thus on 9 May 1950 the French Foreign Minister (1948–53) Robert Schuman proposed, after fairly long preparations, to place the whole of French and German coal and steel production under a common supranational 'High Authority', which would also be open to other European countries. Such ideas went back to the 1920s.

The formation of a Franco-West German economic union had already been suggested by Adenauer in March 1950. The head of the French Office for Economic Planning, Jean Monnet, had a decisive share in the Schuman Plan. With the project the French need for security, which had not been satisfied despite the Ruhr statute, was to be allayed; German domination in the coal and steel sector was to be prevented; France was to be assured of a leading role in Western Europe and also to have considerable independence from the USA; and the political unification of Western Europe was to be given an economic basis. On 30 June 1950, Belgium, the Federal Republic, Italy, Luxembourg and the Netherlands accepted this project as a negotiating basis. The Treaty on the European Coal and Steel Community (ECSC), which was valid for 50 years, was signed on 18 April 1951 in Paris and came into effect on 25 July 1952. The status of the Ruhr simultaneously came to an end with this, whereas the Occupation Statute would remain in place. The ECSC was the prelude to the formation of further communities designed to be supranational.

In the immediate post-war period a 'European Movement' had also formed in the West, finding expression in the founding of a plethora of associations and societies. Federalists called for a European Federal state, constitutionalists for a European constitution and unionists for a union of states. Many dreamed of a 'Europe as a Third Power' between the blocs being formed. This admittedly might have provided a solution to the German question that did not involve division. The European Congress in the Hague in 1948 still held out hope of this. However, the interests of the super-powers and the resurgence of thinking in terms of the nation state acted against these idealistic plans.

It is true that the signing of the statute on the Council of Europe by the representatives of Belgium, Denmark, France, Great Britain, Ireland, Italy, Luxembourg, the Netherlands, Norway and Sweden came about on 5 May 1949. In addition, Greece and Turkey joined in the same year. The institution thus founded, however, fell far short of the expectations of the supporters of Europe, who had hoped for a political community or a constitutional assembly. The Conseil de l'Europe meeting in Strasbourg, with its Advisory Assembly as a consultative body, formed a discussion forum for ambitious projects, which, however, required the agreement of national parliaments. In connection with the Council of Europe the signing of the European Convention on the Protection of Human Rights and Fundamental Freedoms took place on 4 November 1950, with its 11 protocols (effected on 3 September 1953), acceptance of which committed the member states to numerous initiatives on the level of cultural policy, as well as the European Social Charter of 18 October 1961. The Council of Europe was seen from the point of view of supranational wishful thinking as a 'failed attempt at integration'. It stood, however, for a start to European unification in the quest for peace and freedom and functioned as a catalyst. Admittedly this was much more in the sense of a 'United States' for an enlarged Europe rather than the integration of a Western European core led by the Federal Republic. The method of the Council of Europe was a flexible one. It consisted of cooperation and integration. Even if it did not fulfil all the expectations, it did act as a start to the institutional structure for the unification of Europe and created a specifically European milieu for parliamentarians and politicians. It stood for the many and varied 'Europes of the Europeans' (as Wolf D. Gruner puts it).

On 31 March 1950 the invitation was made to the Federal Republic to join the Council of Europe initially as an associate member along with the Saarland. On 2 May 1951 the West German state became a full member. The Council of Europe was an all-European forum (i.e. the only European organization in which, up until the collapse of the Eastern Bloc, nearly all non-communist states of Europe were represented). The General Treaty, which for propaganda reasons was also called the 'Germany Treaty' by the Adenauer government, although it only affected the Federal Republic, was to regularize the ending of the Occupation Statute. This treaty was linked to a further project amounting to a West German contribution to defence that was to come about against the background of the Korean War and the growing fear of the communist threat. What was planned was the control of the newly established German armed forces by integration into a 'European Army' that Churchill had already proposed on 11 August 1950. It then became a French initiative, the so-called 'Pleven Plan', named after Defence Minister René Pleven (1950–51).

As a result of the Korean War the USA had pressed for a military contribution on the part of the Federal Republic. France was opposed to German rearmament from the start but was once again forced to react. Pleven therefore considered a project for French cooperation and proposed the formation of a European Defence Community (EDC). Following tough negotiations the EDC Treaty was signed, providing for the integration of the forces of Belgium, the Federal Republic, France, Italy, Luxembourg and the Netherlands, and creating a common West European defence structure. The terms revealed elements that discriminated against the Federal Republic, which were severely criticized and were subject to further negotiation. The EDC Treaty was passed by the parliaments of Belgium, the Netherlands, Luxembourg, Italy and the Federal Republic.

The effectiveness of the General Treaty, according to Article 11, was dependent on the EDC Treaty coming into effect. The thrust of the treaty, which was also referred to as the Bonn Treaty, was to end the High Commissions of the Western Allies and to give the Federal Republic a sort of internal sovereignty, with the provision of the resolution of the questions of Berlin and Germany 'as a whole', concerning unity and the peace treaty as well as the rights of army units of the Western powers to be stationed and the management of emergencies for the protection of the troop units of the Western allies. The last only lost their importance with the legislation on states of emergency passed in 1968. The General Treaty committed the Federal Republic to the Charter of the United Nations and the Statute of the Council of Europe, and all signatory states to the common goal of the unity of Germany in freedom and of a freely agreed peace treaty for the whole of Germany (Article 7). It also provided for the establishment of the rights and duties of the Allied forces, the financing of the occupation on the part of the Federal Republic and the treatment of questions concerning the consequences of the war.

In Great Britain and the USA the General Treaty was approved in 1952. Following intensive internal political debates and reservations at the level of constitutional law, it was also ratified in the Federal Republic in 1953. However, it was not supposed to come into effect for the time being. Why?

On 30 August 1954 the Assemblée Nationale removed the subject of the EDC from the agenda. The solid communist and Gaullist opposition to the ratification of the EDC was too strong, particularly since the EDC was not only closely linked to the General Treaty but to the project of the so-called 'European Political Community'. This would have been linked to the renunciation of further French rights to sovereignty. Also, the planned construction of an autonomous nuclear *'force de frappe'* was a reason for the rejection of the European Army in France. Adenauer was shocked and should have considered resignation. He was faced with the shattered remains of his European policy.

At the London Nine Power conference of 28 September to 3 October 1954, however, Belgium, the Federal Republic, France, Great Britain, Italy, Canada, Luxembourg, the Netherlands and the USA eventually agreed on a final act, establishing the framework for the setting up of West German armed forces and their integration into the Western European defence system (Brussels Pact, WEU) and forming the basis for the Paris Treaties of 23 October 1954. It recommended NATO membership of West Germany. In a countermove the Federal Republic officially renounced, among other things, the production and use of nuclear, biological and chemical weapons and of heavy armaments (e.g. long-range or remote-controlled missiles, as well as warships and submarines). It was repeatedly insisted that the policy of the Federal Republic was to be in accordance with principles of the United Nations and to refrain from all measures that might contradict the defensive character of the Western defence alliance. At the same time the ending of the right of occupation and the recognition of the internal sovereignty of the Federal Republic and its status as the sole representative of Germany ('claim to sole representation') were to be linked.

Adenauer used the West German contribution to defence as a tool towards the achievement of partial sovereignty in order to increase the area of manoeuvre of his Federal Republic largely prescribed by the occupying powers. Along with British cooperation on the level of security policy and promotion of West German aim of sovereignty, the Federal Chancellor was actively involved in shaping the West German NATO option. Following the ratification of the Paris Treaties, the General Treaty came into effect on 5 May 1955. The German contribution to defence was thus achieved within both a West European and a transatlantic framework – the WEU and NATO – and therefore the presence of NATO on the European continent was assured for decades. As a result of this historic decision, the EU has suffered right up to the present from its relative impotence at the level of security policy, owing to the principle of unity and the lack of common ideas and goals.

3

The Two German States: Bloc Building in Central Europe, 1949/55–61

A Western Military Bloc Preempts the Formation of a Military Bloc in the East

The 'Bundeswehr' ('Federal German Forces')

On 4 April 1949 a military alliance was formed in Washington by the Western Powers with the name of 'North Atlantic Treaty Organization' (NATO), which would provide for economic and political cooperation, the obligation to consult as well as common military defence in the event of an armed attack on one or more of the members, admittedly *without* the automatic obligation to offer assistance, and a permanent political and military organization. The alliance was to be seen against the background of attempts at expansion on the part of the communists in Central Europe (communist seizures of power in Hungary and in Czechoslovakia in 1947–8 and the Berlin Blockade in 1948–9) as well as in South East Europe (civil war in Greece in 1946–7) and threatening scenarios in the global Cold War. Asked by people close to him about the purpose of NATO in Europe, its first secretary general (1952–7) Lord Hastings Lionel Ismay answered: 'To keep the Russians out, to keep us in and to keep the Germans down.' The NATO founder states were Belgium, Denmark, France, Great Britain, Iceland, Italy, Canada, Luxembourg, the Netherlands, Norway, Portugal and the USA. In 1952 Greece and Turkey joined and, in 1955, so too did the Federal Republic. In the course of the militarization of the Federal Republic and its planned integration into NATO, a collective assistance pact was decided within the framework of the Paris Treaties in October 1954 under the name of the Western European Union (WEU); this transformed the Brussels Treaty (West Union: Benelux, France and Great Britain) of 17 March 1948, which had originally been directed towards a resurgent Germany, into a defence alliance completed by the addition of the Federal Republic and Italy. It was to dispel the French reservations about the rearmament of Germany and, in particular, to enable a controlled integration of the Bundeswehr into NATO by means of arms restriction and supervision. The Federal Republic was officially supposed to have equal rights within NATO but its army was totally subordinate to the NATO command. In the WEU the Federal Republic was de facto discriminated against by being placed under a special legal status and subject to impositions.

In regard to the West German forces, according to the Paris Treaties, twelve divisions consisting of 500,000 men were to be established, their strength was not to be increased and their deployment was to be decided in accordance with NATO strategy. The Treaties came into effect on 6 May 1955. Three days later the Federal Republic joined NATO. On 7 June 1955 the 'Blank Office' was renamed the Federal Ministry of Defence. Theodor Blank, a Christian trade unionist who had participated in the war as a former lieutenant in the Wehrmacht reserve, became the first West German Minister of Defence. In June and July the Bundestag passed the first legislation on defence: a law on volunteers, along with a law on the committee for the assessment of personnel that had to decide on the possible reappointment of officers of the German Wehrmacht.

Whereas Adenauer's policy of militarization was clearly rejected by the majority of Germans with a 'Ohne mich' ('without me: count me out') attitude, the authoritarian Federal Chancellor knew how to push it through with his political leadership. The obligation to set up a West German army was automatically linked to NATO membership by the Federal Republic. In the second half of 1955 Adenauer came a considerable step closer to his goal. What the Soviet Union had repeatedly feared in the past became reality: the first units of the Bundeswehr were set up, requiring change to the provisional constitution of 1949.

Legislation completing the 'Grundgesetz' of 26 March 1954 created the basis for the military sovereignty of the Federal Republic and a further amendment of 19 March 1956 integrated West German forces into West German legislation, making the introduction of compulsory military service possible on 21 July 1956 – just over eleven years after the unconditional surrender of the German Wehrmacht. Up until that point, only volunteers could be recruited.

In September 1955 the Federal government announced the plan for setting up the forces. By January 1959 the twelve divisions of the Bundeswehr were to be established and the building up of the air force and the navy was to be completed by January 1960. The total costs were estimated to be 51 billion DM. The date of 12 November 1955 is taken to be the moment at which the Bundeswehr was founded. On that day, the 200th anniversary of the birth of Prussian General

Gerhard von Scharnhorst, the Defence Minister, Theodor Blank, presented the letters of appointment to the first 101 volunteers. At the beginning of 1956 the first 1,000 volunteers reported at Andernach (ground troops), Nörvenich (air force) and Wilhelmshaven (navy). The expensive militarization of the Federal Republic had been achieved.

Circumspection and sensitivity in dealing with the new army were admittedly given a good deal of emphasis. The Bundeswehr was placed under the control of the Bundestag, a defence committee was established and the office of a defence authority that would oversee the upholding of the 'Grundgesetz' was created. The employees of the Bundeswehr were either conscripts, soldiers signed up for a period or professional soldiers. The power of the command lay with the Defence Minister, though in the event of national defence (*Verteidigungsfall*) it passed to the Federal Chancellor. The General Inspector of the Bundeswehr was the highest military advisor to the Federal government. The later established five services (armed forces, Army, Airforce, Navy and Central Medical Services) were represented in command staffs. To insure against any tendencies that might threaten democracy the concept of 'internal leadership' was developed. This sought to integrate soldiers both into society and into the forces, and in the process was to ensure that as few basic rights as possible were being restricted. The personnel of the Bundeswehr enjoyed both active and passive voting rights and the right of association. As early as the consultations of the Parliamentary Council, the right to conscientious objection was accepted as a basic right. Nobody was to be forced to serve in the army against their conscience. In practice, however, the application of the right to conscientious objection was interpreted rather restrictively at times during the Cold War and conscientious objectors were even discriminated against. They were required to carry out 'civilian service' in the health and social services sector; at times this amounted to a period that was more than a third longer and sometimes even twice as long as the conscription period of the Bundeswehr, which included the soldiers having to take part in reserve exercises. The Bundeswehr became an army of the Western alliance.

The National People's Army

It took as long as six years after the founding of NATO, which had been substantially brought about by the USA, for the East to follow the direction of the Soviet Union with the founding of a military alliance. In this process the division of Germany played quite a central role. Shortly after the formal admission of the Federal

Republic into NATO, the signing of a treaty, which was to be known in the history of the Cold War as the Warsaw Pact, took place in the Polish capital on 14 May 1955. Albania, Bulgaria, the GDR, Poland, Romania, Czechoslovakia, the USSR and Hungary agreed this 'Treaty of Friendship, Cooperation and Mutual Assistance' and in parallel to this a 'United Command of Forces'. The founding of the Warsaw Treaty Organization was partly a long-term consequence of the founding of NATO, but above all an answer to alliance politics and the rearmament of the West German partial state that now formed an incontrovertible fact for Soviet policy on Germany. The Warsaw Treaty even directly mentions the 'North-Atlantic bloc' in the preamble. It saw its existence as no longer necessary in the event of the abolition of NATO. Alongside the Council for Mutual Economic Aid, the Warsaw Treaty Organization became the second most important multi-lateral institution of the communist states. The starting point was the militarization of the Federal Republic and its integration into NATO that caused Moscow to secure the right to station its troops in the states of East Central and South Eastern Europe.

It is one of the paradoxes of the Cold War that both the Western and the Eastern alliances defined themselves as defence organizations and in each case imputed an aggressive intention on the part of the other. The Soviet Union saw the aim of the Warsaw Treaty Organization as reacting to the founding of both NATO and the WEU (enlarged by the addition of the Federal Republic and Italy). The economic formation of the Western Bloc in the shape of the ECSC, and the later EEC, followed on after the economic formation of the Eastern Bloc in the shape of COMECON (1949). The formation of the Eastern military Bloc in the shape of the Warsaw Treaty Organization (1955) followed on from the formation of the Western military Bloc in the shape of NATO (1949).

NATO and the Warsaw Treaty Organization fundamentally shaped the Cold War in Europe between 1949 and 1991. Both of them would have been unimaginable without the German partial states. The Federal Republic and the GDR were therefore the central constituents of the militarization during the Cold War in Europe (according to Vojtech Mastny). They were the result of the lack of unity amongst the main victors over the German question and the taking up of contradictory positions on the part of the politicians of the German partial states. The 'rearmament' of the Federal Republic was forced through on Adenauer's insistence and with the decisive support of the USA. The building up of a new German army was to a large extent only possible by former members, particularly officers, of the German Wehrmacht, soldiers who had 'experience of Russia', giving cause for concern in Moscow. For the USSR the Warsaw Treaty Organization fulfilled the aim of bringing the armies of the Communist 'fraternal states' under one umbrella and of binding their states more closely together. The Warsaw Treaty Organization was directed towards the domination of the Soviet Union and hegemony in Central and Eastern Europe. There followed bilateral treaties on the deployment of troops with Poland (1956), the GDR (1957), Romania (1957), Hungary (1957) and what was, by then, called the Republic of Czechoslovakia (October 1968). The Warsaw Treaty Organization committed the member states to consultations, especially in the case of threats to their security, to mutual assistance in the event of aggression towards a member as well as the placing of forces under a common senior command. A 'Political Advisory Committee', comprised of one representative from each of the participating states, acted as the political leadership of the Warsaw Treaty Organization while the military leadership belonged to the Unified High Command based in Moscow that was always led by a Soviet supreme commander.

In the GDR, units of the German People's Police (Deutsche Volkspolizei, VOPO) were at first organized as paramilitaries. In 1952 the People's Police quartered in barracks (Kasernierte Volkspolizei, KVP) were developed from them and only in 1956 was the National People's Army (Nationale Volksarmee, NVA) formed, becoming the military forces of the GDR. Its soldiers wore almost the same helmet as the German Wehrmacht and, to some degree, continued with Prussian traditions. The NVA evolved out of the units of the KVP set up some years earlier and from the naval and air forces built up secretly since the start of the 1950s. The official date of its founding was 1 March 1956, when the first units of the KVP were integrated into the NVA. It had already been decided on 28 January 1956 to accept NVA units within the Warsaw Treaty Organization and to put them under its overall command. Whereas the Bundeswehr saw itself as a 'democratic army', the NVA saw itself as a 'socialist army'. Whereas the Bundeswehr became an essential part of the anti-communist bastion in Western Europe under the leadership of the USA, the NVA, under the leadership of the SED and the USSR, had to fulfil its 'revolutionary task' in the sense of a struggle against the class enemy in the capitalist West.

The schizophrenia of the Cold War in Germany had even reached the military sector by 1955–6. The Ministry for National Defence in the GDR was the supreme command authority and head of the supreme command of the army. The naval forces (Volksmarine) and the air force had their own supreme commands. The building up of the NVA took place after 1955 under the direction and control of the USSR. As with the Bundeswehr, former personnel of the Wehrmacht were called up. They returned mostly from Russia where they had been prisoners of war and had 'enjoyed' anti-fascist instruction. Vincenz Müller, former general in the German

Wehrmacht, also served in the NVA. In the middle of 1956 the officer corps already amounted to 17,500. Of those, 2,600 were former military personnel and approximately 1,600 were non-commissioned officers as well as exactly 500 officers, more than 25 per cent of whom were former Wehrmacht soldiers. They were deployed in the Defence Ministry, training schools and in leadership positions. Out of about 80 commanding positions in the NVA, over 60 were occupied by people who had taken part in the war and by personnel of the Wehrmacht. The head of the SED, Walter Ulbricht, had in 1952 already considered and suggested the construction of a wall to cut the GDR off from the West, consolidating it as a socialist state. That, however, was only possible with the agreement of the Soviet Union and it did not happen until nine years later. Besides, Moscow did not agree to the militarization of the GDR at that time. Not until after the building of the Wall in 1961 did the SED introduce compulsory military service in the GDR, on 24 January 1962 – six years after it had been introduced in the Federal Republic. There was for a time an increased military state of alert on the part of the Pentagon.

Like the Warsaw Treaty Organization in respect to NATO, the NVA also followed the Bundeswehr in details. Formerly, only volunteers had joined the NVA. Enthusiasm for militarization likewise remained limited. The SED and the Free German Youth movement (Freie Deutsche Jugend, FDJ) had to advertise actively up until 1962 to build up the units.

Two German States – Two German Systems

The 'Chancellor Democracy' of the Adenauer–Erhard Era: Societal-Social Integration in Order to Stabilize the Political System of the Federal Republic

In 1949 first a Federal President, then a Federal Chancellor, were elected. The Federal assembly elected the FDP chairman, Theodor Heuss, as the first head of state on 12 September 1949. In the Parliamentary Council he had been involved in the preparation of the 'Grundgesetz'. With Heuss the new office of Federal President gained recognition and respect. Limits were, however, set to his efforts to overcome the ideological and political oppositions. He was unable to reconcile the differences between the CDU/CSU and the SPD, let alone to resolve them yet. A Grand Coalition vital for national unity, as in Austria after 1945, did not come about in the Federal Republic. Heuss acted as a head of state recognized abroad. In 1954 he was confirmed in his office by the Federal Assembly. As a political writer he received the peace prize of the German Book Trade in 1959. He refused a third term of office, for which a change in the 'Grundgesetz' would have been necessary. Heuss died in

Stuttgart in 1963. As already mentioned, Konrad Adenauer became the first Federal Chancellor, the CDU chairman of the British zone who had been elected president of the Parliamentary Council on 1 September 1948 and who was to be in office as Bundestag chairman of the same party from 1950 to 1966. A total of 402 members of the first Bundestag were elected on 14 August 1949. The CDU/CSU received 31 per cent, the SPD 29.2 per cent and the FDP 11.9 per cent.

Out of a total of 402 seats, the CDU, CSU and the SPD had achieved the majority – admittedly the formation of a large coalition did not come about as in Austria, but a conservative Christian Democrat liberal-democratic one did. The German political culture was, roughly speaking, divided between Social and Christian Democracy, and the remainder, between the conservative and liberal-democratic camp. This was relatively fragmented, if one leaves aside the FDP, the Deutsche Volkspartei and the League of People forced to leave the former German Territories in the East. The latter existed as a pressure group for a long time. The result of 1949 to a large extent still mirrors the very fragmented spectrum of voters in the Weimar Republic, in which there was proportional representation and many single parties.

On 15 September 1949 the Bundestag elected the Federal Chancellor. Adenauer received 202 votes and had been elected with the smallest majority. With a majority of a single vote (his own) he became the first head of government and remained in this office until 1963. A total of three times – in 1953, 1957 and 1961 – the CDU/CSU alliance under Adenauer won the Bundestag elections, always with a clear lead over the SPD and, in 1957, with an absolute majority.

On 20 September 1949 the composition of the cabinet was decided. Adenauer formed a bourgeois-conservative-liberal coalition made up of the CDU/CSU, FDP and DP. Thirteen departmental ministers belonged to this cabinet. A Foreign Ministry did not yet exist, because the foreign policy of the Federal Republic was reserved by the occupying powers. Adenauer felt responsible for this, even if his foreign policy horizon was limited or mostly directed towards Western Europe.

One thing that belonged to the pressing issues of Adenauer's first cabinet was the accommodation and integration of the refugees and the people forced to leave the former German territories in the East as well as providing aid to the victims of the war. The state insurance system had to be reorganized and set up on a new financial basis. A separate 'Federal law on public assistance' for the whole of West Germany would deal with assistance to the victims of the war, a law on returning soldiers would deal with their compensation and a law on the equalization of burdens would include the losses of the refugees and the people forced to leave the former German territories in the East, and as far as possible compensate them. The main objective was, above all, to promote the building sector, since the former enemies of Germany in the war had used bombing on a large scale, making many towns uninhabitable.

The catastrophic housing situation caused by Allied bombing was worsened by the approximately fourteen million people who had arrived from the former German territories in the East together with the hard post-war winter of 1946–7. The refugees – apart from some groups who went to the Soviet Occupation Zone/GDR – in the main tended to move to the Western zones. In the largely destroyed towns the rubble first had to be cleared and the buildings that were only partly destroyed had to be reinstated as makeshift accommodation. The reconstruction of homes was one of the prime social political tasks. In 1949/50 over half a million dwellings were finished in the Federal Republic, of which more than 400,000 were within the framework of a state-promoted programme for the building of homes. The first legislation on the building of homes of 24 April 1950 dealt with the reconstruction on a unified basis throughout West Germany and promoted the building of social housing. It was directed at the broad masses of the people and designed to meet their needs. The project was geared to the creation of 1.8 million units of social housing in six years. At the start of the 1950s there was still a need for no less than five million homes. Nearly 900,000 dwellings were built from 1951–2. Approximately one-fifth were financed by the state, the Länder and the local councils. The total subsidies came to almost two billion DM. This was extended on 25 August 1953 and a second piece of legislation on the building of homes on 27 June 1956 more strongly promoted the building of private homes. In the course of the 1950s social housing declined in favour of the building of private dwellings, a first sign of conspicuous prosperity. Legislation for state subsidies on the construction of dwellings in 1952 created further incentives for this.

After the end of the war industrial workers and office employees became involved in production through the leadership of works councils. A trade union organization began to be arranged, leading to the formation in 1949 of the Federation of German Trade Unions (Deutscher Gewerkschaftsbund, DGB). The DGB was made up of industrial unions structured according to the sectors of the economy and saw itself as a united organization independent of political parties, in total contrast to the aligned unions of the Weimar and Wilhelminian periods. The industrial unions demanded to be embedded within legislation going beyond the co-determination set by the European Coal and Steel Community, even for the economic co-determination of employees at the higher levels of the companies.

Under the threat of strikes in the iron and steel industry in January 1951 an agreement was reached between the DGB chairman, Hans Böckler, and Federal Chancellor, Adenauer: the co-determination as practised up to this point was embedded into a law of 21 May 1951, though with reference only to the mining industry. Despite support from the Churches the other union demands were not implemented. The FDP and the DP came out against the law, which could only achieve legal force with the votes of the SPD. The integration of employees and works councils was established on a unitary basis by means of legislation on the constitution within the workplace of 11 October 1952, according to which works councils would be elected and which, amongst other things, would participate in decision-making concerning the workforce, the organization of the workplace, working time regulations and the provision of holidays. In the economic sphere the works councils only had the right to be kept informed. Up to 30–35 per cent of positions on supervisory boards in joint-stock companies were occupied by employee representatives. Thus a decision on rights at work had been reached for the 1950s.

Not until the 1960s would the question of co-determination be taken up again, culminating in 1972 after long debates and negotiations over the extension of employees' rights in legislation on the constitution within the workplace, and in 1976 in legislation on co-determination.

In the first years the Federal government had to provide particularly for people affected by the war. People bombed out of their homes, refugees, people driven out of the former German territories in the East and war widows were numerous and in need of help. Legislation had to be passed to provide aid and reduce the need. In June 1950 a law was introduced on support measures for soldiers returning from the war, including former prisoners of war and their dependants. In December 1950 Federal legislation on public assistance was passed by the Bundestag, dealing with the support of war victims, invalids and their dependants throughout the Federal Republic.

Of extreme relevance was the Law on the Equalization of Burdens, passed on 14 August 1952, which was to compensate the damage and losses to the refugees driven out of the former German territories in the East and from the Soviet Occupation Zone/GDR. Comprehensive and complex legislation was brought in and a large administration with offices for the equalization of burdens was set up for the assessment of damage, determination of losses and the fixing of sums. This dealt with loans for the promotion of settlement and integration, damages for household goods, compensation for damage to property, for pensions, aid for accommodation and support, as well as exchange equalization for the savings deposits of refugees and people driven out of the former German territories in the East. In spite of all the legal effort and enormous achievements (just up until 1980 around 104 billion DM were paid out in compensation aid) it was a long time before the greatest need could be relieved.

Relatively early a development emerged in the Federal Republic towards a social and welfare state, having the effect of adding considerably to political stability. In 1951 social costs took up 36.5 per cent of the budget; in 1955 this had already risen to 42 per cent, amounting to a sum of almost 10 billion DM. This was out of a total national budget of around 30 billion DM. In this year twenty per cent of the population were dependent on social support. One million households were living under the official poverty level of a monthly income of 130 DM. The social system of the Federal Republic was in great need of reform. There were two basic tendencies: trade unions and social democrats demanded a unitary insurance scheme with equal benefits for all professions with a unitary administration; whereas the economic federations, on the other hand, demanded the reintroduction of a structured system providing each group with their own insurance schemes. The supporters of the traditional system were to win out. The unitary insurance scheme was rejected. There had been no solution by 1955, however. Bundestag elections were already set for 1957. Adenauer pressed for a reform which could no longer be achieved in the time remaining. Only a partial reform was still realistic. Pensioners in particular were living in very poor circumstances. A pension reform would therefore tackle the hardest cases and create the basis for cases of social security. The model under discussion was that those in work would pay a portion of their income into the pension pot to be passed on to pensioners, for which those contributing would be given points according to the level of contributions. The value of the pension would be determined on the basis of this and the annual contribution. The link between the payment of a pension and the gross income of those contributing gave rise to the term 'earnings-related pension'.

This concept of a 'contract between the generations' would win out in the confrontation between the political parties and the government ministries. The SPD did distance itself from the unitary insurance scheme. In 1957 the reform was passed by the Bundestag and additional payments and increases were introduced. As regards the insurance of industrial workers, pensions rose by 65 per cent on average, and in the case of office workers, by more than 70 per cent. This reform won an absolute majority for Adenauer's CDU in the elections of September 1957. However successful this was from the party political point of view, this decision on the pensions policy in the Federal Republic would prove to be a fundamental mistake.

With the new legislation, capital recovery within pensions insurance was abolished and pensions were linked to the growth of wages and salaries. The much praised 'contract between the generations' later turned out to be a crucial mistake as regards capital. The 'earnings-related pension' led to an explosion in total social expenditure to an extent that could no longer be financed – a legacy of the Adenauer era. The Finance Ministry, under Fritz Schäffer, and the Economics Ministry, under Ludwig Erhard, were opposed to this pension reform. Erhard believed that a compulsory private insurance system was required in order to build up a stock of capital in savings. To portray the earnings-related pension as a contract between the generations, which was only a complicated and hidden tax deduction, seemed a joke to him. Adenauer, who really had no idea about economics, had been persuaded of the efficiency of the earnings-related pension. As an election handout in the run-up to the polls it served the purpose.

Comprehensive Armament, Anti-Communism and the Banning of the Communist Party (KPD) in Order to Secure and Consolidate Integration with the West

The bourgeois-Christian-liberal coalition contributed to the consolidation and stabilization of political organization in the Federal Republic. A Communist Party of Germany (Kommunistische Partei Deutschlands, KPD) had also been founded in the Western zones. Between 1945 and 1948 it had, on occasion, participated in Länder governments, with the exception of Schleswig-Holstein and Württemberg-Hohenzollern. It pursued a policy aimed at the whole of Germany and emphasized activism in the workplace. It formed a 'working partnership' with the SED in the Soviet Occupation Zone and later the GDR, aiming at a united Socialist Party for the whole of Germany. The KPD rejected the concept of the founding of the Federal Republic as an end in itself. It dreamed of a communist all-German state. In the elections of 1949 it won 5.7 per cent of the votes and had 15 members of the Bundestag.

In the second round of elections, however, the West German communists got only 2.2 per cent of the vote and fell at the 5 per cent threshold clause that had, in the meantime, been introduced as an obstacle to entry into the Bundestag. This regulation was to prevent the entry of small or extremist parties along with splinter parties. From the start of the 1950s the KPD increasingly isolated itself from the other parties and went in for revolutionary activity and anti-capitalist rhetoric. Thus, in class-war fashion it called upon the workers to defend themselves against the 'exploitation of the German people' and the 'lackeys of the imperialists'. Only by toppling Adenauer, who was portrayed as being in the pay of the USA, could German unity be brought about. The aggressively shouted slogans seemed to be undermining the basis and identity of the Federal Republic.

It reveals a lot about the climate of the Cold War, now fully broken out, that this 2.2 per cent mini-party caused concern, consternation, nerves and disquiet in the political establishment of the young and still insecure Federal Republic. The feeling of a communist threat was consciously whipped up by Adenauer's CDU. Anti-communist attitudes had a long history in Germany, such as during the period of the Kaiser Reich, the Weimar Republic and the Third Reich, forming a continuous thread throughout. In this process we are dealing with an anti-communism without communists (according to Josef Foschepoth). What was in fact an insignificant KPD, with its consistently strident criticism of the system, caused the Federal government to have the party investigated by the Federal Constitutional Court (Bundesverfassungsgericht, BVG), leading to it being banned. This intention was to be carried out in parallel with the banning of the right-wing extremist Sozialistische Reichspartei, SRP, led by Otto Strasser, a brother of the social revolutionary National Socialist Gregor Strasser, murdered by the SS in June 1934.

The KPD and the SRP also worried the Western powers with their behaviour and their programmes. However, the planned banning of the parties took a while. In November 1955 the BVG entered into negotiations about the intentions of the Federal government to ban them. On 17 August 1956 the court ruled in favour of the banning of the KPD on the grounds that the party was against the 'Grundgesetz'. Their goal was a 'socialist revolution', to bring about the 'dictatorship of the proletariat'. There have been heated debates about this banning. Elections for the Bundestag, the Landtag of each state and in the local elections in 1953 already clearly indicated that the exaggerated alarmism was uncalled for, since the KPD was an irrelevance. Only in 1968, the year of the student uprisings, was it allowed to be set up again under the slightly different name of the German Communist Party (Deutsche Kommunistische Partei, DKP) by which time its membership had slumped to 7,500. Proscription and isolation had contributed to this. The experience with the KPD and the DKP illustrated, on the one hand, how sensitive and vulnerable the reaction of the new West German republic was to criticism of the system and, on the other, how threatened this new state felt itself to be. In dealing with fundamental opposition from the margins it showed neither self-confidence nor independence. It was still a very young state that saw itself as provisional, though it was established for the long term by its founding father Konrad Adenauer.

Controversy over 'Rearmament'

The question of rearmament troubled the German public from the very start and led to passionate debate in the Bundestag over the need for German armed forces. In 1955, with great difficulty, the Adenauer government managed to push through militarization within the framework of NATO. This was also to be a shift in the direction of the Americanization of West Germany and the division of Germany. The subject of militarization, however, had not yet been settled. In February 1957 the American NATO Supreme Commander, General Lauris Norstad, called for the Bundeswehr to be supplied with atomic weapons. A nuclear arms pact between the USA and the USSR was already in place by this time and the question arose as to whether this would be destabilized by the Federal Republic having atomic weapons. NATO had developed new strategic plans, including tactical nuclear weapons with a range of up to 150 kilometres. Adenauer and his Defence Minister, Franz Josef Strauß, argued for the Bundeswehr to be equipped with atomic weapons in order to strengthen the West and its defence capacity. At the NATO council meeting in December 1957 the Federal Chancellor also called for talks over détente between West and East in order to secure his position in the eyes of the German public.

Starting in 1958 a protest movement on the part of the West German public against the NATO plans was formed. As early as the spring, 18 atomic scientists had come out against nuclear armament in the 'Göttingen Manifesto'. The SPD made it clear that the Bundeswehr should not be equipped with atomic weapons nor should such weapons be stationed on West German soil. In March 1958 an all-party committee supported by the SPD and the trade unions was set up with slogans such as 'Fight Atomic Death'. In the Bundestag the issues were hotly debated. The government parties CDU/CSU and DP decided 'to equip the Bundeswehr with the most up-to-date weapons if this should prove politically and strategically necessary'. The SPD and the DGB mobilized public opinion and organized protests to have the decision withdrawn. Around 10,000 workers from the VW factory went on strike in Wolfsburg. There were demonstrations against Adenauer's armaments policy involving stoppages of work, public gatherings and silent marches. The DGB, however, subsequently kept a low profile on account of the many CDU voters amongst its members. The move by the SPD to institute a referendum on nuclear armament was rejected by the Federal Constitutional Court, which did not want to approve any plebiscites in Germany and this led to a disenfranchisement of West Germans as regards democratic politics.

The anti-nuclear movement finally failed due to the majority in the Bundestag that were in favour of the nuclear arming of the Bundeswehr, as well as due to the absolute determination of the NATO states to implement the agreements made within the Atlantic alliance and to Adenauer's inflexible will as leader. The CDU won the elections in the Landtag of North Rhine-Westphalia in July 1958; the activities by the DGB and the SPD in the campaign against atomic death decreased. The alternative movement lost momentum and was consigned to history.

In the meantime, top secret negotiations had already taken place between the Federal Republic, Italy and France on the construction of a common atom bomb. The project was then immediately stopped by de Gaulle after coming to power in France in April 1958. The French statesman still believed in the formation of a 'force de frappe nucléaire' together with the USA and Great Britain, which did not, in the end, materialize.

The Federal government then decided in October 1958 to acquire the most up-to-date fighter bomber, the Starfighter F 104 G, which was equipped with atomic bombs and was able to fly deep into Soviet Russian territory. The declared 'search for security' (as Eckart Conze calls it) of the Germans in the Federal Republic was to be carried out by means of the creation of a new army and its being equipped with nuclear weapons, giving rise to the contradictory situation that this policy simultaneously led to a threat to military security for Germans in East and West and an increase in their political insecurity, particularly since the potential for conflict and confrontation between the GDR and the Federal Republic was heightened.

With his one-sided and undisguised Western policy and his style of governing, Adenauer shaped an era that was characterized by an American, transatlantic and francophile attitude and, at the same time, conservative and authoritarian models. The main concerns of the Federal Chancellor, who was strongly oriented towards the Rhineland, were the determined concentration on achieving sovereignty for the West German state and the forcing through of Western integration in the teeth of strong opposition from the SPD. Adenauer was consciously prepared to accept the resulting division of Germany by giving the impression in public that unity could only be achieved through Western integration and a 'policy of strength' towards the USSR. This idea, which was only superficially impressive, was not to meet with any success. On the contrary, his policy led to a deepening of the division, not only of Germany, but also of Europe. The Federal Chancellor created a new West German state in a growing Western economic community. Thus he also became the Chancellor of a divided Germany, an outcome that is not often referred to by German historians. Of course for this there also needed to be favourable conditions and a fellow player: Walter Ulbricht, whose policy, with its socialist Eastern state, played into the hands of Adenauer's idea of isolation and distancing. Ulbricht was equally opposed to a unification of Germany at the expense of the GDR system.

The way Adenauer's 'policy of strength' developed contributed to an escalation in the formation of blocs. In this area he was ahead of his 'opponent' Ulbricht in fact and in timing. As early as March 1949 – even before the founding of the Federal Republic – and on several occasions in the summer and autumn of 1950, he expressed his readiness to contribute militarily within the framework of a European army. The Korean War was favourable for Adenauer's policy of the militarization of the Federal Republic, drawing international attention and seemingly making a West German contribution necessary. As a quid pro quo Adenauer demanded sovereignty for his partial state. At the end of August 1950 US High Commissioner John J. McCloy, to whom the Federal Chancellor was distantly related, received a memorandum from Adenauer. From the start he had sought a close attachment to the Western powers. A German military contribution would be useful in this. The social democrats, however, voiced their fundamental opposition to this, led by Kurt Schumacher, who rightly predicted that the one-sided policy of Western integration would reduce the prospects for a unification of Germany and would also therefore damage European unification. Schumacher saw German unity as a precondition for the unification of Europe, and in the long run he was correct: the unification of Germany in 1990 became the basis for the 'enlargement' of the European Union towards the East that took place later in 2004–7.

As long as Germany remained split, Europe was divided. This observation was not lost on the CDU either. Even in Adenauer's own party there was opposition to his one-sided policy. The Minister of the Interior, Gustav Heinemann, resigned on account of the policy of German rearmament that actually meant the militarization of the Federal Republic. Heinemann considered peace in Europe to be threatened by this and saw a deepening in the division of Germany. Adenauer carried the day by raising the spectre of the communist danger and by the assurance that he was not in favour of carrying out 'any experiments', and gained the support of the citizens of the Federal Republic. In the second Bundestag elections on 6 September 1953 the CDU/CSU achieved an increased number of votes and in 1957, as already mentioned, even gained an absolute majority.

Adenauer placed notable emphasis on the establishment of ties with representatives of the state of Israel, tied above all to the recognition and readiness to make reparations. This had already got underway at the start of the 1950s. Likewise, Adenauer sought contacts early on with the political representatives of France. It would be an exaggeration to talk about reconciliation as early as the 1950s. At first it was a matter of tentative exploration and putting out feelers on the part of Georges Bidault and Robert Schuman from the related political party, the MRP (Mouvement Républicain Populaire) in France. At issue was the tricky question of the resolution of the Ruhr question and who the Saarland belonged to. The best one could hope for at this time was a policy of mutual understanding. French suspicion of the Germans was still considerable. One can hardly talk of reconciliation, given the still fresh experience of the war. In France in the first years after the war, the 'German danger' was seen as greater than the potential threat from the Soviet Union – a drastic misjudgement of the situation. It was not until the Elysée Treaty, signed on 22 January 1963 in Paris, wrongly referred to as the Franco-German Treaty of Friendship (it was just called the Franco-German Treaty), that avenues for closer cooperation were opened up, creating the preconditions for a reconciliation.

On the occasion of Adenauer's visit to Moscow in 1955 the leadership in the Kremlin allowed the release of the prisoners of war still in the Soviet Union in exchange for Bonn's taking up diplomatic relations that had not been sought up to this point. In answer to the question of what Adenauer's greatest achievement was in opinion polls more than ten years later, 75 per cent of the citizens of the Federal Republic stated 'bringing home the last prisoners of war', which has entered into mythology. In the middle of his fourth period of office, Adenauer resigned on 15 October 1963 after criticism from within the ranks of his own party had increased in strength. His successor was Ludwig Erhard, the successful Economics Minister, who was similarly mythologized as the 'father of the "Economic Miracle"'.

'Resurrected from the Ruins' – Mass Uprising in the GDR on 17 June 1953

The official foundation of the GDR in the Soviet Occupation Zone, by means of publication of a constitution on 7 October 1949, followed the formation of the Federal Republic with only a slight time delay. The German People's Council, which had emerged from the People's Congress movement on 30 May 1949, was transformed on the same day into a provisional Volkskammer (People's Chamber), becoming the parliament of the East German partial state. On 10 October 1949 the five Länder parliaments of the Soviet Occupation Zone formed a provisional Länderkammer consisting of 34 representatives. The Volkskammer and the Länderkammer elected SED chairman Wilhelm Pieck to be the first President of the GDR.

On 10 July 1945 he had been elected chairman at the meeting constituting the refounding of the Central Committee (CC) of the SPD. Nine days later his name appeared as a co-signatory of an action alliance with the KPD. In the middle of July he signed as a co-founder of a bloc of anti-fascist democratic parties, the so-called 'Anti-fa bloc'. At the start of October 1945 the British occupation authorities prevented him from travelling to the SPD conference in Wennigsen near Hanover. The US and French occupation authorities reacted similarly. Pieck joined the study commission of the CC of the SPD and of the CC of the KPD to work on the 'principles and aims of the party statute of the SED', as a member of the party executive committee of the SED from 1946 and also joint SED chairman after the merging of the two parties. The first elections to the GDR Volkskammer took place on 15 October 1950 on the basis of a single list of the National Front, and delivered the 99.7 per cent 'Yes' votes usual within dictatorships. This system, which offered voters no choice, was practised up to the end of the SED regime in 1989.

The results of the single-list elections to the Volkskammer in the years from 1950 to 1986 (i.e. in the periods of Walter Ulbricht and Erich Honecker), show a cluster of 'Yes' votes developing clearly in parallel and a turn-out in the election giving percentages that look rather suspicious. The numbers were all well over 90 per cent, ranging towards the 100 per cent mark. With a turn-out, for example, in 1986 of 99.74 per cent with 99.4 per cent 'Yes' votes, the suspicion of fraud was obvious. As late as 1988 then this had become apparent. The developments show, in addition, the tendency of the system geared totally towards one party. Showing it diagrammatically makes it clear that it could not be called a universal franchise. The phrase beside it, 'Ich gehe falten' (I'm going to fold) instead of 'Ich gehe wählen' (I'm going to vote), proves that the single-list elections had nothing to do with elections in the usual sense of a real democracy.

The constitution of the GDR was reminiscent of the Weimar one in form. Germany was referred to as an 'indivisible democratic republic' based on Länder. It guaranteed the basic rights of the citizen (e.g. freedom of speech, press freedom, the freedom of assembly and of religion as well as the right to strike). It guaranteed private property and insisted that the economy had to 'serve the wellbeing of the whole people and the provision of needs'. The state was to carry out public economic planning by means of legislative bodies.

Even though it made a claim to represent the whole of Germany and affirmed democratic principles, this constitutional document immediately developed into an instrument for the construction of a socialist partial state using political repression and the persecution of those with differing views. Article 6 was particularly

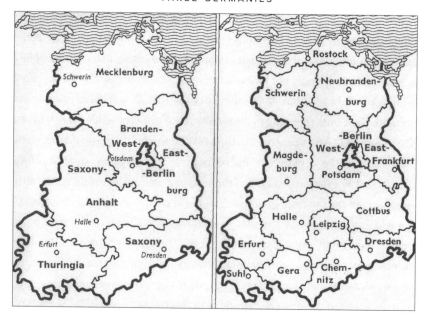

The Administrative Areas ('Bezirke') before and after July 1952.

striking in this respect as it characterized a 'boycott campaign against democratic institutions and organizations' as a crime. The GDR constitution also offered a handy pretext for a justice system that, increasingly, acted politically, proceeding by targeting opponents of this new German partial state and carrying out harsh measures against them. It soon became clear that this constitution was a contradiction with the elements in itself that were based on a state system recognizing legal rights and in contradiction to real democratic conditions. In 1952, without reference to the populations concerned and the representatives of the Länder of Brandenburg, Mecklenburg, Saxony, Saxony-Anhalt and Thuringia, these historic Länder were replaced by fourteen 'Bezirke' (counties). No change to the constitution was considered necessary for this.

In contrast to the Federal Republic, in the GDR authority was not exercised by the state and its organizations, but by a party: the SED and its committees. The SED Politburo was the centre of power. In addition to this came the apparatus of the Central Committee (CC), which had more than 2,000 members and was superior to the administration of the state. The principle in the song composed in 1950 by Louis Fürnberg was the rule: 'The Party, the Party is always right and may it stay like that, comrades! Because whoever fights for what is right, is always in the right against lies and exploitation. Whoever offends against life, is stupid or evil, whoever defends humanity, is always right. So, springing from

Lenin's mind and welded into place by Stalin, that's the Party, the Party!' The SED thus wielded a wide-ranging control over the activity of the state. The CC of the SED, a deviant form of internal party democracy, a pseudo-parliament within the party, convened at intervals of a few months, acted as a mouthpiece for the political edicts of the Politburo, only in a few cases did it make use of the control function theoretically ascribed to it in relation to the all-powerful and complacent party leadership. The low priority the Party of Workers and Peasants gave to the real relevance of the GDR constitution of 1949 for the state can be clearly seen by the fact that in 1968 a new 'socialist constitution' came into effect that more accurately described the system in the GDR, also proclaiming the predominance of the SED in no uncertain terms.

The groupings and sub-organizations of this one-party regime are worth mentioning. The Free German Youth Movement (Freie Deutsche Jugend, FDJ) was the only legitimate youth organization and enjoyed a high status within the framework of the so-called mass organizations. The FDJ was to serve as a recruiting ground for the new generation of the SED and a 'reserve of cadres' for the party. The SED had recognized its leadership role. With its slogan 'Young people, awake, build up, build up, we are aiming for a better future for the homeland', the FDJ was to contribute to the politicization of young people, to work for the 'Socialist Fatherland' and fight the capitalist 'class enemy'.

The FDJ was embedded in industrial plants, places of education and residential quarters, the aim being political and ideological coordination along with the structuring of vocational training and leisure activities. The object was to reach as many young people as possible and get them involved in the FDJ. Linked to this were also the 'Young Pioneers', or the 'Ernst Thälmann' Pioneer Organization, named after the leading communist of the Weimar Period who was persecuted during the Nazi era, arrested and murdered in Buchenwald concentration camp.

The FDJ was founded on 7 March 1946 and systematically built up under the leadership of the later SED general secretary, Erich Honecker, as a youth organization allegedly 'above party affiliation'. Who was this man? Arrested by the Gestapo in 1937, Honecker, a roofer born at Neunkirchen in the Saarland, had survived almost ten years in prison and was liberated by the Red Army on 27 April 1945. In May he joined the 'Ulbricht Group' and as youth secretary of the CC of the KPD built up the 'Antifa' youth committees, which led to the founding of the FDJ in 1946. Its alignment with the KPD and later with the SED was established in the 1950s. After that, it was to promote Marxism-Leninism, carry out the SED decisions and participate in pre-military training.

The FDJ was to number more than two million members. According to official statistics, approximately 70 per cent of young people between 14 and 25 in the GDR were members of the FDJ. The proportion of school pupils and students was particularly high. The officials of the FDJ were often at the same time members of the SED. The secretaries of the FDJ also belonged to the Politburo. The FDJ also formed a grouping in the 'Parliament'. From the 1960s a little under 10 per cent of the members of the Volkskammer belonged to the FDJ grouping. The FDJ was to be a guarantee for the hegemony of the SED.

Agricultural policy was already from the 1950s totally under the control of the socialist restructuring of the GDR. The SED regime forced through collectivization after the model of the USSR. Straight after the end of the war land reform had been introduced, involving the expropriation of agricultural property of over 100 hectares per holding. Large agricultural properties were broken up. Many new farmers were given relatively small areas of land without technical equipment to aid them. The unity party went in for massive propaganda for the founding of collective farms, called Agricultural Production Co-operatives (Landwirtschaftliche Produktionsgenossenschaften, LPGs), which the farmers were to join 'voluntarily'. The extent to which this was voluntary was limited.

After many had only joined with scepticism and hesitation, action against resistant farmers was announced. At the end of the 1950s there was a campaign against anyone who refused. Anyone who did not comply was put under pressure, arrested and physically mistreated. The stream of propaganda continued to be pumped out right up until the spring of 1960; the socialization of the means of production was pushed through in parallel to this and the expropriation largely 'completed'. The LPGs were divided into three types according to the degree of collectivization and the resulting distribution of the collective income: collective agriculture, wherever possible using meadow land and woodland; collective animal husbandry, based on the so-called 'perspective plan'; bringing together all areas of agricultural and forestry use, machinery and equipment and all the livestock. There were restrictions on agricultural land and the numbers of cattle for one's own use (e.g. half a hectare per family). Inevitably, as a result of the forced expropriations, there was wide-scale destruction of the identity, habits and traditions of the farming community, who lost their individuality and now had to function as collective producers. Their own property and individual production lost their value. What mattered now was mass production. Feeling alarmed and insecure, many farmers left the GDR with their families and made for the Federal Republic, which had a negative effect on the supply of food in East Germany.

Ulbricht's state transformed the LPGs into new agricultural units whenever these demonstrated readiness to be involved in cooperation above the level of the unit. The mergers led to 'cooperatives', which were devoted to the cultivation of specific crops and the rearing of specific animals.

The continuing stream of refugees towards the 'free' West illustrated that the SED and their programme were not particularly popular amongst the population. Within the party voices were at once raised against Ulbricht and his practice of going along with Soviet domination. A purge was already underway at the end of the 1940s against former SPD members and those old communists who had come out against the merger of the KPD and the SPD. Their opposition was particularly directed against the restructuring of the SED as a Stalinist cadre party.

Stalin died on 5 March 1953. The mood of the Soviet people was marked both by relief and mourning. There was hope of a reduction of state terror and a relaxation in relations with the Western powers. Changes were also noticeable in the GDR. The dogmatic and intolerant SED general secretary, Walter Ulbricht, who attempted to emulate Stalin in his little German Soviet state, was going to be replaced, judging by the rumours.

The new Soviet High Commissioner, Vladimir Semenov, had instructions from Moscow according to which the SED leadership should show more flexibility. On 28 May 1953 the GDR Council of Ministers still announced a general increase of norms of production, thus fuelling discontent and further encouraging people to flee. In addition there were shortages in the food supply and an increase in state terror as a result of arbitrary arrests. The SED regime under Ulbricht was behaving in a more communist way than the Soviets.

Only after increased pressure from Moscow did the Pankow regime make economic concessions towards their own population and were forced to announce a 'new course', introducing relaxations in the pressure of production, a cancellation of price increases and improvements in the consumer sector. The increase of production norms by 10 per cent scheduled for May, relating to industrial plants and agriculture was not, however, reviewed, whereupon building workers on the Stalin Allee in East Berlin went on strike starting on 16 June.

The next day discontent was reflected in a spontaneous mass uprising all over the GDR, in the course of which there were demonstrations and strikes in more than 560 areas, above all, in the industrial centres. Around 10 per cent of workers played an active part. Initially economic demands were aimed at a cancellation of the increases in production norms. Political demands soon developed from this, calling for the resignation of the SED regime, the removal of Ulbricht, free elections and German unity.

The GDR leadership lost control of the situation. Without Russian backing it would have lost the battle and been strung up. In the end there was no alternative but to put a stop to the movement that had got out of hand by means of Soviet troops. Russian tanks mowed down the angry masses of people in Berlin and other large towns in the GDR. The exact figure of the fatalities varies from between a few dozen and several hundred. Over 1,000 people were given long terms of imprisonment.

The winner of the uprising having been put down was Ulbricht who was able to consolidate his power position and could count on Soviet support for lack of other suitable leaders, particularly since his opponents within the party were arrested.

On 19 June the Western High Commissioners voiced their protest at the Soviet action and called for the restoration of 'normal conditions of life'. They publicly expressed their horror at the brutality and made it known to the East Germans that they sympathized with their fate. The Western press made a great show of supporting those who took part in the uprising and gave the impression that there would be Western involvement and help, but this impression was deceptive.

It soon became clear that Great Britain had no interest in providing East German citizens with any help. The British High Commissioner, Sir Ivonne Kirkpatrick, held the view that the intervention of Soviet troops had been legitimate. For him the USSR also had the right in principle to keep control of their zone if necessary by force. The inactivity of Great Britain must be seen in the light of this stance. It is confirmed by an internal remark of the British Foreign Secretary, Selwyn Lloyd:

> Germany is the key to the peace of Europe. A divided Europe has meant a divided Germany. To unite Germany while Europe is divided, even if practicable, is fraught with danger for all. Therefore everyone – Dr Adenauer, the Russians, the Americans, the French and ourselves – feel in our hearts that a divided Germany is safer for the time being. But none of us dare say so openly because of the effect upon German public opinion. Therefore we all publicly support a united Germany, both on his own terms.

Adenauer was taken aback by the popular uprising. He was at a loss about both the origin and the extent of the potential for protest. On the afternoon of 17 June he expressed on the radio his inner solidarity with the demonstrators. At the same time he called on them 'not to be carried away into doing anything rash in response to provocations'. This hesitant stance was significant; it disappointed the East German population and robbed them of any hope of a reunification in the near future.

The year 1953 had begun particularly successfully for Adenauer as regards foreign policy. On 19 March the Bundestag had ratified the treaty of the European Defence Community (EDC). Only France's signature was missing. Adenauer wanted to avoid a failure of the negotiations at all cost. For this reason he was reserved in his attitude towards the June events in the GDR (he also didn't want to give the USSR any cause for direct accusations of the West). Above and beyond that, uncertainty about the consequences of a possible intervention was too great. Only when, in the next few days, he came under pressure to act did Adenauer address a telegram to the heads of government of the Western Allies on 21 June. In it, he called upon them to do everything 'to put an end to the unbearable conditions in the Soviet Zone and to return the German people to unity and freedom'. Two days later he travelled to Berlin to take part in the memorial ceremony for the victims of the uprising. Afterwards, in front of the Schöneberg Town Hall, Adenauer declared that he would not rest 'until the whole of Germany was united'.

The suppression of the events of 17 June was in fact convenient for Adenauer, particularly since it validated the policy he had been pursuing up until then and to advise against talks at Four Power level in the light of Soviet repression in the GDR and their continuing support for the SED, even though for tactical reasons he publicly called for them. The events of 17 June strengthened his position both in the alliance with the Western powers and in domestic politics, as the elections of 6 September prove. This success created a broad parliamentary basis for his policy of Western integration. Adenauer portrayed himself as the father figure of the whole of the German population. In the autumn of 1953 he achieved an astounding success at the elections. West Germans totally believed in his slogan 'No experiments' and his Western policy, which led to an absolute majority after the elections in 1957.

The 'Oberbürgermeister' of Berlin, Ernst Reuter, reacted more impulsively to the dramatic events. After a delayed return from a visit to Vienna on 18 June, he protested to the Americans. In no uncertain terms, he called for 'the mobilization of all forces to put an end to [the] madness'. Later he declared in a radio speech 'that people can surely not in the long term be held down by martial law, bayonets and tanks'. Visibly shocked at the inactivity of the Allies, he said: 'There is no problem that is as pressing as the reunification of Germany. There will be no rest, no peace until this problem is solved.'

This opinion was shared in particular by the SPD, which kept its sights on the whole of Germany. By means of solidarity campaigns, which were rejected in advance by the occupiers, they demonstrated their solidarity with the East Germans. Annoyed at the lack of obedience, the party members who participated were given a telling off. Even the governing mayor was reprimanded over his behaviour. In the end he was made aware that he could not change anything and his cry for help was falling on deaf ears. On the afternoon of 17 June US Secretary of State John Foster Dulles learnt of the bloody crushing of the East German uprising and recognized that this event would make an excellent propaganda tool. The US President, Dwight D. Eisenhower, who strictly refused to participate in a Four Power conference, now had a strong argument against it. In Washington the question was raised: 'How could Churchill agree to sit down at the negotiating table with a government and trust a partner whose policy had just cost dozens of people in East Germany their lives and which was desperately attempting to keep an incompetent and hated regime in power against the will of the people?'

Why the West remained passive when stones were flying against tanks, and people had to die (the first since the Iron Curtain went up to have risen up against a Stalinist system of terror in Central and Eastern Europe), was for a long time a mystery. In the meantime it has been proved that the uprising as such, in particular the fate of the East Germans, was of secondary importance to Adenauer and the West, or at least was only of instrumental use (i.e. to counteract a policy irreversibly of the Soviet Union that, after Stalin's death, seemed more eager to make concessions in its policy towards Germany and, for the West above all, to bring on the Western integration of the Federal Republic of Germany). The tragedy of 17 June signified for those who took part in the uprising a weakening of the opponents of the status quo of German policy and helped to consolidate Germany as two states. The failure of the uprising served to support all opponents of a compromise between East and West and helped those who had an interest in the maintenance of their positions and thus of the status quo.

The East German population expected more than just a show of human sympathy from the West and that they would take up strong positions. In the main, the failed uprising helped Ulbricht, enabling him to rescue himself and his position by means of the overthrow of a 'group of conspirators' within the party around Wilhelm Zaisser and Rudolf Herrnstadt.

In the case of the Soviets the view subsequently won out that they should not push through the announced liberalization of the GDR any further, that they should support Ulbricht and not continually jeopardize the SED system in favour of an all-German agreement with the West.

After 17 June the proposal from Churchill of 11 May 1953 to work at the highest level with the Kremlin towards an arrangement on a neutral all-German solution was robbed of any basis. He had been convinced that the West could negotiate with the Soviets based on a 'position of strength' in order to ward off the danger of an nuclear war. In fact, Moscow's readiness to take part in negotiations in Western capitals was minimal, even though the events in the GDR before 17 June were seen to reflect completely the Soviet intention of pressing for a Four Power conference on the German question. Churchill's proposal was not regarded as unrealistic in the rest of the West but as unwelcome. The planned summit of the Big Three in 1953 was reduced to a conference of the three Western foreign ministers.

The victors of the Second World War remained Allies, true to their principles, *against* Germany even through the days around 17 June 1953, particularly since they were dealing primarily with the security and consolidation of their areas of interest in relation to both of the German partial states. The actual losers were the weakest element in the game: the Germans behind the Iron Curtain and all those who had hoped for the restoration of German unity.

Historical research has often, in the end, portrayed the events of 17 June against the background of the world-shaking course of events of October and November 1989. When considered in a wider historical context, the process sparked off by the broad masses on 17 June 1953 after protest rallies in Czechoslovakia in May a further – though disorganized and abortive – attempt to stage an uprising behind the Iron Curtain that was important as a precedent and had a long-term effect. A successful revolution could, after all, hardly take place in the conditions prevailing at the start of the 1950s in the Soviet bloc. It was a rehearsal for an actual revolution. The formation of more durable 'revolutionary' forms of organization against the background of a rigid apparatus of state repression was hardly possible. A renewal for the spontaneous uprising of the masses could only be bloodily suppressed by a massive Soviet intervention – it was typical that no leading personality could be identified as being in control of it, unlike in the case of those later in Hungary (Imre Nagy), Czechoslovakia (Alexander Dubček) or Poland (Lech Wałęsa). The failure of the events of 17 June also depended, however, on the fact that the Western powers did not consider any effective support at all for those involved in the uprising, even though they were soon well informed about what was going on. From this point of view, the reason usually given until recently for the failure – 'military intervention by the occupation forces of the Soviet Union' – is only half the truth. Along with its economically inefficient system and long overdue reforms in its own sphere of power as well as a lack of political flexibility, the Soviet Union considerably failed in its (self-)imposed policy on Germany. As long as the primary goal of the Western powers remained the integration of the Federal Republic with the West, however, there was no obstacle set to the integration of the GDR into the East and it could be useful for propaganda towards this goal. The two things were mutually support-ive. To this extent the destabilization of the GDR was not at all, in the end, a means towards achieving this goal. The unification of Germany in the early days of the Cold War could only have meant neutrality for Germany – such a unification was neither ruled out nor impossible, it was admittedly unwelcome to Adenauer, even if it had been still considered possible and practicable within the State Department, for example in Summer 1955.

The events of 17 June, which started as local unrest amongst workers and quickly turned into a mass uprising across the whole republic, threatened, for a short period, to disrupt the process of Western integration because the revolution-ary movement appeared to lead automatically to German unity. More than half a million people came out onto the streets, went on strike or demonstrated.

The American 'roll back' had proved to be impracticable. The psychology and propaganda of the Cold War remained and was supported by humanitarian measures – over five million food parcels were sent to the GDR between 27 July and 3 October 1953 – which in a way even helped to consolidate the Ulbricht regime. From the US point of view the watchword was one of 'keeping the pot simmering but not to bring it to the boil'. The fact that the US also let their opponents follow a policy of 'keep the Germans down', looking on in Berlin as this was carried out, can be regarded as the Machiavellian aspect of the 'roll back' in the case of 17 June. In fact what was practised was 'dual containment': there was an attempt to stem the tide of the communist and the German 'danger', and for the average citizen this subtle game was not obvious. From a psychological point of view, however, it may have had a not inconsiderable effect on the self-image of those involved in the uprising and, in the long run, on the stability of the badly hit GDR system.

To avoid a greater risk, the Western powers had refrained from intervening as the East German population had hoped and limited themselves to protests. The day 17 June was declared a public holiday in the Federal Republic on 4 August 1953, becoming the 'Day of German Unity', and remained as such until 1990. The citizens in the free West made use of this additional public holiday for extensive outings and increased leisure activities. The fate of those involved in the uprising and the actual significance of 17 June as a day of commemoration dropped out of sight or were repressed.

Elimination of the 'Counter-revolutionaries' and the Continuation of the Ulbricht Era

The popular uprising in the GDR was also accompanied by different opinions and increased oppositional tendencies within the SED. Minister of Justice, Max Fechner, was arrested as a result of his criticism of the wave of state terror following 17 June. Only in the second half of the 1950s, when the 20th Party Congress of the Soviet Communist Party initiated de-stalinization, was there for a time any criticism to be voiced in the SED of the bureaucratic and centralized planned economy which had contributed to the failure of the economic plans. Instead of giving space to these well-intentioned moves forward, these critics were denounced as 'counter-revolutionaries' and subjected to vicious treatment. After 1956 there was a tightening up. The philosophers Wolfgang Harich and Ernst Bloch, and the scientist Robert Havemann, who stood up for 'Socialism with a human face', lost their posts and their professional positions. Harich, who knew Bertolt Brecht and was a close associate of the literary figures Gerhard Zwerenz and Erich Loest, had put forward ideas about a 'renewal of the party' and a 'particular German socialism' that would be freed of Soviet Stalinism. He had not reckoned with the German Stalinist Ulbricht and was arrested shortly after the uprising in Hungary in November 1956. In 1957 he was sentenced to ten years' imprisonment on account of the 'formation of a group of conspirators hostile to the state' and was not released until December 1964 under an amnesty. In 1979 he was able to travel on an extended visa to the Federal Republic, Austria, Spain and Switzerland. He supported the peace and environmental protection movement in the Federal Republic. In 1981 he returned to the GDR. After unification in 1990, which Harich welcomed, he spoke out against the right of the Federal Republic to put the iniquities of the GDR on trial and to judge the past of the GDR.

The philosopher Ernst Bloch, who was regarded as the brain behind the 'revisionists', was dismissed from his chair at the University of Leipzig in 1957. He was forced to retire on account of his open criticism of Marxism having become a rigid doctrine in the GDR and his condemnation of the bloody repression of the Hungarian uprising. During his stay in the Federal Republic with his wife he was taken by surprise by the building of the Wall and decided not to go back to the GDR. He subsequently accepted a professorship in Tübingen. He was expelled from the East Berlin Academy of Sciences in 1962. Bloch later belonged to the critics of US policy in Vietnam and the crimes committed there. Along with

Theodor Adorno and Max Horkheimer, Bloch was one of the leading figures of the 1968 student movement.

Robert Havemann – a member of the KPD since 1932, founding member of the resistance group, The European Union, in 1942, arrested by the Gestapo in 1943, liberated from prison by the Red Army in 1945, later professor of applied physical chemistry at the Humboldt University – met with open criticism from the SED Party newspaper *Neues Deutschland* on account of his critical essays (for example, 'The Clash of Opinions Advances Knowledge') and lectures. In 1964 Havemann was expelled from the party and placed under restrictions at the Humboldt University. In 1965 the Hamburg weekly newspaper *Die Zeit* published an article by Havemann entitled 'Yes I was wrong. Why I was a Stalinist and became an Anti-Stalinist.' At this, he was permanently dismissed and was also placed under restrictions in relation to the German Academy of Sciences in East Berlin. In the year after he was removed from its lists, Havemann refused to leave the GDR. In 1975 the SED removed him from their list of 'anti-fascist resistance fighters'. He protested against the treatment of Wolf Biermann, the songwriter and performer critical of the regime and being stripped of GDR citizenship. Havemann was placed under house arrest as a result. In 1979 he was fined 10,000 DM for infringing the law relating to foreign currency. In 1982 he signed the 'Berlin Appeal' of Rainer Eppelmann entitled 'Creating Peace without Weapons'. Up until his death (in the same year) Havemann was systematically isolated socially and politically. The scientists Fritz Behrens and Arne Benary, who were in favour of an 'independent management on the part of producers' on the Yugoslav model, were severely reprimanded by the SED. The SED functionaries, Karl Schirdewan and Ernst Wollweber, lost their positions on the Politburo after they called for the continuation of de-stalinization.

According to the highly idiosyncratic definition of the East German state, the sovereignty of the people was embodied in it. In line with this primitive logic, any criticism and opposition was therefore always therefore directed 'against the people' and had thus to be consistently persecuted. In doing this, the state in its internal affairs tended towards the use of the procedures well known from the French revolutionary tribunal and the guillotine, or then later on also the methods familiar from Nazism of persecution and execution by means of beheading or a shot in the back of the neck in line with the 'elimination of the political opponent'. Opposition to the regime and to the SED against 'rule by the people' was defamed and criminalized in this way. Despite repression and banning, oppositional tendencies to the SED dictatorship repeatedly surfaced. Actions such as the removal of GDR citizenship from the writer and singer Biermann when he travelled to the Federal Republic, the arrest and deportation of the sociologist and writer Rudolf Bahro, the move to the West of the poets Reiner Kunze and Sarah Kirsch and the way the GDR authorities dealt with the peace movement in their own country illustrate the questionable nature of the 'peace-loving' state as regards its internal affairs.

The GDR banished its critical intelligence and rationality of thought from public life within its own country, forced it not only into 'internal emigration' but also into exile and was thus diluted intellectually. That this happened under the former exile politician Ulbricht, shows how little sympathy and understanding this German communist had for people who thought differently.

After the founding of the product of a forced unification between KPD and SPD, the SED, Walter Ulbricht initially became its deputy chairman and member of the Central Secretariat after Grotewohl and Pieck. In 1950–53 the trained carpenter rose to the post of general secretary of the party and thus took over the de facto leadership of the SED. After 17 June 1953 he was appointed First Secretary of the CC of the SED and held this office until 1971. In 1955 he became first deputy chairman of the Council of Ministers and thereby also consolidated his position within the GDR state apparatus. Also a member of the 'Volkskammer' from 1949, after the death of the first State President, Pieck, he became chairman of the Council of State newly created in 1960 and at the same time chairman of the National Defence Council. Thus, all the relevant functions of the East German state were united within a personal union in Ulbricht's hands. For more than two decades Ulbricht, like no-one else, determined the fate of the German state at the behest of Moscow. After eliminating all opponents within the party he became the most powerful and influential politician in the GDR. According to official pronouncements, the GDR under his leadership would become the second most powerful industrial state in the so-called 'Eastern Bloc', at least the most loyal and trustworthy vassal state to the USSR. The East German Communists were as a rule more communist and more conforming with Moscow than their comrades in Poland and Hungary.

Ulbricht outlived Stalin and Khrushchev and also proved to be an obedient satrap for Brezhnev. He shared his doctrine, according to which military interventions were to be carried out in 'fraternal socialist states' in the event of 'counter revolutions' and always steadfastly supported *externally* the positions of the USSR. From the middle of the 1960s he attempted to boost the role of the GDR in COMECON and the Warsaw Pact and to achieve a certain loosening of the dependence on the Soviet hegemony in Central Europe. In 1968 he was an outspoken supporter of the military repression of the Prague Spring reforms of Communism in Czechoslovakia.

In 1963, one year before the fall of Khrushchev, he initiated an economic reform under the control of the SED, thus portraying himself as a German socialist statesman who had conceived his own model of Socialism in the GDR that would be an example for modern industrial states. This tendency towards self-aggrandizement caused irritation and bad feeling in the Kremlin, which joined the growing criticism in the Politburo of the course Ulbricht was taking and supported his removal. Allegedly 'for health reasons', mainly, however, as a result of Soviet requests and pressure from within the Party and putsch-like manoeuvres by Erich Honecker, Ulbricht resigned as First Secretary of the SED on 3 May 1971, making way for the ambitious FDJ activist. He had to give up his chairmanship in the National Defence Council and he lost all political influence, even though he retained the purely nominal office of chairman of the Council of State up until his death on 1 August 1973 in East Berlin.

Escape to the West and the GDR as a Retreat for Refugees

Already in the last weeks of the war and after the occupation zones had been set up, the German population started to flee westwards from the areas occupied by the Red Army. Even the founding of the GDR could not alter this in any way: on the contrary, many Germans from Central and Eastern Germany were not able to identify with this 'Russian state' and turned their backs on it. Individual, family and material reasons also played a role in this. Already in 1949, the year that the GDR was founded, emergency camps were erected in West Berlin and the Federal Republic, containing over 100,000 refugees. The numbers continued to rise in the 1950s. The events of 17 June 1953, with the beginning of a wave of arrests and terror, represented the high point of people 'voting with their feet'. In the year of the bloody suppression of the uprising by workers and the people in the GDR more than 300,000 people crossed the inner-German border; which, strictly speaking in terms of international law, was not a border but only a demarcation line between the occupation zones until such time as the victorious powers had negotiated a definitive resolution of the question of Germany in the form of a peace treaty.

To this extent, not only was the Federal Republic an 'occupied Ally' (as Hermann-Josef Rupieper calls it) with a provisional outer border with the second German state, but so too was the GDR. In that respect, there were two 'occupied Allies', (i.e. by the Soviet Union and the Western powers including the USA). To be precise and honest, one would have to call them satellite and vassal states under the control of East and West.

Even in the years after 1953, the number of illegal emigrants ('Republik-flüchtlinge', i.e. 'deserters of the Republic') continued to be very high. The loss of population was a thorn in the side of the GDR. The exodus threatened to bleed it to death, particularly since it was mainly the younger and middle generations of working age who 'went West'. Approximately half of the refugees were young people under the age of 25, nearly 60 per cent were of working age and fewer than 10 per cent were of pension age. The harder stance of the SED regime and the forced collectivization of agriculture boosted the numbers of refugees in 1960, and in 1961 this was to see a dramatic development.

In August 1961 another 47,433 people sought refuge in the West via East Berlin. Less than two months after Ulbricht put out the false information detailed below, the GDR blocked the border between the Eastern and Western sectors of Berlin and began work on the Wall in Berlin, subsequently developing it by the use of a sophisticated system of border areas, guard dogs, tall barbed wire, automatic firing equipment and watchtowers, the so-called 'death strip'. In front of the Brandenburg Gate in West Berlin demonstrators shouted 'Open the gate!' The mayor of West Berlin, Willy Brandt, insisted: 'The Soviet Union have given their guard dog a bit of play on his leash. They have allowed him to move his troops into the Eastern sector of this city. The Soviet Union have given their guard dog the power to break international law. The tanks that were mobilized to stop the mass flight from the Zone, these tanks have crushed under their tracks the binding Four Power status of the whole of Berlin.'

However, Ulbricht defended the 'anti-fascist protection wall'. The GDR leadership had been aware of the social and economic catastrophe for a long time. As early as 1952 Ulbricht had considered building a wall, but did not have Stalin's agreement to this. In 1957, along with a tightening of controls, travelling between the two halves of Berlin had also been restricted and the crime of illegal emigration ('Republikflucht', i.e. 'desertion of the Republic') was introduced. With the construction of the Wall, the GDR was able to prohibit all links between the Soviet sector and the three Western sectors and stem the flood of refugees.

From the founding of the East German state in 1949 up to 13 August 1961, a total of 2,686,942 people were recorded as having sought refuge in the West, representing a seventh of the East German population. Without the building of the Wall and the border areas, the GDR would have been largely depopulated.

In the months leading up to 13 August 1961, the day on which the building of the Wall in Berlin began, more than 155,000 GDR citizens came to the West. Since then, as many as 52,000 refugees left the illegitimate state under risk of death in

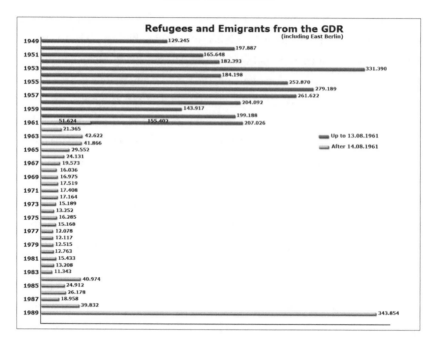

Refugees and Emigrants from the GDR
(including East Berlin)

Year	
1949	129.245
	197.887
1951	165.648
	182.393
1953	331.390
	184.198
1955	252.870
	279.189
1957	261.622
	204.092
1959	143.917
	199.188
1961	51.624 / 155.402 / 207.026
	21.365
1963	42.622
	41.866
1965	29.552
	24.131
1967	19.573
	16.036
1969	16.975
	17.519
1971	17.408
	17.164
1973	15.189
	13.252
1975	16.285
	15.168
1977	12.078
	12.117
1979	12.515
	12.763
1981	15.433
	13.208
1983	11.343
	40.974
1985	24.912
	26.178
1987	18.958
	39.832
1989	343.854

Up to 13.08.1961
After 14.08.1961

Refugees and emigrants from the GDR (including East Berlin).

1961 alone. The majority managed to cross the borders between the sectors and reach West Berlin at great risk, after being assembled in refugee camps there they were flown to the Federal Republic. Only very few wanted to stay in the 'trap' that was West Berlin, many of them were afraid of threats and persecution on the part of East German Communists. For years the SED regime had triumphantly announced that only 'class enemies' would leave the 'Workers' and Farmers' State'. Since the end of the war approximately two million people had already left the GDR. Rumours circulated that the last opportunity to seek refuge in West Berlin would not be long in coming. Ulbricht wanted to deny them this opportunity.

On 15 June 1961 the chairman of the Council of State had lied in reply to a question from a representative of the Press: 'I take your question to mean that there are people in West Germany who want us to mobilize the building workers of the capital of the GDR to construct a wall. I am not aware of any such intention, [but] the building workers in the capital are busy enough building homes and they have their hands full with the work . . . Nobody has the intention of building a wall!' When this interview became known, the number of refugees shot up again.

The dark columns in the diagram above show the statistics from 1949 up to the building of the Wall in August 1961. The figures per year rose from 130,000 (in 1949) to 200,000 and even more than 300,000 in the year of the people's uprising of 17

June. As mentioned before, a high number was recorded for 1961, totalling over 200,000. But what is the explanation for the later, still remarkable, statistic of tens of thousands leaving the GDR after 1962? There were fewer and fewer refugees, but there were still emigrants. By means of negotiations with the GDR, the Federal Republic was able to bring about opportunities for visits and emigration to the West of Germany (by paying ransoms, organizing family reunions and allocating financial grants). In total, 5.2 million East Germans applied to come to the Federal Republic against the background of the Cold War, which was a remarkable trend.

'Go and see how you like it in the GDR!' was the usual taunt on the part of rightwing conservatives directed at West German critics of the Federal Republic. There were quite a lot of people who went in that direction as well. For a long time the (recently published) results of research by Bernd Stöver were not taken up: that a considerable number of West Germans also moved over to East Germany, 'internal German migrations' as Stöver terms them, people who 'went over there' as they used to say. In 1950, for example, about 40,000 people moved over to the GDR; even in 1953, the year the people's uprising was crushed, there were more than 22,000 people, and in 1961, the year in which the Wall was built, there were still as many as 20,000, in 1983 an additional 1,344 people. For the whole period up until 1990 there were a total of approximately 500,000 citizens of the Federal Republic who apparently found the GDR interesting enough to turn their backs on the West: the attractions of socialism, the guarantee of a job and accommodation, political and military career motivations, comprehensive childcare, family connections and, last but not least, love affairs. Those 'who went over there' were suspected, on the one hand, of being 'drop-outs', 'criminals', the 'losers' of the 'Economic Miracle' or 'traitors'. In the fight for recognition by the two states, on the other hand, they served to highlight the right to exist and the legitimation of the GDR. Many of them were, however, disappointed by the GDR and returned. The greatest cause of frustration on the part of many of the emigrants was, according to Stöver, individual experience with the SED regime and German communism following the Moscow line, which deeply affected ordinary everyday life. This inflexibility, as well as the lack of readiness to adapt to the prevailing conditions, became a largely insoluble problem – not just for the immigrants and those who had sought refuge there – as did the 'Economic Miracle' in the West and the building of the Wall in the East. After 13 August the GDR further lost credibility. Exact figures of those who returned 'full of regret' to the Federal Republic are unknown.

Opposed Foreign Policies of the Federal Republic and the GDR

The Hallstein Doctrine, West European Integration and the Construction
of the Wall as Impasses of German Policy

Soon after its founding, the West German state declared itself to be the sole legitimate representative of German interests and the only one entitled to speak for all Germans in the East and the West. This was the basis of the 'claim to sole representation' on the part of the Federal Republic. The assertion of this prerogative was linked to the isolation of the East German state and the devaluation of the GDR, which was not yet called by that name and only later put in inverted commas. This claim was justified by the argument based on democratic policy that only the Western part of Germany had a government that resulted from universal, free, equal and secret elections, whereas in the GDR, as it were, a unity party functioned by means of irrelevant 'bloc parties' (that is, there was rule by the dictatorship of one party).

Stalin had hesitated a long time before deciding on the definition and the role of the East German state. Moscow left its status undecided until the middle of the 1950s. Only after the integration of the Federal Republic into the Western military alliance did Khrushchev, along with the other Allied states and the GDR, proclaim the idea of 'peaceful coexistence' as an overriding principle and within this context the so-called 'two-state theory', according to which two sovereign German states had now emerged on the territory of the former German Reich.

The Federal government tried every means to challenge this view and prevent other states following the Soviet Union in opening up diplomatic relations with the GDR and thereby recognizing it as a state. Bonn, however, aided and abetted this development by its forceful policy of integration of the Federal Republic with the West. When Federal Chancellor Adenauer visited Moscow in September 1955, he was able to bring about the release of the last German prisoners of war as a quid pro quo for the opening up of diplomatic relations between the USSR and the Federal Republic. The exchange of ambassadors was agreed. The USSR had already established diplomatic relations with the GDR in 1954.

Adenauer had barely left when a GDR delegation arrived in Moscow and the official relations of the USSR to the two German states were clarified demonstratively and definitively. Adenauer had justified the opening of diplomatic relations with the Soviet Union with the argument that it was one of the Four Powers and that the hope was to bring about the release of the German prisoners of war who were still in Soviet camps (which had already been offered by

Moscow earlier, but Adenauer had delayed out of concern over the effect of a Russian success of prestige on West German public opinion preventing the ratification of the Western treaties).

On the journey back to Bonn the West German delegation wracked their brains on how to construct a barrier to the expected series of diplomatic recognitions of the GDR. The Freiburg expert on international law and head of the political section of the Foreign Office, Wilhelm Georg Grewe, and Walter Hallstein, the State Secretary of the Foreign Office and a former professor of private and company law at the universities of Rostock and Frankfurt am Main, developed an idea that was to be called the 'Hallstein doctrine'.

The doctrine was announced in the government declaration of 23 September 1955. Its aim was to isolate the GDR as an illegal construct. It subsequently developed into a dogmatic position of West German foreign policy. Based on the 'claim to sole representation of the whole German people', the Federal Republic declared that it would not open up or maintain diplomatic relations with any state in the world that had diplomatic relations with the GDR or that would enter into such relations.

Supported by the enormous economic potential and the massive payments of development aid to the so-called Third World in contrast to the economically modest GDR weakened by Soviet exploitation, this doctrine initially proved to be useful to thwart the recognition of the GDR by non-communist states. Aiming at the diplomatic isolation of the GDR, this strategy soon proved unworkable. Thus, Bonn had to break off relations with Yugoslavia in 1957 and with Cuba in 1963 because they had recognized the GDR. In the medium and long term, the Hallstein doctrine led to a self-isolation of West German foreign policy and hindered a more flexible and open diplomacy. Via channels linked to the Austrian Federal Chancellery on the Ballhausplatz in Vienna and its network throughout Central and Eastern Europe urgent attempts were made to assess the situation.

The Hallstein doctrine came very much into question when, in 1967, the Federal Republic opened relations with Romania and, in 1969, even with Yugoslavia, both states that had long recognized the GDR. The Hallstein doctrine had led to an untenable situation where, up until that time, there were no German embassies in Belgrade, Budapest, Bucharest, Prague, Sofia and Warsaw and thus no relevant information was being gathered in these countries.

Adenauer's German policy had been forced down a blind alley by the Hallstein doctrine, culminating in the Berlin Wall. At the same time it meant the failure of his 'policy of strength'. After the formation of the SPD-FDP coalition in 1969 the direction of West German policy towards the East changed fundamentally. In the light of the German-Soviet Treaty of 1970 and the 'Grundlagen-Vertrag' of 1972, in which the Federal Republic recognized the GDR as a state but not a foreign one, the Hallstein doctrine became totally obsolete. The concept had proved to be impracticable after not only the neutral Austrians, but also Western diplomacy, had pressed Bonn to give up this idea. The name Hallstein, however, has positive associations in the context of West European integration. As a prisoner of war of the US, he had set up a camp university in 1945, reopened Frankfurt am Main University in 1946 and, two years later, had held a post as a visiting professor at Georgetown University in Washington. In 1950 Adenauer commissioned him as State Secretary for Foreign Policy with leading the West German delegation at the Paris 'Schuman Plan' negotiations. Six states came together in April 1951 in order to form the European Coal and Steel Community (ECSC). On 25 March 1957 the representatives of the same states signed the so-called Treaties of Rome on the Capitol of the Holy City. For Adenauer, 'this union' was 'the most important post-war event'. The agreements, which came into effect on 1 January 1958, founded two more European communities: the European Atomic Energy Community (EURATOM) was to facilitate scientific research and the peaceful uses of atomic energy (which was only partly successful) and the European Economic Community (EEC) was to establish a 'common market' involving competition policy and a customs union.

Raising the standard of living and an intensification of trade and economic policy were the goals. The Common Assembly of the ECSC was to become the European Parliament, admittedly not directly elected until 1979. In the Council of Ministers there were representatives of the governments of the national states. The specialist ministers met according to their departmental affiliation. Decision-making lay with the Council, in which majority decisions would be valid only after a transition period, a principle that the President of France, Charles de Gaulle, scuppered with his veto policy. The Commission, which is made up of government officials from the member states, was the organization initiating and guaranteeing treaties. The decisions of the Council had to be put into practice and supervised by the Commission. Hallstein was President of the Commission from 1958 to 1967. As a result of continuing resistance by de Gaulle and his so-called concept of 'l'Europe des patries' in contrast to Hallstein's dream of a European Federal state, Hallstein, citing health reasons, resigned as Commission President.

De Gaulle, who at that time was regarded as a French 'nationalist', an opponent of integration and a eurosceptic, nevertheless accepted the 'Treaties of Rome' as trade treaties and an opportunity to free the French economy from isolation and modernize it, as well as to strengthen its competitiveness against the German economy and as a means towards the achievement of financial support from the Federal Republic. At the end of the 1960s Bonn was admittedly no longer prepared to accept these financial demands. De Gaulle attempted to deprive the EEC of its political content and get around its supranational character, by coming up against Hallstein's vision. The EEC should not dominate France, but France should dominate Europe, and do so by means of continuing to control Germany. The Customs Union of the EEC was up and running and already brought about the reduction of internal tariffs in 1968. The Common Agricultural Policy was financed, as a result of a massive policy of lobbying on the part of France, by a European Agricultural Guidance and Guarantee Fund, in the end by German money. In 1967 the executives of the ECSC, EURATOM and the EEC were united by the Merger Treaty so that, from then on, common organizations were at the disposal of all three communities: the European Court of Justice, the European Parliament, the Council of Ministers and the European Commission.

After the death of Kurt Schumacher, the party leader in 1952, the SPD went through a transformation with regards to labour and to its programme. At the party congress in Stuttgart in 1958 a third of the executive committee were newly elected, amongst them Willy Brandt, Helmut Schmidt and Gustav Heinemann. The Heidelberg Programme of 1925, which had been adhered to up until then and had only been supplemented by temporary action and election programmes, was seen as obsolete. In January 1959, the party presidium agreed to focus its debates and to hold an extraordinary party conference at which a new programme would be discussed and decided upon.

The Bad Godesberg Party Conference took place from 13 to 15 November 1959. Herbert Wehner was the leading figure and was decisively involved in reforming the programme. After returning from exile in Moscow and Sweden, he joined the SPD in 1946, worked for a party newspaper and was supported by Schumacher as a member of the Bundestag and in important offices within the party up until 1983. The politically controversial Wehner was to set the SPD on its Western course. Marxist principles were abandoned in favour of the new goals of 'freedom', 'justice' and 'solidarity'. In place of the abolition of 'capitalist conditions of production' by means of nationalization and a planned economy, 'co-determination' (or 'worker participation') was introduced as a control on the power of entrepreneurs.

The Godesberg Programme was an expression of basic approval of Adenauer's policy on NATO and Western integration. The SPD had to live with the normative power of the prevailing facts. The new type of programme was unanimously called for. The acceptance of the social market economy and Western integration represented a break in the party history in West Germany and a belated reconciliation on the part of the SPD with Adenauer's policy – the Soviets saw it quite differently. With their plan for Germany of the same year, the social democrats won no approval in Moscow. A speech in the Bundestag on German policy by Herbert Wehner in 1960 signalled the new position of the SPD.

At Bad Godesberg, the SPD attempted to bridge the historic divide between, on the one hand, a Marxist programme and revolutionary rhetoric and, on the other, social democratic practice. The overcoming of opposition to the churches and a clear commitment to the defence of the country illustrated the transformation. Thus, the social democrats also became more popular with academics and intellectuals and lost their image as being a pure party of the workers. The SPD now became more electable for middle-class sections of society. The party changed from a workers' to a catch-all party. The Godesberg Programme smoothed their way from a socialist opposition party to a social democratic coalition and government party.

From 'Germans, get round one table!' Participation in the Common Market to the Consolidation of Division by the Wall to the End of the Adenauer Era

The SED, under Prime Minister Otto Grotewohl, had linked its policy on Germany since the 1950s to the slogan 'Germans, get round one table!' The two German states should accordingly negotiate on German unity independently of the victorious powers. On 30 November 1950, the Federal Republic replied to the demand put by the GDR for a counter-proposal for the holding of free all-German elections under the supervision of the United Nations, that admittedly, against the background of the Korean War, was on the side of the USA and served as a Western tool in the Cold War. Bonn insisted on its position: only under this condition could there be talks with the GDR. Involvement by the UNO, in view of its pro-Western position, would be tantamount to a capitulation on the part of the Eastern regime before the enemy philosophy.

The SED offensive went back to the Foreign Ministers conference in Prague in 1950, at which the foreign ministers of the 'fraternal socialist states' raised objections to the rearmament of West Germany and to the integration of the Federal Republic with the West, as well as having called for an 'all-German Constitutive Council' consisting of delegates from both East and West Germany on an equal footing, which would lay the foundation for the formation of an appropriate government. The Western Powers supported Bonn's demand. At their request the United Nations instituted a commission on 20 December 1951, which would oversee the preconditions for free elections in both parts of Germany. The GDR did not permit them entry.

With Stalin's note of 10 March 1952 there began a new phase in German policy. Adenauer immediately dismissed this proposal, which was not directed to him, but to Western ambassadors in Moscow, before the West had time to react. He did not think in terms of the whole of Germany. Nevertheless, the premature dismissal was one of his most serious mistakes because he thereby made his policy more difficult and opened himself up to the accusation that he did not even want exploratory talks on German unity. This was a 'missed opportunity' (as Rolf Steininger puts it). Adenauer's supporters, however, thought him right to have rejected the 'attempt at deception and disruption', because Stalin only wanted to bring a neutral and united Germany under his control. Here, however, one was forgetting that the USSR had not even succeeded in doing this in the cases of neutral Finland and Austria. Why was this? A NATO climb-down was sufficient motivation for him and was all that was needed. The SED leadership was concerned by Stalin's offer and started their campaign of 'Germans, get round one table!'. Adenauer was also concerned, but he managed to dissuade the Western powers from engaging in exploratory talks in Moscow or only in order to appear to be negotiating with Stalin.

By the time the ESCS Treaty came into effect (in 1952) and West Germany joined NATO (in 1955), Bonn was firmly embedded in the West. The signing of the 'Treaties of Rome', which founded the EEC and EURATOM (in 1957), were a further step towards the integration of the Federal Republic with the West.

These treaties were interpreted by SED propaganda in the context of the division of Germany, of the East-West conflict, American foreign policy and against the background of re-colonization and neo-colonialism. The usual hostile images and propaganda models seemed to be confirmed by this assessment. Even if interpretations, according to which the 'Treaties of Rome' were the expression of aggressive US foreign and economic policy, lacked any basis, the thesis that they would increase the political division of Europe could not be dismissed, particularly since, as a result of their signing, Western Europe was already divided as regards trade and customs policy, not to mention the whole of Europe. It was a problem that the 'Treaties of Rome' were portrayed by the SED as contributing to the division of Germany, since the protocol annexed to the EEC Treaty provided for trade between the Federal Republic and the GDR being considered internal trade (trade between the two Germanies would become part of the 'Common Market' and thus the GDR would become a 'secret EEC member', at least as regards trade and customs policy). Looking at the philosophy of the 'working population' in the 'freedom-loving workers' and 'farmers' state', accusations levelled at Bonn of 'militarism', 'imperialism', 'colonialism' and 'exploitation of the workers' could only deepen the division. With these standard propaganda slogans, the EEC and EURATOM were portrayed according to the usual negative stereotypes and seen as tools under the control of Washington, directing Western Europe in the interests of the USA. Once one gets away from the propaganda, one can see a kernel of truth in this. When, for example, the SED newspaper *Neues Deutschland* argued that Germany was going to be supplied with atomic weapons and this would possibly aggravate relations between European countries, one cannot deny that there is some historical evidence for this, particularly since between 1956 and 1958 there were secret tri-lateral negotiations held between the Federal Republic, France and Italy over the development of a common atomic weapons capability. The suspicions pointing in that direction expressed by the GDR were not so wide of the mark. Nor was there any lack of evidence about the assumed connection between the EEC, EURATOM and NATO, that was repeatedly being suggested parallel to this. All six founder members of the EEC were founder members of the Atlantic Alliance. When, the day before the signing of the 'Treaties of Rome', *Neues Deutschland* talked of the fact that 'the German imperialists would support the crumbling French colonial regime in North Africa in order to seize the opportunity of replacing their French competitors' and gain 'influence over the African and Asian colonies of France, Italy, Belgium, Holland and Portugal', there was an element of truth in relation to the incorporation of French overseas territories within the Common Market financed by the Federal Republic. Far too big a role was, however, being attributed to West German policy (it was being suggested that West Germany had imperialist and hegemonic ambitions). GDR propaganda consisted in highlighting its own innocence over the division of Germany and Europe and in laying the blame for the split solely at the door of the Adenauer government. The aim was to discredit and disqualify the direct competitor, the 'Federal Republic', in the process of which the larger global context involving Anglo-American colonial policy also played a role (according to Andreas Pudlat). The fact that the GDR benefited from the 'Treaties of Rome' was not mentioned (see below). The term 'inter-zonal trade' was then also replaced by the term 'inner-German trade'. This referred to the exchange of goods between the Federal Republic and the GDR.

The Frankfurt agreement on 'inter-zonal trade' had already been decided as early as 8 October 1949 after the founding of the two German states. Two years later, on

20 September 1951, the economic relations between the Federal Republic and the GDR, including the two divided parts of Berlin, had been established. The agreement was revised after the setting-up of the EEC Customs Union in 1968 and was in force right up until the unification of Germany.

In order to resolve the differences in currency, based on the rate one Western Mark = four Eastern Marks, the clearance of payments took place by means of central clearing accounts at the Deutsche Bundesbank in Frankfurt am Main and the Staatsbank in the GDR. Acting as organizations were the Trust Body for Industry and Trade in West Berlin and for the GDR the Ministry of Foreign Trade in East Berlin. Inner-German trade was at first neither foreign nor internal trade. As independent and differing currency areas were involved, it had to be arranged separately. The special position of inter-zonal trade had to be taken into account in the founding of the EEC. In terms of the 'Treaties of Rome', inter-zonal trade was judged to be internal trade ('inner-German trade'). The GDR enjoyed EEC privileges as a secret member of the European Community. Lists of goods were drawn up annually. The Federal Republic supplied machines, electronic and chemical products as well as wooden articles and mineral oil products.

The integration of the Federal Republic and of the GDR into their respective military blocs, as already mentioned, led to the establishment of German forces in both German partial states.

After 1955/6 politicians in the East and West were keen to push for the German partial states, whenever and however possible, to bring an end to the military alliances. This involved disarmament proposals and the creation of nuclear-free zones in Europe designed to overcome the 'balance of horror'. The plan put forward by the Polish Foreign Minister, Adam Rapacki (1956–68), at the United Nations General Assembly on 2 October 1957, for a disengagement from the 'gulf opening up between the blocs' and for the formation of a nuclear-free zone in Central and Eastern Europe, in its original version involved Poland and the two German states. The use of nuclear weapons against these territories would be prohibited, the agreement would be binding for these states themselves and for the atomic powers, France, Great Britain, the USSR and the USA. The time was well chosen as, in parallel to this in the Federal Republic, the differences of opinion surrounding the supply of atomic weapons to the Bundeswehr (Federal Armed Forces) and the activities of the 'Anti-Atomic Death' campaign were in full swing.

The USSR only took this proposal fully on board when the West rejected it. The GDR leadership joined the campaign and, for its part, promoted the idea of a confederation of both German states on the basis of equality, something that the

Federal Republic, with its 'claim to sole representation', did not accept. In the West the Rapacki Plan was prematurely interpreted as an initiative to loosen Poland's dependence on the USSR and Rapacki misinterpreted as an 'agent of Krushchev'. In fact it was designed to stabilize the status quo and, in the process, the Soviet embassy in Warsaw had been consulted, but not the government of the USSR.

On 14 February 1958 a second amended version of the Rapacki Plan was put forward, now to include Czechoslovakia as well as Poland and the two German states. It provided for a ban on the production, storage and deployment of nuclear weapons or any equipment or installations associated with them, in addition for comprehensive control and inspection mechanisms as well as for the withdrawal of occupation forces from these states. Above all, the installing of US medium-range missiles in the Federal Republic would be stopped.

This Rapacki Plan was also rejected by NATO, the WEU and the government in Bonn. The FRG was afraid of endangering the question of the recognition of the GDR as well as of the German-Polish border. The Hallstein Doctrine was opposed to the acceptance of any further variations of the Rapacki Plan of 4 November 1958 and of 28 March 1962. Thus the first proposals for political détente by an Eastern Bloc politician, taken up by the West and also partly recognized, were condemned to failure.

The leading Western powers rejected Rapacki's proposals, chiefly arguing that they would alter the military balance in Europe as a result of the conventional superiority of the USSR in favour of the Warsaw Pact.

In the debate about the future of Europe and a reduction in the military blocs, Pankow spoke out, putting forward in several notes directed towards Bonn the idea of a 'confederation' of the two German states on the basis of equality as a preliminary stage to a later unification. These moves backed by the USSR were rejected by Bonn in agreement with the Western powers and were interpreted as an attempt to force the Federal Republic out of the transatlantic and West European alliance. Adenauer considered an 'Austrian solution' for the renouncement of reunification, but only for the GDR to make the conditions there easier for the people. The attempts by the Austrian Federal Chancellor, Julius Raab, with his plan for Germany involving a Four Power settlement bringing the Federal Republic and the GDR together, were not successful either, as both Bonn and Pankow were against it.

In autumn 1958 Nikita S. Khrushchev, head of the Soviet Party and government, went on the offensive. In a speech on 10 November 1958 he made clear that the Western Allies no longer had any right to station their troops in Berlin, something that caused a stir. On 27 November he doubled down by setting the Western powers an ultimatum, demanding that Berlin be transformed into an 'autonomous political unit' and turned into a 'demilitarized free city'. Negotiations would take place within six months on this status, otherwise the USSR would reach a settlement with the GDR, whereby it could exercise its due sovereignty, also in relation to Allied military transports.

Even before the ultimatum, the People's Police (VOPO, 'Volkspolizei') of the GDR had begun to check, block and impound US transports through East German territory. This put the Supreme Command of NATO on a state of alert, and internally the use of force against the VOPO was even considered.

At the meeting of the NATO Council in December 1958 Khrushchev's demands were rejected. In a note on 10 January he emphasized that the restructuring of Germany was at issue and that the Western powers should withdraw. He presented the draft of a Peace Treaty based on two German states and a demilitarized 'free city of Berlin'. Bonn reacted with counter proposals which in the case of the maximum demands to the Eastern side amounted to the status quo and above all were to stimulate the Western powers to reject the ultimatum and to strengthen their guarantees over Berlin. The remarkable thing was the fact that the moves initiated by the Eastern side now also set off a movement in German policy in West Germany. Neither the government's 'Globke Plan' (named after Hans Globke, the State Secretary in the Federal Chancellery and former participant in the formulation of the 1935 Nuremberg Race Laws) nor the SPD's 'Germany Plan' excluded recognition of the GDR outright. The 'Globke Plan' admittedly immediately rejected the idea of a demilitarized Federal Republic, in the case of Berlin as one big unit, but it did recognize the possibility of such an entity. After an interim period, according to this plan, free elections would take place in the whole of Germany and measures towards German unification would be introduced. The 'Germany Plan' started from the basis of Rapacki's arms control zone, but in relation to Berlin it did not go as far as the 'Globke Plan' in developing ideas. As in the case of the latter, it should usher in a unified Germany, ideas that were supported by the SED proposals of a 'confederation'. In the case of both of the West German initiatives it was probably, above all, a matter of getting Moscow to engage in negotiations. On 11 May 1959 Soviet Foreign Minister Andrei Gromyko agreed to a conference of foreign ministers. Here it was noticeable that the Soviet Union would not insist on keeping to the ultimatum deadline of 27 May. In June 1959 a Four Power conference was called in Geneva and once more Germany and the Berlin question were the subject of negotiations. The two German partial states were represented by delegations of observers sitting at the side tables.

The conference took place in two sessions between 11 May and 20 June and between 13 July and 5 August 1959. Three days before the start, US Secretary of State Christian A. Herter came out decisively in favour of German reunification on US television. The Federal government had already rejected criticism by the Soviet Union clearly directed against nuclear arming of the Bundeswehr. At the foreign ministers' conference in Geneva, Herter proposed giving the United Nations the task of controlling subversive activities in the two parts of Berlin.

In Geneva there was, in the end, no sign of a breakthrough in the struggle for a solution to the German Question but there was a change in the climate of East–West relations. Russian threats declined. Khrushchev and US President Eisenhower arrived at a decision to reach an agreement over an open-ended commitment to talks on Berlin. The USSR appeared to be able to accept the status quo in the former capital of the Reich.

On the morning of 13 August 1961, the SED regime began putting up barriers on the border area and building the Wall that would cut off the Eastern sector of Berlin. Construction work was supervised by the VOPO and the NVA. Traffic links between the parts of Berlin were severed. There were strict controls on all the borders to West Berlin and the Federal Republic. Representatives of Berlin and Bonn were powerless to react to what was happening and were unable to help. The urgent calls for protests on the part of the Western Allies against the building of the Wall came too late and proved to be ineffective.

In the Federal Republic the Bundestag election campaign got underway for September 1961. It was also the focus of interest for Adenauer who decided it was not a good idea to go to Berlin immediately and show his solidarity with his oppressed and hard-pressed fellow countrymen. As with the events of 17 July Bonn was keen not to allow proceedings to escalate and to prevent the population going in for spontaneous action. Willy Brandt, the Governing Mayor of Berlin, was in favour of a clearer policy. Adenauer went ahead with his election campaign in Bavaria and only on 16 August did he visit the divided Berlin, conduct which brought him in for criticism. In a speech in Regensburg he referred to Brandt disparagingly as 'alias Frahm', by which he drew attention to Brandt's illegitimate birth and his role as an 'emigrant' during the war.

The Western powers were kept informed about the events in the East via their intelligence services. As early as the start of the summer of 1961 they had indicated to the Soviet side that they were giving them plenty of rope in the Eastern sector. The Soviet Union had after all agreed to the sealing off of the GDR because it did not see any alternative for stabilizing the economic position of the GDR. The

First Day Cover commemorating John F. Kennedy's visit to Berlin.

Pankow Republic and Moscow took the short-lived outburst of criticism in the West in their stride.

The building of the Wall helped to stem the tide of the threatened exodus from the GDR, led to its stabilization and at the same time marked the end of Adenauer's 'policy of strength', which turned out to be a policy of German weakness and Western refusal of an active German policy. Adenauer's disappointment at US policy on Germany led to a rapprochement with de Gaulle and the Franco-German Treaty of 22 January 1963. Kennedy's visit to Berlin in the summer of 1963 with his famous statement 'Ich bin ein Berliner' could not hide the fact that the West did not see German unity as a priority. Egon Bahr, head of the Press and Information Ministry in West Berlin, had recognized that the Germans could not rely on the Western powers and had to play an active role themselves. The moment of recognition was a speech in the Protestant Academy of Tutzing that spoke of 'change through rapprochement'. The logical consequence of this was banal and simple: if you want something from someone, you have to approach them and talk to them.

After the building of the Wall, the USSR officially kept to the major goal of the incorporation of the whole of Berlin within the GDR, but came to terms with the prevailing balance of power in Berlin, particularly since the Western powers adhered to the political guarantees in relation to West Berlin and the security of the access routes and insisted on their right to enter the Eastern sector of the city freely. Brandt saw the danger of Berlin acquiring neutral status separate from the Federal Republic.

As a result of his pressure bypassing the Federal Chancellor and the Foreign Office in Bonn, by means of a direct initiative to US President John F. Kennedy, he managed to obtain a renewed US declaration guaranteeing the status of Berlin.

The definitive division of the city was, however, unaltered by this, both East and West having come to terms with it. Those supporters of Adenauer, who had naively believed that Western integration would lead to reunification and that the Western powers would be committed to German unity, had to accept this bitter reality. The GDR was, however, triumphant after the building of the Wall, which the SED propaganda deceitfully lauded as the 'anti-fascist protection barrier' and celebrated as the victory of socialism over 'imperialism'. There were also a number of misguided, but also convinced, GDR citizens who actually believed this propaganda.

After the Bundestag election, Adenauer was again able to form a government (albeit for the last time), a short-term cabinet as the FDP, partner in the coalition, made the premature departure of the Chancellor the condition for a coalition. It was beset with crises. The worst of these was the *Spiegel* Affair in October 1962. The magazine had published a report on NATO manoeuvres, following which the magazine's offices were searched and journalists such as Conrad Ahlers and Rudolf Augstein were arrested. Hermann Höcherl, the Minister of the Interior, declared that one could not go around carrying the 'Grundgesetz' under one's arm. Five Free Democrats resigned. After Franz-Josef Strauß, the Defence Minister, misled the Bundestag, he too had to go.

This Federal Republic was shaky and nervous at the centre of the Cold War in Europe. In December 1962 Adenauer announced that he would be retiring from office in the autumn of the following year. The end of the Adenauer Era was already evident from the abortive attempt to stand for Federal President in 1959 and it was decisively accelerated by the *Spiegel* Affair. On 16 October 1963 the Bundestag elected the former Federal Economics Minister Ludwig Erhard as the new Federal Chancellor.

4

Germany as Two States, 1961–72

The Internal Stabilization of the GDR and Continued Integration of the Federal Republic with the West

On the Road to being a 'Socialist Nation': Political and Economic Consolidation of the 'Protestant' GDR and the Agreements on Border Passes

With the building of the Wall there began a phase of economic and political stabilization in the GDR. The last loophole for getting into the so-called 'free West' was now sealed. From now on the East German population had no more opportunities to escape to the West. In the main, they submitted to the prevailing situation, accepted their fate and more or less came to terms with the political circumstances in the second German state of 'real existing Socialism'. The social disintegration caused by their voting with their feet and the mass exodus were brought to a definitive end by the building of the Wall, and the paralysis in the economic reconstruction of the GDR was overcome.

The regime run by the SED now promoted the idea of solidarity even more than before. It appealed for cooperation and held out the prospect of better working and living conditions. In order to reform and optimize the economic conditions and the political system of organization, the Central Committee of the SED and the GDR Council of Ministers decided on the introduction of the 'New Economic System of Planning and Management of the National Economy'. State planning committees were to establish long-term objectives and develop annual timetables with subordinate institutions. In this the state-owned enterprises (Volkseigene Betriebe, VEBS, or People's Enterprises) played an important role. Incentives were created by means of bonuses. Higher productivity, the stimulation of investment and the payment of productivity-related wages were the goal.

With these more flexible methods, combined with the promotion of competitive thinking, the deficiencies of the hitherto centrally managed planned economy were to be avoided. With the so-called 'New Economic System' reminiscent in a way of Lenin's New Economic Policy of the Soviet Union in the early 1920s, the GDR attempted to become a pioneer of economic reforms ahead of the other 'socialist fraternal states' in Central and Eastern Europe, something that these states did not always welcome.

East German communism and its representatives were viewed with suspicion and scepticism in the socialist camp, largely because of their earnestness and efficiency in putting Marxism-Leninism into practice as well as their efforts to build a socialist model state on German soil, but above all because of their subservience to Moscow. German *Spiessersozialismus* ('petty socialism'), with its almost ubiquitous state apparatus of surveillance and spying on the population, was surely one of the worst features of 'real existing Socialism' in Central, Eastern and South-Eastern Europe. The external borders of the GDR were in any case the strictest and the most inhumane compared with those of the other fraternal states. In the last phase of the period under Ulbricht and Honecker, however, there were also attempts, albeit on a small scale and short-lived, at emancipation from the Soviet Union. They were carried along by the absurd idea, indeed the illusion, of knowing better than and being able to outdo their communist masters in the Kremlin. Hence, these attempts were bound to fail. The GDR was not just a product of the Soviet policy of occupation in Germany but its existence was, to a great extent, dependent on the goodwill and approval of the USSR. It was Brezhnev who warned Honecker against German arrogance towards the neighbouring states. Poland was concerned about a unified socialist Germany. The relations between Warsaw and East Berlin were not without strains and conflicts. The far lower standard of living in Poland played a role in this.

The New Economic System led to a 'normalization' of conditions in the GDR. Thus, a foundation stone was laid for the development of the GDR on the road to becoming the second most powerful industrial nation within COMECON, and propaganda by the SED correspondingly helped to promote this impression and excessively inflated its self-image as being the 'tenth most powerful industrial power in the world'.

In this new economic policy, the expenditure side was subject to bias being focused on certain sectors, thereby producing distortions: for example, bottlenecks in supply in the area of consumer goods arose. These difficulties were soon felt by the population and led at the start of the 1970s to a suspension of economic reforms. Even if the GDR was still far behind the Federal Republic as regards standard of living, the existence of the East German state was nevertheless assured for the time being. With the Wall around West Berlin (in effect a walling-in) and the accompanying isolation, West Berliners were cut off from any chance of meeting up with members of their families and friends in East Berlin. At the same time East Berliners and GDR citizens were unable to continue with their jobs that, up until then, they had been doing in the Western part of the city. This involved around 60,000 people. Now they had to seek jobs in the Eastern sector of Berlin or, in the GDR, to replace the ones that they had lost in the west of the city. Attempts by the Senate of West Berlin to ease the isolation just for the weeks around Christmas 1963 helped bring about negotiations with the SED regime leading to a first agreement on border passes with the approval of Bonn directly between the West Berlin Senate and the GDR authorities on 17 December 1963.

'If you want something from another person, you have to talk to them', was the basic idea, perhaps a simple one, but a successful motto on the part of Egon Bahr, adviser to West Berlin's Governing Mayor Willy Brandt. Thanks to these agreements, 28 months after the building of the Wall, West Berliners had the chance to visit their relatives in the Eastern sector between 19 December 1963 and 5 January 1964. The result was a mass rush on the offices where the coveted border passes were to be obtained. Over one million people came to East Berlin. The GDR proved to be generous and favourable.

With the agreement worked out by Bahr the second German dictatorship in the twentieth century sought to give the appearance of a normal state that was attempting to interpret it as an agreement in accordance with international law and thus exploit it for international legitimation. Bonn and West Berlin were, on the contrary, extremely keen not to allow such an impression to be given and treated the process as a purely technical administrative agreement. These efforts aimed at recognition and prestige in the area of legal protocols between states were to become characteristic of the anomalies in the relations between the two Germanies and were to be repeated in the following years. New agreements on border passes were to follow in autumn 1964, at New Year 1964/5 and 1965/6 as well as at Easter and Whitsun 1966. In this way more than four million West Germans were able to see their friends and relatives living beyond the Wall. Not until years later was a more permanent and fundamentally improved system of personal contacts between West Berlin and East Berlin established.

The governments following on after Adenauer from 1963, led by Ludwig Erhard (1963–6) and Kurt-Georg Kiesinger (1966–9), unlike their predecessor, attempted to reform and normalize their relationship with the socialist states other than the GDR, which motivated the SED regime to do everything to highlight the autonomy and independence of the partial state of East Germany.

The history of the division of the two German states cannot be fully appreciated without acknowledging the doctrinal division into two German belief systems: that the denominational dividing line ran through the centre of Germany. The GDR was clearly dominated by the Protestant and Lutheran section of the population whereas in the Federal Republic, particularly in the South and West, there was a majority of Catholics. As a result of the influx of refugees from Eastern Germany the number of Protestants in the Federal Republic admittedly increased but a disparity between Roman Catholics, on the one hand, and Lutheran Protestants, on the other, is evident. Even if both sides still sought to maintain unity by means of the national churches, they had increasingly gone their separate ways since the 1970s.

In the middle of the 1960s the GDR was successful in gaining a degree of respect, gradually causing doubts in Bonn to arise as to the chance of success of the much invoked Hallstein Doctrine. In 1965 Walter Ulbricht, chairman of the State Council, went on a state visit to Egypt and in the same year, Josip 'Tito' Broz, the former partisan leader and then Yugoslav head of state, paid an official visit to East Berlin. These achievements gave the GDR the aura of a state and, along with the stabilization produced by the New Economic System, served to boost the self-esteem of the East German Communists by consistently highlighting the autonomy of the GDR.

In 1967–8 Willi Stoph, chairman of the Council of Ministers, even held negotiations with the Federal Republic over an agreement aimed at the recognition of the GDR as an equal German state, which was, however, rejected (at least for the time being) by Bonn. At the same time this policy was supported within the state and by the constitution by a Law on Citizenship of the GDR of 20 February 1967, thus indicating a distancing from the Federal Republic.

In the following year Pankow made the presentation of a passport and visa obligatory for journeys between the Federal Republic and both West Berlin and the GDR, a rule that also applied to transit journeys between the Federal Republic and West Berlin. In addition the SED regime established a minimum currency exchange of 10 DM per day per person for a stay in the workers' and peasants' paradise as well as 5 DM for a desired stay in East Berlin.

Comprehensive state reforms in the GDR followed. According to a referendum, the constitution of 7 October 1949 was replaced on 6 April 1968 by the new socialist constitution. At the end of an eight-week 'popular consultation' out of around 98

A GDR boundary post with the GDR's national emblem.

per cent of those entitled to vote – as is usual in dictatorships for internal support and external legitimation – approximately 94.5 per cent voted in favour of the new constitution. The first and only popular vote in the history of the GDR served, above all, to establish the claim to power and leadership of the one-party system.

Officially and formally there were several parties, along with the so-called mass organizations appealing to a range of different adherents and voters, but their function was limited to representing and furthering the interests of the SED. Politics was considered a 'communal act'. Opposition to the SED was seen as an offence against the state punishable as a crime.

The GDR parliament, the Volkskammer ('People's Chamber'), consisting of 500 representatives, was characterized as the 'highest state organ of power'. Its actual political influence remained marginal. Since 1950 it had been elected every four years on the basis of unified lists of the parties organized within the so-called National Front and of the mass organizations. The Volkskammer could point to several groupings, but only that of the SED mattered. Besides the SED and the four 'Blockparteien', ('bloc parties'), which were jokingly referred to as the 'Blockflöten', the '(flute) recorders', there were also the Free German Trade Union Association

(Freier Deutscher Gewerkschaftsbund, FDGB), the Free German Youth Movement (Freie Deutsche Jugend, FDJ), the Democratic Women's Association of Germany (Demokratischer Frauenbund, DFB) and the Cultural Association (Kulturbund, KB). The Volkskammer had to discuss and pass laws, meeting every two months for this purpose. Thanks to its resolutions, which as a rule were passed unanimously, it was a compliant organ of the dictatorship by the SED.

In the new GDR constitution – in contrast to the one passed in 1949 – a number of basic rights had been removed: the right to emigrate, the free choice of employment, private property, the right to strike and the right to contest, individual liberties and the non-imposition of press censorship. However, basic social rights were extended: the right to work, education, medical treatment, recreation and living space. The development and structure of the organization of the state were laid down comprehensively and in detail in the new GDR constitution.

After Pieck's death a State Council was set up in 1960 whose chairman took over the former duties of the State President. Resolutions and decrees became law as soon as they were announced. The chairman of the State Council was Walter Ulbricht. He interpreted the constitution and the laws and supervised the Supreme Court. The Council of Ministers and the State government presided over economic matters. Their members came principally from the ministries of industry and economics. The functions of party and the state were closely bound together so that the public committees had to implement the aims of the SED. The members of the Party had to carry out their directives and the Party's resolutions were binding on the Council of Ministers and the apparatus of the state.

This questionable system of 'democratic centralism' did not allow for any political or social alternative and oversaw the increasing psychological and ideological uniformity and overall control of the citizens. The close interconnection between the state and the 'Unity Party' (a contradiction in terms) and the subordination of all of its organs to the hegemony of this one party had a very prejudicial, at times paralysing, effect on the creativity and originality of the political conditions in the GDR. The state apparatus controlled by the SED was only able to react rather inflexibly to the social, economic and political challenges and changes of the 1960s.

In its new constitution the GDR characterized itself as a 'socialist state of the German nation'. For the time being it still clung to the possibility of a future unification of Germany, on the basis of socialism of course. The 1970s, however, saw a growing turn of GDR foreign policy towards ideology, with a deliberate 'isolation' from the Federal Republic legitimized on the basis of the socio-political antagonism between socialism (in the GDR) and capitalism (in the Federal Republic). By means of a putsch-like manoeuvre Walter Ulbricht was replaced in 1971 by Erich Honecker as First Secretary of the SED. All he retained, until his death in 1973, was his function as chairman of the State Council, and he rapidly lost influence. This power shift was a decisive turning point in the history of the GDR, combined with a shift in the internal political situation illustrated by the phrase 'Unity of Economic and Social Policy'. It contributed, in the wake of a policy of treaties between the two Germanies, to the arrival of the GDR on the world stage.

On 7 October 1974 there followed remarkable modifications to the 'Socialist Constitution' of the GDR. Not only was the term 'of the German nation' dropped but also any hint of a unification of the two German states had disappeared. Under Erich Honecker, the 'socialist nation' of the GDR was to advance the sole claim to the title of Germany.

The Federal Republic of Germany in the split between Paris and Washington – The Elysée Treaty with an emphasis on the Atlantic Relationship

While the policy of continued and deepening integration of the GDR with the East was renewed after 13 August 1961, Adenauer was to drive the policy of Western European integration steadfastly forward. However, he inevitably came to realize that his 'policy of strength' – to seek German unification in association with the Western powers, particularly with the Anglo-Americans – had failed; if, that is, the Chancellor of the Federal Republic wanted unification at all.

The seizure of power by Charles de Gaulle in France in 1958 at first undermined the project that was already underway between France, Italy and the Federal Republic, working together on the development of nuclear weapons systems and the construction of the common atomic bomb. Immediately after his second entry into government in June 1958, de Gaulle had put a stop to the secret trilateral negotiations, which provided for cooperation in the development of nuclear military technology, in the event that the signatory states were not given a full say in the deployment of Anglo-American atomic weapons. US President Dwight D. Eisenhower had at first welcomed de Gaulle's coming to power as a guarantee of the stabilization of France. Whereas de Gaulle not only sought a leading position on the continent but also wanted to loosen military integration within NATO and thus to remove the claim of the USA to a leading role in Europe, Adenauer was not prepared to put the nuclear guarantee of the USA at risk to protect the Federal Republic and West Berlin. In order to prevent France and Germany from acting independently as regards nuclear armament, in September 1958 Eisenhower gave the go-ahead for the formation of a Multilateral Force, by which the Army of the Federal Republic (the Bundeswehr) would automatically have access to tactical nuclear weapons in the event of war; thereby de Gaulle's plan had achieved partial success.

The French President, however, also rejected the idea of a supranational Europe. What he envisaged was '*l'Europe des patries*', in which France would enjoy a position of hegemony. Was Adenauer also prepared to accept this? Following the disappointment that the Chancellor of the Federal Republic had to suffer over the passive stance of the Anglo-Americans in the Berlin crisis (1958–61), he turned towards France. There were further meetings with de Gaulle, who had already received Adenauer as the only politician and state guest at his private residence IN Colombey-les-Deux-Églises in 1958. After the unsuccessful bid on the part of de Gaulle for French participation in the Anglo-American '*liaison nucléaire*', he vetoed Britain's entry into the EEC. On 14 January 1963 he uttered his '*Non*' publicly at a press conference. A further consequence of the French refusal to admit the British to EEC membership was the Elysée Treaty of 22 January 1963, an ambivalent document of European bilateral policy. This added up to the status quo of membership of the EEC, in other words an implicit 'keep the British out', and thus was not particularly favourable towards enhancing the interactions between the UK and the other member states.

In this treaty Bonn and Paris committed themselves to permanent consultation and regular meetings to discuss questions of foreign, economic, defence and cultural policy. One aim was increased exchanges between young German and French people, leading to Franco-German youth projects. Twice-yearly meetings and conferences were also arranged by the successor governments.

The frequently (wrongly) dubbed 'treaty of friendship' was without doubt a remarkable event as it marked a new beginning; an overcoming of the traditional enmity between the two countries. Nevertheless, there were differences in the interpretation and significance of existing treaties and the resulting consequences that one could identify in the preamble to the Elysée Treaty. Jean Monnet, already at this time an arch-enemy of de Gaulle with excellent relations to the USA, managed to put pressure on members of the Bundestag (the Parliament of the Federal Republic) via Washington for a preamble to be added to the Elysée Treaty. In Bonn, after the so-called Atlanticists, in addition to those on the Left, formed the majority, as opposed to the Gaullists on the Right, Monnet's intervention was successful in achieving its goal.

The preamble was to keep to the principle that the rights and duties of the multilateral treaties entered into by the Federal Republic were to remain 'unaffected' by the Elysée Treaty, which was an affirmation of the pro-Atlantic orientation of the Bonn Republic, and thus again gave a pro-US tone to the working out of the treaty between the Federal Republic and France. Whereas de Gaulle was for a more autonomous policy on the part of Europe, even towards the United States, and France was to withdraw from military ties to NATO in 1966, Bonn also repeatedly emphasized its close tie to the USA and NATO in regard to West Berlin. For de Gaulle the way the preamble was formulated was a touchstone for the question of a possible emancipation of the Federal Republic from its guardian. To de Gaulle's disappointment Bonn did not pass the test and sought refuge in its asserted dependence. In spite of this, the Elysée Treaty became an important foundation stone of the cooperation between the Federal Republic and France. In the area of foreign policy Adenauer's successor Erhard, against a background of emerging détente between East and West, made moves towards a normalization in relations towards the socialist states of Europe. In a peace message on 25 March 1966 he offered an agreement to renounce the use of force, though he committed a diplomatic and political blunder. He did not include the GDR in this plan and stuck no less than before to the Hallstein Doctrine, which doomed the initiative to failure. As Atlanticists, Erhard and the Foreign Minister Gerhard Schröder continued to maintain close contact with the USA and gave priority to the alliance with the USA over the idea of Europe held by de Gaulle, who talked of 'fading roses'. Relations with France grew weaker under Erhard. But the Gaullists in the CDU/CSU, with Franz-Josef Strauß in the lead, aimed for stronger cooperation with Paris.

Inter-German Differences in the State Cultural Policy, the Structure of the Media and the Literary Scene

The Federal Republic, in line with federalism, guaranteed the cultural sovereignty of the Federal Länder. The Federal government therefore allowed the right of competing legislation for the protection of German cultural activity in order to prevent the export of cultural capital as well as to promote education and research. By means of framework legislation, the state nevertheless exercised its influence through financial subsidies via the cultural departments of the Foreign Office as well as other resources. Part of its remit was brought together in the area of responsibility of the Federal Ministry for Scientific Research; later there were ministries for Education and Science as well as Research and Technology.

In the GDR cultural policy was centralized. Schools, educational establishments and vocational training were run by the Ministry for People's Education. The

Ministry of Culture was responsible for public cultural institutions including film production, and there was a corresponding ministry responsible for universities and polytechnics.

In the West of Germany, Allied control and compulsory licensing in the area of the media were abolished in 1949. In the same year the news agencies of the Western zones united to form the German Press Agency (Deutsche Presseagentur, DPA). Former publishers and publishing houses were able to reinstate their printing works and organizations and publish their products for the press. The big newspapers in the main cities dating from before 1933–9 were not revived, unlike the local and regional newspapers, the so-called 'homeland press' as well as the quality papers that went beyond the region, such as the *Frankfurter Allgemeine Zeitung* (*FAZ*), *Die Welt* or the *Süddeutsche Zeitung* (*SZ*). In the early 1950s there were papers that were sold on the street. One paper in particular came to prominence: the tabloid *Bild-Zeitung* (comparable to *The Sun* in Britain) gained increased sales and became the leading mass circulation paper of the German popular press, with its sometimes questionable investigative methods and corresponding quality. Daily party newspapers were no longer published. The process of concentration of the publishing industry into fewer and fewer hands had already in the middle of the 1950s led to a reduction in the number of independent newspapers from 225 to no more than 120 at the end of the 1970s. The total circulation doubled in the same period from around 12.5 to 25 million, above all as a result of the increased circulation of the newspapers available on sale.

At the end of the 1940s, set up by the occupation power and Land legislation, new radio stations developed from the radio stations of the Allied military authorities with the right to public broadcasting: North West German Radio (Nordwestdeutscher Rundfunk, NWDR) in Hamburg, Bavarian Broadcasting Service (Bayer- ischer Rundfunk) in Munich, Radio Bremen in Bremen, South Radio (Südfunk) in Stuttgart, South West Radio (Südwestfunk) in Baden-Baden and West German Radio (Westdeutscher Rundfunk) in Cologne. These were followed in 1955 by Saarländischer Rundfunk (SR) in Saarbrücken and North German Radio (Norddeutscher Rundfunk, NDR) in Hamburg. The 'Deutsche Welle' and 'Deutsch- landfunk' were stations under the legal control of the Federal government. At the start of the 1950s there began cooperation between the stations as regards programming, sharing financial burdens and technology in the so-called 'Working Party of the Publicly Controlled Radio Stations in the Federal Republic' (ARD). In 1952 a regular television channel was set up in Hamburg. It was to be called the ARD 'German Television' channel two years later. The tremendous interest shown by Federal politics, or at least by Adenauer, at the creation of the media structure and their corresponding influence is clear from the fact that, for the Federal Chancellor, ARD was too much oriented towards the SPD). After much wrangling, in 1963 at the end of his period of office the 'Second German Television' channel (Zweites Deutsches Fernsehen, ZDF) based in Mainz came into being, founded on the basis of a national treaty made two years previously between the Länder, which tended more towards the CDU and CSU (in Bavaria).

The number of listeners increased after the end of the 1950s from 14 million to 18.5 million by the end of the 1960s, and this was to increase by the end of the 1970s to over 22 million. The number of television viewers was still relatively small at the end of the 1950s at approximately 700,000. With the successful onward march of 'the box' in the course of the 1960s there were already 13 million viewers by 1967 and by the end of the 1970s there were over 20 million. The figures were to more than double in the following decades, as the result of an explosion in the supply of private television channels and pay-TV, which put publishing and the print media under enormous pressure, leading to reductions in circulation and losses in advertising revenue and thus to a profound change in the structure of the media in Germany.

In the East of Germany the press and publicity developed in a completely different way: the system of control and licensing of the SMAD was continued after the founding of the GDR. Every periodical had to be approved by the Press Department of the Prime Minister of the GDR. The main organ of the dominant party was *Neues Deutschland*, which also appeared in the 14 local Bezirk organizations of the SED. In total there were around 40 daily newspapers in the GDR with a combined circulation of around eight million copies.

The centrally controlled press was the publishing house of the SED, the 'VOB Zentrag'. As early as 1946 in the Soviet Occupation Zone, long before the Federal Republic, the ADN (Allgemeine Deutsche Nachrichtendienst) News Agency was founded. In 1953 it was already placed under the Prime Minister and the Press Department. The radio system in the Soviet Zone was likewise already centralized in a General Supervisory Body, but after reorganization in 1952, this was divided in 1968 between the two broadcasting media, a State Committee for Radio and a State Committee for Television. There were two radio stations, the European service *Voice of the GDR (Stimme der DDR)* and the overseas service *Radio Berlin International*. After 1952 there was a first channel, after 1969 a second channel – and this is how it remained up until 1989. Only in the chaotic weeks of the 'Wende' ('change') in that autumn was an alternative TV channel introduced, *11–89*, whose effect on the GDR turning towards reform was limited. The number of radio listeners at the end of the 1950s was around five million and only went up to a little over 6.2 million in the course of the 1960s. This figure did not increase substantially later on, female citizens of the GDR preferring to tune in to Western radio programmes, which were more popular. The number of TV viewers was still limited at the end of the 1950s (approximately 70,000). The numbers rose at the end of the 1960s to 3.6 million, reaching five to six million by the end of the 1970s. These figures continued to rise, but the story was the same for television as for radio: because of the increasing possibility of receiving West German television stations, people in East Germany formed their own image (often a distorted one) of the Federal Republic, since the GDR media were seen as vehicles for political activism, manipulation and propaganda towards a 'socialist direction of consciousness' created by the party. This bias was blatant in comparison with the Western media, which was highlighted by the programme *The Black Channel* (*Der Schwarze Kanal*). The former head of NWDR, Karl-Eduard von Schnitzler, who moved to the Soviet Occupation Zone in 1947 and then joined the SED, went in for his own brand of 'counter-propaganda' by replaying specially selected negative reports from West German TV clips. His opponent was the right-wing conservative TV journalist Gerhard Löwenthal, who mounted a counter-attack, and in his programme 'ZDF-Magazin' exposed denials of human rights in the GDR and acts of mistreatment by the SED regime. The Cold War in the media reached a bizarre peak due to the fact that, since 1959, the GDR had been running a station in Turkish from Leipzig called *Bizim Radyo*, run by Turks from Bulgaria, which was aimed at inculcating 'guest workers' from Turkey in the Federal Republic with anti-capitalist and communist ideology and thus contributing to the destabilization of the Federal Republic and stirring up unrest. The station was on air up until 1989, but did not achieve any tangible success; one reason for this was because WDR in Cologne in the 1960s began to broadcast pro-capitalist Western programmes, also in Turkish, in order to immunize 'guest workers' against the propaganda being pumped out by the GDR.

The West German media overall were not free and independent either but run by interest groups, particularly those that were involved in the conflict between the systems in the East and the West (that tended to align themselves strongly with a pro-American and transatlantic position). This was not conducive to unbiased reporting. Only after 1989–90 did a change take place in the media world shaped by the old Federal Republic in the direction of open, critical and neutral reporting, such as was usual for example with ORF in Austria or the Swiss Radio and Television Corporation (SRG) even at the height of the Cold War. Thanks to many new private stations there was not just a more pronounced privatization of what was on offer to viewers but also a diversification, internationalization and pluralization of television programming.

German creative writing and literature after 1945 were marked by the consequences and the end of the Nazi dictatorship. Exiled writers like Bertolt Brecht, Alfred Döblin, Thomas and Heinrich Mann came into their own. Young authors, on the one hand, attempted to reconnect with the period before 1933 but also, on the other, tried a radical new start (Wolfgang Borchert or Wolfgang Weyrauch) or turned towards a revival of religion and a renewed Christianity (Elisabeth Langgässer), while yet others critically engaged with the Nazi regime or the persecution of the Jews (Carl Zuckmayer, Heinrich Böll). The leading post-war authors joined together in 'Gruppe 47'. In the 1960s the trend intensified towards a critical coming to terms with the National Socialist past and the Second World War (Günter Grass, Peter Härtling, Martin Walser, Gerhard Zwerenz) or with the persecution of the Jews (Ilse Aichinger). The student unrest of the 1960s brought about stronger criticism in literature of the social context and political conditions (the war crimes of the US military in Vietnam and the military intervention of the Warsaw Pact states in Czechoslovakia in 1968). Concern with the world of work in the form of historical and non-fiction reportage was most strongly characterized by Günter Wallraff, who passed himself off as a journalist for *Bild*, thereby highlighting their questionable reporting. Issues relating to the peace movement, as well as psychology and psychiatry, likewise played a role on the West German literary scene.

In the GDR literature was bracketed under the heading of the 'Construction of Socialism'. A new literary term was coined, 'socialist realism', based on the communist writers returning from exile (Johannes R. Becher, Bertolt Brecht, Stephan Hermlin, Stefan Heym, Anna Seghers). As early as July 1945 the Cultural Alliance for the Democratic Renewal of Germany was founded by the SMAD, after 1958 known as the German Cultural Alliance. It was organized in local groups, circles of friends, working and interest groups, consisting of 200,000 members and represented in the Volkskammer by their own grouping. The first chairman was Johannes R. Becher (1945–58). He was the mouthpiece of a socialist-oriented party political and centrally controlled cultural policy.

The high points of the creative writing and literature in praise of the SED and the GDR were the 'Bitterfeld conferences' in 1959 and 1964, which would found the concept of the 'worker as writer' as an amateur movement in literature and would praise writers for taking part in a 'VEB' or 'Ppeople's enterprise'.

Despite political influences, state intervention through SED edicts and an office for copyright and censorship, with the building of the Wall there developed a critical GDR literature on the part of young authors (Hermann Kant, Günter Kunert, Heiner Müller, Ulrich Plenzdorf, Brigitte Reimann, Christa Wolf) who took on society, the Party and the state more directly than the earlier Communist literature by previously exiled writers. Subjects that were absolutely taboo, such as depression, 'desertion of the Republic' ('Republikflucht'), criticism of state officials, the mismanagement of the economy, escape into private life, despair and suicide, were dealt with. It went so far that the state and party leadership was obliged to authorize writers in order to check tendencies that were destabilizing, or threatening the system (Wolf Biermann, Peter Huchel, Reiner Kunze, Sarah Kirsch). The policy of setting limits changed. After repression and liberalization, there was a period of greater restriction. Some of the members of the protest movement by citizens in 1989 were recruited from those in literature and the arts who had been involved in this criticism.

The Short Chancellorship of Ludwig Erhard (1963–6) and the Grand Coalition under Kurt-Georg Kiesinger (1966–9) as Transition Phases

Ludwig Erhard had joined Adenauer's government as Economics Minister in 1949 and was in all the cabinets up to 1963. With the 'social market economy' he had a considerable share in the upturn of the West German partial state. As an 'election locomotive' he helped the CDU/CSU to victory in all the elections to the Bundestag, providing them with a clear win over the SPD. In 1961 Adenauer, the 85-year-old Federal Chancellor, who had become rigid but no less resolute, had committed himself under pressure of the FDP coalition partner to give up office halfway through the new legislative period. The CDU/CSU grouping proposed Erhard as successor even though Adenauer was strongly opposed to his candidature. He did not consider him suitable to be a Federal Chancellor. Adenauer's time, however, was over and his influence had become minimal. Thus, Erhard took up office from October 1963 and in September 1965 he won the elections to the Bundestag for the CDU/CSU.

Even while the government was being formed, however, the first differences with the FDP arose, which was opposed to having Franz-Josef Strauß, the right-wing conservative chairman of the CSU as a member of the government. In the field of political economy the government of Erhard experienced a suddenly occurring recession in 1966, causing unemployment and setting off a budget crisis. In the conflict over the settlement of the budget the coalition with the FDP collapsed. The ministers all resigned on 27 October 1966. Following a serious CDU election defeat in North Rhine-Westphalia in July 1966, Erhard was already being questioned in his own party circles. When elections to the Landtag of the states of Hesse and Bavaria in November 1966 demonstrated considerable popularity for the extreme right-wing NPD, senior politicians of the CDU/CSU began negotiations with the SPD about a Grand Coalition. Behind the back of the Federal Chancellor in office, they decided that Kurt-Georg Kiesinger, Minister-President of Baden-Württemberg, would be the successor while Erhard still ruled with a minority cabinet.

It is significant for the degree of criticism and loss of confidence towards Erhard that this economics expert was no longer apparently entrusted with solving the crisis. As a result he resigned and in the following year he also gave up his chairmanship of the CDU to Kiesinger. By his election as honorary chairman the leadership of the party attempted to rehabilitate him but this did not compensate for the loss of his authority and the damage to his image. As the 'father of the German *Wirtschaftswunder* (Economic Miracle)', Erhard, who died in 1977 in Bonn, nevertheless became a political icon of the postwar history of West Germany.

Kiesinger, a trained lawyer, historian and philosopher, first practised as a barrister at the Berlin Supreme Court and was, from 1940–45 an academic assistant and vice-controller of the radio division in the Foreign Ministry. After being interned in Ludwigsburg during the first postwar years, in 1948 he was to become local executive leader of the CDU for the state of South Württemberg-Hohenzollern. He was a member of the Bundestag (Federal German Parliament) from 1949 until 1958 and finally Minister-President of Baden-Württemberg. He was elected Federal Chancellor and presented his government. The worsening economic crisis, with a large budget deficit, growing unemployment, combined with the concern about the spread of right-wing radicalism, led to a political change. At the same time it showed how insecure the Bonn political establishment was. It seems significant that a solution for this political crisis was hoped for from a former member of the Nazi party such as Kiesinger. The party-political motives were even more significant on the part of the CDU and the SPD towards the formation of a Grand Coalition, offering all the advantages in overcoming the economic crisis. This form of government was designed for that purpose and was therefore limited to this single task.

Following the change of direction within the CDU, the Bundestag elected Kiesinger to be Federal Chancellor on 1 December 1966. Willy Brandt, chairman of the SPD and Governing Mayor of Berlin, became Deputy Chancellor and Foreign Minister. Kiesinger mediated between the diverging political forces within the

Grand Coalition, who were eyeing each other up suspiciously and sharing power only tentatively.

Both the change of government within one legislative period and a Grand Coalition were new for the still young republic in Bonn. It was seen as an unavoidable necessity and a temporary government. There was no lack of criticism since the usual relation between government and opposition could no longer be taken for granted. A total of 49 FDP members of Parliament were opposed by 447 from the CDU/CSU and SPD.

Solving the problem of the budget and overcoming the economic recession were the goals of the new government. A 'stability law' and 'concerted action' were the chosen methods of tackling the problems. Karl Schiller (SPD), the economics minister, and Strauß, the finance minister, got on well together and enabled the success of the new form of government. Reform projects over social reform and renewal of the state became possible: a reformed financial system regulated the tax income between the state and the federal states (Länder) anew and laid down common responsibilities that were to be borne and paid for by both the Federal government and the Länder. In the field of culture and research the state took over more competences. The setting-up of universities, the structure of education and the promotion of research above the level of the individual Länder were to be common enterprises. A reform of penal justice led to a reduction in the use of prisons and a loosening of sexual conventions.

The Law on the Promotion of Stability and Economic Growth of 8 June 1967 formed an important basis through the use of public invitations to tender and state-sponsored project contracts to check the negative economic development. The central state and the federal states, which were to develop a medium-term financial forecast, were, due to the stability law, dedicated to the much quoted 'magic quadrilateral': currency stability, balance of the external economy, full employment and economic growth. By means of the stability law, the 'concerted action' lying at the basis of this and the appointment of an economic committee for public enterprise, the government was able to overcome the economic crisis. A committee of experts formed on models abroad recommended 'concerted action', which was organized and carried into practice by Schiller. All the institutions and bodies decisively involved in the economic process were drawn in: employers' organizations, trade unions, regional bodies, representatives of the Federal government, the Länder and the local authorities, as well as those involved in agriculture. The activity was discussed and agreed on by means of 'orientation data'. The 'concerted action' brought about in this way proved its worth and worked for a decade beyond the Grand Coalition. The unions only pulled out in 1977 after the employers had challenged the Law on Worker's Representation before the Federal Constitutional Court in 1976.

While the economics and finance ministers worked well together, there was not any wider consensus within the Grand Coalition on the policy towards the East and the question of Germany. While Kiesinger, faithful to continuing Adenauer's line, was unwilling to tamper with the claim of the Federal Republic to be the sole representative of Germany, Foreign Minister Brandt was on the lookout for new ways to foreign policy orientation and worked for a more flexible policy towards the states of Central and Eastern Europe, including the GDR.

When in September 1967 Willi Stoph, chairman of the Council of Ministers of the GDR, proposed negotiations on the normalization of relations and the recognition of the existing borders, Kiesinger opposed this initiative and only indicated his willingness to enter into 'talks' on increased contact between people in East and West Germany. The Grand Coalition did not develop any really promising initiatives in its Eastern Policy as regards its 'brothers and sisters' in the 'Zone'.

It is true that Kiesinger supported the building of trust towards the USSR and the People's Republic of Poland, but he and his government did not officially depart from the Hallstein Doctrine. The Federal Republic alone was to have and retain the right 'to speak for the whole German people'. The fact that the dogmatic position of the Hallstein Doctrine could not be maintained for much longer was demonstrated in 1967 by the example of the taking up of diplomatic relations with Romania, carried out by the Foreign Office. Cautious soundings and an unsuccessful exchange of letters between Kiesinger and Stoph were in the end too modest to find a way out of the impasse that was the policy on Germany of the Adenauer era.

Foreign policy was not the only area of conflict for the Grand Coalition. There were problems in other areas as well. In the run-up to the elections of 1969 one could hardly identify any common areas at all between the CDU and the SPD. A change of direction was already marked by the election of Gustav W. Heinemann, earlier an opponent of Adenauer, as Federal President on 5 March 1969. Heinemann was the Minister of Justice who had left the CDU and gone over to the SPD. He was elected with votes from the SPD and the FDP in the third round against the Federal Defence Minister Gerhard Schröder, the CDU/CSU candidate also supported by the NPD. Heinemann had also gained the majority of FDP votes. This was taken as a clear signal of the readiness for a coalition of the SPD and the FDP. The governments led by the Christian Democrats for over two decades had come to an end.

The Grand Coalition was, in this respect, also a government on the way out. It collapsed following the Bundestag elections of September 1969.

The Grand Coalition had achieved considerable reforms in domestic politics, amongst other things contributing to the modernization of West German society; in foreign policy, however, it remained relatively rigid, as it had been under Adenauer. The formation of a government from the CDU/CSU and the SPD, supported by over 90 per cent of the Members of the Bundestag, resulted in internal political conflicts no longer being debated in parliament in the way that they had been before. The lack of a real opposition in the Bundestag contributed to the emergence of the so-called extra-parliamentary opposition (Ausserparlamentarische Opposition, APO). It is true that Kiesinger was able to achieve a remarkable success in the election, with almost 46 per cent of the votes against the SPD's 42.7 per cent. Before the polls, however, the SPD and FDP had announced their intention of working together to form a government; this meant that Kiesinger and his party were condemned to the opposition despite their victory in the election.

The New Faces of the Federal Republic: 'Guest Workers', Extremism and the 1968 Student Movement

The tremendous economic development of the 1950s brought about an equally fast reduction in unemployment. Soon there was even a shortage of workers, for example, in the building sector or in small businesses as well as in agriculture. The Federal government came to the employers' aid and started with the targeted recruitment of workers in offices specially set up for the purpose in Southern European countries and Turkey. They were very well received in the West German labour market. They already numbered over 1 million by 1964 when the first Portuguese was welcomed in the land of the economic miracle. At the start of 1970s twice the number of 'guest workers', as they were called, were recorded (the term 'guest workers' making it clear that West German society presumed that all these labourers would eventually go 'home' again). There was no acceptance of the fact that West German society should become a society of immigration. At first, immigrants were employed in firms and protected by law. Before long, however, many of their dependants were to join them. Thus, issues of social integration soon followed, amongst other things in education and employment. During the economic crisis (oil crisis, economic slump, collapse of the international finance system) of the years following 1973, the situation in the employment market worsened even in the Federal Republic.

With rising unemployment the relationship of people in the Federal Republic to the 'guest workers' also changed, which was thoroughly predictable. The Federal government had taken no precautions for this and consequently had no plan either. These 'foreigners' were less in demand now. They were increasingly made scapegoats for the problems of society and the welfare state. It was not long before social rejection reared its head. Social conflicts led to xenophobia and hostility towards foreigners. Politically extremist and rightwing radical groups took particular advantage of this, stirring up violence and agitation.

A party with such a tendency, the German Reich Party (Deutsche Reichspartei, DRP) had, however, already been in existence since 1950, independent of any problems relating to immigration and in the first elections had gained 1.8 per cent of the votes and five seats in the Bundestag. The 5 per cent clause introduced in 1953 had prevented any other such extreme splinter parties being represented. In 1949 the Socialist Reich Party (SRP) split away from the DRP. It was devoted to the idea of a Führer and advocated Nazi propaganda. In the elections to the Landtag of Lower Saxony in 1951 they got 11 per cent of the vote and in Bremen just under 8 per cent.

The Federal Constitutional Court consequently banned this party in 1952 as a successor organization to the National Socialist Party. Some of its supporters went back to the DRP. In Hanover the National Democratic Party of Germany (Nationaldemokratische Partei Deutschlands, NPD) emerged from the fusion of the DRP and other dispersed right-wing groups. It was to become a focus of recruitment for Neo-Nazi circles. Against the background of the economic crisis it attracted protest votes and in the elections to the Landtag in Hesse in 1966 it experienced a surprising surge in support, with just under 8 per cent of the vote; and this was not to be exceptional. In this and the following year the NPD was represented in six Länder parliaments. In Baden-Württemberg in 1968 it achieved its best result of just under 10 per cent of the vote, admittedly by stirring up a combination of German nationalism, hostility to immigrants and the idea of a strong state. In addition the NPD pressed for the reunification of Germany in Europe. A re-establishment of the Eastern border and a retrieval of the territories handed over to the Poles were also part of their programme, along with a demand for an end to the trials of Nazi criminals. In the elections to the Bundestag in 1969 the NPD fell below expectations with a little more than 4 per cent of the vote, below the stated percentage barrier.

The success in the Länder was not to be repeated either. At the start of the 1970s the NPD lost all its seats in the Landtag of the various states; in the elections to the Bundestag in 1972 it was forced to accept a loss of votes and declined to less than 1 per cent. The problems surrounding 'guest workers' that initially became more and more acute as a result of the changed economic climate therefore had little connection to the development of extreme political parties, since these continued to lose influence in the 1970s. However, right-wing extremism and Neo-Nazi support remained ideologically and intellectually alive in the Federal Republic, unlike in the GDR, where comparable currents and tendencies could not come to the surface owing to the structure of the dictatorship and the police state.

At the end of the 1970s Neo-Nazi groups made more of an appearance again and carried out acts of violence, for example, by the Defence Sports Group, Hoffmann, tolerated by the State government of the Free State of Bavaria under Franz Josef Strauß or the Action Front of National Socialists/National Activists, banned in 1983, with its leader, Michael Kühnen, a former lieutenant in the Bundeswehr (Federal Army).

Right-wing tending parties such as the Republikaner ('Republicans') under the former Waffen-SS member and popular journalist from Bavarian Radio, Franz Schönhuber; the German People's Union (Deutsche Volksunion, DVU) with the influential publisher Gerhard Frey; and the revived NPD under Günter Deckert, had gained more support towards the end of the 1980s in the various Landtag and local elections and were able to send members to the respective parliaments. Even in the 1990s there were such tendencies, which increased in strength in the new Länder of Eastern Germany after German unity. With the difficult background these parties had of course no chance up until then at the Federal level. They did not play a part in the Bundestag, let alone in any government. It is therefore advisable from the historical perspective not to overrate the problem of right-wing extremism and Neo-Nazism in the Federal Republic, which remained politically stable. The shock of 1945, the disavowal, indeed the perversion of German national ideology by Hitler and the Nazi Party and the associated lessons of German history in the first half of the twentieth century continue to resonate to the twenty-first century, thanks also to the continued influence of the media making public opinion sensitive in respect to the Holocaust.

The experience of left-wing extremism, including terrorism, was a different matter. The student movement in Germany was not unusual in this respect: left-wing protest was at that time both a European and a global phenomenon. In the United States the protest was directed against the war and US aggression in Vietnam and supported civil rights in the 1960s. These currents also affected Europe. There were riots in Berlin, Paris and Rome. At the Free University in West Berlin students protested against the dated structures. The modest opposition to the Grand

Coalition in the Bundestag encouraged discontent, together with the protest groups. This tension led to the formation of protest cells, outside of the Bundestag, which entered the history of the Federal Republic as the 'extra-parliamentary opposition' (Ausserparlamentarische Opposition, APO). In the process they questioned the whole system of the Federal Republic. They were mainly young people in search of a new style of life and turning against authoritarian ways of thinking. The unrest affected families, schools and universities.

The protest movement (that arose simultaneously in other Western industrial states) had its origin in the dissatisfaction of young people with social conditions of the Adenauer and Erhard republic. The discontent was not just politically motivated but affected many areas of life. The APO saw itself as 'anti-authoritarian' and wanted a 'cultural revolution'. The power structures of marriage and family, schools and universities, companies and administration were not only to be questioned but also destroyed. Values and forms of behaviour changed, yet social power relations remained essentially unchanged. The APO was substantially made up of students but it had an impact on apprentices and school students as well. It inspired the women's movement and brought about changes within the SPD, the FDP and the trade unions.

The protest was also directed at dictatorial forms of government worldwide. When the Shah of Iran, Reza Pahlevi, visited the Federal Republic, students in West Berlin demonstrated against his regime and his bodyguards attacked the protestors with wooden planks. The Berlin police were also mobilized. On 2 June 1967 the student Benno Ohnesorg was killed by a police bullet in the back of his head. As was only revealed in 2009, the West Berlin plain-clothes policeman and weapons enthusiast who killed Ohnesorg, Karl-Heinz Kurras, had also worked for the Stasi from 1955 until at least 1967.

The fatal shooting by Kurras and his acquittal led to a radicalization. The situation escalated and the protest spread to many towns and their universities in the Federal Republic. Blockades, sit-ins and stopping the traffic were typical protests. There was also violence against property. Axel Springer's newspaper empire was held up as 'the press system'. Fire-bombings of the publisher's building in West Berlin, and also of department stores such as the one in Frankfurt am Main on 3 April 1968, caused a slide in the protests towards criminal activity.

The Frankfurt School around Theodor Adorno, Max Horkheimer and Herbert Marcuse had a stimulating effect on the protest with their writings on critical theory, thus indirectly encouraging many students to invade centres of the 'system' and take action against 'repressive tolerance' and 'consumer terror'.

Following an assault by Josef Bachmann, a young temporary worker, on Rudi Dutschke, the leader of the student protest movement, on 11 April 1968 – hitting his victim twice in the head and once in the left shoulder – demonstrations against the Springer concern increased once again. Bachmann had cuttings from the *National-Zeitung* on him with the headline 'Stop Red Rudi Now'. A protest march in Bonn in May 1968, in which tens of thousands of demonstrators took part, was directed against the emergency constitution (*Notstandsgesetze*).

Although the student movement claimed solidarity with the working class, it did not really gain any acceptance with them. They could not identify with the actions of the students. Only in the campaign against the emergency laws was there a temporary alliance with the trade unions. The student movement clearly decreased in 1969 and continued to decline. Smaller groups were not willing to give in, becoming more radical, going underground and drifting towards terrorism.

As a result of the troubled events of 1967–8 the political climate in the Federal Republic experienced a noticeable change. Patterns of policing started to harden against the background of a political radicalization of right and left. Members of the APO and their sympathizers joined the SPD. Very few went to the FDP, many joined the German Communist Party (Deutsche Kommunistische Partei, DKP) or the Maoist 'K-groups' ('Kampf-Gruppen', hardcore radical groups).

The debate about the introduction of emergency legislation that had been going on since the end of the 1950s was controversial. According to the new version of the treaty on West Germany of 23 October 1954, the former occupying powers, France, Great Britain and the USA, were now to hand over their remaining responsibility for protection and security of their forces stationed in the Federal Republic to the German authorities – as soon as these authorities had been given authorization by German legislation guaranteeing the security of those forces. This meant that this increase in sovereignty on the part of the Federal Republic also required legislation to be passed in relation to an emergency and this had to be included in the Grundgesetz. Bills put forward by the Ministry of the Interior in 1958, 1960 and 1963, leading to a strengthening of the rights of the executive, did not receive the required assent of the Bundestag. The Grand Coalition in power from 1966 gained the majority and passed the emergency laws by which the Allied privileges should be abolished. With the SPD, the CDU/CSU succeeded against the FDP opposition in passing the newly drafted legislation on 30 May 1968 with the necessary two-thirds majority. The discussions generated a great deal of heat, both in the Bundestag and amongst the public. Trade unions and students feared an illegitimate growth in the power of the state and took part in demonstrations across the Federal Republic. On

28 June the introduction of the emergency legislation nevertheless came into force. The competence of the legislation and the authority to issue state directives were extended in relation to the Länder in the event of defensive action. There was the possibility of considerably curbing individual basic rights in the case of either an internal emergency or a catastrophe. Even if the government was keen to avoid any misuse of this constitution, a wave of protest against it developed, considerably boosting the student movement. The radical core morphed into the RAF, a leftwing terrorist organization.

Change of Power in Bonn: The Social-Liberal Coalition Brandt-Scheel (1969–74)

The Launch of the New Government and the New Industrial Constitution Act

As Governing Mayor of Berlin (1957–66), Willy Brandt was very popular inside and outside of Germany. In the Bundestag elections of 1961 and 1964 he still lost against Adenauer and Erhard. As chairman of the SPD from 1964 he then, in 1966, became Deputy Chancellor and Foreign Minister in the Grand Coalition. In the Bundestag election on 28 September 1969 the CDU/CSU achieved 242 seats, the SPD 224 and the FDP 30. Brandt then announced his intention of working to bring about an SPD-FDP coalition. The FDP agreed to the coalition. After the election it was Brandt who, as Federal Chancellor, formed a social-liberal coalition with the FDP.

Walter Scheel (FDP) was given the position of Foreign Minister. Under Adenauer and Erhard, Scheel was the Minister for Economic Cooperation, Deputy President of the Bundestag from 1967–9 and he had been chairman of the FDP since 1968. In 1974 Scheel was elected President of the Bundestag with the votes of the SPD and the FDP, winning against the CDU/CSU candidate, Richard von Weizsäcker.

In the government declaration of 28 October 1969 Brandt spoke of putting a comprehensive plan of reform under the slogan 'daring more democracy' into practice. This has been described as the start of a policy that was 'mad about modernization' (Andreas Rödder). In this process there were a number of successes: the new Industrial Constitution Act of 15 January 1972 replaced the old act from 1952. It regularized the position of the trade unions and enabled them to have a greater involvement within industry. Moreover, works councils were set up. The employees' representations that were already in existence were given additional rights to take part in decision-making. Workers' participation was increased. Rights to a tribunal, to make complaints and to make proposals were added to this.

The Meetings between Willy Brandt and Willi Stoph in Erfurt and Kassel

Brandt and Scheel immediately set out on a new policy towards the East (Ost-politik). In their German policy they accepted the GDR as another German state and offered negotiations at government level. In their foreign and security policy the SPD-FDP coalition referred back to Erhard's peace message of March 1966 and Kiesinger's government declaration of December 1966. The signing of the Nuclear Non-Proliferation Treaty was announced. Parallel to this, a confirmation of the transatlantic alliance and a declaration of loyalty to the USA followed. Brandt linked this to an expectation of establishing a basis for talks with the Soviet Union and other Warsaw Pact countries that would lead to a rapprochement.

One means towards a softening of Adenauer's and Ulbricht's Cold War policy consisted in the idea of the renunciation of violence, which Erhard had already offered to the states of Eastern and Central Europe in 1966, but now referred to the existing borders by including the GDR as well. That was equivalent to a political recognition of the Oder-Neisse Line as the Western border of Poland and of the GDR as a second German state. Unlike their predecessors Adenauer and Erhard, Brandt and Scheel actually pursued an active Ostpolitik so as to maintain unity of the German people and at the same time in the process repudiate the desire of the GDR for recognition in international law. In the government declaration of 28 October 1969 Brandt put it like this: 'Even if two states exist in Germany, neverthe-less they are not foreign to one another; their mutual relations can only be of a special kind.' Representatives of the opposition attacked Brandt in the Bundestag on account of this and saw it as a 'dark hour for this House, for this people'.

The main idea of this new Ostpolitik was the attempt on the part of the social-liberal coalition to maintain the tie between people in the Federal Republic and the GDR and to secure the existence of West Berlin. The USSR, Poland and the GDR had indicated that they were prepared to start negotiations. Talks between Bonn, Moscow and Warsaw on the subject of treaties had already taken place when in January/February Brandt and Stoph exchanged letters, arranging meetings on 19 March 1970 in Erfurt and 21 May 1970 in Kassel.

The preliminary negotiations proved to be extremely difficult, however. It had been 23 years since the conference of minister-presidents in Munich in 1947, during which no official meeting between East and West German political repre-sentatives had taken place. This was a clear proof of the Cold War that had dominated between the two German states, of which the Federal Republic was in search of security, according to Eckart Conze. Security could not, however, be achieved by confrontation. This search now took place with increased vigour under Brandt-Scheel, also meeting with the approval of wide sections of the population.

In Erfurt, citizens of the GDR broke through police barriers to show Brandt their sympathy; in Kassel, however, right-wing extremist groups demonstrated against the FRG's Ostpolitik. The Erfurt meeting, which took place in a good atmosphere, contrasted with the meeting in Kassel, which ended coolly. Inflexibility was still strongly marked on both sides and their points of view were irreconcilable. Pankow insisted on total recognition in international law while Bonn stressed the commitment to national unity. Brandt recognized the equality of the GDR and the exchange of representatives, but not of ambassadors.

The Moscow and Warsaw Treaty

There were parallel talks between Bonn and Moscow aimed at a normalization of the relations between the Federal Republic and the GDR. Thus, the contacts between Bonn and East Berlin were strengthened at the insistence of Moscow. The 20 points brought up by Brandt in Kassel as a draft for a treaty between the two Germanies formed the foundation for the 'Grundlagen-Vertrag', which was signed later. Egon Bahr had been holding preliminary negotiations in Moscow since January 1970. While the Soviets at first emphasized the recognition of the GDR in international law, Bonn aimed at a renunciation of violence. The Federal government approved Bahr talking about the borders. The Federal Republic, by giving in on the frontier guarantees demanded by Andrei Gromyko, caused Moscow to drop the recognition of the GDR in international law.

The document that was published in a West German magazine as the 'Bahr-Paper', which had been leaked due to an indiscretion, caused a considerable row in internal politics. The opposition thought they had found the proof that the social-liberal coalition was acting prematurely and had surrendered irrevocable principles. The government was burdened with this but did not waver in its course.

On 12 August 1970 the heads of government, Brandt and Kossygin, along with Foreign Ministers Scheel and Gromyko, signed the treaty in Moscow. It was intended as a contribution to the normalization of the situation in Europe and as a boost to peaceful relations between all European states. It was a statement in favour of the renunciation of force and the recognition of the territorial integrity within their boundaries of all the states of Europe, and contained a declaration that no territorial claims existed against anyone and would not be made in future. The inviolability of the borders, including the Oder-Neisse Line, forming the Western border of Poland, and the confirmation of the border between the Federal Republic and the GDR, were fundamental agreements. In a 'Letter on German Unity' Scheel made it clear to Gromyko that this was not a contradiction of the declared goal of the Federal Republic to work for a state of peace in Europe 'in which the German people will regain their unity in free self-determination'. The letter was accepted by Moscow without reservation and became a part of the treaty.

At the same time as the talks in Moscow, negotiations were also held on a treaty with Poland. This was signed on 7 December 1970 by Brandt and the Polish Prime Minister Jószef Cyrankiewicz, along with Foreign Ministers Walter Scheel and Stefan Jedrychowski. The commitment that took place in Potsdam, according to which the Oder-Neisse Line 'forms the Western state border of the People's Republic of Poland', was confirmed politically. Both sides likewise upheld the 'inviolability of their existing borders now and in the future' and pledged to respect without qualification their territorial integrity and declared that they were prepared to renounce all territorial claims. Renunciation of violence, normalization (exchange of ambassadors) and the comprehensive development of relations were further principles. In an appendix Poland expressed its readiness to permit the exit of its inhabitants of German origin in the cause of reuniting families. The government in Warsaw also upheld a declaration referring to Germany as a whole made on 24 August 1953 by which it had renounced claims to the payment of reparations after 1954.

During a visit to the Polish capital on 7 December 1970 Brandt laid a wreath on at the memorial to the victims of the ghetto uprising by the Jews. To the astonishment of all those watching, and prompted by a spontaneous impulse, he knelt before the memorial for a minute's reflection. The images went around the world. This symbolic act was welcomed as a gesture of reconciliation but in the Federal Republic the 'Kniefall' ('Warsaw Genuflection') caused much political controversy. There were several days of verbal battles as the Ostverträge (Eastern Treaties) were discussed in the Bundesrat and the Bundestag in February 1972.

Transit Agreements and the Traffic Treaty between the Federal Republic and the GDR

As early as March 1970 the policy of détente made talks between the Allied powers about a new agreement on the question of Berlin possible. The American, British and French ambassadors to Bonn and the Soviet ambassador to the GDR met in the former building of the Allied Control Council in West Berlin. No session had been held there for 22 years. Two Berlin crises (1948–9 and 1958–61) had led to fear and insecurity. The situation of West Berlin in the centre of the GDR was uncertain. Even after the building of the Wall, the traffic between the Federal Republic and Berlin was often interrupted. The GDR repeatedly practised a policy of petty irritation. Bonn and the Western powers wanted to solve these problems and guarantee the viability of West Berlin.

Following the signing of the Moscow and the Warsaw Treaties, the Federal Republic with the agreement of the Western powers made the ratification of the Moscow Treaty dependent upon a package deal over a satisfactory resolution of the Berlin question. The Kremlin had its sights on a pan-European security conference (CSCE) and was unwilling for the Moscow agreements to be further contested. Such a conference also presupposed the participation of both German states.

These pressing circumstances contributed to the reaching of a Four Power agreement on Berlin by the ambassadors on 3 September 1971. It was the first agreement by the Allies since the start of the Cold War, which both German states had so rashly gone along with. It established the rights and responsibilities of the Four Powers so firmly, while safeguarding their different legal principles, that the agreed conditions could not be altered by any side. The presence of the Western powers in West Berlin was accordingly set in stone. The USSR agreed not to interrupt the transit of civilians and goods between the Western sectors of the city and the Federal Republic by road, rail and water across the territory of the GDR. Thus, Pankow was deprived of the sole right of control over the movement of traffic to Berlin, which it had often used as a means to apply pressure. From the perspective of the Federal Republic, a limitation of the agreement was the fact that the Western sectors of Berlin would continue not to be part and parcel of the Federal Republic and not to be governed by it. The critical situation of this city on the frontline of the Cold War, which had been a place of insecurity for 25 years, was eased and stabilized by the Four Power agreement, which now became the basis for further agreements.

Since March 1971 there had already been talks between the West Berlin Senate and the GDR leadership on the regularization of travel and visitor traffic from West Berlin to East Berlin and to the GDR, which were concluded on 20 December 1971. Secretary of State Egon Bahr and GDR Secretary of State Michael Kohl negotiated concurrently a transit agreement designed to regularize traffic movement between the Federal Republic and West Berlin and signed it on 17 December 1972 in Bonn, followed by a general treaty on traffic on 26 May 1972. Both agreements came into force, completing the Four Power agreement, on 3 June 1972. Berliners and people in the Federal Republic and the GDR welcomed these agreements. Visits to East Berlin and the GDR increased after 1972.

The 'Grundlagen-Vertrag' (Basic Treaty) and the Treaty with Czechoslovakia

The SPD-FDP coalition had from the start made it clear that it was interested in a new regularization of the relations between the two German states. In Kassel, Brandt had handed Stoph a draft for a treaty. As in the case of the transit agreement and the treaty on traffic, the negotiations were led by Bahr and Kohl. On 16 August 1972, the official negotiations began on the agreement – also called the 'Grundlagen-Vertrag' (Basic Treaty) – that was concluded on 8 November 1972 with the signing in Bonn and on 21 December with the signing in East Berlin. Normal neighbourly relations on the basis of equality deriving from the UN Charter, mutual renunciation of violence and the threat of such as well as the inviolability of the common border, regard for the respective territorial integrity and respect for the independence and autonomy of each of the two states in their internal and external affairs were explicitly emphasized. The Federal Republic and the GDR declared themselves to be in agreement over encouraging peaceful relations between the states of Europe and to participate in controlled international disarmament. The exchange of permanent representations was also agreed on. Accompanying documents concerned the work of journalists, the easing of travel restrictions and issues relating to the reuniting of families. The 'Basic Treaty' also made it possible for both states to be members of the United Nations. As in the case of the Moscow Treaty, the Federal government handed over a 'letter on German unity'. On 22 September 1972, with nine abstentions on the part of the CDU/CSU, the Bundestag unanimously passed the traffic treaty negotiated by Bahr and Kohl. It came into force on 17 October 1972 and was the first treaty between the two German states that they carried out in their own right and not within the framework of Allied agreements. In this treaty all the technical questions of road, rail and water traffic were settled. In the course of the easing of travel, relatives and acquaintances in the GDR could be visited several times a year and GDR citizens were able to travel to the Federal Republic in the case of pressing family matters. Up until then only retired GDR citizens had been able to do this. The SPD–FDP government were to this extent successful in achieving treaties within international law with Moscow and Warsaw as well as to bring the associated Four Power agreement on Berlin into force and to effect the signing of the 'Basic Treaty' with the GDR before the Bundestag elections were called in November 1972. In the context of the Ostpolitik consistently pursued by the social-liberal coalition, following the Moscow and Warsaw Treaties along with the 'Basic Treaty', negotiations had been started with the government of Czechoslovakia, already preceded by tough talks ongoing since 1971. One particular difficulty was the question of whether the Munich Agreement of 1938, by which the German Reich, Italy, Great Britain and France had forced Czechoslovakia to give up the Sudetenland that was populated in the majority by Germans, was to be considered as no longer valid 'from the start' ('ex tunc'), or only retrospectively, as it were from now on ('ex nunc') or generally. Prague insisted on a declaration of validity 'ex tunc'; Bonn saw in this unforeseeable consequences bearing on national and private property laws.

The West German position was maintained in the negotiations, according to which the Munich Agreement was characterized as 'null and void' in the treaty, so no liabilities could arise in relation to injured parties or material claims on the part of Czechoslovakia. Renunciation of violence and inviolability of the borders were the principles that had already proved effective. On 11 December 1973 the heads of government, Willy Brandt and Lubomir Strougal, along with Foreign Ministers Walter Scheel and Bohuslav Chnoupek, signed the German–Czechoslovak Treaty in Prague. Simultaneously, diplomatic relations between the two countries were established. Ten days later it was announced in Bonn, Sofia and Budapest that diplomatic relations had also been established between Bulgaria, Hungary and the Federal Republic of Germany. Thus, the Hallstein Doctrine in its programmatic definition was set aside as a viable tool of diplomatic history and a new era in German–Soviet diplomatic history was ushered in.

The Failed Vote of No Confidence Against Willy Brandt

Brandt was awarded the Nobel Peace Prize in Oslo for his contribution to political détente in Europe as early as 1971. He had been able to push through Ostpolitik only against the stiffest internal resistance. Egon Bahr, Brandt's political advisor over many years, had largely envisaged, shaped and developed the Ostpolitik of the SPD. His involvement was decisive in talks and in exploratory and preliminary negotiations in Moscow and in East Berlin. The way he conducted negotiations angered the CDU/CSU opposition, supported by some newspapers, who whipped up a storm in the press. Criticism was repeatedly voiced that legal positions that had been established and maintained by the CDU/CSU were being unnecessarily abandoned. There were even accusations of 'selling Germany out', 'national betrayal' and collaboration with the socialist states of the East. The Western Allies followed the progress of Ostpolitik not without some scepticism and concern, yet the social-liberal coalition was keen to develop a policy of East-West détente and to pursue this with the agreement of the USA under President Richard Nixon and Foreign Minister Henry Kissinger. The CDU/CSU knew this. It remained their clear objective, however, to bring down the rather weak parliamentary majority of the government coalition (this stood at 254 to 242 votes). Every step Brandt took had to be made in a tough struggle with the CDU/CSU opposition, who still kept to Adenauer's Western approach. The major emphasis of the Brandt-Scheel government was without a doubt Ostpolitik, and this provoked the CDU/CSU into massive opposition. This absorbed a lot of energy and the government was not able to push through the internal reforms announced. In the course of the social-liberal period of government, some FDP members of the Bundestag went over to the CDU or CSU over the question of Ostpolitik. Three sitting members of the conservative wing of the FDP – in October 1970 the former FDP chairman, Erich Mende, in January 1972 the SPD member, Herbert Hupka, chairman of the Association representing the former German territory of Silesia, and, on 23 April 1972, FDP member Wilhelm Helms – changed over to the CDU/CSU, in each case holding on to their seats. The majority of the government coalition disappeared. Gains in the elections to the various Landtag parliaments prompted the CDU/CSU to topple Brandt as Federal Chancellor by means of a constructive vote of no-confidence. The CDU and the CSU argued that the government did not have a majority for their policy any longer. The Bundestag were called upon to elect the chairman of the CDU/CSU grouping, Rainer Barzel, as the new Federal Chancellor and to request the Federal President to dismiss Brandt. The opposition hoped to gain further votes from the social-liberal coalition in a secret ballot on 27 April 1972.

It was a failure. The ballot gave Barzel only 247 votes instead of the necessary 249. The two missing votes had been paid for by the Stasi for 50,000 DM each. The process provided for by the 'Grundgesetz' (Basic Law) of a constructive vote of no confidence was controversial with a section of the population and had been rejected because the result of the Bundestag election of 1969 had been ignored without consulting the voters. A number of demonstrations and work stoppages against the vote of no confidence followed.

After the failure of the vote of no confidence, the factions within the Bundestag nevertheless thrashed out a 'common decision' over common positions on the treaties with the East. However, the decision did not succeed in achieving a broad majority for the ratification of the treaties that 491 members agreed to. In the final ballot on 17 May 1972 248 members agreed to the Moscow Treaty, ten voted 'No' and 238 abstained. Likewise 248 members agreed to the Warsaw Treaty. This time there were seventeen 'No' votes and 231 abstentions. With the majority of the CDU/CSU grouping abstaining – only a single one of them was for it, Richard von Weizsäcker – the treaties were therefore passed by the Bundestag. On 19 May the Bundesrat, the Federal Council, also ratified the two treaties with the East, the Länder run by the CDU/CSU abstaining. The government did not have a majority any more, however, to push through the budget. Brandt asked for a vote of confidence on 20 September and thus brought about the premature dissolution of the Bundestag and new elections. On 19 November 1972 the coalition received a resounding confirmation. Brandt achieved a victory for the SPD with over 45 per cent of the votes, becoming the most powerful grouping in the Bundestag. The government coalition, with a clear majority of 271 members (to 225 CDU/CSU members), was able to resume its work with vigour.

5

'Change Through Rapprochement': Détente and Normalization, 1972–9

Enlargement of the EU, UN Membership of the Two German States and the CSCE Process

Through the fusion of the organizations of the ECSC, the EEC and EURATOM, the European Community emerged in 1967, now having a common Council of Ministers, a Commission, a European Parliament and a European Court of Justice. After 1974 there was also the European Council as a governing body of the heads of state and governments meeting at least twice a year. The Federal Republic together with some other EC members aimed for a political union in Western Europe. France, however, rejected such a policy and opposed the entry of Great Britain, which, according to de Gaulle's point of view had ties that were too close to the United States.

After the founding of the EEC, the United Kingdom, together with Denmark, Norway, Austria, Portugal, Sweden and Switzerland, had founded the European Free Trade Association (EFTA) in 1960, which entered into competition with the EEC but remained limited in its political scope. The subject of enlargement continued to be a goal of West German European policy after de Gaulle's resignation in France. At the Hague summit conference in 1969, Willy Brandt was successful with his proposal of setting up negotiations on entry with Great Britain, Denmark, Ireland and Norway. In the meantime, the Customs Union of the six EEC member states had already been established. Plans for an economic and monetary union were agreed. In 1973 Great Britain, Denmark and Ireland became new members of the EC; in Norway the population voted against entry into the EC. In 1979, for the first time, the deputies to the European Parliament could be directly elected.

In a protocol annexed to the 'Grundlagen-Vertrag', the Federal Republic and the GDR had agreed to make a coordinated application to join the United Nations. The simultaneous application did not create any more serious obstacles in the Eastern and Western political spheres. On 18 September 1973, within the framework of the 28th General Assembly of the United Nations in New York, the GDR was admitted as the 133rd and the Federal Republic as the 134th member of the international organization, founded in 1945. Foreign Minister Walter Scheel emphasized that the Federal Republic would be committed to human freedom and dignity and would show solidarity with the poor of the world. A precondition was a policy of détente, which would be to everyone's benefit and in which the Federal government would be involved. Through the reduction of the potential for conflict, new energies could emerge that would be useful for dealing with social injustice and the alleviation of economic need. The admission of the GDR into the United Nations took place with less ambitious world-political goals and, above all, else marked its worldwide recognition. With this step, the Hallstein Doctrine was definitively put to rest internationally.

The policy of détente addressed by Scheel had already been underway since the end of the 1960s. The idea had originally started on the Eastern side and was then taken up and supported by the neutral states of Europe, particularly Finland. The USSR had, as early as 1954, and the Warsaw Pact finally in 1967 put forward the proposal of a European security conference that all the states of the continent were to take part in. The Soviet Union wanted to prevent the integration of the Federal Republic with the West and thereby the formation of a West European bloc but, as expected, it met with rejection on the part of the Western powers who did not want to lose the potential of West Germany for their interests. From the middle of the 1960s, more Soviet initiatives appeared for such a conference to be called in Europe. NATO again reacted coolly and replied with the demand for a simultaneous discussion of questions on human and civil rights. In 1968 the NATO states reacted positively. Against the background of the departure from Adenauer's 'policy of strength' and of the new Ostpolitik under Brandt and Scheel, who signed treaties of non-aggression with the USSR, Poland and the GDR, a real basis for a Europe-wide security structure was established. The treaty agreed between Washington and Moscow on Strategic Arms Limitation Talks (SALT-I) offered a further important precondition for a Conference on Security and Cooperation in Europe (CSCE). The CSCE referred to the international meetings following preliminary talks, contacts and discussions from 22 November 1972 up to 8 June 1973. They were formally opened on 3 July 1973 in Helsinki with a meeting of foreign ministers, continued from 18 September 1973 up to 21 July 1975 in Geneva and were finalized on 1 August 1975 by the heads of state and governments through the Helsinki Final Act. The 33 European states as well as Canada and the USA were taking part. What contributed

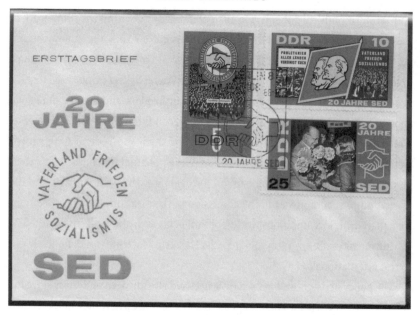

Twenty years of the Socialist Unity Party (SED) commemorated on a First Day Cover.

to the policy of détente of the 1970s, along with the Ostpolitik of Brandt and Scheel, was Austria's active policy of neutrality under Federal Chancellor Bruno Kreisky, who cooperated closely with Sweden's Prime Minister Olof Palme. In the CSCE three bundles of subjects had been central to the debates: 'Basket I' included among other things security questions; 'Basket II' implied cooperation in the sectors of economics, science, technology and environment; while 'Basket III' concerned human contacts, cultural exchanges and the sharing of information. 'Baskets' I and III were subjects of dispute in which the 'non-aligned and neutral states' successfully played a mediating role. There followed a further phase of the CSCE from September 1973 up to July 1975 in Geneva devoted to the writing of the final documents.

At the summit conference in Helsinki from 30 July up to 1 August 1975, the heads of state, government and political parties from the participating states signed the final act which admittedly did not represent a binding treaty but nevertheless contained common declarations of intent on the part of the participating governments. The treaties that were signed by the Federal Republic at the start of the 1970s to a great extent anticipated the guiding principles of the CSCE (renunciation of force, inviolability of borders, territorial integrity, peaceful resolution of conflict, non-interference), in which respect for human rights, basic freedoms, equality and the right of self-determination of peoples and cooperation between states formed further important principles. Confidence-building measures (including the notification and observations of troop manoeuvres) as well as economic and technical cooperation and the promotion of human contacts across frontiers likewise formed part of the agreements.

The Guillaume Affair as a Pyrrhic Victory on the Part of the GDR – SED Policy of Isolation – Continuation of the Social-Liberal Coalition under Schmidt and Genscher

25 April 1974 was a black day for Willy Brandt. The Office of the Federal Director of Public Prosecutions announced that a close aide of the Federal Chancellor had been arrested under suspicion of having acted as a spy for the GDR. This involved Günter Guillaume, who had come allegedly as a refugee to the Federal Republic in 1956. In fact, he was a member of the GDR Stasi from the start and an officer in the NVA and had been active since then within the SPD for the Eastern intelligence service. In 1970 he had joined the Federal Chancellery and working in Brandt's office he had organized the head of government's diary as well as correspondence with the party since 1972.

Brandt was disappointed at the human level and politically shaken. The opposition demanded an explanation. On 6 May Brandt took personal responsibility for 'negligence' in the affair and announced his resignation. The SPD reacted by appointing the Finance Minister, Helmut Schmidt, who was elected the new Federal Chancellor by the Bundestag on 16 May 1974. Guillaume (and, in 1975, his wife) were sentenced to thirteen and eight years in prison respectively for high treason and in 1981 they were transferred to the GDR, where Guillaume was formally welcomed by Markus 'Mischa' Wolf, the foreign head of the Stasi, as a 'hero of Socialism' in the struggle against the 'class enemy'. Guillaume died on 17 April 1995.

For the GDR, the unmasking of Guillaume and the associated fall of Brandt was admittedly a pyrrhic victory, because a West German politician associated with détente and the normalization of relations had to give up the highest position in the government and the CDU/CSU opposition gained further impetus thereby. Brandt remained as SPD Party chairman (up until 1987) and in 1976 also became chairman of the Socialist International and from 1977 to 1980 chairman of the international North-South Commission together with Bruno Kreisky and Olof Palme.

The years 1971–2 represented a double break in the history of the GDR. In 1971 the change of guard within the SED was completed and in 1972 the 'Grundlagen-Vertrag' was signed. After Ulbricht's death in 1973 Stoph, who had been Prime Minister up until then, became chairman of the Council of State. In 1976 Honecker, who held the offices of head of the party and General Secretary, took over this position while Stoph again took over the chairmanship of the Council of Ministers. Following the 'Grundlagen-Vertrag' the GDR was recognized by nearly all the states in the world. This was also linked to admission to the United Nations. The SED regime had achieved its goal of international recognition. The associated increase in exchange and the growth in contacts that were inevitable in the wake of the normalization of relations with the Federal Republic aroused fears within the East German leadership as regards internal stability. Therefore, the GDR forced through a stronger policy of isolation towards the Federal Republic.

Whereas Bonn emphasized the unity of the German nation and a common German history and culture, Pankow highlighted the differences in the political and social spheres in relation to the Federal Republic. Shortly after Walter Ulbricht's fall, initiated by Erich Honecker, his successor had expressed at the eighth Party Conference of the SED 'that the process of isolation between the two states was becoming deeper and deeper in all areas of social life'. The GDR stood accordingly for a 'socialist nation', while the Federal Republic represented a 'bourgeois nation'. The euphoric reception by the citizens of Erfurt gave Brandt on the occasion of his visit resulted in, among other things, a fundamental reform of the constitution on the part of the GDR leadership in October 1974, in which all the references to commonalities in respect to the German nation were erased. The 'Socialist Constitution' of 1968 had still referred to the 'whole German nation', the 'ending of the division forced on the German nation by Imperialism' as well as a 'rapprochement between the two German states towards their unification on the basis of democracy and Socialism' to come about step by step. In 1974, by contrast, it said that the GDR was 'a solid component of the Socialist community of states' and was allied 'for ever and irrevocably' with the USSR. Many institutions and organizations in the GDR had their names changed. Terms such as 'German' or 'Germany' were removed. The prevailing anxiety on the part of the state that the population might make contact with Western journalists led in 1974 and 1979 to a tightening-up of the law in political matters. Giving information 'counter to the interests of the GDR' was punishable as 'treasonable transmission of intelligence', even if such information was not being kept secret. The widespread interpretation of the term led in practice to a ban on contact by GDR citizens with visitors and journalists from the West. Publishing in the West was punished by severe penalties. Critics of the regime such as Robert Havemann, Rudolf Bahro and Wolf Biermann were subject to repressive measures ranging from being permanently watched through to house arrest and even imprisonment and deportation.

With legal methods of exerting pressure the SED regime attempted to control and direct information about the GDR. Strict restrictions were imposed on Western reporters, limiting journalism by means of a regulation of 11 April 1979 requiring the compulsory authorization of discussions and expressions of opinion of any kind. In individual cases the East German state ordered the deportation of undesirable reporters and the closing of editorial premises.

From the interpretation and application of the freedom of speech and of the press it became increasingly clear that the GDR did not deserve the name 'Democratic Republic' and that it was a totalitarian dictatorship, even if apologists, former representatives or nostalgists were unwilling to admit this or even denied it outright. In 1976 Honecker took over the chairmanship of the Council of State and therefore the office of the head of state, having already forced Ulbricht out of the top job of First Secretary of the CC of the SED five years earlier. Thus, he was at the helm of the Socialist Party dictatorship.

On 16 May 1974 the Bundestag elected Helmut Schmidt as the new Federal Chancellor with the votes of the SPD and the FDP. On the previous day the Federal Assembly had elected the former Deputy Chancellor and Foreign Minister Walter Scheel as the Federal President after Gustav Heinemann had renounced a second candidature.

The son of a schoolmaster, Schmidt took part in the war, and afterwards studied political science and became a member of the SPD in 1946. As a member of the Bundestag he stood out as a defence expert. As Hamburg's Senator for Interior Affairs (equivalent to a Minister in the other larger Länder), Schmidt became well known for his crisis management during the flood catastrophe of 1962. Having been chairman of the parliamentary grouping from 1967, in 1969 he became Defence Minister and in 1972, after Karl Schiller's resignation, for a short time he became Minister for the Economy and Finance.

Born in Reideburg near Halle an der Saale in 1927, the lawyer Hans-Dietrich Genscher was, after 1945, at first a member of the LPDP in the Soviet Occupation Zone. In 1952 he went to the Federal Republic and from 1954 worked as a lawyer. As party manager of the FDP and from 1965 a member of the Bundestag, from 1969 he was Minister of the Interior in the social-liberal coalition government and in the course of this he introduced measures in the area of environmental protection. In the coalition formed by Schmidt in 1974, Genscher served as Foreign Minister and Deputy Chancellor and, after Scheel became Federal President, he also replaced him as chairman of the FDP.

With the slogan 'Continuity and Concentration', the new government wanted to continue the social-liberal policy of Brandt and Scheel. The CDU/CSU mobilized and pressed forward with its concerted opposition. Within this a change of political leadership had taken place. Barzel, who had failed in the Bundestag election of 1972, resigned from his positions as CDU/CSU Federal chairman and chairman of the CDU/CSU parliamentary grouping. At a special CDU Party conference in June 1973 the Minister-President of Rhineland-Palatinate, Helmut Kohl, became the new party chairman. Kohl was also a candidate for the post of Chancellor in the Bundestag elections of 1976 and after the election defeat he took over the chairmanship of the parliamentary grouping. The opposition of the Christian Democrats continued to be directed against the policy of détente. The political legacy of Adenauer's almost non-existent Ostpolitik was difficult for them to cast off. They had considerable problems over the normalization of relations with the GDR and the states of the Eastern Bloc; this was at the same time a natural consequence of the failure of the policy of confrontation. With its fundamental rejection of the CSCE, the CDU/CSU forced itself, not just into political isolation internally, but also into international isolation. There was no doubt criticism to be made about the Helsinki Final Act of 1 August 1975, particularly since the East-West conflict continued in its basic structures, but declarations of intent were expressed in the CSCE principles that the communist states also had to take on board.

While upholding the Western alliance, the Schmidt/Genscher government kept to the Ostpolitik of the Brandt/Scheel government and developed it further. While against the background of the world financial crisis some reform projects had to be put on hold, the policy of détente was consistently followed. After the Bundestag elections of 1976 and 1980, won by the SPD-FDP coalition, Schmidt became Federal Chancellor once again. In dealing with terrorism he showed tenacity and strength of leadership, particularly in a period when the Federal Republic was in a state of flux on the edge of constitutionality as a result of the exceptional situation. Thanks to his economic expertise and his ability as a statesman, Schmidt enjoyed great respect at home and abroad. Along with his friend, Valéry Giscard d'Estaing, he continued the policy of understanding with France and with the founding of the European Monetary System (EMS) and the introduction of the European Currency Unit (ECU) he decisively contributed to the deepening of European integration.

Oil Crisis, Limits to Growth, Unemployment and the 'Unity of Economic and Social Policy': The Socio-Economic Situation in the Two German States

Policy under Federal Chancellor Brandt and particularly that under Helmut Schmidt was marked by 'crisis management' (Andreas Rödder). Against the background of the Israeli-Arab War of October 1973 oil was used as a political tool to exert pressure for the first time after the Second World War. The Arab oil-producing states not only pushed up the oil price but imposed increased restrictions on production. They declared a boycott against the United States and the Netherlands on account of their pro-Israeli position, with immediate painful results for other Western states in Europe as well. The Organization of Petroleum Exporting Countries (OPEC), which also included non-Arab oil-producing states, joined in with this policy. The price of crude oil, which still stood at $1.40 per barrel (158.8 litres) in 1970, had quadrupled three years later. Western oil concerns benefited from the reduced supply of oil and increased their profit margins.

Since the Federal Republic was lacking raw materials, the consumption of energy had to be reduced. The Federal government declared four car-free Sundays in November and December 1973. The temporary introduction of speed limits ('100 KPH max' on the autobahns) was to follow. The population came to realize for the first time the dependence of society and the economy of their country on oil.

The oil shock of 1973 triggered the most serious economic crisis, not just in the Federal Republic, but in the other Western industrial states as well. After 1974 OPEC increased oil prices several times. The revolution in Iran in 1979 caused a further oil shock. The price of crude oil rose to just $23 per barrel, which was not, however, the highest it was to go. In October 1981 it reached $34. In the wake of the oil crisis in 1973 the Federal Republic experienced a decrease in employment and in demand for goods as well as increasing inflation (also referred to as stagflation).

The oil price rise led to a flow of money from industrial nations to oil-producing states. The world economic crisis must also be seen within the context of the collapse of the world monetary system established at Bretton Woods in 1944, of the negative effect on the dollar and of the USA's costly Vietnam War, which had provoked opposition in both parts of Germany. The combined effect of these crises clearly demonstrated the weaknesses of the Federal Republic. In the Ruhr, the region of the German Economic Miracle of the 1950s, particularly in the traditional coal and steel industries, there was a tremendous overcapacity. Added to this were the Japanese products in the micro-electronic and optical sector, but also in car production, which represented dramatic competition for the German manufacturers. Textile producers from the so-called Third World, who could count on far lower wages and social costs than their German competitors, aggravated the situation.

Compared with other Western industrial nations the Federal Republic was relatively better able to weather the situation. The SPD–FDP government under Schmidt attempted to come to terms with the crisis both within the framework of an international economic summit and on the domestic level.

With the collapse of the international monetary system and the oil crisis of 1973–4 a global crisis had come about, affecting all Western industrial countries. As in the 1930s there was a great risk that the states would solve the economic problems by going it alone and returning in the process to protectionism (i.e. putting up tariff barriers or introducing other trade restrictions).

Schmidt sought to overcome the developing economic crisis by means of national and international measures. State borrowing was increased and unemployment was successfully tackled with public programmes for stimulating activity. After the 'concerted action' of 1977, Schmidt was keen to work with trade unions and employers to bring about economic equilibrium. On the international level the Federal government sought agreement on economic policy. One goal was the prevention of protectionist measures on the part of individual states, protecting their own market and thereby hitting trade in general. One thing that helped this was participation in economic summit conferences of the most important Western states, which took place annually after 1975. Economic cooperation with the Communist states was developed at the same time. It was France's President Valéry Giscard d'Estaing who invited the heads of states and governments of the Federal Republic, the United Kingdom, Italy, Japan and the USA to the château of Rambouillet near Paris from 15 to 17 November 1975 to discuss the pressing economic questions. At the next conference in June 1976 in Puerto Rico, the Prime Minister of Canada took part. The economic summits were from then on held every year between May and July in one of the seven participating countries, including Bonn in 1978 and 1985 and Munich in 1992. Giscard and Schmidt called for agreement on economic and finance policy on the part of the participating countries and resistance to protectionist measures. This proved as much beyond their reach as the reduction of the USA's ballooning deficit, which was the cause of both higher interest rates for West European states and of economic damage in developing countries.

Despite the meagre results from these economic summits, which were the basis for the later G7 and G8 summits, there remained the possibility for meeting and the exchange of information on the part of the most important statesmen of the Western world. With the conference at Williamsburg in the USA in 1983, after pressure from the USA, the original limiting of the points of the agenda to economic and finance policy was abandoned and political questions were also included. Even if the economic summits only achieved relatively little, nevertheless the internal measures in the Federal Republic met with some success. The programmes for stimulating activity admittedly pushed up debts again on the part of the state and encouraged inflation, but this policy was successful to the extent that in 1978 there was a drop in the unemployment figures. In the following years unemployment fell to less than 900,000. Unemployment in Germany was then now at its lowest level since reunification in 1990, according to the offical statistics.

In 1972 the 'Club of Rome' presented a report on the limits to growth and warned of the destruction of the world through unrestricted economic growth. The report had relatively little effect, society in the Federal Republic as in the rest of the Western industrial world being too caught up in the euphoria surrounding growth.

The Austrian cultural historian Friedrich Heer, a perceptive observer of the Federal Republic, noted that an effective social life could not be based and built on 'efficiency', 'productivity' and 'rationality' alone. In his opinion, along with a loss of faith there was the threat of a loss of security. This development was expressed in the Federal Republic in the flight towards material values. The concentration on new (alleged) securities, according to Heer, went hand in hand with an impoverishment of spiritual substance, which he clearly described and characterized in detail in his book 'Why is there no spiritual life in Germany?' – in his words: 'a critical declaration of love directed at the Germans'. In the Federal Republic he identified a lack of spirituality and life of the soul, linked to an increasing materialism. The 'Now Society in the Federal Republic' did not constitute 'a nation, have any spiritual life, any culture – it does not have any health, its life is without tact and without contact, an untidy, uncouth living for today. A life without any background. Without roots.' Heer also regretted the neglect of history and of the historical amongst the Germans and characterized a large part of their life as an escape. Inarticulacy found expression in 'debased language', a language which would also make increasing use of anglicisms and ignore its own vocabulary.

The social consensus and political stability of the system in the Federal Republic were biased towards an emphasis on thinking in terms of productivity and permanent economic growth, particularly since the distribution of income and wealth purely reflected the rates of growth. The oil shocks had shown that this raw material could become more scarce and expensive. Since the end of the 1970s there was an increasing awareness that the euphoria surrounding growth might prove naive, even dangerous for humanity and nature.

Environmental protection on the part of the state had been underway since the start of the 1970s. Preventive measures in order to avoid new damage to the environment were introduced. Gradually there was the start of a recognition that environmental protection involving the application of new technology could also create employment. In the 1970s it also became apparent that the gulf between the rich industrial states of the Northern and the poor countries of the Southern Hemisphere could be more dramatic and more dangerous than the East-West conflict, which had often since the Adenauer Era been portrayed in an unbalanced fashion. Enormous population growth in the Third World led to food crises and famine catastrophes, while the First World squandered enormous sums on conventional and atomic weapons and was responsible for surpluses in production. The necessary resolution of the stark inequalities, within the framework of a 'North-South dialogue' – demanded particularly by the Social Democrat parties in the context of the Socialist International – did not receive the necessary attention (e.g. in the context of the conference taking place in Paris in 1975 on international economic cooperation with the so-called underdeveloped states). They demanded the stabilization of crude oil prices and access to the markets of the industrial states. In 1977 an independent North-South Commission chaired by Brandt was set up that presented proposals for achieving an equilibrium in the partnership between North and South but which admittedly did not have much effect on the political reality. The indebtedness of the 'developing countries' continued to increase as a result of the US policy of high interest rates.

The development policy of the Federal Republic in the 1970s might be summed up under the heading 'aid towards self-help', which was reminiscent of the days of the Marshall Plan but could not be compared with that programme. The improvement in living conditions, the overcoming of unemployment and the deferment of foreign policy interests, the securing of peace and the procurement of 'tomorrow's trading partners' were the focus.

A comparison of the employment and occupational structures in the two German states shows how little movement there was in the GDR and how much more change there was in the economy of the Federal Republic.

Diagrams show an agriculture and forestry sector that does not move from the end of the Ulbricht Era and the start of the Honecker Era up to the fall of the Wall. In the manufacturing sector too the values are relatively unchanging, similarly in the area of transport and information and in the other areas. We see a society showing

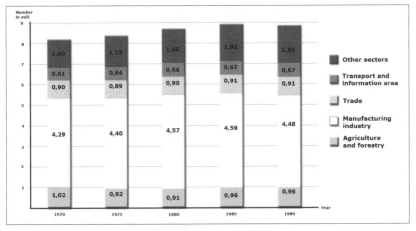

Those in employment according to areas of the economy in the GDR.

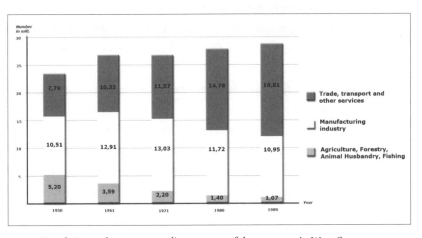

People in employment according to areas of the economy in West Germany.

little dynamism, social mobility or change. In the GDR, in comparison with the West, the transformation towards the manufacturing sector appears not to have taken place at all. Comparison with the West German territory, on the other hand, shows that sectors one, two and three were switched over and agriculture and forestry were almost irrelevant, the service sector, however, becoming all the more important.

The areas of the economy in the Federal Republic show a reduction in the agricultural sector. The manufacturing sector has remained stable, while the areas of services and trade indicate a doubling of the number of people employed in them. There are clear shifts from the primary to the secondary and tertiary sectors.

The world economic crisis of the 1970s did not leave the second German state unaffected either. At the end of the 1960s the SED regime already had to acknowledge that despite the economic reforms initiated after the building of the Wall it had not been able to make up for the lag in growth behind the Federal Republic or, for that matter, to achieve anything like the prosperity of the citizens of West Germany. At the eighth SED Party congress from 15 to 19 June 1971, Erich Honecker, still seemingly oozing self-confidence, had sarcastically referred to his predecessor Ulbricht's 'greater-than-target economic miracles' and promised a turn towards a 'more realistic' policy. There followed a change of course, going under the slogan 'Unity of Economic and Social Policy'. Honecker's policy was aimed in a collectivist sense at focusing state propaganda on the successes of the social achievements of the GDR as opposed to the standard of living of the individual. Working mothers were encouraged. Minimum pensions and minimum wages were increased; the building of homes was financed; stable prices for basic foodstuffs and rents were guaranteed. These social measures were sold as an improve- ment in wages, by means of which the lag in the level of wages and pensions behind the Federal Republic would be overlooked. It was a policy at the expense of third parties (principally the Federal Republic), forcing the GDR into the self-imposed trap of massive debts. These were debts that, unlike those in the care of Western currencies, could not be made up for by currencies' convertible assets. In the first half of the 1970s one still did not have this impression, however, particularly since a not inconsiderable growth rate was achieved. The real income of GDR citizens experienced a rise of approximately 30–35 per cent from 1971 to 1975. Despite this trend the supply of goods could not sufficiently keep pace. The SED regime had to make concessions: in line with new legislation on foreign exchange, after 1973 citizens of the GDR were able to buy goods from the West in the 'Intershops' that had been in existence since the start of the 1960s, although admittedly only if they used Western currency. Thus the socialist state was, to a certain extent, painting itself into a corner, even if Honecker, the head of state, insisted that the Intershops would not be a permanent feature of socialism. Nevertheless, they drew attention to the attractiveness and desirability of capitalist products in the GDR and proved the greater productivity and economic superiority of the West German market society. Deutsche Marks (DM) were obtained from West Germans visiting East Germany and became an auxiliary currency in the GDR, which was a quicker and more efficient way of paying for everyday needs, not only for purchases in the Intershops, but also in the area of services and tradesmen. Owning DM or Western currency sometimes increased opportunities and the feeling of self-worth of the citizens in the GDR more than the achievement of higher incomes in the East German economy. Despite Honecker's appearances putting on a show of self-confidence and marked optimism and his insistence on the inevitability of the socialist ideology, the economic situation of the GDR worsened in the second half of the 1970s. The oil price shocks hit the state which had few raw materials and lacked foreign exchange, particularly since there was very little investment left available to the economy and its development. The state measures designed to promote the area of social policy contributed to the worsening of this situation. The GDR was caught up in the increasing dilemma of its deficit policy.

The first deputy chairman of the Council of Ministers, Werner Krolikowski, referred to Honecker's and Günter Mittag's borrowing 'socialism of pump and pomp' in January 1980 with surprising candour and in a note of unmistakeable clarity. According to Helmut M. Müller: 'When Brezhnev was in Berlin for the thirtieth anniversary of the GDR in 1979 – the GDR had at that time around 30 billion exchange-Marks of debt to the West – he banged his fist the table in front of the whole of the Politburo and quite seriously accused Honecker of driving the GDR into bankruptcy by his debts to the West.'

These were clear expressions from the centre of power but Honecker, the East German communist, was outwardly unfazed by these warnings. With the aid of further financial support from the Federal Republic, controversial loans amounting to billions of DM, and from Western countries, he thought he could continue this risky (and at the same time ruinous) policy. Behind the facade of this would-be humane and progressive Workers' and Farmers' state – as allegedly one of the most productive industrial nations in the world – was in fact concealed a bankrupt and corrupt system, exploiting its own citizens and run by party bosses who awarded themselves all kinds of privileges and enjoyed Western consumer goods in their villas out of sight of the public in Wandlitz. Even their rubbish collections were supervised so as not to give rise to any discontent at their lifestyle.

GDR social policy created a higher degree of economic equality for the broad masses and thus considerably helped towards the political legitimation of the domination of the SED, even if the material privileges of the party elites and those close to the state and the rising costs associated with these presented a cynical contrast. The satisfaction of basic needs was manifested in price supports for basic goods – luxury goods were an exception and excluded – and in the areas of health and construction. In the course of time, the level of prices and the supply of necessities to society corresponded less to the increased demands of the population and so became less and less effective.

In the 1980s indications that the East German state and its citizens were living far beyond their means and that its resources were largely exhausted became stronger. A supply system based on paternalism predominated by far over the principle of productivity. The policy of a socialist welfare state attempted by Honecker was no longer sustainable without injections of Western finance. Externally SED propaganda constructed one Potemkin village after another, according to which the citizens of the GDR were socially secure and happy as if the state was politically and economically sound. Nevertheless, the cracks and warning signs could not be ignored, pointing towards the economic decline and the political erosion of the system in the second half of the 1980s. Only under pressure from the ever-present state security service (the Stasi), the system of spying involving a large number of secret and unofficial collaborators, a total surveillance state and an inhumanly strict (zonal) border with the Federal Republic, could things be held together. How the regime would react if the discontent and anger were to be expressed on a massive scale was still an open question. That the SED regime was able to keep going at all was only possible as a result of fear, intimidation and terror, by means of which the SED apparatus of repression created a semblance of law and order. Added to this was one of the most closely guarded borders in the world, which could only be crossed at great risk to one's life. The GDR was to fail as a result of this murderous dividing line between one population with the same language. The people involved in the areas near the border and the surviving victims and their families would, however, still suffer as a result long after the fall of the Iron Curtain.

The Main Recording Centre in Salzgitter, the Decree Against Radicals, Bans on Admission to Professions and the 'Red Army'

The Federal Republic created an institution that would serve to record all the events occurring on the demarcation line between the two states. It went back to Brandt, the Governing Mayor of Berlin, who in Berlin in August 1961, a few days after the measures setting up the barrier conducted by the 'state organizations' of the GDR, had called for the securing of evidence and recording of acts of mistreatment carried out on the inner-German border.

The 'Main Recording Centre' (Zentrale Erfassungsstelle, ZESt) was situated in Salzgitter, a town in Lower Saxony near the border, from 1961 to 1989. The background to this was that there were limitations to the validity of the 'Grundgesetz': it only involved the territory of the Federal Republic. The Federal government had no direct possibility of influencing events in the GDR, or on the demarcation line either. Thus the ZESt was to take on the role of a registration centre. It was not a Federal agency but was set up by the Länder. The material for dealing with the events recorded was passed to the Directors of Public Prosecutions following a judicial hearing. The securing of evidence involved the establishment of various facts: all acts of violence as well as lethal acts against refugees; perversion of justice; mistreatment within the justice system and penal institutions of the GDR along with political denunciations by informing on persons to the Volkspolizei or the Stasi, the Ministry for State Security (MfS).

Detention pending trial was often justified in the GDR under the term ('danger of desertion'), which in theory did not actually exist, or could not exist. The core of the whole problem was the approximately 42,000 preliminary judicial enquiries. The ZESt was associated with a vitally important political acknowledgement and designation as well as with a moral acknowledgement of those suffering at the hands of and the victims of the GDR regime. The work of the ZESt was admittedly controversial on the political level, but it increased the pressure on the SED regime for justification. Thus, the GDR called the ZESt a 'relic of the Cold War'. Honecker put down four points in his 'Gera Demands' of 1980 directed at Bonn: first, the Elbe border would run along the middle of the river between Lauenburg and Schnackenburg, and second, the citizenship of the GDR was to be recognized by the Federal Republic. This would have made the speedy and unproblematic reception of GDR refugees more difficult and would have also meant the application for asylum by Germans in Germany. Third, the transformation of the Permanent Representations of the two German states into embassies which would have implied the establishment of international relations between the Federal Republic and the GDR and would have been equivalent to a recognition by Bonn of the GDR in international law. The SPD-FDP and the following CDU-FDP coalition rejected this demand. Bonn continued to talk of 'particular relations', 'inner-German relations' or 'inter-German relations'. Fourth, Honecker demanded the abolition of the ZESt, which indirectly highlighted its political relevance as well as its effectiveness in German political terms. Later on there were SPD circles around Egon Bahr, Gerhard Schröder or Hans-Jochen Vogel, who wanted to pursue Honecker's Gera Demands, but there was opposition within the party as well as from the CDU, CSU and FDP, so the ZESt in Salzgitter remained operational. Between 1952 and 1989, hundreds of people met their death on the inner-German border as a result of landmines in the death strip, automatic firing devices on the barbed wire several metres high or being shot by GDR border guards, who in the event of a 'danger of desertion' had to 'make use of weapons': the equivalent of an order to shoot. Thousands of escape attempts failed. Conditions prevailing between the two Germanies were completely abnormal. In the Federal Republic the political climate also became more intense as a result of the Cold War.

Following the political radicalization at the end of the 1960s, the Federal government under Willy Brandt, together with the Federal Länder, adopted resolutions on 28 January 1972 relating to the membership of extreme organizations by state employees. Accordingly, the suitability of applicants being considered for a career in the civil service was to be checked. Civil servants were obliged to pledge allegiance to the 'Grundgesetz' and to commit to the free and democratic basis of the social order. In the public debate these measures were criticized for being a 'decree against radicals'. In practice, there were actually bans on admission to professions (*Berufsverbote*). There were fears in CDU/CSU circles that the left-wing extremist groups emerging from the student movement were a danger to the state. The leaders of the student movement had in fact used the slogan of 'the long march through the institutions' and by their activities had themselves contributed to the creation of these fears and worries. SPD and FDP politicians expressed reservations at the decree on extremists and its questionable application, particularly on account of the checks on thousands of applicants by the Office for the Protection of the Constitution. The Federal Constitutional Court in Karlsruhe finally ruled in 1975 that the decision about the suitability of a candidate was not dependent upon membership of a party, judged as unconstitutional or even banned as being opposed to the constitution but, rather, it was in the end dependent on the conduct and personality of the applicant. The draft bill passed by the social-liberal government in the Bundestag amending the regulations on the legal position of the civil service failed as a result of the CDU/CSU majority in the Bundesrat (Upper House). The Federal Länder did not, however, agree amongst themselves. While the Länder dominated by the CDU/CSU insisted on the decree on extremists in its original form, the SPD Länder and the Federal government applied the more liberal regulations of the failed Bill.

For more than two decades the 'Red Army' faction (Rote Armee Fraktion, RAF, also known as the Baader-Meinhof Group) had spread fear and had been largely successful in carrying out terrorism: founded in 1970 after the student revolts of the 1960s by Ulrike Meinhof, Andreas Baader and Gudrun Ensslin, this left-wing extremist group left a trail of blood in the wake of their violent actions. The RAF aimed to oppose what they saw as the 'exploiting', 'fascist', 'imperialistic' and 'repressive' state. They declared war on 'Imperialism' and 'Mono-Capitalism' and attempted to destroy its social order.

It began with an arson attack on a department store in April 1968 in Frankfurt am Main as a statement against the USA's Vietnam War. Baader and Ensslin were arrested; as a result of intervention by the left-wing journalist Meinhof, they were, however, immediately released. All three united and formed the core of the RAF.

They followed the example of Latin American city guerrilla fighters, trained with Palestinian terrorists and continued the 'armed struggle' underground. The three leaders of the RAF were soon caught and locked up in the high security wing at Stuttgart/ Stammheim. However, they managed to organize a 'second generation' of terrorists from their prison cells.

In West German history 'Stammheim' has become a synonym for the judicial debate about the terrorism of the RAF. A court building with expensive security provision had been set up at the prison site, where on 21 May 1975 the trial against the leaders of the RAF, Baader, Meinhof, Ensslin and Jan-Carl Raspe was held by the Highest Land Court of Stuttgart. The court and the Public Prosecutor were faced with the challenge of applying criminal law to the criminal activities of the accused, who claimed the status of prisoners of war and demanded to be tried by court martial. The defence made several challenges on the grounds of bias. After the 85th objection in January 1977 the judge was relieved of the case. There followed lengthy boycotts of the proceedings on the part of the defence counsel as well as a hunger strike by the accused. The law applied legally questionable measures, such as dismissal of all but one of the lawyers chosen by the defendants, continuing the proceedings in the absence of the accused and bugging the conversations between the lawyers and the accused. On 25 April 1977 the sentences were passed. Baader, Raspe and Ensslin received life sentences for several cases of murder or at least attempted murder as well as for forming a criminal organization. Meinhof had already committed suicide in May 1976. The sentences had no legal force as the defence appealed, which was, however, rendered superfluous by the suicide of all of the accused in October 1977. This had been preceded years before by a dramatic development, culminating in 1977.

With the abduction of the CDU chairman, Peter Lorenz, on 27 February 1975, a terrorist group from the 2 June Movement demanded that five jailed fellow terrorists be flown to South Yemen. As the terrorists already had sufficient funds at their disposal through bank robberies, it was suspected that the main reason for the abduction of Lorenz was to force the release of the jailed fellow terrorists. Already in the case of the earlier attack on Günther Drenkmann, President of the Berlin Kammergericht, in November 1974, and the later murder of the banker, Jürgen Ponto, on 30 July 1977, the security authorities had presumed that the murder victims must originally have been kidnapped and that they were only shot after they put up stiff resistance.

In the 'German Autumn' of 1977 terrorist violence escalated. At first Siegfried Buback, prosecutor in the Baader-Meinhof trials, was murdered in April. Then

Ponto, head of the Dresdner Bank, was shot by Susanne Albrecht, Christian Klar and Brigitte Mohnhaupt at his own front door. The climax came in October with the murder of the head of the German Employers' Confederation, Hanns-Martin Schleyer.

The RAF gave the term 'internal security' a new meaning in the Federal Republic. From this point on the justice system was to change fundamentally. The legislation and justice were influenced by events in the criminal history of the Federal Republic as never before. The terrorists provoked the government under Schmidt to walk a tightrope on the edge of democracy, legality and constitutionality. The Anti-Terror laws of 1974 and 1976 were extended in the 'German Autumn'. During the abduction of Schleyer the Law Banning Contact was passed, which was designed to prevent prisoners from entering into contact with each other and with their defence counsel. Access to their clients was rendered impossible for the defence counsel despite judicial resolutions. The order of an injunction on information on 8 September 1977 prevented the RAF from communicating their motives, ideas and aims to the general public. The abduction squad in addition should not be informed about the investigations through the media. It was largely possible for the state to achieve its intentions, but the secrecy gave rise to feelings of terrorism in the imagination of the public, causing the RAF to have more power ascribed to it than they really had. The media voluntarily submitted to the controls imposed and even passed on information from the terrorists, which had been sent to the agencies for the Federal Criminal Bureau of Investigation to be made use of. The systematic implementation of these measures was made possible by crisis teams that were outside of parliamentary control. The executive and the legislative were combined in these decision-making bodies and the politically elected bodies were largely excluded. The Federal Chancellor enabled and justified the partial bypassing of democratic and constitutional principles. In the exceptional situation, in which people felt collectively under threat, a strong consensus arose whereby the state was given the sole ability to act in countering terrorism and succeeded in communicating that its interests overrode individual civil rights. The forces of political opposition lost importance, the media their role as a check on the situation. The area of involvement of the authorities was extended. The Federal Bureau of Criminal Investigation and the Office for the Protection of the Constitution saw an increase in personnel and budget.

The RAF, however, remained largely isolated in society, apart from a few leftist splinter groups and extremist apologists for violence. In the larger population they were dismissed, though sympathizers could always be found, some of whom were committed to the integration of the imprisoned RAF members into regular prison.

The attempts by the RAF to provoke acts of solidarity in the German population through their assassinations therefore failed. This was also put down to the power of the state acting decisively. According to surveys, the policy was welcomed by a large part of the population. The overwhelming majority were for the introduction of the death penalty. The battle against the RAF also became a way of dealing with things: critics of the state's policy were often denounced as aiding and abetting the terrorism of the RAF and thus any opposition to the politics of the Federal Republic was eliminated.

After 1972 when the hard core of Meinhof, Ensslin, Raspe and Holger Meins were in custody, the goal of freeing them became the focus of the RAF's supporters. With the aim of freeing those jailed at Stammheim, four terrorists – Stefan Wisniewski, Peter-Jürgen Boock, Sieglinde Hofmann and Willy Peter Stoll – abducted Hanns-Martin Schleyer on 5 September 1977 in Braunsfeld near Cologne. The RAF kidnappers had pushed a pram onto the road, forcing the column, consisting of three cars, into braking; they then immediately opened fire at Schleyer's security guards from a VW van with a sub-machine gun. Schleyer's driver and three accompanying policemen were killed. The head of the German Employers' Confederation was then driven off in the kidnappers' own vehicle.

The international dimension of the RAF terrorism, which was taking on a postmodern character, was illustrated when a Palestinian commando group hijacked the Lufthansa plane 'Landshut' on 13 October with 86 passengers and a crew of five on board. Their goal was to reinforce their demand for the freeing of those jailed in Stammheim. On 18 October 1977, however, a West German elite unit from the anti-terrorist squad GSG-9 succeeded in carrying out a surprise attack on the terrorists.

The GSG-9 had been set up after the Palestinian attack on the Israeli team at the Olympic Games in Munich. The attack on 5 September 1972 directed against the delegation of Israeli sportsmen and women in the Olympic Village gave rise to a serious shock: it resulted in 17 deaths (including 11 Israeli athletes) and it was caused by Arab terrorists. At Fürstenfeldbruck airport in Bavaria the planned attempt to free the captives got beyond control of the forces of law and order. It ended in a fiasco, which would lead to the formation of a professional task force. That was the origin of the GSG-9, which seven years later was to storm the 'Landshut' parked at the airport of the Somali town of Mogadishu in a lightning assault: they freed all the hostages from the Lufthansa Boeing 737 unharmed and killed three of the four terrorists. After this, Baader, Ensslin and Raspe committed suicide at Stammheim. Meinhof had already hanged herself in her cell before this. Schleyer was murdered on the same day by several shots from the kidnappers after 43 days of captivity as a hostage. His body was discovered in the boot of a car in the town of Mulhouse in Alsace.

After the end of the 1970s the RAF was on the defensive. To avoid increased search measures, most of their members went abroad, leading to a big change in the personnel involved. Many were arrested, some went to the GDR and new ones came in their place. Brigitte Mohnhaupt, Peter-Jürgen Boock, Rolf Clemens Wagner and Sieglinde Hofmann were caught in May 1978 in Yugoslavia, but as a result of diplomatic differences between Belgrade and Bonn they were not extradited. After six months they travelled on to Iraq. Wisniewski was arrested in Paris at the same time. In a period marked by internal differences, the RAF withdrew to Aden in South Yemen. From there they wanted to continue to provide proof of their ability to act. This was to be demonstrated by an attempt to kill General Alexander Haig, the Supreme Commander of NATO, on 25 July 1979, but the attack failed and he was unharmed. Originally, leading representatives of the Federal Republic had been targeted by the RAF; now the terrorists aimed at US authorities and military installations. There followed an attack on the headquarters of the US Air Force at Ramstein on 31 August 1981, and 14 days later General Frederick Kroesen, the Supreme Commander of US forces in Europe, was targeted. He survived the attack with slight injuries.

The process of dissolution of the RAF, however, went ahead in the 1980s. By summer 1980 the GDR leadership had provided their members with the opportunity to defect in order to assume a new identity and start a new life. In the wake of German unification this was revealed in June 1990; the 'drop-outs' were then arrested and put on trial. After fellow citizens and Stasi agents gave them away, the drop-outs from the RAF were arrested, Susanne Albrecht in East Berlin, Inge Viett in Magdeburg, Monika Helbing and Eckehard Freiherr von Seckendorff-Gudent in Frankfurt an der Oder. They had led a seemingly respectable and inconspicuous life in the GDR. The Ministry of State Security had assisted in their application for citizenship; they had been integrated and provided with accommodation and employment. They benefited from the 'chief witness ruling', which provided for a mitigation of the conditions of punishment and shortened sentences in cases where comprehensive statements were made. The SED regime thus sought to keep potential opponents of the system in the Federal Republic in reserve, which raises the question of whether this did the Federal Republic a favour.

Up to 1993 RAF terrorism had claimed dozens of victims and 60 deaths. 34 people had been murdered by the terrorists (mainly bodyguards, ordinary policemen or soldiers, as well as high-ranking politicians and representatives of industry), approximately 230 people were injured and around €250 million of damage was caused. About eleven million pages of investigation files and approximately 1,500 convictions are the horrendous total of this unique disaster of German left-wing extremism. Following the battle against terrorism, experience from the Stammheim Trial has led to changes in the criminal justice system limiting the rights of the accused and the defending counsel.

Citizens' Initiatives, Women's Emancipation, Worker Co-determination, Alternative Energy and the Broadening Out of the Traditional Party Spectrum in the Federal Republic

The first citizens' initiatives were set up in the Federal Republic as early as 1968–9. These were action groups run by parties and associations of people of similar political and ideological persuasion who wanted to further specific causes. The starting point for such campaigns were actual inadequacies in the areas of housing, culture or education, transport and civic affairs or the protection of nature. Initially initiatives were focused on local problems and were often informal rather than professional, but subsequently gained in strength of organization and profile and became wider in scope. The two oil shocks of 1973 and 1979 had shown the dependence of the Federal Republic on imported energy and also highlighted the increased importance of nuclear energy. The government policy was directed towards a reduction in the consumption of oil and was based on natural gas, home-produced coal and nuclear energy. The construction of nuclear power stations, however, met with rejection and opposition in the population, particularly in the vicinity of planned sites for power stations. Local or regional citizens' initiatives demonstrated and protested or campaigned using legal means. An anti-nuclear power station movement developed throughout West Germany. There were heated confrontations, occupations, large demonstrations and police involvement in places such as Wyhl in Baden or Brokdorf in Schleswig-Holstein. The problems in Wyhl, Kalkar or Brokdorf forced repeated construction stoppages. In Gorleben in Lower Saxony there was opposition to a decision that had already been made by the Land government against a nuclear reprocessing plant.

These planned programmes had to be reversed, particularly since the need for energy proved to be less than had been originally thought. The number of atomic power stations was reduced. The unresolved question about the disposal of radioactive waste caused particular discontent. As the so-called 'permanent storage' did not provide total protection for people and the environment, this problem set off a political argument. Unlike nuclear energy, research into alternative energies (biogas, earth warming, solar energy and wind power) received only very little attention and support in the Federal Republic. Having said that, energy saving was promoted as a result of the shortage of resources and for environmental protection. The replacement of home heating units, making use of the natural heat of the earth and use of solar energy and the insulation of buildings, are examples of ideas of new energy use.

The citizens' initiatives successfully opposed the construction of a car test-track at Boxberg in the Odenwald and caused the firm of Daimler-Benz to modify their projects. They had also put a stop to a referendum due to the constitutional right protecting the free movement of individuals, and it was only after a change in the law a decade later that data protection was introduced.

The declaration of equality enshrined in the 'Grundgesetz' made men and women equal, but in fact women were disadvantaged in West German society as regards their representation in the workplace, and they were discriminated against in the social hierarchy. This fact had been noticeable for decades in the areas of education, professional development, pay and appointment to public and political office. At the end of the 1960s, in the wake of the student protest movement and the influence of the new women's movement in the United States, an autonomous, left-leaning women's organization got under way, attempting to continue progressive trends from the nineteenth and early twentieth centuries. It soon split along social and feminist lines. The latter sought to overcome the historically anachronistic dominance of the male gender as regards the state and society. This branch of the movement opposed patriarchy. The former operated more within the existing system.

The struggle within the movement was reduced by common action on the part of women in favour of the politically controversial abolition of paragraph 218 of the legal code regulating abortion. Following a 1976 reform of this section of the law that was disappointing for the women's movement, feminist groups largely withdrew from direct political confrontation and became involved with women's self-realization and the organization of self-help groups. Women's refuges, centres and journals emerged. A notable medium was the magazine *Emma*, founded in 1977 by Alice Schwarzer, one of the main representatives of feminist women's culture. Based on the specific needs of women, *Emma* called for a fundamental change in social norms, particularly in the allocation of traditional roles. This high-profile respresentative voice of the women's movement only involved a small section of women in the Federal Republic at the start but, by politicizing the subject matter, it brought about increasing social acceptance and change.

Unlike the 1968 movement, which had been marginal and in the background, feminism became an essential part of the alternative movement and had a decisive share in the foundation and evolution of the Green Party, and was not without influence either on other parties.

Following the Bundestag election of 1972 the government also had to address the problem of worker co-determination in the workplace. There were unbridgeable differences between the SPD and the FDP, as the liberals wanted to leave employers' rights unchanged. After tough negotiations a compromise was reached that provided the basis for legislation on worker co-determination coming into force on 1 July 1976: according to this, supervisory boards in firms with more than 2,000 employees were to be made up of equal numbers of representatives of shareholders and of employees. The trade unions could delegate at least two employees to this committee; the remaining employees' seats would be distributed among the workers, office employees and senior managers. When the legislation came into force, there was no end of debate. The trade unions complained that the law was being circumvented by tricks such as dividing up firms. The bosses' side considered the right to property was being ignored and lodged a complaint with the Federal Constitutional Court, but was unsuccessful in this attempt.

The increase in citizens' initiatives and protest actions was a serious factor for party and government policy. Their existence highlighted the failure of political decisions and raised doubts about the nearness of politicians to the citizens. In the end it was questionable whether people's thinking was being represented by the political parties any more. Civil rights activists contributed to a change in the political climate in the Federal Republic. The claim by the parties to be the sole representatives of the people was questioned. The citizens' initiatives also influenced the parties. Subjects that hitherto were not really taken into account or were ignored were now taken on board and discussed. The citizens' initiatives could not, however, change anything substantial about the fundamental structure of the political system in the Federal Republic. This disappointing experience added to the fact that by the end of the 1970s ideas about an alternative party got under way. These thoughts originated with citizens' initiatives, protest groups such as the women's movement, the squatter scene and the unemployed. They were only loosely connected. In the area of politics there were connections, particularly with the women's movement. The scene was characterized by cultural, social and economic projects, often communally organized in presses, bookshops, craft areas or organic and environmentally friendly food outlets.

The year 1968 did not, however, represent a turning point in the trend towards the increasing employment of women. This had already begun and had been on the rise from the 1960s, and this long-term trend was to continue. In this context it is worth pointing out that women played an exceptional role in the reconstruction after 1945, leading at least temporarily to changes in their role in society.

The proportion of working women between the ages of 15 and 64 in the Federal Republic showed a progressive development rising to more than 50 per cent in the 1980s. A slight dip at the beginning of the 1980s is noticeable followed by a further rise reaching 57 per cent. At the start of the 1980s the dilemma over the decision between a career or a family caused a brief change in the trend which can be explained in terms of the 'turn towards conservatism' on the part of the CDU/CSU-FDP government: more women again decided in favour of a role in the home and in the family. The trend is nevertheless generally clear as more and more women were employed in the workplace and no longer exclusively chose the path of bringing up children and domestic life. Approximately two-thirds of German women were employed long-term.

The citizens' groups, the emancipation of women and above all the environmental movement produced 'green lists' of candidates standing for local and Landtag elections in the Federal Republic of the 1970s. Through the merging of these various heterogeneous alliances in the Green Action for the Future group and participation by the women's and the alternative movement, the party referred to as 'The Greens' emerged at a federal level at the start of the 1980s. Their platform was to be 'ecological – social – based on democracy – non-violent'. They successfully promoted the conservation of nature as the basis for human life. Earlier and more keenly than the other parties, they turned this into the object of politics and questioned the principle of the necessity for continual economic growth. Their basically pacifist position made the greens an important part of the peace movement. They rejected military blocs and called for the Federal Republic to leave NATO. This was a totally different approach and brought a breath of fresh air to the rigid party and government structures.

6

New Confrontation, Disarmament and Erosion of the Defence Blocs, 1979–89

Détente in Crisis, the Intervention by the USSR in Afghanistan, NATO Twin-Track Decision, the Peace Movement and the Deployment of Missiles

By the time of the CSCE Helsinki Final Act on 1 August 1975 the subject of détente had been on the table for some time. It then went through various phases: at issue initially was the reduction in the potential for tension and confrontation (up to 1977/8), then dealing with the internal crisis and avoiding a collapse of the CSCE against the background of the intensification of the Cold War (1979–83) and finally support for the course of reform by the new general secretary of the CC, Mikhail Gorbachev (1985–91), as well as the ultimate development of a mechanism for absorbing the crumbling Warsaw Pact. The mutual recognition and normalization of relations between the Federal Republic and the GDR were substantial building blocks for the process of détente, but neither state was the engine or the vehicle of the CSCE. Thus, above all, the non-aligned and neutral states contributed to the détente and cooperation between states in Europe. The CSCE stimulated the treaty partners to engage in cooperation, indirectly opened up possible Western influences on the societies of the East, supported groups working for civil rights there and sped up the process of erosion of the post-Stalinist regime in East and Central Europe. After Helsinki there followed successive conferences in Belgrade in 1977–9 and Madrid in 1981–3. A 'Conference on Confidence and Security-Building and Disarmament in Europe' (the Stockholm Conference) took place in Sweden between 1984 and 1986. The third CSCE successor conference between 1986 and 1989 in Vienna was attended by the Foreign Ministers of the 35 participating states including the United States and Canada.

In the debate about the enactment of the principles agreed in the CSCE Final Act, the Western representatives raised serious objections to the abuse of human rights by the Eastern Bloc. The fact that political changes in this area, in particular as a result of the Soviet policy of perestroika, were having positive effects was reflected in the closing document of the conference on 15 January 1989. It recognized progress in questions of basic human rights and in humanitarian cooperation on the part of individual participating states. At the same time it was decided to hold negotiations for a treaty on conventional forces in Europe (CFE).

The policy of détente, to be sure, suffered another serious crisis in the second half of the 1970s. From 1976/7 the USSR had replaced their older intermediate-range missiles directed at Europe with modern Type SS 20 missiles, each carrying three warheads. Bonn saw this as a challenge to the balance of political security in Europe. Chancellor Schmidt called for a reaction from NATO. In Washington, which paid hardly any attention to this question at first, interest rose in strengthening its own position in relation to the USSR by installing US intermediate-range missiles on the continent for the first time. By this it was clear that only Germany would be a possible future battleground. It also became evident that the Federal Republic would play a role in the confrontation between East and West, as it already had in the 1950s. Unlike in the Adenauer Era, which had contributed decisively to the escalation of the Cold War in Europe, lasting and consistent protest was expressed against further armament on German soil. The decision made by NATO Foreign and Defence Ministers on 12 December 1979 to increase arms consisted of two elements and was therefore also called the NATO Twin Track Decision: first, the deployment of ground-based intermediate-range atomic weapons (108 Pershing II missiles and 464 Cruise Missiles) in Europe by the end of 1983; second, the offer to the USSR on negotiations with the USA on intermediate-range weapons in Europe. Implementation of the deployment of weapons would depend on the result.

Negotiations began on 30 November 1981 in Geneva. In the meantime, since the start of the 1980s a peace movement had got under way in many of the NATO states, which aimed to make governments back off from further armaments. Another action carried out by the Kremlin led to a further escalation of the situation: the invasion of Afghanistan by Soviet troops on 25/6 December 1979, which caused a clear worsening of East–West relations.

An all-German phenomenon came about at the start of the 1980s. A peace movement emerged in both German states, even though this had different roots and ways of expressing itself. In the Federal Republic it was informal and loosely organized and encompassed a multifarious, broad spectrum of groups of different social origins and political persuasions. Trade unions, religious organizations, doctors, Green initiatives, the DKP and sections of the SPD and groups from the

CDU were involved. There were close connections to the alternative and women's movements as well as to the environmental protection cause. In the Federal Republic this pacifist trend developed into a mass political movement with the slogan 'Make peace without weapons!', which, in view of the worldwide build-up of nuclear weapons, called for a stop to arms production.

Within the SPD opposition to further armament increased. The pressure on Federal Chancellor Schmidt from the left wing in his own party opposed to further armament reached such a point that this was to contribute to the change of government in autumn 1982. The largest demonstrations in West German history, of around 250,000 people, took place on 10 October 1981; on 10 June 1982 in Bonn some 300,000 to 350,000 marched to the provisional capital of the FRG.

The GDR was the only state in the Eastern Bloc to have its own peace movement, 'Swords into Ploughshares', which, alongside the official propaganda aimed at the 'evil' Western armaments, also protested against armaments as such. Peace groups associated with the Protestant Church called for disarmament in East and West, but were subject to state control and repression. Nevertheless, there was already a protest by citizens here which, along with the alternative and environmentalist groups, was to feed into the opposition to the SED dictatorship in 1989/90.

Even though the peace movement failed and, with the calling-off of the unsuccessful Geneva talks and the deployment of US intermediate-range missiles after November 1983, did not achieve its goal, its political effects were enormous. Shortly before the missiles were stationed, a 'week of action' was organized throughout the Federal Republic in October 1983 in which, according to the organizers, approximately three million people took part and by means of demonstrations extending beyond their regions formed a human chain from Stuttgart to Neu-Ulm. A mass movement had emerged from isolated groups, opposed to the parties represented in the Bundestag and playing a considerable role in shaping the public debate on questions of security right up to the end of the Cold War.

Opposition Victory: Constructive Vote of No-Confidence against Schmidt, the Conservative 'Change' under Kohl and the Setting Up of the Greens

In the controversy with the CDU/CSU surrounding their Chancellor candidate Franz-Josef Strauß, the Social Democrats and Free Democrats had been able to win the Bundestag election on 5 October 1980 and continue in government. The FDP, in their commitment to resist Strauß and their promise to continue the coalition with Schmidt, had been able to increase their share of the vote from 7.9 per cent in 1976 to 10.6 per cent. The SPD had only slightly improved from 42.6 per cent to 42.9 per cent, while the CDU/CSU dropped from 48.6 per cent to 44.5 per cent. It was their worst election result since 1949.

At the top of the FDP, particularly in the case of the party chairman and Foreign Minister Genscher, the realization meanwhile grew that they would not be able to be successful in the next elections any more with the Social–Liberal coalition, particularly since the SPD appeared to be in a decline. Having friendly relations with Kohl, Genscher made provision for a change of coalition. Unlike Strauß, who rejected an association with the FDP, Kohl had for quite some time been a supporter of an alliance with the FDP, particularly since he did not think an absolute majority was possible for the CDU. A coalition with the FDP would from Kohl's perspective limit the influence of the CSU under Strauß, which for him was not always desirable.

In the Social–Liberal coalition after 1980 there increasingly arose different points of view over the question of dealing with unemployment and the economic crisis. The FDP wanted to reduce borrowing by the state far more, make definite savings in social benefits and prevent the supplementary levy on higher incomes that the Social Democrats intended to bring in. The government policy seemed to be losing its Social Democratic character. The gap widened between Federal Chancellor Schmidt, who had reached the summit of his worldwide reputation, and the party, which continued to be led by Brandt. Both were widely recognized and respected, but Brandt was in addition very popular, causing bitterness in the ruling Chancellor. Cutbacks in the social area led to protests from sections of their own party. In the SPD criticism grew of the coalition partner sticking to a liberal economic course, but also of the savings policy of their own party, which appeared to take less and less of the interests of employers into account. Differences in thinking became clear in the planning of the federal budget for 1982.

In a letter to FDP members in the summer of 1981, Genscher called for a 'change' in West German politics. A break up of the social–liberal coalition came about in September 1982 in the aftermath of the deliberations on the budget for 1983. A paper prepared by Hans Tietmeyer for the Economics Minister, Otto Graf Lambsdorff (FDP), had strengthened this tendency. In this, in comparison to the way the coalition was going, very deep cutbacks in the social state were called for. When Schmidt indicated that the sacking of the Economics Minister was an option, the four FDP ministers, Genscher, Lambsdorff, Baum and Ertl, resigned on 17 September 1982. Schmidt took over the Foreign Ministry and now led a minority government. In the FDP and their parliamentary grouping heated debates on the question of whether they should stay with the alliance with the SPD or whether they could put up with an SPD minority government began. Genscher's supporters wanted a coalition with the CDU/CSU. He was able to win out. After rapid negotiations with the CDU/CSU parties an agreement on a coalition was reached.

In the context of a renewed constructive vote of no confidence against the SPD head of government, the Bundestag elected the chairman of the CDU, Helmut Kohl, as new Federal Chancellor on 1 October 1982. This was heralded as the 'change'. Schmidt was thus toppled, but he remained a respected personality and was repeatedly the centre of attention thanks to the important opinions he voiced.

Despite all the criticism of Schmidt on the part of the CDU/CSU there was subsequently a continuity in policy on foreign affairs and security. Egon Bahr was positively surprised by the fact that the new government policy carried out by the CDU/CSU did not vary in the slightest from the Ostpolitik of the Social-Liberal coalition. As regards domestic policy too, Kohl's undeniable desire for renewal was limited.

Born the son of a customs official in 1930 in Ludwigshafen on the Rhine, he studied history and political science and after gaining his PhD he worked in industry. As a co-founder of the Junge Union, the Christian Democrat youth movement, in 1946 in Ludwigshafen, he joined the CDU in 1947 and held several posts in the Junge Union and the CDU. In 1959 Kohl was elected to the Landtag of Rhineland-Palatinate, of which in 1963 he became chairman of the CDU parliamentary grouping, from 1966 also becoming chairman of the CDU in the Land and in 1969 Minister-President of Rhineland-Palatinate. After Barzel's resignation Kohl became chairman of the CDU in 1973. In 1976 he was put forward as the candidate for Chancellor by the CDU and the CSU.

The Christian Democrat Union parties achieved the second best election result in their history with 48.6 per cent of the vote, but the SPD-FDP coalition survived. Kohl resigned from the office of Minister-President of Rhineland-Palatinate and went to Bonn as chairman of the CDU/CSU parliamentary grouping. For the election for the Bundestag in 1980 Kohl did not stand as a candidate, but he remained opposition leader in the Bundestag, from where he got the chance of becoming Federal Chancellor by means of the constructive no confidence vote and the change of coalition by the FDP to the CDU/CSU.

The second prominent figure of this new government was Hans-Dietrich Genscher. In the new government made up of the CDU, CSU and FDP formed in October 1982 and confirmed in the following Bundestag elections of 1983, 1987 and 1990, Deputy

Chancellor Genscher again took over the post of Foreign Minister. He retained this until 1992 and became the longest ever serving Foreign Minister to date.

The third prominent personality of the Kohl Era was Richard Freiherr von Weizsäcker. He had belonged to the CDU since 1950, was active in the Bundestag from 1969 to 1981 and was already the top CDU candidate in Berlin in 1979. After elections that had been brought forward in 1981 he became the governing Mayor of Berlin. In 1984 he was elected Federal President by a broad majority of the Federal Assembly. As such he won recognition at home and abroad as a result of his authority going beyond party allegiance and as an important source of stimulus. The new coalition government was clearly confirmed in office by the Bundestag elections that had been brought forward to 6 March 1983. The promised boom showed itself in a real invigoration of the economy, yet within three years between 1982 and 1985 there was a rise in unemployment from 1.8 to 2.2 million.

It is remarkable that Kohl did not change anything about the much criticized and dismissed policy of détente and Ostpolitik of the Social–Liberal coalition under Brandt-Scheel and Schmidt-Genscher. Genscher was a guarantee of a successful continuity in the foreign and German policy of the Federal Republic. Added to this was the definite commitment to the Atlantic alliance and to the NATO Twin-Track Decision. Against the great resistance of a broad peace movement with which the SPD also associated itself, the CDU-FDP government pushed through the deployment of US intermediate-range missiles in the Federal Republic.

After the Greens had only obtained 1.5 per cent of the votes in the elections of 1980, in 1983 with 5.6 per cent of the votes they were able to get over the 5 per cent clause hurdle and entered the Bundestag. In 1987 the Greens even got 8.3 per cent of the votes in the Bundestag elections. The ongoing passionate struggle between the two wings within the party – the Fundamentalists (the 'Fundis') who categorically rejected any sharing of power and the Realpoliticians (the 'Realos') who favoured forming a government with the SPD – not only influenced their image with the public, but also hampered their activity and threatened to lead to a split. After a period of consolidation the Greens also managed to win seats in the Landtags and to form coalition governments, as for example in Hesse, where admittedly the coalition with the SPD did not last long and ended in failure.

The INF Treaty and the 'Shared Responsibility of Both German States'

An escalation of the East–West conflict came about after the Soviet invasion of Afghanistan in 1979 and also as a result of the developments in Poland, where the independent trade union Solidarność was formed after mass strikes in the summer of 1980. In the West everyone expected another military intervention on the part of the USSR but this did not happen. US President Ronald Reagan, in office after 1981, once again pursued the policy of confrontation with the USSR from the period of the Eisenhower-Dulles administration in the 1950s. The end of the policy of détente seemed to be near. It is a surprising fact that, against this background of a heightened conflict situation, both German states set out to mitigate the consequences of renewed East–West opposition and did not want them to leave their mark on inter-German relations. The relations built up by Brandt-Scheel and Schmidt-Genscher were not only adhered to, but strengthened. Kohl continued to build consistently on the basis of the previously maligned Ostpolitik. The change of government in Bonn in autumn 1982 therefore did not represent a break in policy on German affairs, particularly since Kohl's CDU-FDP government continued to develop the German policy of the Social–Liberal coalition.

A raft of practical questions were settled. After Federal Chancellor Schmidt's visit to the GDR in February 1982, the GDR brought in relaxations over travel to the Federal Republic. When in 1983 West German banks approved loans of billions to a GDR teetering on the verge of bankruptcy and dependent on foreign exchange and this was even guaranteed by Bonn, the Bavarian Minister-President Strauß was decisively involved; this was the same impulsive and emotionally engaged politician who had still roundly condemned the Ostpolitik of the SPD-FDP government in the 1970s. While the GDR was stabilized and kept going politically by this intervention and financial support, the CDU/CSU-FDP government stepped up its policy of increased NATO armament in the hope that this would force the USSR into being more conciliatory.

The SPD party conference in Cologne in November 1983 decided against the deployment of missiles in the Federal Republic by a clear majority. The CDU/CSU and FDP, however, would not be moved from their stand on the NATO decision. They relied on a breakthrough in the negotiations in Geneva, but they were also determined to go ahead with the deployment of US missiles in the event of failure. The Western alliance was not to be exposed to any threat and was to be held together. Absolute loyalty to the alliance clearly ranked ahead of any possible risk to security.

Whether this policy, coming under Eckart Conze's heading of the 'pursuit of security', is representative of the history of the Federal Republic, a policy of going along with the increase in atomic weapons to the point of nuclear overkill, is very much an open question. In any case, it was highly controversial for the people who lived through it.

Discontent at the increase in armaments, which was seen as a false and counterproductive security policy, brought the Greens more popularity. They had been represented in the Bundestag since the elections of 1983. Their acceptance as a party grew when they formed a coalition government for the first time with the SPD in Hesse in 1985.

Geneva did not bring an agreement between the USA and the USSR, even though the leaders of the negotiations had pointed the way to a solution. On 22 November 1983, in a show of premature allegiance to the alliance after two days of heated discussion with a majority of the CDU/CSU and FDP, the Bundestag agreed to the deployment of nuclear missiles in the Federal Republic. In the following days the USA began installing the Pershing II missiles, at which the Soviet Union broke off the negotiations in Geneva.

Not until March 1985 were the negotiations on the global reduction of all American and Soviet intermediate-range missiles resumed and finalized two years later in the Treaty on Intermediate-Range Nuclear Forces (INF). Tough negotiations and two American-Soviet summits, in November 1985 in Geneva and in October 1986 in Reykjavik, led to the signing in Washington on 8 December 1987 by US President Ronald Reagan and the General Secretary of the CPSU, Mikhail Gorbachev, who had been in office since 11 March 1985. The agreement was aimed at a total and worldwide reduction of all American and Soviet land-based intermediate- to long-range missiles, including launch facilities, within three years. The treaty was welcomed as a breakthrough in efforts towards disarmament. It involved not just the control of armaments with specific upper limits for nuclear weapons, but the abolition of whole categories of missiles on both sides, linked to a unique agreement on effective control procedures.

The INF Treaty was welcomed by both the Federal Republic and the GDR – the two states mainly affected by the threat of annihilation by nuclear weapons. Both Honecker and Kohl had kept up their relations during the interruption in the negotiations and further developed their contact. Behind the scenes both sides had made the need for the abolition of intermediate-range missiles clear to their respective dominating powers. It was obvious to both German republics, Bonn as well as Pankow, that in the event of an atomic war, that is in the event of a first strike and the corresponding counterattack, the existence of both was at stake and that not much would be left of either the pro-American or pro-Soviet oriented satellite states. The INF agreement not only improved the climate between the super-powers but also opened up new perspectives for a further normalization of inter-German relations.

The view is often stated that the firm and uncompromising stance of the West over the deployment of missiles contributed to the break-up of the USSR, but this is doubtful and one-sided. The economic decline of the Soviet Empire and its allied satellites had been evident since the middle of the 1970s. Global competition with Asia and Latin America was already a big challenge. The process of détente had already demonstrated weaknesses and rifts in the Soviet Bloc. In 1978 China had turned its back on the USSR.

Remembering the World Wars: The Controversy between Historians and the Question of Emigration

In 1984/5 in the Federal Republic there were commemorations of the outbreak of the First World War, but above all of the end of the Second World War. The First World War manifested itself in a particularly German and French commemorative symbolism that we shall return to. Compared with earlier memorial days in 1955, 1965 and 1975, both the victors and the losers of the Second World War paid greater attention in 1985 to the anniversary of the surrender of the German Wehrmacht on 8 May 1945. It was a matter of controversy whether it had been a 'zero hour'. Not only was the Germans' sense of history weighed down by National Socialism but any sort of national pride and patriotism had become suspect as well, not to mention German nationalism. This led to decades of silence and unease about their own view of history – far more in the Federal Republic than in the GDR, where people behaved in a thoroughly 'national' and patriotic manner. The West German public was reminded far more about the Holocaust and the Nazi crimes, while in the first half of the 1980s the GDR focused on the 'positive' sides of German history: the commemoration of Martin Luther, the unveiling of the monument of Frederick the Great on horseback in Unter den Linden in Berlin, and a definite appreciation of Prussia and its reforms, including the tradition of close contacts with Russia. There was no debate about history in the GDR that was both public and controversial.

The debate about the surrender of the German Wehrmacht in 1945 was a subject of controversy in the Federal Republic. Was it the liberation of Germany and therefore also a contribution to freedom in Europe? Was it not rather the collapse of the Reich and the downfall of Germany? While the SPD and the trade unions judged the 8 May 1945 from the positive side to have been a day of liberation from National Socialism, the Christian Democrats and Conservatives also saw it as the end of freedom and the beginning of oppression in the Eastern part of Europe. Other interpreters pointed to the 8 May as the definitive end of the German national state and as the beginning of the division of Germany. Both were wrong: the history of the German national state was neither over, nor had the division of Germany in 1945 been fixed for good. The reconciliation between France and the Federal Republic reached a high point in 1984 with the meeting of Federal Chancellor Helmut Kohl and French President François Mitterrand on the former First World War battlefield at Verdun – following on from meetings between Adenauer and de Gaulle in the 1960s. This meeting at which the two politicians shook hands had led to a recognition and appreciation on both sides and to the sealing of a friendship. By contrast, the meetings laden with historical and political significance between Reagan and Kohl in the Federal Republic in May 1985 were partly fraught.

The wish expressed by the US President for a visit to the memorial site of the concentration camp at Dachau was rejected by Kohl as inappropriate. (Kohl was later also to refuse to be present at the inauguration of the Holocaust Memorial in Washington as being a 'place of German shame'). Still, Reagan did not want, on the other hand, to give a speech on 8 May in the Federal Republic and preferred to speak to the European Parliament in Strasbourg on that day. Kohl finally suggested visiting a military cemetery together, an idea that was well received in the White House. Along with the American President, on 5 May the Federal Chancellor visited a German military cemetery at Bitburg in the Eifel. When it became known beforehand that members of the Waffen-SS were also buried there, there were strong protests, particularly from representatives of Jewish organizations, and it caused a storm in the press in the USA. Following this, a visit to the former concentration camp at Bergen-Belsen was quickly added to the President's itinerary on the morning of 5 May, acting as a sort of compensation – a remarkable and exceptional 'deal' in history policy illustrating Bonn's continuing difficulties with the 'shadow of history'. Kohl had won out against his critics over Bitburg and Reagan had kept his word. In the aftermath of these embarrassments, stubborn positions and contortions, the speech by the Federal President on 8 May 1985 before the plenary of the Bundestag provided relief and boosted confidence. In an impressive speech that was courteous and conciliatory but still unambiguous and uncompromising, Weizsäcker impressed the German and the foreign public. His words carried weight. Looking back, he declared 8 May to be a 'day of liberation' which had freed everyone from the inhumane Nazi tyranny. But no one would forget the widespread suffering that continued after it. One should not, however, see in the ending of the war the cause for seeking refuge, being driven out and for losing freedom. Rather, it lay in its beginning and in the beginning of the tyranny that led to war. 'We should not see the 8 May 1945 in isolation from the 30 January 1933', he explained in regard to cause and effect in history. Remembering was important and reconciliation was only brought about by it. There had never been a 'zero hour', 'but we had the opportunity to begin again'. This was made use of, 'the best we could'. In place of a lack of freedom, democratic freedom had been established. Weizsäcker expressed confidence about the future of the German nation, saying 'that the 8 May is not the last date in our history which is a commitment on all Germans'.

A heated debate was sparked off the next year by a statement of the Berlin historian, Ernst Nolte, who saw in the 'racial murder' by the Nazis – the Holocaust – a parallel to the 'class murder' that had started earlier under the Bolsheviks with the gulags. This factual precursor and 'Asiatic' prototype had led to a sort of putative self-defence on the part of the Nazis by their use of 'Russian methods'. The so-called 'Historikerstreit' (historians' dispute) resulted in not just historians, but also philosophers and political theorists taking part. Jürgen Habermas accused Nolte of wanting to let the Germans off the hook and relativizing the Nazis' crimes by the comparison with the Gulag. The historian Hans-Ulrich Wehler accused Nolte of trying to throw off the German past. The debate, which was unproductive and devoid of any new sources, ended with Nolte being stigmatized and boycotted. The taboo of the comparison, even though it was partly discredited by Nolte's arguments, had in the end been successfully broken. Comparative research into genocide became possible without one having to face the permanent accusation of minimizing or playing down the Nazis' crimes, though in their case mass murder on an industrial and highly organized scale remained exceptional.

The question of the people forced out of the former German territories in the East, also broached by Weizsäcker, likewise became a subject of debate in the second half of the 1980s. Despite Germans having been forced out of the former German territories in the East on a massive scale, hundreds of thousands of people of German origin and mother-tongue were still living in the Central and Eastern European states, particularly in Poland, but also in Romania and the Soviet Union. According to the 'Grundgesetz' of 1949 (Article 116, paragraph 1), these people and their dependants (women and children) were entitled to German nationality.

On leaving these states and on arrival in the Federal Republic at the reception camp at Friedland, these ethnic Germans returning to Germany were officially referred to as 'emigrants' (*Aussiedler*). There was almost no interest in emigrating to the GDR. Since the 1970s, in the wake of détente and the normalization of relations with the socialist states and even treaty agreements such as in 1975/6 with Poland, all the Federal Länder governments had been calling for the implementation of emigration for these ethnic Germans. In the second half of the 1980s the Central and Eastern European regimes showed more readiness to allow their ethnic German population to emigrate. Thus in 1987/8 around 200,000 arrived in the Federal Republic from Poland, more than 60,000 from the USSR and around 27,000 from Romania and under a thousand emigrants each from Czechoslovakia, Hungary and Yugoslavia. Many of the younger ones could not speak a word of German. Above all economic reasons played a role in the decision to move to the Federal Republic. The authorities were totally unprepared and overstretched in face of the massive influx. There were problems with organizing German courses, providing accommodation and employment in a country with high unemployment. Because of the tight housing market and the approximately two million people already unemployed there was plenty of cause for friction and unrest. In September 1989 Bonn was forced to present a bill by which the payment of unemployment benefit to the ethnic German emigrants as well as people moving to Germany from elsewhere was replaced by a unified provisional sum of around 1,000 DM a month. A restructuring of the process of asylum had to be carried out in 1993 on account of the enormous flood of new asylum seekers and on account of the tighter social conditions in the Federal Republic.

Chernobyl and the Anti-nuclear Movement – Protests Against the Nuclear Reprocessing Plant at Wackersdorf

On 26 April 1986 a calamity with long-term consequences took place at the nuclear power station at Chernobyl in the Soviet Republic of the Ukraine. There had been a meltdown in the core of the reactor. A fire broke out and a large amount of radioactive material escaped. The disastrous accident only became known to the public in the outside world days after the event due to the USSR policy of secrecy and censorship. In distant parts of Europe as well as in the Soviet Union an increase in radioactivity was recorded.

Chernobyl became a symbol of the problems surrounding the use of nuclear energy. There started in the Federal Republic a broad public discussion about its direction and value. The Greens felt totally confirmed in their rejection of nuclear power stations. The SPD then supported their demand for the shutting-down of all power stations, having preferred the use of coal up to this point while being in favour of a further development of nuclear energy. Now the social democrats also backtracked on this. The CDU/CSU and FDP only partly withdrew their support for nuclear energy, not wanting to give it up as a 'transitional technology' that would take Germany into the twenty-first century.

Apart from the previous flashpoints of anti-nuclear protest at Brokdorf, Gorleben, Kalkar and Wyhl the protest was now focused on the nuclear reprocessing plant under construction at Wackersdorf in the Oberpfalz region of Bavaria. After the accident with the reactor at Chernobyl, Wackersdorf became the target of mass protest activity. It led to violent clashes between demonstrators and the police. Several motivations were involved here: fundamental opposition to nuclear energy; reasons of cost, since the reprocessing of spent nuclear rods would be more expensive than permanent storage; and the protection of nature. Strauß, the Minister-President of Bavaria (CSU), was inflexible and stuck stolidly to the project. The protest by thousands of anti-nuclear campaigners, however, continued. The cessation of construction on 30 May 1989 owed as much to considerations of the cost of energy production as to the continual demonstrations. Cooperation with the French firm Cogema developed, which allowed Germany's spent nuclear material, temporarily, to be stored more cheaply at La Hague on the Normandy coast. The permanent storage of atomic waste remained a problem, however, particularly since the radioactivity of uranium lasts millions of years. The controversial permanent storage was supposed to take place in a former salt mine in the vicinity of Gorleben.

Progress in the Policy of European Integration

Without the full involvement, the massive financial investment and the political support of the Federal Republic, the process of the unification of Western Europe in its concrete form would have been unimaginable and hardly possible. The Bonn Republic was not just clearly oriented towards 'Europe', it was also always aimed at the enlargement of Europe: in 1981, with its support Greece was admitted into the EC, in 1986 Spain and Portugal. Spain's admission to NATO also played a not insubstantial role, particularly in Kohl's way of thinking. Other Mediterranean countries, including Turkey, which had been seeking full membership since 1987, and more than 60 so called Third World states, had for some time been linked to the EEC or EC by association agreements.

In 1985, with support from Bonn, a renewed attempt was made to promote European unification. A government conference was given the task of 'bringing about concrete progress on the road to European Union' and developing the Single European Act (SEA), which would come into force in 1987 through enactment by the twelve member states. It brought about a re-evaluation of the community organizations, an increase in majority decisions in the Council of Ministers and stronger participation by the European Parliament in legislation, with the responsibility for decision-making remaining with the Council of Ministers. What was up until then modest 'European Political Cooperation', linked to the prospect of a common foreign policy, became part of the task of forming European treaties. The most ambitious goal was the achievement of the Internal Market by 1992.

This new attempt at a policy of integration led to consequences in the Soviet Bloc. The Council for Mutual Economic Aid (COMECON), which the East European states belonged to, established official relations with the EC in 1988. After more than three decades of non-recognition of the West European community institutions, this was a novelty and already indicated the change in international relations and the ending of the East-West conflict. In development policy there were shifts of emphasis. One of the basic features of the Christian Democrat-Liberal Federal government was that development aid would be an element of a globally oriented policy, one that was directed towards compromise, peace and stability. The Christian commandment 'love thy neighbour', 'solidarity between human beings', but also the self-interest of a Federal Republic geared towards exports, played a role in this. The states of the EC established a unified direction of development policy involving different agreements with what had in the meantime become 70 'associated states' in Africa, the Caribbean and the Pacific. Products from the associated states, except for agricultural produce, would be given free access to the Common Market of Western Europe. Financial support was considerably increased in a Lomé agreement, the fourth, in 1989.

Increasing Unemployment, Public Debt, Scandals in Bonn: The Flick Affair (Party Donations) and the Barschel Affair

In 1981/2 the gross national product had already diminished and by 1982 it was only equivalent to the size it had been in 1979 in real terms. Unemployment grew from 1.3 million in 1981 to 1.8 million in 1982. This was one of the main reasons why the social-liberal coalition broke apart in 1982. Yet, the government led by the CDU/CSU-FDP under Kohl was no more able to solve this problem. It is true that the

GNP grew again in 1983/4 and also that it was possible to reduce inflation as well as public-sector borrowing, but unemployment stood at its highest figure of 2.2 million. The trade unions called for a cut in working hours, arguing that with increasing productivity but no increase in sales the number of jobs was inevitably decreasing. Tariff negotiations on a reduction of the working week from 40 to 35 hours led to labour unrest in the metal and pressing industry that lasted for weeks in 1984. The agreed compromise at 38.5 hours with flexible working time was also adopted by other branches of industry.

The debate on the economic situation of Germany altered the prospect for a further reduction in the working week to that of the preservation of jobs – this was despite ongoing high unemployment. High wage and production costs were pointed to as adversely affecting competition on the part of the employers. Flexible working time and using machines to full capacity would guarantee higher productivity. Possibilities of reducing working hours through part-time work became more general, but they moved a share of the responsibility for a fair distribution of labour from the state to the individual. Unemployment was not to decrease. In addition was the high public debt of the Federal Republic, which led to an extension of the working life of civil servants through an increase in the number of hours worked per week.

The history of the Federal Republic was not without scandals affecting public life, since they are also revealing about political culture and socio-political conditions. The *Spiegel* Affair has already been mentioned. In the 1980s new scandals rocked the Bonn Republic with the growth of party favours and sleaze. In 1975 one of the most influential commercial groups in the Federal Republic, the Flick Group, earned proceeds of 1.9 billion DM from the sale of Daimler-Benz shares, on which they would normally have paid tax at the maximum rate of 56 per cent; however, 1.5 billion DM of this was immediately invested again. The Flick Group legally applied for tax exemption. The application was approved. Federal Economics Minister, Hans Friderichs, and his successor, Otto Graf Lambsdorff, (both FDP), had asserted that the investment was particularly valuable for the economy. In 1983 the Federal Public Prosecutor in Bonn instituted proceedings against both ministers on the grounds of bribery. Eberhard von Brauchitsch, formerly personally associated with Flick, was accused of the same offence. According to the charge, by means of payments of around half a million DM to Friderichs and Lambsdorff he had influenced decisions on tax concessions. After the start of the main proceedings in 1984 Lambsdorff resigned. The Land court in Bonn passed a legally binding judgment in February 1987 according to which all three of the accused were acquitted of the charge of bribery or corruption, but they were found guilty of tax evasion or of aiding and abetting it: Brauchitsch was given a suspended sentence of two years and a fine of 550,000 DM, Lambsdorff a fine of 180,000 DM and Friderichs a fine of 61,000 DM.

The Flick Affair led to the resignation of Barzel, the President of the Bundestag, in 1984. It took place in the context of party donations, in which it was soon revealed that the CDU, CSU, FDP and SPD had illegally accepted untaxed donations, which were often channelled through charitable organizations and therefore contrary to the rules on the declaration of large donors. The attempt by the Christian Democrat-Liberal government to pass an emergency bill giving amnesty to donors and party officials was rejected by the Free Democrats on a party basis. The influential firm Flick, which had already attempted to influence party politics through financial inducements in the 1930s, became a symbol for decadence, sleaze and the moral decline of party democracy. In the public debate the question was raised whether the Bonn Republic was corrupt and whether policy was being manipulated by the financial influence of powerful individuals. The close interconnection between the economy and politics was publicly criticized in the media, but only very little of substance was to change structurally, as the scandal of party donations to the CDU revealed in 1999 was to show.

Another case of party political impropriety shook the Bonn Republic with the events in Kiel. The Federal Republic's Watergate was the 'Waterkant' (Baltic and North Sea coastal region) Affair. On 12 September 1989, shortly before the elections for the Landtag in Schleswig-Holstein, the television and radio as well as the next edition of *Der Spiegel* put out an incredible story: Minister-President Uwe Barschel had apparently given Reiner Pfeiffer, his media secretary and the head of his election campaign, the task of bringing a charge of tax evasion against Björn Engholm, the chief representative of the SPD and leader of the opposition. He also had him followed by a detective agency and placed a bug in Barschel's office telephone in order to smear the SPD and Engholm. The Landtag elections on 13 September brought about the loss of an absolute majority for the CDU so that there was an equal number of seats in comparison with the other parties. Barschel denied all the accusations and gave his word of honour on TV. He called them 'smears and lies', despite the fact that an investigating committee and judicial enquiries were against him. In the end he drew the conclusions from the debate that had been going on for weeks and resigned as Minister-President at the start of October 1987. Ten days later journalists from the German weekly *Der Stern* found Barschel's dead body in his room at the luxury Beau Rivage hotel in Geneva. The

Swiss press argued that it was suicide and even maintained this after the family of the deceased claimed it was murder on account of the dubious circumstances. The closing report of the investigating committee of the Schleswig-Holstein Landtag of 5 February 1988 said 'that sections of the chancery and the press office of the Land government' had been 'put to illegal use in the course of the election campaign for the CDU leading candidate'. The critical investigation by the press was recognized and a raft of changes to the constitution of the Land were suggested. There were mutterings about 'dirty deals' going beyond the election campaign in Schleswig-Holstein, including weapons sales with the GDR and blackmail attempts associated with this. Years later, Engholm as the new Minister-President of Schleswig-Holstein, had to admit that he had known about the scandal much earlier than he had originally said and had more or less let the matter go in order to make party political capital out of it. He too had to pay the political price and in 1993 he also resigned from office as Federal chairman of the SPD.

The intricate Barschel-Engholm Affair produced shockwaves in the Federal Republic. The murky background has yet to be explained. After the Flick Affair the case was another fall from grace of the Bonn Republic in the 1980s. The pursuit of absolute success, the infringement of laws, the criminal undertakings, the lust for power and the abuse of justice raised the uneasy question whether this political system was at all able to take sufficient precautions against such activities on the part of individual politicians and their paid accomplices. The CDU/CSU and FDP coalition survived the strains of the affairs that various Federal ministers were involved in. The successful slogan of the Kohl era was 'ride out any unresolved problems'.

Neither Glasnost nor Perestroika in the GDR, Honecker's Visit to Bonn, Repression by the SED, Opposition from the Churches and Signs of Erosion

Against the background of the NATO Twin-Track Decision and the controversy over the deployment of US intermediate-range missiles in the Federal Republic, both German states emphasized that a war should never again start on German soil. The talk was of an 'inter-German community of responsibility'. Even after the change of government in Bonn, the SED regime kept to the task of not allowing the increased tension between East and West to affect the inter-German relationship too much. At the start of 1984 the West Berlin Senate took over from the GDR the running of the S-Bahn overhead railway in West Berlin. In the same year more than 10,000 GDR citizens were able to have their wish and travel to the Federal Republic.

Numerous cases of spying in 1985 did little to influence the relations between Bonn and Pankow. One had become accustomed to Germany being two states and regarded this as 'normal'.

After the quick succession of Yuri Andropov and Konstantin Chernenko following Leonid Brezhnev, Michail Gorbachev became the new General Secretary of the CC of the CPSU. Glasnost (openness and transparency) and perestroika (restructuring) were the catchwords of his policy, which was directed towards reforms in the economy, politics and society of the USSR. The economy, which lagged behind the West, would experience an increase in productivity through the abandonment of central control mechanisms, the sanctioning of limited private property and elements of the market economy. Besides the economic innovations, at the same time as keeping the dominating monopoly and the leading role of the CPSU, a democratization of the political system was introduced, which included the putting forward of several candidates for elections and the emphasis on self-reliance at all levels. The comprehensive reform process would, according to Gorbachev, be set in train and stimulated by the opening up of society and a broad-based discussi on. By means of glasnost all the media would contribute to the public debate and political transparency: that is, they would render transparent the formation of opinion and decision-making and would allow objections and criticism on the part of the public, for example on weaknesses within the system and structural deficits as well as on the supply of consumer goods or on conflicts such as questions about minorities. A critical light was now also shone on the history of the USSR under Stalin. In the international context the CPSU abandoned its hegemony within the Communist parties, moved away from the Brezhnev doctrine and from now on backed the concept of the sovereignty of the Communist states.

In this concession the GDR saw the basis for arguing in favour of a distancing from Gorbachev's glasnost and perestroika and continuing on their political course independently. In the economic area the SED argued that many of Gorbachev's reforms had already been carried out in the GDR, that they did not have the defects of the Soviet economy and that they had a leading position amongst the socialist states. With this position, based on the status quo and its delusion over political power, the ageing, often aged, leading clique of the SED wasted the historic opportunity to start on a publicly effective policy of renewal in the GDR, which could still at least have been instituted between 1985–6 and 1988–9 and would therefore have been able to be put on display. Such a policy of 'change' would possibly have been able to absorb, soften or otherwise influence the direction of the actual change (or 'Wende') that happened abruptly in 1989/90. A really thorough-going reform policy à la Gorbachev in the USSR, however, was still not possible in terms of structure or personalities in the GDR. The repressive apparatus was too deeply implanted, the SED neither ready nor willing to give up its historical dominating monopoly, the substance of the state largely exhausted and its economy hopelessly indebted to the West. The system thus lacked not only the readiness but also the ability for renewal. Added to this was the seemingly great foreign policy success in gaining recognition by the invitation of Honecker to Bonn, which gave many GDR citizens the feeling of being fully recognized on a totally equal footing with the Federal Republic, and filled them with satisfaction and pride. The GDR appeared to be at the summit of its success and power; in fact, however, it was teetering on the edge of a precipice and for a few years it was faced with total collapse.

After longwinded and tough exploratory talks, a remarkable inter-German meeting came about. For the GDR leadership, the working visit by the chairman of the Council of State and General Secretary of the SED to the Federal Republic that took place between 7 and 11 September 1987 meant the culmination of international prestige. In the Bonn Republic Honecker was received with the full diplomatic honours due to the head of state of a sovereign nation. Talks took place in Bonn between Honecker, Weizsäcker, Kohl and other high-ranking politicians. The GDR potentate promised to continue promoting the 'normalization' of relations between the two German states. In Neunkirchen in the Saarland, Honecker's birthplace, he gave vent to his feelings and declared that one day the borders 'would no longer separate, but unite' the Germans. At the state reception in Bonn, Kohl remained controlled and used courteous but clear words. In his after-dinner speech on 7 September 1987 he insisted, in his manner marked by pragmatism and Realpolitik: 'Let us in these days concentrate on what is practicable, and let us also remain agreed not to put questions in the foreground that are at the moment insoluble.' He also spoke as a German and a patriot, however, when he insisted: 'The people in Germany are suffering because of the division. They are suffering because of a Wall literally blocking their way and repelling them.' As well as Bonn and Neunkirchen, Honecker visited North Rhine-Westphalia, Rhineland-Palatinate and Bavaria. In Trier he visited Karl Marx's childhood home. Honecker's foreign policy triumph in the Federal Republic could not, however, eclipse the fact that the system in the GDR was not just economically exhausted but was falling apart politically.

Ten years earlier, on 6 March 1978, at a meeting with the board of the Protestant Church Alliance, Honecker had conceded a modification of the SED position on the decay of religion within socialism and a recognition of the Church in the GDR as an independent, largely autonomous organization of social importance within social-ism. Despite allowing religious programmes on the radio and television, controversies and disagreements continued in the relations with the SED. As the 'Church within socialism' the Church leaders insisted on the unbridgeable philo-sophical gulf separating them from the state and the party, but, as an overall organization as opposed to individual Church members, renounced a policy of opposition.

Annually on 15 January in the GDR there was an official commemoration of the murders of Rosa Luxemburg and Karl Liebknecht committed by the members of the right-wing extremist Freikorps in 1919. Luxemburg and Liebknecht had founded the German Communist Party, belonged to the guiding commemorative figures of the GDR and provided substance for the legitimation of the 'Workers' and Farmers' State', the first socialist state on German soil. The marking of the anniversary turned out differently in 1988. In the course of the official rally on 17 January there was a counter-demonstration by people who wished to travel to the West, civil rights campaigners and individual citizens who pointed back to the democratic legacy of Luxemburg, carrying banners with the slogan 'Freedom is always the freedom to think differently'. The GDR regime grew nervous, as it had already arrested members of these groups because of their criticial view on the regime and had taken them into temporary custody. Therefore, they interpreted the courageous appearance of these counter-demonstrators as a 'counter-revolu-tion' and reacted brutally. Over 120 demonstrators were seized and in fast-track trials some received prison sentences of up to one year for 'banding together'. Some 54 GDR citizens were put on trial for 'treasonable activity'. They were deported to the Federal Republic with the option of returning to the GDR later on, an opportunity that was taken up by, for example, the songwriter Stefan Krawczyk and the director Freya Klier.

After the brutal intervention of the State Security Service against the Parish of Zion in East Berlin in 1987 and against the counter-demonstrators during the Luxemburg commemoration in 1988, more militant forces came to the fore within the Church. The protests were above all carried out by the young. They were directed against the arbitrary use of power by the state, the surveillance and arrests by the Stasi, and the deportation of opposition figures. The discontent and anger led to packed church services and rallies under the protection of the Church, at which people remembered those in prison by praying and holding vigils. The GDR was to face the greatest internal test of strength since 17 June 1953.

7

Return of the 'German Question' and the Unification of Germany, 1989–90

Background and Pre-conditions for Changes in East Germany

The revolutionary transformations in Central and South-East Europe reached their culmination in 1989. The Communist systems had to give up their monopoly of power and one by one they collapsed. The permanent economic crisis of state Socialism, the policy of détente in the CSCE process and the targeted embargo, as well as the costly NATO policy of building up armaments, all contributed to the political and ideological fiasco.

In his New Year's address of 1990, France's President François Mitterrand expressed the opinion that the importance of the events went beyond anything that had been experienced since the Second World War and ranked with the most outstanding moments of history. A few weeks earlier, on the island of Malta, the General Secretary of the CPSU, Mikhail Gorbachev, and US President, George Bush, had announced that the Cold War was over, and this was declared officially on 21 November 1990 in the Paris Charter for a New Europe. The US political scientist Francis Fukuyama misleadingly talked of the 'end of history'. He meant the victory and triumph of Western liberal democracy and the disappearance of ideological oppositions, but this ideal was questionable, since 1989 also saw a rebirth of radical Islamic fundamentalism following the revolution in Iran in 1979. What was over, however, was bi-polarity in international relations.

Honecker had still been claiming in all seriousness in January 1989 that the Berlin Wall would still be standing in 50 or 100 years. The Soviet Union had to force the GDR to sign the closing document of the successor conference to the CSCE, providing, among other things, for the right to travel abroad from any country along with the possibility of returning. Honecker was described by the later president of the Bundestag, Wolfgang Thierse, as a 'stubborn, insensitive and short-sighted human being and politician'. He neither understood Gorbachev nor what had happened in his own country as regards changes, opposition and internal differences within the SED. He seemed a sad and aged figure at the end.

During Kohl's visit to Moscow between 4 and 6 July 1983, the aged successor to Brezhnev, Yuri Andropov, threatened a Third World War and the construction of a missile shield. After Andropov's death, there was once more an old man with health problems at the head of the USSR, who died soon after his appointment: Konstantin Chernenko. The advisor to the Chancellor, Horst Teltschik, remembers how happy people were in Western capitals 'when after three old Soviet leaders at last a healthy young man came to the helm in Moscow'. The Federal Chancellor did not find the right tone at first. Looking back, Kohl called his disastrous interview with Newsweek on 27 October 1986 a 'monumental stupidity', in which he had compared Gorbachev to Nazi and Reichsminister of Propaganda, Goebbels, signalling a cooling of relations between Moscow and Bonn. The General Secretary of the CPSU then wanted to isolate the Federal Republic and teach the Federal Chancellor a lesson. Relations were strained once more. Even after this was resolved, there remained a residual suspicion felt by Gorbachev towards Kohl – still even in 1990, the year of German unification. Here a decided anti-Americanism influenced Soviet policy on Europe and the USA.

On his visit to the West of Berlin on the occasion of the 750th anniversary of the city on 12 June 1987, Reagan gave a speech in which he intentionally and pointedly called upon the Soviet leader: 'Mr Gorbachev, tear down this wall.' The appearance of the US President was accompanied by protests from young people and students and was only possible with the strictest security measures. The trip by Richard von Weizsäcker to Moscow between 6 and 11 July 1987 then brought about a normalization of the relations between the Federal Republic and Russia. Gorbachev put it to the Federal President that history would settle the German question and thus it was declared an open question. Kohl then found a common language with Gorbachev. On his visit to Moscow from 24–7 October 1988 the ice was broken. He travelled to the GDR privately in the same year in an attempt to understand the country and the people. On his visit to the other part of Germany, which drew much attention, he was able to make contact with people individually. It was from this time at the latest that the Chancellor followed a long-term strategy in solving the German question. In June 1989 Gorbachev visited Bonn and in front of the town hall declared to a cheering crowd of people that the Wall was not built forever and that without the Federal Republic a 'common European house' was not possible. A joint declaration recognized – for the first time from the Soviet side – the right to national self-determination for all Germans as well as the validity of international law at home and abroad. It was evident to the Federal Chancellery that these comments had to affect the GDR.

The changes in the GDR did not take much longer to come. They fell into the period of revolutionary events in Central and Eastern Europe. The Germans did not start the movements in order to overthrow the system but, rather, followed in the steps of the Poles and the Hungarians. The Polish trade union organization Solidarność had already contributed to the weakening of Communist domination in Poland since 1980. In Hungary a noticeable liberalization of the economic and political system had been underway since 1987–8. The opening of the Berlin Wall on 9 November 1989 then created a further thrust for the upheavals in Czechoslovakia and Romania. The freedom movements, which had already led the way in Poland and Hungary before 1989, had a stimulating effect on the developments, bringing about fundamental change in the GDR and Czechoslovakia. The revolutionary events, which did not always produce immediate outcomes, had several causes. The most important of such backgrounds was the attempted reforms after 1985 by Gorbachev, the newly appointed CPSU General Secretary. Glasnost and perestroika were supposed to lead not only to a renewal of Soviet society but also to gaining considerable importance within the Bloc and in foreign policy. The consequence was a partial withdrawal of Moscow from global responsibilities as well as a readiness on the part of the Kremlin for disarmament. The so-called Brezhnev doctrine, which never represented an official policy, was abandoned and for the first time autonomous development of internal conditions was granted to the socialist 'fraternal states'. Gorbachev's attempts at reform in the Soviet Union gave those who thought differently in the socialist 'fraternal states' a political motivation and moral legitimacy.

The trade union movement Solidarność in Poland could only be blocked by the declaration of martial law in December 1981 and even then only temporarily. As a power base it became more and more of a threat to the regime and was banned, but it continued to function underground. In Hungary reformist Communists had introduced elements of the market economy into the economic policy. The civil rights groups that had been forming since the middle of the 1970s, such as Charter 77 in Czechoslovakia, pointed to the CSCE Final Act of 1975 and demanded democratic rights to freedom from the Communist one-party regimes.

One can also cite Western integration as another of the preconditions to the upheavals of 1989. With the Single European Act (in effect from 1987) the twelve members of the European Community had committed themselves to the creation of the Internal Market by 31 December 1992. In addition to this there was the project of the European Economic Area (EEA), which in the shape of a multilateral association of EFTA and EC states was to form the largest single economic area in the world and would be copied by NAFTA in the USA and by MERCOSUR in Latin America. The effect of the economic unification via the four freedoms (persons, goods, services and capital) of the European continent in the West was attractive to the Soviet Union and its allies.

Economic Collapse, Occupations of Embassies, Radicalization and Successful Escapes via Hungary, Austria and Czechoslovakia

For a long time the GDR was considered 'stable'. In reality its economic situation was already highly precarious in the 1980s. The fact that the East German state did not have access to sufficient foreign exchange – there was enough paper money for domestic purposes but this only concealed the underlying economic facts – and was practically bankrupted as regards foreign exchange was not realized for a long time by people either in the East or the West. The level of debt was dramatic and a creeping erosion of ideology was beginning to set in. Consumer socialism was almost finished.

The economic development of the Federal Republic in comparison to the one in the GDR is immediately recognizable when one looks at the weakened growth rates of real national income (GDR) and real GDP (Federal Republic). The growth rates of the latter fell by approximately 8 per cent in the post-war period to one third. The downward trend began in the 1950s, but then settled down at a rate of around 2 per cent in the 1970s. A clear decline in growth occurred in the national income of the GDR up until the construction of the Wall. A phase of stabilization followed, ending again with a downward trend in the Honecker period. From the 1980s – here the billions in loans made by the Federal Republic played a role – there was a slight increase once again. The GDR accordingly was living beyond its means. Its level of consumption was too great. Both German states were hit by a declining trend in the growth of GDP or national income (GDR). Growth took off again but not as strongly as before.

The economic development of the Federal Republic and the GDR in comparison show significant trends. The productivity of the GDR fell dramatically up until the construction of the Wall. The exodus of people of working age was one of the most serious problems. Young people, gainfully employed workers, skilled workers, people with a future and ambition, left the GDR. After the construction of the Wall there was a consolidation of productivity. The level of 1961 was maintained, but then fell again at the start of the 1980s and declined from 4.3 to 3.4 per cent. Surprisingly the Federal Republic also experienced a decline in productivity, albeit not such a drastic one. From the high level of the years of the Economic Miracle in the 1950s, the 1960s saw a decline and a review. Since the 1970s the world economy had been in a crisis marked by oil shocks and declines in economic activity. From the 1980s the Federal Republic maintained the level up until German unification. In the West productivity dropped and then remained at a lower level. After the construction of the Wall the GDR experienced a stabilization of its previously dramatic crisis of productivity.

From the growth rates of exports it is clear that West German exports decreased. One wonders whether we are dealing with a 'world champion in exports' here, when the growth rates of the 1950s went down from 13.5 per cent to around half of the original data in the 1960s. They picked up again in the 1970s in the wake of the world economic crisis. Then the growth rate remained relatively consistent up until German unification. The growth rates of GDR exports sharply declined. It was less than half of the basic data up until the construction of the Wall, then the level is held. There followed a further decline in the 1980s relating to globalization and competition from East Asia on the world markets. The actually existing Communist states could not keep up, even with the backing of the Soviet Union, and recorded enormous export losses along with rising levels of public debt.

From the growth rates of imports the development of the GDR ran parallel to that of exports. There was a downward trend up until 1961, another from 1971–81 and then it went up slightly. The GDR was more dependent on imports in the 1980s than the Federal Republic. The latter, on the contrary, had to import less and less so the development since the 1970s has stayed at approximately the same level. In the case of the Federal Republic one can say that there was no negative foreign trade balance. Even if growth in exports declined, the decline in imports was no disadvantage in this case, so that again a balance could be achieved. In the case of the GDR it was different. Only with loans of DM was the GDR again able to import more. The East German state was increasingly dependent on its West German opposite number as regards foreign exchange policy and finance.

Since the 1970s people from the GDR who were being oppressed and imprisoned had their freedom bought by the Federal Republic at the cost of 600 million DM (rising to 1.5 billion) per annum. The SED state became more and more dependent on the Federal Republic. Despite the planting of mines on the internal German border after 1952 and the construction of the Wall in 1961 the citizens of the GDR still continued to think in terms of the whole of Germany. This orientation was more pronounced than in West Germany. An estimated 4.5 to 5.2 million people had left the GDR since the start of its existence, the largest movement of refugees since the Second World War. The SED regime, however, never gave a thought to removing the borders or pulling down the Wall until well into 1989. The Party had at times up to 3.5 million members. By means of it and the 'mass organizations' aligned with it uniformity was the rule and stability appeared to be guaranteed.

However, since the start of 1989 lack of understanding and protests aimed at the SED system could no longer be ignored. On 11 January a group of GDR citizens determined to travel to the West occupied the Permanent Representation of the Federal Republic in East Berlin and succeeded in gaining their exit. They not only managed to get freedom from punishment but also acceptance of their applications to travel to the West. But the SED state remained obdurate and unrepentant. In February and March it reacted to renewed attempts to escape by shooting at refugees. Chris Gueffroy, at only 19 years of age, was the last victim of the infamous order to open fire. He died on the night of 6 February 1989 from ten bullet shots from the wall snipers. His friend, Christian Gaudian, was seized and badly wounded. Both had attempted to go along the Britz canal linking Treptow in East Berlin with Neukölln in the West of the free city. They did not succeed. Four border guards were given an achievement award and a 150 DM bonus each. After the unification they were charged by the Berlin Land court. Gueffroy's mother would not give up and made sure that the 'trial of the Wall sharp-shooters' came about. The outcome was not, however, very satisfactory. In 1992 two of them were acquitted; one was given a suspended sentence. Ingolf Heinrich, who had fired the deadly shot to the heart, was sentenced to three and a half years in prison. In the appeal in 1994 the sentence was reduced to a two years' suspended sentence. The police officer, Sven Hüber, who did not shoot, but was responsible for the section of the border guarded by Berlin brigade 33 (Treptow), went on to hold a leading position in the Federal Police Force. Approximately 100 people died on the inter-German border in Berlin, including eight soldiers shot by their own comrades.

Protests from civil rights campaigners against the blatant rigging of the local elections by the authorities in the GDR on 7 May 1989 expressed broad discontent, ushering in peaceful mass demonstrations in East Germany. The escalation of events got underway at the same time.

In Hungary democratization had gone the furthest after Poland. In January 1989 the representatives of the Hungarian people had agreed to the formation of new parties. In February 1989 there was a new constitution in which the monopoly of the Communist Party was no longer enshrined. In April the first Soviet troops left the country. In May 1989 a start was made with the removal of the border installations to the West, immediately exploited by people on holiday from the GDR to escape, after their upkeep and renewal had proved to be too expensive and no longer worth paying for on the part of the Communist regime. On 27 June the Foreign Ministers of Austria and Hungary, Alois Mock and Gyula Horn, openly crossed the Iron Curtain in front of the cameras. TV broadcasts of this were shown around the world and could also be seen in the GDR. While over the summer months hundreds of GDR citizens crowded into West German embassies in Budapest, Prague and Warsaw, demanding to be allowed to travel to the West, on 19 August hundreds of GDR holidaymakers in Hungary used a 'Pan-European Picnic', organized by reformist Communists and under the protection of Otto von Habsburg on the Austro-Hungarian border near Šopron, to escape to freedom. For a few hours the border was open. In the same month more than 100 GDR occupiers of the embassy in Budapest, which like other embassies had to be closed on account of overcrowding on 14 August, were flown to Vienna. This was the signal for a wave of escapes that rose sharply and was illustrated by further embassy occupations in Prague, Warsaw and Budapest as well as the Permanent Representation in East Berlin. A few days later the GDR refugees holed up in the West German embassy in Budapest got permission to leave. The Hungarian government emphasized that the question of refugees had to be settled by both German states. On 11 September they put aside an agreement made with the GDR on travel by reference to the CSCE Final Act and, with the definitive opening up of the border, opened the way for all GDR citizens in Hungary who wanted to travel to the West.

Since the second half of the 1980s there had already been close contact between the Chancellery in Bonn and the Hungarian reformed Communists, in order to explore the situation within the Bloc and discover how Moscow was thinking. Shortly before the opening of the border the government, under Miklos Németh, had received undertakings of sums in the billions. Up to 1 October approximately 25,000 East Germans reached the free West via Hungary. Pankow, which was preparing for the fortieth anniversary of the founding of the GDR on 7 October, chose to deny reality and did not react to the movement of refugees. The official GDR news agency ADN carried a statement by Honecker from the party newspaper *Neues Deutschland*: 'and we shall weep no tears for them'.

While the exodus from the GDR was taking place, circles in Bonn were still concerned with their own affairs. When Hungary opened up its borders at 7 pm on 10 September, thus allowing GDR citizens to go to the West, at the party conference being held at the same time in Bremen the opponents of Kohl within the CDU (Kurt

Biedenkopf, Heiner Geißler, Lothar Späth and Rita Süssmuth) had planned to topple Kohl. Aware of his threatened position, Kohl made the Hungarian decision publicly known and thus took the wind out of the sails of all his opponents. The Germans from East Germany were to come to his aid. Looking back, not without bitterness, the former Chancellor put it this way: 'At a moment when the whole world was looking and the framework of the Warsaw Pact was cracking apart, we spent 17 hours chatting about the most extraordinary things.' This Bonn Republic was much too provincial and too concerned with itself to correctly assess the changes in world politics taking place on German soil and correspondingly was not prepared to react.

In the course of September 1989, when the movement towards escape via Hungary became intense, thousands of GDR citizens crammed into the grounds of the German embassy in Prague and hundreds into the one in Warsaw. On the evening of 30 September, Foreign Minister Genscher broke the news to the approximately 6,000 GDR refugees present that their road to freedom was possible. From the balcony of the embassy in Prague the Foreign Minister made a statement calmly and very objectively, which he was not able to finish because he was drowned out by cheering: 'We have come to you to tell you that today your exit [here a sudden outburst of enthusiasm on the part of thousands of GDR citizens in the West German embassy compound could be heard] has become possible.' Genscher, admittedly, on the occasion of this moving event in his political life had to give the information that the refugees would be transported to the Federal Republic in special trains of the East German Reichsbahn via GDR territory. That was one condition that the SED regime had still made, demonstrating thereby its would-be power, which caused much consternation among those wishing to travel to the West. A few weeks after a heart operation on a visit to New York, Genscher had found out that the GDR refugees would not be transported via the Bavarian-Czechoslovak border but had to go via the GDR. He was aware what fears this would arouse and decided to travel in one of the trains in order to act personally as a guarantee. However, the GDR leadership was against this. Genscher in the end did not want to 'risk anyone in East Berlin finding a loophole and see the whole thing go wrong at the last minute'. The process went ahead without difficulty, with GDR citizens standing by the track and cheering their fellow citizens. On 4 October another mass exit took place with more than 7,000 GDR refugees from Prague, a day after journeys between the GDR and Czechoslovakia without a visa were suspended.

For the first time since the construction of the Wall in 1961 GDR citizens had the chance to express their desire to travel to the West and turn their backs on the East

German state. Not many suspected that, by 'voting with their feet' and escaping spectacularly, they would be contributing to the imminent fall of the unpopular SED system. Between July and November 1989 tens of thousands of East Germans made use of the route via Hungary and Austria in order to move to the longed-for Federal Republic, which most of them only knew from television images in the West and tempting advertisements.

In the GDR protest actions by opposition groups started, growing into mass marches. They criticized the SED leadership's unwillingness to reform and held them responsible for the mass escapes. With banners reading 'We shall stay here' and 'We are the People' the demonstrators gave vent to their feelings and demanded reforms. The escapes via Hungary no doubt had the effect of putting pressure on and threatening the SED regime. The transport of the refugees holed up in the Prague embassy via GDR territory was another serious mistake by the SED leadership. The celebrations of the anniversary of the Republic seemed particularly questionable when people clearly wanted to leave the country in droves. The thousands of refugees thus undermined the authority of the state. The GDR leadership openly criticized the 'betrayal by the Hungarians' and were irritated by the 'Soviet Union bystanding and looking on'. The party leadership was faced with the alternative of introducing speedy reforms or pursuing a policy of force with a new Wall on the borders with the neighbouring socialist states. They decided on the latter. On 3 October 1989 the border with Czechoslovakia was closed and on 7 October, the national holiday, demonstrators in Berlin were brutally beaten with police truncheons. With the prospect of the Monday demonstrations breaking out in Leipzig there was the danger of a 'Chinese solution'. Honecker and Mielke wanted to 'stop people banding together'. The mass exodus from the GDR that got underway in the summer of 1989 and, at the same time, the citizens taking to the streets there illustrated that the East German state had failed in its aim of achieving acceptance and legitimation from its citizens. The question of whether to stay or go stirred up the population. Those young people who were regarded as 'indoctrinated' were particularly affected and were up in arms. Unlimited freedom to travel and Western lifestyles made the Federal Republic seem like a dreamland for many of them; in this dream naked economic competition and the sometimes oppressive social conditions resulting from mass unemployment were not appreciated.

The 40th Anniversary of the GDR and the Collective Resignation of the Central Committee under Honecker

The SED regime, focused entirely on the 40th anniversary of the existence of the East German partial state, celebrated itself and 77-year-old Erich Honecker's recovery from an operation for gallstones in the parliament building, the Palace of the Republic. When Gorbachev had landed in East Berlin and was being driven into the city in his black limousine, he became increasingly troubled. Up until now the GDR had been seen by him as a haven of stability. In fact many spontaneously produced placards saying 'Gorbi' were to be seen and one could not avoid hearing people by the side of the road chanting 'Help us!' and 'Save us!' He could remember only one placard saying 'Erich – keep up the good work!'

Gorbachev, along with Honecker, underestimated the extent of the pressure for change; he overestimated the attractiveness of a reformed Socialism, but above all he underestimated what GDR citizens were after: political freedom and German unity. He had initially taken it for granted that the people in the East German state were better off than those in the Soviet Union and that they would therefore be totally satisfied with their situation. Gorbachev saw the events from the point of view of a hegemonic world power without recognizing that his own position was crumbling. The German question was not his first priority. It ranked behind the social and economic reforms as well as the problem of nationalities in the USSR.

In his official speech on 6 October 1989 Honecker devoted not a single word to the refugees and the associated problems with the infrastructure of the GDR. The next day there was a meeting with Gorbachev at Schloss Niederschönhausen; he did not mince his words with Honecker and the Politburo. Courageous decisions were needed and any delay would lead to defeat. Accordingly the General Secretary of the CPSU impressed upon 'Comrade Honecker' that he considered it 'very important, not to miss the opportunity and waste any chance'. Gorbachev went on: 'If we hesitate, life will immediately punish us.' 'Far-reaching decisions' had to be made and these had to be 'well thought through', 'so that they bear rich fruit'. The experiences with Poland and Hungary had shown that: 'If the Party does not react to life, it is condemned by it.' There was 'only one choice': 'to go forward decisively'. Honecker brushed aside all warning requests in his reply, which made Gorbachev speak even more pointedly and brought the discussion to an abrupt end. Gorbachev's spokesman, Gennadi Gerassimov, put together from the General Secretary's words the famous statement at the following press conference on 7 October: 'Life punishes those who are late.'

During the celebrations of the Republic young people had protested on the Alexander Platz in East Berlin against the rigging of the local elections in May 1989, which they had expressed by a chorus of whistling on the seventh day of each of the preceding months. They marched to the Palace of the Republic where Honecker and the official guests were. The crowd, which had swollen to several thousand people, chanted 'Gorbi, Gorbi' and held vigils for political prisoners. When they came to the ADN news agency, the demonstrators shouted 'liars, liars' and 'freedom for the press'. Police cars arrived. Scuffles and arrests followed. The Schönhauser Allee railway station was closed off by the police and units of the State Security. At a late hour the security forces intervened and forcibly broke up the demonstration. Similar incidents took place in Arnstadt, Dresden, Ilmenau, Jena, Karl-Marx Stadt, Leipzig, Magdeburg and Plauen. 'Stasi into production!' and 'We are the People!', the demonstrators chanted. The violent intervention by the police and the Stasi units against peaceful demonstrators on this 7 October in the 'Capital of the GDR' and other towns brought about international protests.

The upheavals in the GDR were like a revolution. It was a Protestant revolution and first and foremost an urban revolution in Saxony. On 2 October between approximately 10,000 and 20,000 people demonstrated in Leipzig. The police intervened, resulting in arrests and injuries. On Honecker's orders, hospitals were cleared for the Monday of the following week, 9 October, several hundred of the NVA were mustered, factory action squads and the People's Police, the Volkspolizei quartered in barracks – 8,000 men altogether – were put on standby. The atmosphere was highly explosive. To everyone's surprise and horror, instead of the expected 20,000 to 30,000, 70,000 demonstrators came on 9 October, marching peacefully on the Leipzig Ring chanting such things as 'No violence' and 'We are the People'. 'We were ready for anything, except for candles and prayers', an internal report of SED heads said. At the same time the order beforehand had been 'if necessary make use of weapons in order to defend the achievements of Socialism'. Western journalists were not allowed to go to Leipzig – only one had gained access 'illegally'. After the failure of the anniversary celebrations of the socialist state there were further mass marches after the Monday prayers in Leipzig on 9 October, in favour of a renewal of the GDR. On 16 October there were 120,000 people taking part in the Monday demonstration, on 23 October, 200,000, on 30 October, 300,000 and on 6 November, 500,000. On 13 November – after the opening of the Wall – the 150,000 people taking part chanted 'Germany, one Fatherland'. Factory action groups, the NVA, the Stasi and the Volkspolizei were powerless against these masses. The date of 9 October was the decisive turning-point of the revolutionary events in the GDR.

Banners from demonstrations in the GDR in the autumn of 1989.

Volkspolizei and security forces were in the end passive. As we now know, no order was given by Egon Krenz to shoot and kill, but the aged head of the Politburo and chairman of the State Council in the first half of October had still wrongly assumed that the Soviet military would send in tanks. The Brezhnev doctrine, however, was no longer applicable. As early as late summer, Foreign Minister Edvard Shevardnadze had pushed through an order in Moscow not to become involved in the event of mass demonstrations in the GDR and to exert an influence on the NVA in this direction. The responsible 20 Garde-Mot Division with their 271 tanks kept to this instruction when Leipzig erupted in revolt. Gorbachev acted, by all appearances, as if he was directing the state without the use of force. One was dealing initially with a revolution in Saxony. On 8 October in Dresden, demonstrators, a 'group of 20', made contact with the SED leadership and decided to attempt a mutual dialogue. Oberbürgermeister (Lord Mayor) Wolfgang Berghofer played an important role in this. In the small town of Plauen on 7 October around 15,000 of the 70,000 inhabitants were on the streets: a quarter of the total population. In the following days in every area of the GDR territory hundreds of thousands of people demonstrated in favour of democratic reforms. Calls of 'We are the People' were heard everywhere. Writers, theatre people, singers and musicians came out with resolutions calling upon the SED regime to be serious about reforms in order to bring about an end to the flood of refugees. Protestant churches played a decisive role as places of refuge as did enlightened and courageous pastors such as Pastor Christian Führer in Leipzig who, after preaching the Gospel, told the churchgoers before they left the service: 'Whoever puts their life on the line and loses it, will gain it.'

The SED Politburo, reacting in a sclerotic and sluggish manner, met for crisis meetings on 10 and 18 October. For the first time there was criticism of Honecker's stubborn style of leadership, which was seen as being totally inflexible. When the chairman of the State Council and General Secretary of the SED again opposed all the necessary attempts at reform, a number of Politburo members called for his replacement. On 18 October Honecker resigned as General Secretary. Politburo members Günter Mittag and Joachim Herrmann were likewise removed from office. Egon Krenz became the new SED General Secretary, announcing the 'Wende' (the 'turning point' or 'change') in a speech on television, admittedly in the same breath calling for the 'development of the socialist society'. On 24 October Honecker was removed from power completely. He was succeeded by Krenz as chairman of the State Council and chairman of the 'National Defence Council'. Thus, a lightning process of erosion of political power began in the GDR, continuing on 8 November with the collective resignation of the Politburo of the SED. Honecker's chosen candidate, Krenz, was a further mistake. For the GDR civil protest movement he was just as bad as his predecessor. A more credible reformer such as Modrow would have produced a different outcome.

The Opening of the Wall on 9 November 1989 and Kohl's 'Ten Point Plan'

After Honecker's fall one event quickly followed another. His successor, Krenz, was elected as chairman of the State Council on 24 October by the Volkskammer with 26 negative votes, despite strong objections among the population. He had welcomed the bloody suppression of the student protests by the military and tanks on the 'Square of heavenly Peace' (Tiananmen Square) in Peking on 3 and 4 July. Subsequently, there was the fear of a 'Chinese solution' in the GDR. Krenz pursued a new style of leadership by offering 'dialogue' on all sides. He announced the 'easing of travel' as a first reform and tried to win trust. On 27 October an amnesty was declared for refugees and demonstrators and proceedings were instigated against members of the police and the Stasi relating to the events of 7 October. From 1 November unrestricted travel to Czechoslovakia without a visa was introduced, which meant that the number of refugees and of people travelling to the West went up again.

Demonstrations in many towns followed. On 4 November in East Berlin around 500,000 people demanded free elections, the end of the SED's monopoly of power as well as freedom of the press, freedom to express one's opinion and to travel. The SED leadership had lost its credibility long ago. Krenz and his new leadership were no longer trusted. They were looked on as *Wendehälse* (turncoats), a term that the writer Christa Wolf coined in response to the 'turning point' announced by Krenz. On 7 November the Council of Ministers chaired by Willi Stoph resigned, the day after the whole Politburo would do the same. The CC of the SED had elected a new Politburo reduced from 21 to 11 members. Amongst these was the head of the Dresden Bezirk, Hans Modrow. Krenz was still confirmed as General Secretary. Modrow, who was judged to be a 'reformer', was the new man; however, admittedly he was the one who had deployed police units on the railways station in Dresden when the GDR refugees from Prague were being transported to the Federal Republic, preventing by force people who wanted to depart for the West from jumping on. For many Communist supporters of a new and better GDR Modrow, nevertheless, represented a 'figure of hope'.

Since the middle of the 1970s there had been discussions within the SED on the mounting structural problems. The GDR was faced with bankruptcy several times in the 1980s, which was only averted by billions in new loans from the Federal Republic. During Krenz's visit to Gorbachev in Moscow on 1 November 1989 the topic of the GDR's economic plight was brought up, causing considerable concern. In the exchange the representative of the SED had asked 'Comrade Mikhail Sergeyevich' whether the Soviet Union still recognized paternity in relation to its child, the GDR, at which Gorbachev at first fell silent, then whispered and finally, taken aback, wanted to know what sort of a question Krenz was asking. He said he did not know anyone who wanted reunification – not even Kohl. The interpreter then repeated a Russian proverb that Gorbachev was quoting: 'however long the string is, it will eventually come to an end'. The decisive factor about this meeting was to be the aid of the USSR that Krenz urgently appealed for, which Gorbachev, however, refused to give. Krenz returned home from Moscow deeply troubled. The GDR had constantly lived beyond its means.

The economic crisis led to an underlying government crisis. This in turn brought about an insecurity within the Politburo, which left them speechless. On

31 October 1989 the facts of the economic situation were revealed to be catastrophic: productive capacity was used up, there was an inability to pay, they were on the verge of definitive bankruptcy. Only by lowering the standard of living by 25 per cent could the situation be saved. A loan of 12–13 billion DM was needed. Bonn considered it and was only ready to offer one in exchange for making the Wall more porous. Secret talks were held between the GDR negotiator Alexander Schalk-Golodkowski, who had also been responsible for acquiring foreign currency, Minister of the Chancellery Rudolf Seiters and Minister of the Interior Wolfgang Schäuble.

The new SED leadership was forced to negotiate and acted when it was already too late: on 1 November it lifted the ban on travel to Czechoslovakia. On 4 November the Politburo gave the green light for GDR citizens to leave Czechoslovakia after Prague had protested in East Berlin about the 'mass migration through our country' and had demanded their direct exit. On 8 November Kohl indicated his readiness, in exchange for the introduction of further freedoms, to secure economic aid for the GDR on a totally new level. Shortly before starting a visit to Warsaw the Federal Chancellor gave the Bundestag a 'report on the national situation', in which he promised the GDR 'comprehensive economic aid', once 'a commitment to fundamental reform of political and economic conditions' in the GDR had been made. This included, said Kohl, the abandonment by the SED of its monopoly of power, the legalization of independent parties and the definite setting-up of free elections.

Events followed in rapid succession. When it became clear that the Volkskammer would reject the legislation on travel put forward by the government, allowing GDR citizens to travel to the West but linking this to bureaucratic procedures and financial requirements, the SED leadership under Krenz rushed ahead and planned the opening of the border crossings. On the evening of 9 November Günter Schabowski, a member of the Politburo, at a hastily called press conference in reply to the Italian journalist, Riccardo Ehrmann, unexpectedly announced to those present that all GDR border crossings to the Federal Republic and West Berlin would be opened. When another man from the press enquired on what basis and when this would take effect, Schabowski, who was badly prepared, stammeringly confirmed his announcement saying 'as far as I know, immediately'. This was a misunderstanding, as the opening of the sector borders was planned for 10 November. The announcement was to be made on the radio at 4 am. In this way the new regulation on travel to the West was already announced in advance at the press conference the evening before. The decision took place without consultation (i.e. without Moscow's

A model reconstructing the scene of the opening of the Wall in Berlin on 9 November 1989.

agreement), and would have considerable consequences. The USSR and the GDR lost an important bargaining chip for possible inter-German negotiations, and the opening of the Wall was to be the beginning of the end of the Pankow regime.

However, it was not the press conference with Günter Schabowski's announcement but the information in the Western media with the headline 'GDR opens border' in the ARD news bulletin by Hanns Joachim Friedrichs that anticipated the fall of the Wall. Fiction became reality. The SED leadership was paralysed. The opening of the Wall could no longer be prevented. The one-party state was on the verge of an unintentional self-dissolution (as Hermann Hertle puts it). The people beat the regime to it.

The opening of the Wall was a surprise for everyone. People were totally unprepared for it – people opposed to it as well as politicians in the East and West. The first border crossing to be opened was the Bornholmer Strasse. That very evening people assembled there to cross over into the west of the city. Thousands of GDR citizens queued at the border crossings, where the border guards, who were unprepared but who acted in a controlled manner, were totally outnumbered and forced to open the barriers. There were outbreaks of spontaneous dancing for joy and tearful encounters between East and West Germans.

Helmut Kohl had to interrupt a state visit to Poland, which was apparently quite difficult to explain to the Poles. However, the Federal Chancellor was not to be dissuaded. The journey to Berlin proved to be complicated. As flying over GDR territory was not allowed, he first had to travel to Hamburg. From there he went on by a US military plane to Berlin, which was subject to Four Power control. It was in a chaotic state. The parties had not been able to agree on a common rally. The Senate, made up of Socialist and Green members, organized one in front of Schöneberg Town Hall; the CDU later organized one on the Breitscheidplatz. Kohl was very upset with his own party, as the international press had congregated at the first venue. Kohl was mercilessly jeered there (for him this was 'a left-wing mob'), creating an extremely bad impression, whereas Willy Brandt was very welcomed. Later he let us know what he thought: 'Now, that which belongs together will grow together. Now we are seeing and I thank God that I am here to witness it: the parts of Europe are growing together.'

After the announcement of the opening of the border hundreds of thousands of GDR citizens flocked to visit West Berlin and the Federal Republic. Approximately two million GDR citizens were to visit West Berlin by the weekend of 12 November. Around 500,000 enjoyed the freedom to travel by visiting West German towns. The GDR Ministry of Defence announced on 13 December that, with immediate effect, all border zones along the Berlin Wall and the whole of the border with the Federal Republic were to be opened up.

Cars passing through the Wall, seen on a First Day Cover.

Mass demonstrations, however, continued in the GDR. In the meantime the call 'Wir sind ein Volk' ('We are one People') and the associated desire for a united Germany grew louder. Because of the protests by East German citizens, Federal Chancellor Kohl was forced to act. On 28 November he put forward a Ten Point Plan in the Bundestag, neither in discussion with Foreign Minister Genscher nor in consultation with the Western powers. It appeared to be aimed in the long-term at German unity by means of stages, not for the moment in concrete form, consisting of a 'contractual community and confederation-like structures'. Thus, Kohl seized the initiative. It was a clever move by which he gave a timely answer to the German question that was now in flux. The plan provided initially for immediate measures in regard to cooperation in the area of environmental protection, as well as the extension of the telephone and railway network. In the next stage, following a change in the constitution giving the GDR a new franchise, the conditions would be created for the market economy. In another stage the 'contractual community' suggested by Prime Minister Modrow would be set up on the widest level and, following free elections, a state alliance, talk was of 'confederation-like structures', would be created opening up the way to a German Federation or an organization along Federal lines. The question as to the concrete form of a 'reunified Germany' Kohl did no go into, but pointed to the relevance of the European context for an inter-German unification process. The Ten Point Plan did not mention a timetable so as not to cause too much alarm. The opposition in the Bundestag agreed with the plan in principle but, along with the FDP coalition partner, regretted the Chancellor's going it alone. Above all they criticized the absence of a clear declaration of a guarantee on the Western border of Poland. The GDR bloc parties likewise reacted with criticism: in reply, counter to the suggested unity, they pointed out the autonomy of the GDR.

Crisis in the SED, Civil Rights Groups, the Transitional Government of Modrow and the 'Round Table'

By their placards and chants the demonstrators drew attention to the fact that the SED had lost its credibility and could not regain it by simply replacing some of their top representatives or removing them from the SED. Honecker's successor, Krenz, did nothing to build up confidence, particularly since his critics held him responsible for rigging the local elections in May 1989. On 13 November the representatives of the Volkskammer voted for a new President. The successor to Horst Sindermann (SED) was the chairman of the Democratic Farmers' Party (Demokratische Bauernpartei,

DBD), Günther Maleuda. After the dissolution of the old Council of Ministers which, by resigning, wanted to keep open the option of a 'renewal of Socialism', the Volkskammer elected Modrow as the new Minister-President. On 17 November he presented his 'government of peace and Socialism' in the Volkskammer and promised profound changes in the economy, education and the administration. He verbosely glossed over the development that had been actually underway for some time and stuck to the inter-German status quo. The GDR and the Federal Republic would continue to develop the 'community of responsibility' with the aim of 'qualified good neighbourliness' and 'cooperative coexistence' becoming a 'contractual community' that would go beyond previous agreements.

Krenz and Modrow initially had a good number of opportunities for unlimited action since organized opposition groups were still pretty thin on the ground. By comparison with Czechoslovakia and Hungary, these formed relatively late in the GDR. In the second half of 1989 the party political spectrum became more diversified.

The citizens' initiative group 'Neues Forum' was set up on 9–10 September under Bärbel Bohley, only two weeks after being rejected by the old GDR Ministry of the Interior as being 'hostile to the state'. In the following days and weeks it experienced a leap in support. After the opening of the Wall Neues Forum warned against the looming sell-out of the GDR and expressed opposition to unity.

The citizens' movement 'Demokratie jetzt' (Democracy Now), which started on 12 September, called on both Christians and Marxists to work together to bring about a democratic restructuring of the GDR as well as measures to protect against the serious pollution of the environment.

Other activists made a historic step on 7 October by founding the Social Democratic Party of the GDR (SDP). After the forced unification of the SPD and the KPD into the SED, there was now a Social Democratic Party in existence once again. The citizens' group 'Demokratischer Aufbruch' (Democratic Renewal), founded at the start of October, was constituted on 16/17 December 1989 with Wolfgang Schnur as the chairman of the party. Schnur later turned out to have been a Stasi spy and quickly disappeared from view, like Ibrahim Böhme, who first made a name for himself with the SDP/SPD. Alongside the Green Party there was also a United Left, which continued to support the autonomy of the GDR and repudiated the trend towards unification.

The civil rights' groups clearly rejected the SED regime. They did not, however, agree over the question of whether to go for a reformed autonomous 'Socialist GDR' or a rapid 'German unity'. After the fall of the Wall differing concepts of the survival of the GDR were current within the opposition camp, resulting in broad sections of the population losing faith in the opposition.

On 1 December 1989 a pivotal event took place when the Volkskammer of the GDR dropped the monopoly of leadership by the SED from the constitution. Protest actions on a mass scale, however, continued to increase. Within the SED criticism of Krenz grew so strong that he and the party leadership also had to announce their resignation. At the same time the majority of the former party and state leadership, including Honecker and Mielke, were expelled from the SED. A few days later, on 6 December, Krenz also resigned from his position as chairman of the State Council.

The Chairman of the Council of Ministers, Modrow, gained recognition, but, in face of the power relations that were now completely out of control, he was only a transitional figure. Civil rights groups and opposition figures became more and more self-confident and demanding. In this turbulent phase they demanded a share in the decisions made by the government. After the example of Poland, on 7 December a Central Round Table had to be set up in East Berlin, which consisted of representatives of the opposition, the parties in the Volkskammer and the government. In the following weeks it grew to become the most important decision-making body in the GDR. Measures on working out a new constitution and the announcement of new elections for 6 May 1990 were agreed. In a 'government of national responsibility', formed on 5 February 1990, the Round Table appointed eight ministers without portfolio and agreed on a social charter which would avoid being in favour of the union of the economies and currencies. At a final meeting on 12 March they voiced their opposition to an acceptance of the 'Grundgesetz' for the GDR and put forward their own draft for a GDR constitution.

Inter-German Meeting in Dresden: Opening Up of the Brandenburg Gate, Weeks of Silence in Moscow and the Avoidance of Chaos

After it became evident that no more economic aid was to come for the exhausted GDR from Moscow, Krenz had immediately requested a meeting with Kohl. The latter, however, declined after Gorbachev had made it known that he should not meet with Krenz. Krenz would not survive the next party conference, proving the head of the Kremlin right. Therefore a meeting came about between Kohl and Modrow in Dresden. The political representatives of the Western states and the Soviet Union observed the events gathering pace in East Germany with growing concern, particularly since they did not have any real chance of doing anything

The Brandenburg Gate, now open again.

about it. The first official meeting between Federal Chancellor Kohl and the GDR Prime Minister that took place on 19 December 1989 in Dresden had a calming effect, for the time being. The representatives of the two German states behaved responsibly in respect to the international community, which viewed the inter-German developments either critically or negatively. Despite calls, that could not be ignored, for unification from both parts of Germany the representatives of the Bonn and the Pankow Republics did not undermine the fact of two existing German states and initially agreed to a 'contractual community', which would be finalized in spring 1990. Kohl and Modrow came out in favour of holding a CSCE summit conference next. The pair also agreed in Dresden to open the Brandenburg Gate to pedestrians before Christmas.

People anxious to witness the event and television crews from all over the world had been waiting for weeks at the historic place for the day when the symbolic process of the opening would take place. Finally on 21 December work began, on the East German side, demolishing the Wall. Shortly after midnight, at exactly 00.37 am, a first break through the Wall was achieved. For the celebration on 22 December nearly half a million people from the city and guests from East and West had come to the central point of the division of Europe to listen to the speeches in the driving rain. Modrow – unlike Erich Honecker who had opined months before that the Wall would stand for another 100 years – now talked in his capacity as a conciliator of the monument as a 'gate of peace'. Kohl called upon Germans in the East and West to exercise 'patience and judgement'. The mayors of the city, Walter Momper of West Berlin and Erhard Krack of East Berlin, emphasized the new role of the city in a period in which the two hitherto divided parts of Germany would grow together.

After the highly popular visit by Kohl to Dresden, where he was rapturously received with his speech outside the Frauenkirche ('Church of Our Lady') that had been badly destroyed by Allied bombing in the war, Modrow paid a return visit to Bonn on 13 February 1990, with 17 ministers, including as many as eight representatives of the opposition belonging to the 'government of national responsibility' formed on 5 February. The political situation remained uncertain. The election deadline originally set for the GDR could not be met, lending little credibility to Modrow's government, as it had only a few weeks left before it was brought to an anticipated end.

The delegation led by Modrow had put forward a unique request in inter-German history: it asked for 'immediate aid' as a 'solidarity contribution' in the shape of a sum of 15 billion DM; Kohl and his team turned this down. The look on Modrow's face after the meeting with Kohl was plain to everyone in the television broadcasts. The result of the exchange of ideas was only the decision to set up a commission that would prepare an economic and currency union.

Gorbachev, who wanted to reform the USSR and socialism, carried out a consistent staged withdrawal in his German policy in 1989–90. Externally he reacted positively to the opening of the Wall. Internally he agreed to the unification at the end of January and at the start of February 1990 publicly as well, after Foreign Minister Shevardnadze had still referred to Kohl's 10 Point Plan of 28 November of the previous year as a 'diktat, that not even Hitler would have dared to put forward'. Everything had clearly happened too quickly for the Soviet Foreign Minister.

After the meeting with Bush in Malta, German unity was no longer a taboo subject for Gorbachev, but the process, the timetable and the modalities were still open. For the Soviet military, however, the situation was anything but settled. On 15 January 1990 there came all at once a stop to the reception of foreign guests in the Kremlin and a ban on contact. Suddenly there was radio silence. Not until the end of January did Kohl receive notice of a date set for a visit for the beginning of February. What was going on? Shevardnadze later revealed that a passionate internal discussion was taking place over whether to mount a military intervention in the GDR. In January the former Stasi building in East Berlin had been invaded; a critical moment. The situation was uncertain, but the Soviet Union under Gorbachev again did not react by intervening with force. On 26 January a high-ranking ad hoc meeting took place in the Kremlin which agreed to reunification; admittedly, Gorbachev said, this should not happen for another 10 years. He was wrong, since developments had already become too fluid and the Soviet Union depended on Western aid.

The economic situation in the USSR was extremely strained, as Kohl knew. In January 1990 the Federal Republic supplied the Soviet Union with 220 million DM worth of food, including thousands of tonnes of meat. In a move agreed upon by Finance Minister Theo Waigel, Agriculture Minister Ignaz Kiechle and the Soviet ambassador in Bonn, aid was dispatched to people suffering from hunger in Russia by means of a unique logistical undertaking involving hundreds of goods trains and freezing facilities.

Despite the spectacular opening of the Wall and the clear readiness for reform on the part of the Modrow government, the flood of refugees from the Pankow Republic did not let up. Many did not believe the promise of a 'change' or 'turning point', the negative experiences in the Stasi state were too deeply ingrained in them, the disappointments and frustrations with the SED state were too deeply embedded. The despised party admittedly renamed itself the 'Party of Democratic Socialism' (Partei des Demokratischen Sozialismus, PDS) but this was felt by many GDR citizens to be hocus-pocus and looked upon as a delaying tactic. The ongoing conflict over the removal of the Stasi was an unmistakable sign for many that a credible change of course was not to be expected.

The fact that forced both sides to act – in East as well as West Germany – was that in February 1990 an end-of-year estimate said that around a million GDR citizens would be rushing to West Germany. Horst Teltschik, advisor to the Chancellor, admitted: 'This was the decisive fact that made things go very quickly.' It was GDR citizens that forced action to be taken. For the GDR it would have meant an irreparable loss of young and employable workers. In the short term the Federal Republic would not be able to provide either accommodation or jobs for so many people. It was a question of avoiding chaos on both sides. The main worry in Bonn was, however, that Gorbachev might decisively lose power. A package had to be put together to help him. In May the Soviet Union was guaranteed a 5 billion DM loan by Bonn.

The Heavy Legacy of the Stasi and the Bringing Forward of Elections to the Volkskammer

The informal continued existence of the structures of the disbanded State Security Service (the Stasi) formed a heavy burden for the new GDR government. In the wake of the erosion of domination by the SED in autumn 1989 the indignation of the masses was strongly directed at the ubiquitous Stasi, which for decades had spread out its tight, tentacle-like and all-pervasive spying system all over the Pankow Republic. Nothing seemed to have escaped it. In almost all imaginable areas GDR citizens were observed, controlled and under surveillance. Approximately 91,000 full-time and hundreds of thousands of so-called 'unofficial co-workers' (*inoffizielle Mitarbeiter* or IMs) had worked for the Ministry for State Security (Ministerium für Staatssicherheit, MfS) – far more personnel than the Gestapo (Geheime Staatspolizei) had in the Third Reich for a population three times as large. Husbands spied on their wives. Children denounced their parents. Brothers and sisters mutually betrayed one another. No-one could be trusted. The deformation of East German society had become considerable. IMs were everywhere: workplaces, factories, hotels, restaurants, church groups, the cinema and the theatre as well as in the NVA and naturally in all the party organizations – finally even amongst the civil rights' groups and demonstrators, giving rise to the suspicion that the Stasi had influenced the revolutionary events, if not even partially brought them about. This is questionable, but it is a fact that the opposition groups were infiltrated by IMs. It seemed to many GDR citizens that there was no area of political or private life that was not controlled and influenced.

However, the Stasi was not at the core of the problems of this deformed society. Both the state and State Security were products of the SED. It had created the GDR and been in command of the Stasi (which people referred to as 'the firm of Listen and Look'). The public was, therefore, enormously suspicious, particularly in relation to the Stasi, less so in relation to the party. The whole Stasi experience weighed heavily on the new GDR, which was oriented towards reform.

Many new-style politicians from the newly born parties had to give up and withdraw, if there were any signs of 'cooperative activities' in connection with the Stasi that could not be disproved. The main person responsible for the petit bourgeois, small-minded and totalitarian surveillance state was the 'anti-fascist' Erich Mielke. Back in the days of the Weimar Republic on 9 August 1931, along with his friend Erich Wichert, he had shot the policemen Paul Anlauf and Franz Lenk in an ambush in Berlin in a retaliation attack against a hated police unit. Mielke then escaped to the USSR. He was not sentenced for this crime until 1993. As the successor of Ernst Wollweber, Mielke had been Minister for State Security in the GDR for over 30 years, since 1957. After Honecker, the 'second Erich' was one of the first leading representatives of the system to be dismissed by the Volkskammer.

In an embarrassing appearance on 13 November before the same body, after he had been requested by one of the members not to address all the members of the parliament as 'Comrades!', he replied: 'But I love them all – all people – but I do love them – I stick up for them.' Noisy protests resulted from these statements by the man who was co-responsible for the whole apparatus of repression and killing in the GDR, including the order to shoot on the inter-German border and the Wall. Probably he only meant to declare love for 'socialist people'.

The indignation of people against state terror, even if it was a pale shadow, could not be mitigated or stopped. On 15 January 1990 a crowd of protesters stormed the headquarters of the Stasi in Normannenstrasse in East Berlin. One reason for this was the wriggling by the Modrow government in relation to the disbandment of the Office for National Security (Nationale Sicherheit, Nasi), which had replaced the Ministry of State Security. The question of the storage and evaluation of the MfS files became the subject of continuing controversy. Civil rights activists occupied the MfS building to prevent their transfer to the Federal Archive in Koblenz. There were millions of personal files relating to GDR and West German citizens. It led to their storage in local branches of the Federal Archive on East German territory. One year after unification a Federal Authority for the Documents of the State Security Service of the GDR was set up in Berlin by means of separate 'Stasi Document legislation'. Pastor Joachim Gauck, an opponent of the SED regime and co-founder of the New Forum, became head of the authority, followed by Marianne Birthler and Roland Jahn.

The growing impatience of GDR citizens with the change in the system soon also manifested itself in relation to the Modrow government so that the Volkskammer elections had to be brought forward to 18 March 1990. The election campaign that soon got underway was dominated by West German parties and their representatives, who enjoyed greater popularity, stronger support and a broader appeal than the still largely unknown candidates of the newly founded parties in the GDR. The West German SPD soon found an ally in the Social Democratic German Party in the GDR (Sozialdemokratische Deutsche Partei, SDP), newly founded by representatives who appeared to be untainted.

The West German Christian Democrats initially had a more difficult time. An 'Alliance for Germany' (Allianz für Deutschland) was put together under instructions from the party headquarters in Bonn, which would consist of the Eastern-CDU, a former Bloc party, and the Democratic Social Union (DSU) created with the support of the Bavarian CSU, and the opposition group Democratic Change (Demokratischer Aufbruch, DA). The FDP supported a liberal alliance. They were all agreed on the direction of the GDR towards an ecologically oriented social market economy and a unified Germany.

The bringing forward of the election date did not leave the new, still very young, parties and community groups in the GDR enough time to present their candidates and put forward their manifestoes. The 'Round Table' had rejected party-political support from the Federal Republic but the election campaign was in the end largely dominated by West German financiers, parties and politicians. Critical observers soon felt confirmed in their judgement of a coming 'sell-out' and a political dependence 'on the West'.

Against the predictions about the allegedly traditionally Social Democratic leaning regions of the former GDR (Saxony, Thuringia, Berlin), the CDU proved the clear winner with almost 41 per cent of the vote. In the common Alliance for Germany with the DSU (6.3 per cent) and the DA (0.9 per cent) it fell just short of an absolute majority. The SPD only got 21.9 per cent while the successor party to the SED, the PDS, achieved a remarkable 16.4 per cent. The Alliance of Free Democrats got 5.3 per cent while Alliance 90 disappointed its supporters with just 2.9 per cent. The turn-out was extremely high, amounting to 93 per cent. From the pie chart below it is clear that the Alliance for Germany, with 163 seats, was the winner of the elections. Clearly behind was the alliance between the SDP (GDR

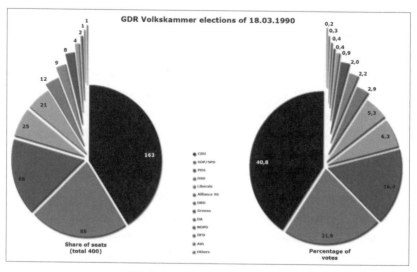

GDR Volkskammer elections of 18 March 1990.

Social Democrats) and the SPD. The share of the vote amounting to 66 seats on the part of the SED successor party, the PDS, was not inconsiderable. Here it is very clear that there was only a relative majority for the Alliance for Germany. There remained a strong counterweight: if the SDP, SPD and the PDS votes were added together it comes to 38.3 per cent, close to the Alliance's result. The victory for the supporters of unification in the still existing GDR was not so clear cut as it might seem. A relatively strong share remained on the left.

The result revealed two things: there was still a considerable number of former sympathizers with the state and the party of the GDR left. The majority of the citizens, however, had come out in favour of a speedy unification with the Federal Republic and of the Deutsche Mark. The date of 18 March did not just mean the end of the Modrow regime but also de facto the end of the GDR. The (Eastern-)CDU President Lothar de Maizière formed a coalition of the Alliance, the Liberals and the Social Democrats (i.e. a Grand Coalition), the form of government necessary for a unification of Germany, which the West Germans up to that point had used only once in their history (1966–9).

On 5 April 1990 the first freely elected Volkskammer of the GDR was constituted and elected Sabine Bergmann-Pohl (CDU) as its president, who thus became head of state as well. As its first act, the Volkskammer abolished the Council of State and on 12 April elected de Maizière as Minister-President.

Inter-German Currency Union and 'Two-Plus-Four Negotiations'

As early as April 1990 negotiations got underway on a currency union and an economic and social union between the Federal Republic and the GDR. The Federal government in Bonn immediately set about this task in association with the new, democratically legitimated, GDR government. On 18 May 1990 the State Treaty was signed in Bonn by the finance ministers of both German states. With effect from 1 July 1990, the DM became the sole, official means of payment in the GDR. Wages, salaries and pensions were converted at the rate of 1:1. Children's savings accounts up to 2,000 DM, adults' savings accounts up to 4,000 DM and senior citizens' up to 6,000 DM were likewise converted at 1:1. All further savings accounts as well as debts were converted at a rate of 2:1. For Waigel there was no alternative to a currency exchange of 1:1, 'unless we had made a new border' (i.e. as regards customs and currency policy), which according to Kohl's estimate of the situation would have meant 'quite a difficult psychological situation' for the people in the former GDR. The decision for an exchange rate of 1:1 or 2:1 was therefore a political one.

At the same time market economic conditions were introduced and an assimilation of the GDR social security system into that of the West German social insurance system. In the Bundestag and the Federal Council, the Bundesrat, the sitting members, including the majority of the SPD, agreed to the State Treaty despite criticism and reservations (unemployment, massive public debt). The SPD candidate for Chancellor, Oskar Lafontaine, had expressed considerable reservations as well as putting forward enormous objections, giving voice thereby to doubts as to the sense of a rapid unification. With his prognosis that was not unrealistic from the perspective of economics, however, he had no chance in the election campaign. People wanted a message of change and confidence. Kohl's evocation of a 'flourishing landscape' (which turned out later to be exaggerated optimism) was more attractive. The writer Günter Grass, who always sympathized with SPD chancellors and politicians, even went so far as to make an analogy between the historical fact of Auschwitz as a warning from history and the ruling out of German unity. Later it was revealed that the much respected Nobel Prize-winner for literature and bearer of the German guilty conscience had hidden his membership of the Waffen-ss from the public for decades: he only mentioned it in his novel-memoir *Peeling the Onion*, which appeared in 2006.

The rapidly unfolding move towards unification of the two German states awakened historical memories of the Second World War on the part of a number of neighbouring states about the period when, for example, Germany in 1940 had won control over half of Europe in a few weeks. Poland feared there would be no definitive recognition of their Western border. Their leadership reacted coolly and with reserve to the inter-German development, suspecting German revisionism, if not revanchism, since a rapid recognition of their Western border did not come about – how would it happen and by whom? The small states of Europe were worried, above all, that the old Federal Republic, already the leading economic power, after its imminent expansion by acquisition of the 'new Länder' to nearly 80 million inhabitants, would become not just an economically but also a politically dominant power in Europe. In Israel there were fears summoning up warning memories of the Holocaust.

The revolution in the GDR, which had passed off peacefully, as well as the end of the domination of the SED were, in general, welcomed by the European public, but the political establishment and national representatives reacted with anything but enthusiasm (i.e. with scepticism and hesitation, if not even denial).

The 'Iron Lady' Margaret Thatcher's reaction was somewhere between keeping her distance and rejection. She thought of Germany as the belated victor of the

Second World War and was of the view that Kohl had no feeling for the sensitivities of others in Europe. According to her, he seemed to have forgotten that the division of Germany was a result of the war that Germany had started. She was horrified to see the members of the Bundestag standing up after the opening of the Wall and singing 'Einigkeit und Recht und Freiheit' (the national anthem). Her fear of the Germans was atavistic, but it also had concrete motives: she was worried about the position of Gorbachev, whom she saw as 'her child', and about European security on account of the western border of Poland. The diplomats of the Foreign Office, who argued for an open and pragmatic approach, were frustrated by the positively antagonistic and emotional position adopted by the Prime Minister. Kohl simply referred to her as 'this woman'.

François Mitterrand's love for Germany and friendship with Kohl were likewise limited. In January 1990 the French President was still of the opinion that the sudden opportunity for unity had caused the Germans 'a sort of mental shock', turning them back into those 'bad Germans' that they once had been. He realized earlier than Thatcher, however, that it was the Soviet weakness that brought about the newly strengthened German position: 'La faiblesse soviétique fait la force des Allemands' (according to Ulrich Lappenküper).

The Italian Prime Minister, Giulio Andreotti, to Kohl's disappointment, showed anything but Christian Democrat solidarity. The Dutch Premier, Ruud Lubbers, spoke out openly against unity. Kohl took his revenge later when he came out against Lubbers's nomination as President of the EU Commission and successor to Jacques Delors (i.e. by supporting the Luxemburger Jacques Santer instead).

In the end all the critics had to come to terms with the facts created by the East Germans, which were irreversible. The fact that the Federal Republic was a member of NATO and of the EC, whereas the GDR belonged to the Warsaw Pact, made it inevitable that unification could not be achieved from the West German side single-handedly or even through a 'policy of strength' à la Adenauer, but only with both German states; and beyond that, in consultation and coordination with the victorious powers as well as later with bilateral treaties with the Czech Republic and Poland. The four victorious powers of the Second World War were called upon. They also pointed out their responsibility for 'Germany as a whole' as well as for Berlin. In February 1990 at the first mutual conference, in Ottawa, NATO and Warsaw Pact countries arranged 'Two-Plus-Four negotiations' between the two German governments and the four victorious powers and ensured the embedding of a united Germany within Europe, which would take place within the framework of a CSCE meeting. Differences existed over the question of the western border of

Poland and particularly in relation to any alliance to which a united Germany might belong. The GDR delegation returned to East Berlin with a disappointing impression and crestfallen. The West German government under Kohl no longer accepted the Modrow government as it had in December 1989. The Chancellor emphasized that Modrow was no longer an equal partner and that he would only enter into fundamental agreements with a democratically elected GDR government. The negotiations with the USSR were to prove difficult. It was anything but simple and straightforward to win their agreement to the geopolitical changes in Central Europe. Poland and Hungary were important precursors of the revolutionary events in the GDR. However significant and important Solidarność and Hungarian-reformed Communism had been, the GDR had been the trophy of victory for Moscow. In the Second World War the Red Army had defeated 'Hitler fascism'. The GDR was the most Western bastion of the socialist camp. It was something to hold on to – according to general feeling, and to the extremists in diplomatic circles and the party such as Valentin Falin and Igor Ligachev. In total contrast to Poland and Hungary, the German question was always of special significance for Moscow: extremely sensitive, fraught with emotion and also relevant to internal politics. Now the GDR was at issue. The once-victorious Russian troops were faced with withdrawal from Germany.

Gorbachev himself at first wanted neither to give up the GDR nor see its unification with the Federal Republic. The idea that he was seeking and promoting German unity is one of the historical myths believed by Germans in both East and West. For anyone who knows the history and the Realpolitik, it was clear that Moscow, with its agreement to German unity, would be giving up the GDR (i.e. the Western perimeter of its area of influence and its security zone). At first the Kremlin was not prepared to do this. In January 1990 Gorbachev reminded the German public of Stalin's note of 10 March 1952 in relation to the seriousness of the offer and proposed a neutral Germany as a whole (i.e. a reciprocal troop withdrawal of Soviet and Western Allied troop units from both German states). Modrow took up this idea and after his visit to Moscow in February put forward a bloc-free and neutral Germany as 'his idea'. For the US President who, unlike the State Department on the question of German unification, was the most open and positive amongst the Western powers, a significant condition for a rational stance on German unification soon became clear: Germany as a whole should remain in the Western Alliance (i.e. in NATO). George Bush senior and his Secretary of State, James Baker, with this precondition gave their full backing to Kohl – against this, Mitterrand and Thatcher had no chance with their opposition to a rapid German unification.

Moscow hemmed and hawed for a long time, particularly since giving up the GDR was out of the question from the point of view of security policy. Between the end of May and the start of July 1990 Gorbachev admittedly moved on and finally agreed to the right of self-determination for the Germans and their free choice of alliance, which meant de facto membership of NATO for Germany as a whole.

Completely geared towards Western financial aid, the USSR was also therefore politically dependent on loans and payments on the part of the Federal Republic and the USA. Thus, on the occasion of a meeting between President Gorbachev and Federal Chancellor Kohl on 16 July in the Caucasus the Soviet Union definitively gave its agreement to a unified Germany staying within NATO, which was received as something of a sensation.

Despite Moscow's concessions one could not call it a sell-out of Soviet interests, since Gorbachev managed to negotiate a few advantages: Russian troop units were to remain for the time being in East Germany (until 1994), the cost of repatriation and their accommodation in the Soviet Union was to be paid for and (non-German) NATO units were not to be deployed on the territory of the former GDR. In agreements made in Moscow Kohl, on his part, declared in relation to a unified Germany the renunciation of nuclear, biological and chemical weapons and committed himself to set a limit of West German forces at 370,000 men. As long as Soviet troops were on the territory of the former GDR, no NATO units would be stationed there. A total of 350,000 members of the Red Army were stationed on GDR soil, in Hungary and Czechoslovakia approximately 150,000, half a million soldiers in total. They would not be leaving for another four years and the Federal Republic would provide for their return home, accommodation and preparation for civilian life.

Gorbache's acquiescence with NATO membership of a united Germany on 16 July opened the way for the conclusion of the Two-Plus-Four talks on the status of a unified Germany. In the end, Kohl, Bush, Mitterand and Thatcher and the non-Soviet Warsaw Pact states were all for Germany's NATO membership. Again it was the question of limiting the German potential that led to this unholy alliance. A neutral Germany seemed unpredictable, a NATO Germany, on the other hand, controllable. The Atlantic Alliance provided a better guarantee of security than neutralization. Gorbachev realized that Germany had to remain a NATO member, not out of fear of the Soviet Union but on account of Germany's neighbours, who would feel safe if the united Germany were embedded in the Western alliance. This is the argument put forward even by the German negotiators to the Soviet head of state and the party. Again the Germans were, like Adenauer, prepared to 'limit themselves', which was remarkable. In the dramatic years of change, 1989–90, Kohl's strategy consisted chiefly in doing nothing that might weaken Gorbachev and rob him of power. The same strategy was also followed by Washington.

On 12 September 1990 in Moscow the foreign ministers of the four victorious powers, along with Genscher and de Maizière, signed the Sovereignty Treaty (Two-Plus-Four Treaty or the Treaty on the Final Settlement with Respect to Germany) for the newly unified state territory. The foreign ministers had already agreed to suspend the rights of the Four Powers on 3 October – even before the ratification of the treaty by the parliaments. The unified Germany was thereby now given its complete and unlimited sovereignty in fact. Linked to this was also the recognition that the older Federal Republic had only limited sovereignty: it was dependent on the Western powers. On 13 September the foreign ministers Genscher and Shevardnadze signed a German–Soviet treaty of partnership that was basically equivalent to a mutual non-aggression treaty or an implicit treaty of neutrality. Thus, Moscow got what it wanted, at least partly in respect to its traditional concern of Russian-German cooperation by means of a guaranteed policy of neutrality on the part of the united Germany which was neither discussed nor particularly taken note of by historians in the West.

The unification of the two German states that had rapidly got underway had also awakened fears in the Polish population: a strong unified Germany could seek a revision of the German–Polish border. These fears were nurtured by the view – repeatedly voiced publicly by West German politicians – that according to international law, until there was a peace treaty, Germany still consisted of the territory within the borders of 1937. The GDR, by the Görlitz Treaty of 1950 with the People's Republic of Poland, had already recognized the Oder-Neisse Line as an 'inviolable border of peace and friendship'. In the Warsaw Treaty in 1970 Poland and the Federal Republic had designated the Oder-Neisse Line as the Western border of Poland and had affirmed 'the inviolability of its existing border now and in the future'. The new Polish regime under Tadeusz Mazowiecki, for the first time a non-Communist one, expected a final declaration of a guarantee from Bonn and reacted with concern when Kohl repeatedly drew attention to the fact that the decision of a future all-German government could not be prejudiced as a result of the legal position. Kohl had considerable emotional reservations in relation to a (premature) recognition of the Oder-Neisse Line, which became clear on his visit to Moscow on 10 February 1990.

Warsaw wanted to secure participation in the Two-Plus-Four negotiations but it failed to have this wish granted by the Four Powers. As the international powers expected an unequivocal declaration from the Federal Republic, on 21 June 1991 both German parliaments, the Bundestag and the Volkskammer, declared in an identical resolution on the German-Polish border that 'the position of the border between the unified Germany and the Republic of Poland will be finally settled by a treaty under international law', which would be based on the treaties of 1950 and 1970. The German–Polish Treaty of Friendship and Good Neighbourliness was signed on 14 November 1990, through which it was possible to bring a definitive end to the resentment.

Kohl as the 'Chancellor of Unity' and His Contrasting Policy to that of Adenauer

The reservations on the part of the Western European partners about Kohl's Ten-Point-Plan, which aimed at unity in the medium and long term, were a bitter experience for the German Federal Chancellor. That the potential for trust in the Federal Republic on the part of Europe built up in the past decades would be so slight over the decisive question of the nation in 1989 was astonishing for the chancellor and at the same time sobering. His reaction was a highly sensitive and resentful one, particularly since the question of the achievement of German unification was not only the 'central concern', but a passionate affair for him. The right of the Germans to be reunited after being separated for decades was taken for granted by him and was not to be questioned by anyone or any state in the world.

The motto of Adenauer, who had been very much appreciated in the West, had been 'no experiments', which in the 1950s had led to the complete dead-end of his German policy as well as contributing to the construction of the Wall in Berlin and also to the hopelessness of the Germans in the East. It was left to Kohl and his Chancellorship 40 years later to help shape the political change and bring about a revolutionary renewal, started by the East German population, in which he adopted quite a different tone as regards policy on Germany than the founding Chancellor of the Federal Republic.

Born in the Palatinate, having studied history and being a politician oriented towards the history of the whole of Germany, married to a woman from Leipzig, he had a different perspective from that of Adenauer, the administrative lawyer characterized by Rhineland Catholicism and former 'Oberbürgermeister' of Cologne who harboured an aversion towards the 'Junkers east of the Elbe' and Prussia. In 1988, 'in a private capacity' and accompanied by his wife, Kohl visited the other part of Germany, with the strictest security arrangements and surveillance measures by the Stasi, and made contact with totally astonished GDR citizens who could hardly believe their eyes. Kohl was at that time convinced about the East Germans' feelings that they were part of the whole of Germany. Among other things he attended the Semperoper in Dresden and a soccer match between Dynamo, his favourite team, and Carl Zeiss Jena. When in late autumn 1989 a chance of unification was on offer, he self-confidently identified the matter, which was still unresolved, as his task and seized the initiative. In contrast to those, both at home and abroad, who had misgivings and who wanted to apply the brakes he developed an active German policy and acted in pursuit of the goal. By means of the Ten-Point-Plan he mastered the situation, acting partly independently, partly unilaterally, negotiated on German unity directly with the Soviet Union with US backing and in the end also accepted the inevitable Four-Power framework on the settlement of the German question.

Without a previous agreement with the USSR, a solution also to the German question in terms of 'unity in peace and freedom' was not possible. Adenauer's biased Western connection had excluded any Ostpolitik aimed at unity. Thus Kohl was acting and, without being aware of it, he walked into the Austrian pattern (i.e. the method of negotiation of the 'Austrian solution', as when Federal Chancellor Julius Raab with his coalition partner Adolf Schärf first travelled to Moscow in Spring 1955 in order to bring about a 'One Plus Four' solution with the four victorious powers of the Second World War and Austria in Vienna). For Germany in 1990 this became 'Two Plus Four'.

Adenauer had flatly rejected direct negotiation with the Soviet Union on German unity, participation by the GDR and also the Four Power framework and even sought to prevent them. In this regard Kohl's German policy was fundamentally different in approach and method to that of the political founding father of the FRG. It proved to be more liberating and productive for the Germans east of the Elbe. Not just that: whereas Adenauer's policy of Western integration was a renunciation of a united Europe, Kohl with his active policy of German unity also opened the door to a unification of the continent which just like Germany had been divided for decades. To put it another way, if the division of Germany was more or less the precondition of Adenauer's policy towards the formation of West European integration through the European Coal and Steel Community (1951–2) and the EEC (1957–8), then Kohl succeeded in carrying off a double trick through willingness to experiment, determination, readiness to take risks, toughness and audacity – qualities that Adenauer neither possessed nor was willing to develop in his German policy. Kohl not only pushed through the project of 'German unity' consistently as far as the unification of the whole state was concerned but he was able to combine the German national solution and the further development of European integration: the unification of Germany with the German currency union was linked to a considerable push forward of the European communities which subsequently developed into the European Union and the European currency union. By this policy Kohl set up a monument to himself. In 1998, during the Austrian presidency of the EU Council, the heads of state and of government decided to make him an 'honorary citizen of Europe', an honour that, up until then, had only been accorded to the Frenchman behind the European Coal and Steel Community, Jean Monnet. Kohl became the 'Chancellor of Unity', while Adenauer achieved the internal sovereignty of the Federal Republic and its integration with the West but became the Chancellor of the division, something that the historical accounts of the Federal Republic as a rule skim over or are silent about.

Legal Completion of Unification according to Article 23 of the 'Grundgesetz'

The Preamble of the 'Grundgesetz' emphasized in the last sentence the precept of unification. It reads: 'The entire German people is called upon to achieve, by free self-determination, the unity and freedom of Germany.' Legal and constitutional experts made it clear that German unity could only be achieved in two ways. According to Article 146 a new constitution would be worked out replacing the 'Grundgesetz', or Article 23 would come into effect, according to which other parts of Germany could join the jurisdiction of the 'Grundgesetz'. The decision not to have the unification of Germany unnecessarily delayed by constitutional lawyers won out. A pragmatic solution was found to be acceptable: the concept of a rapid unification in line with the thinking of the vast majority of the citizens in the GDR. Motivations concerning domestic and foreign policy were to be of prime importance in rapidly exploiting a unique opportunity.

The date of 3 October 1990 was to be decisive: on this day the 'Grundgesetz' came into force in the five newly established Länder. These were Brandenburg, Mecklenburg-Western Pomerania, Saxony, Saxony-Anhalt and Thuringia as well as East Berlin. The accession of the GDR to the Federal Republic at the same time made a series of changes to the 'Grundgesetz' necessary. A new formulation of the Preamble was required, after unity and freedom had been forced through by the East Germans. Article 23 was rescinded and the number of votes in the Bundesrat (Article 51) had to be changed. Article 146 was modified, offering the possibility of a new constitution in the future but not enforcing any obligation on this. The pragmatic solution hastened unification. The negotiations on the second State Treaty that would establish the conditions for the accession of the GDR to the Federal Republic were accepted as early as July and finalized on 31 August 1990 by the signing of the 'Treaty on Unification'. There was consensus between Kohl and de Maizière that this was the way to create the national unity sought for by the Germans, particularly in the East, more quickly than by the working out of a totally new constitution that, according to Article 146 GG, would have necessitated the calling of a referendum. In the event of such an alternative, numerous blockages and obstacles to unity would also have built up. In a chaotic session, the still existing Volkskammer of the GDR agreed the accession of the GDR to the Federal Republic on 3 October 1990.

On 31 August the leaders of the negotiations, the West German Minister of the Interior Wolfgang Schäuble and the State Secretary of the GDR Günther Krause, signed the so-called 'Treaty of Unification' in East Berlin. By this legally binding document, consisting of 45 articles and three comprehensive appendices, the 'Grundgesetz' was partly amended and thus came into effect in the former GDR on 3 October. It stated that Brandenburg, Mecklenburg-Western Pomerania, Saxony, Saxony-Anhalt and Thuringia would be new Länder of the Federal Republic from the same date. Berlin was established as the 'capital of Germany' – about which there would still be reservations and resistance in Bonn circles, as it was stated in the 'Treaty of Unification' that the question of the location of the parliament and the government would be decided after the achievement of German unity.

The question of abortion (Article 218 of the 'Grundgesetz') was still a subject of controversy. A new version of the Article had been passed in the Federal Republic in 1976 with the votes of the SPD and the FDP and provided for the legality of the termination of pregnancy under specific social and medical circumstances. The GDR had introduced a more liberal law on abortion in 1972. The 'Treaty of Unification' called for a harmonization of practice by 1992. Until that time the respective regulations were in force in the old and the new Federal Länder. The new version set out in the Bill for a Law on Abortion and Support for Families of 1992 provided for abortion within a fixed term with obligatory counselling. It was declared partly invalid by the Federal Constitutional Court following a resolution put forward by Bavaria and the majority of the CDU/CSU grouping. The court ruled that, although abortion was in principle illegal, it was permissible on medical grounds and it was also otherwise legal if it took place within twelve weeks and there had been counselling previously. An illegal termination should not be paid for by the health insurance system. In 1995 the Bundestag passed a new version of Article 218 along these lines.

The date of 3 October was declared the Day of German Unity, an official, legal and purely procedural date without any emotional association or significance attached to it. 17 June, which recalled the uprising by workers and the people in the GDR in 1953 and which had up until then been observed in the old Federal Republic as the Day of German Unity, was – somewhat mysteriously – dropped. The date of 9 November (the date of the Fall of the Wall) was not considered as a remembrance day, because the Hitler Putsch in Munich had also taken place on this day in 1923; it was also the anniversary of 'Reichskristallnacht' (night of broken glass) in 1938, when there had been attacks against Jews all over the Reich. The Central Council of Jews in the FRG objected to 9 November as a possible national holiday. Thus remained the sober and boringly official 3 October – probably quite consciously and intentionally, so as not to give rise to any nationalistic show of feeling.

Federal President von Weizsäcker declared on 3 October that unity was not forced upon anyone but was agreed peacefully. It was part of a historical process involving the whole of Europe, with the goal of freedom for its peoples and a new peaceful order for our continent. Weizsäcker went on: 'We wish to serve this goal. Our unity is dedicated to it. We now have a state that we ourselves no longer regard as provisional and whose identity and integrity is no longer questioned by our neighbours. On this present day the unified German nation takes up her recognized place in Europe.' The Federal President thus pronounced the end of the inter-German provisional situation. With the unification of Germany a natural state of affairs was achieved again. The partial state constructs of the Federal Republic of Germany and the GDR, even if they were recognized by the entire world, were anything but a normal state of affairs.

On 4 October 1990 the German Bundestag of the new Germany, enlarged by the 144 members delegated by the Volkskammer, met for its first session in the Reichstag in Berlin. National and external unity had to be followed up by a social and internal unity between East and West Germans. The GDR had been 'swallowed up'; the old Federal Republic had become a different place through the accession of the new Länder.

The loss of the Central and Eastern European trading area as well as the Russian market for goods accelerated the decline of the East German economy. The rapid introduction of the DM also made the export of their products more expensive. Added to this were the pressure of competition from the West German economy and a tendency to buy up goods. All these factors came together and forced the collapse of the economy of the former GDR. Massive aid from the Federal Republic followed, which was not without negative consequences for the mood and the relationship between the Germans in East and West.

Chancellor Kohl had already given the impression in the Bundestag election campaign in 1990 that the required support would be possible within the usual financial framework, which was not the case. In this way, he did not seize the opportunity to call upon all citizens and social groups in this historic moment to carry out an act of national solidarity. The necessary financial sacrifices on the part of the West Germans for their fellow countrymen and women were not exactly procured willingly, let alone enthusiastically. German 'Gemütlichkeit' (sociability) was in short supply when it came to paying for unification. The 'Ossis' (Easterners) felt dependent on the 'Wessis' (Westerners) and obliged to be grateful on account of the 'Solidaritätszuschlag' or solidarity surcharge (the 'Soli'), the additional tax levied throughout Germany to finance the economic recovery in the East. In addition to this, there were the activities of the so-called 'Treuhand' body in the ex-GDR, which contributed to a negative image of the economic consequences of unity.

8

The Consequences and Burdens of Unity: Transformation, Stagnation and the End of the Kohl Era, 1990–98

The First All-German Elections and the Price of Unity

The first all-German Bundestag election of 2 December 1990 brought a clear victory for the 'Chancellor of Unity' and his alliance of parties. The German national extreme right-wing Republikaner (Republicans) under the former TV journalist Franz Schönhuber were paradoxically unable to benefit from national unity and were not represented. The government coalition under Helmut Kohl, consisting of the CDU/CSU and the FDP, were also again able to decide the election on 16 October 1994, even though opinion polls beforehand had given the SPD candidate for Chancellor, Rudolf Scharping, a lead in the number of votes. The FDP coalition partner had not been able to get into any of the parliaments in the Länder elections in 1994. Scharping was not, however, to be a convincing candidate. Leadership discussions took place amongst the Social Democrats. Here, Oskar Lafontaine and Gerhard Schröder played an important role. The economic position of Germany and the crisis of the welfare state were central issues in the public confrontation between the parties. While the SPD and the trade unions emphasized the social element of the market economy, the FDP called for a purely liberal market economy freed from state influences. The CDU/CSU placed their arguments somewhere in-between. The West German 'Greens' were unsuccessful in the first all-German election in 1990. They fell foul of the 5 per cent threshold. Only in the new Federal Länder was the coalition of Alliance 90/the 'Greens', standing under different conditions, able to enter the new Bundestag with eight members. The 'Greens', who had joined together as a party in 1993 with Alliance 90, formed for the Volkskammer election in 1990, were from now on an established party. In the 1990s they were represented in the Länder governments. Alliance 90/the 'Greens' emerged from the Bundestag elections of 1994 as the third largest party with 7.3 per cent of the votes. Four years later they were to win 6.7 per cent and to form the Federal government along with the SPD.

The victories of the Christian Democrat–Liberal coalitions in the Bundestag elections of 1990 and 1994 secured Kohl a further eight years in government. However, the structural problems of the unified state (budget deficits, mass unemployment, integration of people with an immigrant background, backward technology, etc.) remained largely unresolved. The ability to deal with these problems was limited above all by the burdens of the social and economic consequences of German unity.

The long-term consequential damages of the German division and the price that had to be paid for this in the event of unification were not discussed in the Adenauer Era or by the succeeding West German governments, but were consistently swept under the carpet. This possibly also had its advantage, as since the material thinking of many Germans was bound up with the DM, German unity would probably otherwise never have been attempted or accepted. The unimaginable financial burdens of a unified Germany caused by the diverging and unbalanced orientations of the two social and economic systems, particularly the complex and difficult legacy of the 40-year SED dictatorship, initially went unnoticed in the euphoria of the unification in 1990.

It soon became clear that the transformation of the GDR economy, together with its housing, roads and waterways, and communication links, as well as the reorganization of public institutions in the health and social area, and above all dealing with the considerable environmental damage, presented the new Federal Republic with a heavy burden. These serious considerations were also ignored or underestimated by those who pointed to a new German danger for Europe and the world. From now on all Germans were called upon to take upon themselves communally the material burdens of the division for which the East–West opposition and German policy also bore a share of the responsibility. They would be enormous efforts on an unimaginable financial scale. Some of these were inadequate in the first years.

As early as May 1990 the new state and its Federal Länder agreed on a Fund for German Unity from which the new Länder would receive just under 161 billion DM in total up to 1994. Already after the founding of the currency, economic and social union it became clear that the previous economic support programmes would not be sufficient to deal with the production deficits and structural problems of the East German economy. A Joint Programme for Eastern Regeneration was set up in 1991 to co-ordinate all the aid measures, handing out nearly 25 billion DM in 1991–2 for East Germany to enable the modernization of local institutions such as hospitals, children's nurseries, churches, cultural institutions, schools and universities. Work-creation programmes were set up by means of wage subsidies. The focus of support was the improvement of the infrastructure for industry and technological plants, in order to encourage private investment. The aim was to reduce the obstacles to investment and narrow the gap in productivity of the ex-GDR economy as well as to deal with old environmental damage and prevent new problems.

As the need for finance arose again and again, a solidarity additional deduction was introduced in July 1991, initially for one year, in the form of a 7.5 per cent levy on income and company tax that had to be imposed again after 1995, in fact for an unlimited period.

The 'solidarity pact for the reasonable financing of German unity' put the financial sharing of burdens by the Länder on a new basis. Preference was given to all measures towards speedily setting up new productive and innovative medium-sized businesses. Material compensation for the damage caused by the nationalization of private property and wealth in the days of the GDR was also one of the commitments by Germans to dealing with the consequences of the SED dictatorship. It was also necessary to take on responsibility towards citizens who had suffered repression, persecution and imprisonment. A 'compensation fund' was set up to mitigate the suffering that such citizens had experienced.

In summary, unimaginable sums were raised for the financing of the new Federal Länder, for the renewal and modernization of their towns and localities, in the first half of the 1990s: the transfer of finance between 1991 and 1995 amounted to a gross sum of 812 billion DM. After deduction of tax and administration revenues, this left a net sum of 615 billion DM for the new Federal Länder. Over 50 per cent of this money came from the Federal government. The annual gross transfer came to more than 5 per cent of the West German GDP. Every second DM spent on investment for improvements in transport infrastructure went to the new Federal Länder. Despite this considerable transfer, this was still not enough for the modernization and reorganization of East Germany. Payment continued right into the twenty-first century.

Twenty years after German unification one could draw up a comprehensive balance sheet: if one puts all the social transfers since 1990 together and adds the total of the expenditure on the old debts of the GDR, the development of the infras-tructure and the financial compensation and subsidies, one arrives at a gross sum of approximately 2 trillion euros – a gigantic sum. With deductions for the return flows in the form of tax revenues to the Federal government from the East one is left with a net transfer of €1.6 trillion. The total was spread over public authorities, policy on the employment market and social policy, stimulation of the economy (including the activities of the 'Treuhand' body) and the development of the infrastructure. The sum corresponded approximately to the mountain of debt of the Federal government, the Länder and the local authorities.

Allocations in the case of privatization gradually came to an end, in the case of social security, by contrast, they increased. The West German population, to a large extent, accepted the necessary effort at reconstruction, even if further aid was required. While the net income in the new Federal Länder reached more than 80 per cent of the Western level in 1998, GNP per capita stagnated from the middle of the 1990s at around 61 per cent of the West German level. The economic process of catching up had come to a standstill. The number of unemployed in the East was twice as high as in the West. In 2001 the state and the Federal Länder agreed a Solidarity Pact No. 2, by which 306 billion DM would be invested into the East German Länder from 2005 for 15 years (i.e. until 2020). Then, the special payments for East Germany should have come to an end, but this did not happen.

The 'Treuhand' (Trust Agency): Whipping Boy and Scapegoat – Balance Sheet of a Unique Economic Transformation

Already agreed to by the reform government of the GDR, in 1990 the so-called 'Treuhand' body was given the task of winding up, privatizing and reorganizing the 'state-owned enterprises' (VEBS). In this, the largest shift of property and wealth in post-war German history, large trading, industrial and financial institutions would be sold to West German firms. This transfer was largely based on the unequal distribution of capital and power between East and West. The DM, introduced on 1 July 1990, mercilessly exposed the weaknesses of the GDR economy. The inability of the enterprises to pay wages in DM and to provide corresponding salaries was only temporarily compensated by subsidies from the state 'Treuhand' body.

The unbalanced nature of things increased unemployment, which could only be glossed over as 'part-time work' for the time being. The state finances of the GDR had to be supported by billions in loans from the West German budget. The 'Treuhand' was given a central political and economic role in directing the process of transforming the centralized state planned economy of the GDR into a capitalist market economy on the model of the Federal Republic. It acted on behalf of the Federal Republic as a key to the opening up and reorganization of the East German economy. Its remit had already been laid down by the GDR Volkskammer. Detlev Karsten Rohwedder, second President of the 'Treuhand' body, insisted: 'Rapid privatization, determined reorganization and a cautious winding-up of anything that can't be reorganized any more.'

The activities of the 'Treuhand' were made up of various phases: in 1990–91 it became the temporary owner of about 8,000 former 'combines' and state-owned enterprises. These were associations of state-owned enterprises with tens of thousands of industrial plants. By taking over more than 4,000 Socialist Agricultural Production Co-operatives (LPGs) and forestry enterprises, around 4.3 million hectares of land of agro-economic use and forests came into the possession of the 'Treuhand'. Assets finally taken over included units that had been for the use of the NVA, the Mfs, the SED and the FDGB. The area controlled by the 'Treuhand' at times covered more than half the territory of the GDR. There was neither a track record nor a clear idea as to the transformation of the conditions of ownership and a total political economy. Learning by doing and power play were the two guiding principles. Experience had to be built up and rules worked out. There were misfortunes and hiccups, particularly in the first phase. In the period of activity by the 'Treuhand' from 1991 to 1994, privatization in the restructuring of the economy of the former GDR had absolute priority. Time was of the essence.

Of approximately four million employees of the former state enterprises, about 50 per cent were catapulted onto the free market. About a fifth of them became unemployed. The rest found new jobs or became self-employed, were retrained or pensioned off. The painful consequences for those affected caused much indignation and anger directed at the 'Treuhand', which in both East and West became the 'whipping boy' and scapegoat for all the grievances and wrongs of German unity. This perception created a distraction from the real political difficulties and mistakes.

In the new Federal Länder there soon grew the suspicion that the 'Treuhand' had deliberately smashed the East German economy and 'flattened the lot' so as not to allow an alternative political system to the capitalist economic system to arise in the first place. Instead of reconstructing and developing, it was claimed that the 'Treuhand' had de-industrialized the country and thus structurally disadvantaged the new Federal Länder.

In the old Federal Republic the 'Treuhand' was often criticized for wasting West German resources and taxpayers' money on clapped-out firms that were ripe for the scrapheap. There were objections that the new Federal Länder had forgotten what hard work was during the period of socialism, which had provided them with everything they needed. Criticism from the Eastern side ignored the fact that there was hidden unemployment in the GDR, at times extending to around a quarter of the working population (industrial workers and office employees); sometimes this was the so-called 'unemployment at work', characterized by early 'knocking off' and 'shortage of material to work with'. Criticism from the Western side edited out the fact that the industries that had been subsidized for decades by the SED state and freed from international competition could hardly be integrated within Western markets overnight, and that their traditional sales markets within the states of the former COMECON and the USSR were removed. The COMECON was to be abolished and the Soviet Union imploded. Both of these things happened in 1991. These losses could not be made up for in a hurry. The necessary renewal of the production plants and the associated adaptations to modern practices required time and could not be carried out rapidly in just a few years following unification in order to keep up with the world market. It is a remarkable fact that, as a rule, despite increasing discontent and growing protests, development in the new Federal Länder took place without violence and peacefully.

After finishing its work, the other tasks of the 'Treuhand' were divided up among four smaller state institutions as successors. The balance sheet after four years of the 'Treuhand' was mixed. By the end of 1994, under Rohwedder and his successor Birgit Breuel, it had fulfilled its chief role. Approximately 14,500 concerns and parts of industries were sold. These were not sales of whole combines or state-owned enterprises after the pattern of the GDR. They were newly set up industrial units that had been put together on a smaller scale by means of decentralization of previously large complexes. About 850 business concerns went to foreign investors. Approximately 80 per cent of the businesses sold were acquired by medium-sized buyers. Just under 4,000 industrial units and companies were wound up and closed down. Over 4,000 medium-sized trading and craft businesses that had been nationalized since 1972 were returned to their legal owners, in other words they were re-privatized. The 'Treuhand' was able to net proceeds from privatizations of more than 70 billion DM. Undertaking of investments of over 200 billion DM and jobs for 1.5 million employees were achieved. The 'Treuhand' judged it to be a success that 15 per cent more jobs were able to be created than had originally been promised. In fact the sums invested were about 20 per cent more than the contractually agreed figure. The deficit for all the financial transfers not covered by income, such as settlements, investment aid, renovations, reorganizations, bridging payments and other support, amounted to around 270 billion DM by the end of the 'Treuhand's' activity. As we know, this did not come to the full contingent, but it was still a price that was to be paid for unity. For the citizens of the new Federal Republic this money was regarded as the price of unity, along with the financial transfers still to come; it was effective as investment in an unavoidable modernization of the economy of East Germany and the future viability of the whole of Germany.

The mass unemployment caused in the new Federal Länder, something that was unknown as a social condition in the previous GDR, darkened the mood in the East of Germany. Economic collapse led to a sobering experience. The euphoria over unity soon dissipated. Added to this was the bad economic situation in the West of Germany, where from the middle of the 1990s unemployment likewise increased, limiting the area for manoeuvre on the part of the state in respect to the 'construction of the East'.

A state-controlled planned economy could not be transformed into a capitalist market economy overnight, not to mention the habits and mentality of the GDR population that had grown up over decades. These psychological factors made it extremely difficult in the 1990s to win hearts and minds for unity.

The unity of the two partial states into a whole state had been achieved in 1990, but the process of Germans from the East and from the West merging to form one 'barrier-free' society would take much longer. Even if the Berlin Wall was soon to disappear, the Wall in people's minds could still not be eradicated for a long time. The 'Wessis' (West Germans) were often seen as 'Besserwessis' (West German know-it-alls). The 'Ossis' (East Germans), often the 'losers', were regarded in the West as profiteering from unity and as 'social parasites'. Should one be surprised?

The Federal Republic and the GDR looked upon one another in isolation and hostility for decades. In the West, people for a long time only heard and talked about the 'Zone' and the 'GDR' in quotation marks; in the East 'the Federal Republic' was referred to as the 'haven of fascism and capitalism' and 'the class enemy'. These patterns of thinking from the Cold War had become fixed in people's minds, so that the relations between people in East and West were fraught with loaded baggage and were out of sync. The West Germans looked back on the old Federal Republic positively and were not particularly interested in the conditions in the East of the country in the decades before 1989. The citizens of the GDR had a split relationship to the SED state. Externally they acted in conformity with the party, showed themselves to be loyal and came to terms with the conditions. They meanwhile compared their prospects and life-chances with those of the Federal Republic and were much better informed about what was going on 'in the West' via Western television than their Western compatriots were about the East.

The attempt to come to terms with the legacy of the Stasi exposed further differences between East and West. Indifference and complacency on the part of those unaffected in the old Federal Länder were matched by disappointment and bitterness on the part of the victims of the Stasi in the East. The debate about how to deal with the whole Stasi aftermath also acted as a distraction from the totalitarian character of the GDR as a whole and from the arbitrary nature of the SED domination and its supine Bloc parties.

Against this background feelings of nostalgia emerged, which is referred to as 'East nostalgia' ('ostalgie'), which went partly hand in hand with a whitewashing of the SED dictatorship (according to Hubertus Knabe). In the GDR there were admittedly a certain number of outlets for improvisation, imagination and creativity in everyday life as well as in artistic practice, which had to bow to taste, fashion and economic pressure after 1989–90, giving rise to a blurring of memories of the time when 'we did not have it so bad after all'.

From Provincial Town to Metropolis: Berlin Becomes the New Capital – Bonn Remains the Federal Administrative Centre

With the events of 3 October and the accession of the GDR to the Federal Republic, according to Article 22 of the 'Grundgesetz' Berlin now became the new capital of the new Federal Republic of Germany, after more than 40 years of the Bonn Republic. Berlin had of course been the capital of one of Germany's previous iterations, the German Reich founded by Bismarck in 1871.

As a result the events of 9 November 1989 Berlin had taken on a new dimension again after the historic events of 1918, 1933, 1938 and 1945: Budapest in 1956, Prague in 1968 and Gdansk in 1981 were no doubt pre-revolutionary experiences and important stages towards the cataclysmic changes of 1989. What makes the German capital special as a European *lieu de mémoire* is that its position on the front line of the Cold War made it a symbol not only of the division of Germany, but of the division of the whole continent. It was only from there that the German and European division could be overcome. Besides, it was the East German workers on 16 June and the broad masses of the population on 17 June 1953 who were the after protest rallies in the Czech town of Pilsen first behind the Iron Curtain to rehearse the uprising against a Communist regime put in place at Moscow's behest. Uprisings and unrest such as those in 1956, 1968 and 1981 only came later. The fact that, most symbolically, the 'Wende', the 'turning point' or 'change', in 1989 took place in the former capital of the German Reich, at the birth of a new Germany and a European Germany, underlines the historical dimension of that year and this place.

As a result of the Second World War and against the background of the Cold War, the division of the country and, as a consequence, the division also of Berlin took place – not without German involvement. As early as 1944/5 the Allies had decided on the separation into three, later four, sectors and a special legal situation, which was set up by the Four Power status. It was from there that the division of the spoils of war was organized. Instead of peace being organized from there, Berlin became a focal point of the Cold War. Independently, after the Berlin Blockade was lifted, the SED leadership declared the Soviet sector of the city to be the 'capital of the GDR'. The Federal Republic, newly founded on 23 May 1949, came out in an official declaration in favour of Berlin as capital, while Bonn became the seat of the Federal government and of the parliament as a 'provisional capital'. There, over the course of years and decades, governmental representatives had settled in and made themselves at home and witnessed the revolutionary changes in the East of Germany with surprise and wonder. Despite this official declaration the Western powers had never recognized Berlin as the capital of the Federal Republic. The important thing for them was the Four Power status just as Adenauer also approved this special situation. He knew about the SPD electorate there, fearing it on account of the narrow majority situation of his own government. At his insistence West Berlin would not be an issue in the election of members of the Bundestag. Up until unification, the Western part of the city was not officially part of the Federal Republic. Also in Bonn's 'Grundgesetz' there was no mention of the question of the capital.

For 40 years West Germany was called the 'Bonn Republik', after a town where the joke among foreign guests and diplomats was that it either rained or the railway barriers were closed. Bonn became a symbol of introspection and provinciality, a byword for the politically peaceful and unthreatening Rhineland-West German Republic. Most Germans in the 1980s accepted that what was provisional had become permanent. Thanks to the peaceful revolution in the GDR in 1989 and the unification of Germany set in motion by the East Germans, a heated, one could almost say a typically German, debate over which one was now to be the capital for the future began – Berlin as the place of the peaceful revolution and location in the European memory or Bonn as the town of the would-be 'provisional' capital.

The fact that the name Bonn stood not only for the second and seemingly successful German democracy but it had also become the location of a state with

'Leaving Bonn': the capital returns to Berlin in the summer of 1991, illustrated by
a First Day envelope.

political parties, could be seen from a different perspective. All across the party-
politicians were for the retention of Bonn as the seat of parliament and
government, habit and pride coming together here with narrow-mindedness and
provinciality. The town was said to have distinguished itself over 40 years and
gained great respect worldwide. Besides, the larger, reunified Germany was looked
on with concern by its neighbours, they said. Berlin as capital might encourage
fears that an economically and politically resurgent Germany would be associated
with the status of a great power and thus unpleasant memories would be reawak-
ened. The supporters of Berlin dismissed these fears as irrelevant. Bonn had always
been provisional up to the time of German unity. Berlin as capital would incorpo-
rate the new Federal Länder much more strongly into the new Federal Republic
than Bonn.

The Bundestag decided the question of the capital with a nominal vote after a
debate lasting several hours on 20 June 1991. A very narrow majority of 338 members
were for Berlin and 320 for Bonn. The losers still attempted to challenge the decision or even to postpone it, pointing in particular to the high cost of moving the
ministries. The Federal government under Kohl, however, stood firm, insisted on
the decision to move and started on the reconstruction of a government quarter in
the bend of the river Spree in Berlin. For financial reasons not all ministries were
to be given new buildings. The Foreign Ministry used the former building of the

CC of the SED. The former Reichstag building was converted for the Bundestag. Bonn became a Federal town and was given important political areas. Some ministries remained there, such as the Ministry for Families, Society and Agriculture and the Defence Ministry; some institutions stayed, such as the Federal Cartel Office, or were even transferred there, such as the Federal Audit Office. The Bonn area received compensation payments for the loss of the seat of parliament.

With the decision of the Bundestag, however, Berlin had not by any means become a city for all Germans. The grafting together was not totally successful. The decade-long division of the city was also reflected in how people behaved in the elections. The PDS, the successor party to the SED, was strongly represented in the Eastern part of the city; in the Western part of the city it was insignificant. It was also manifested in the failure of the unification of the Länder of Berlin and Brandenburg. Even in the days of the GDR it was the not unjustified concern of the people of Brandenburg that Berlin would profit at the expense of the surrounding Land. On 5 May 1996 they rejected a merger.

In summer 1999 the Bundestag and the Federal government moved from Bonn to Berlin. The Bundesrat reviewed its original decision to remain in Bonn and also moved. The Federal President had already moved his office there the year before in 1998. The quarter in the bend of the river Spree in Berlin around the Reichstag was mostly complete. The Reichstag building housing the Bundestag was covered over by a glass dome – an attraction for many visitors. Numerous views through glass panels give the parliament an open and transparent appearance. The former frontline city of the Cold War was experiencing a transformation into a global metropolis. As a tourist city, Berlin in 2003 held third position in Europe, attracting the most visitors after London and Paris.

Stagnation and Crisis in the Social and Welfare State

Since the 1990s the economic, financial and political conditions have worsened as regards the continuing existence of the social and welfare state of the Federal Republic. The enormous financial requirement of the 'construction of the East' following German unification, the burden of the social insurance system, the increasing unemployment – in the middle of the 1990s it had risen to four million people – and the resulting shortfall in tax considerably limited what was possible for the budget of the Federal government. In addition the German economy felt increasing pressure from global competition. Added to this was an ageing population, associated with a higher expenditure on pensions and an increased demand for healthcare services, as well as a decline in the working population required to satisfy these needs through their social contributions.

The population pyramid comparing 1 January 1990 and 31 December 2006 produces revealing findings. By superimposing both pyramids one can see how the age structure has gone up. The birth rate fell sharply and the number of elderly people increased considerably. It was a trend that was maintained and within 15 years it increased again. In addition, the Federal Republic had far more 80- and 90-year-olds. Life expectancy shot up enormously. Birth rates did not keep pace with this ageing development.

This development in the birth and death rates in the Federal Republic from the 1950s up into the era of Helmut Kohl at the end of the 1990s – relating to the territory of the old Federal Republic; the GDR is not yet included – is deliberately represented in diagrams as area segments and the rates are superimposed on one another, allowing one to see exactly in which years between 1970 and approximately 1990 there was a clear negative surplus (i.e. more people died than were born).

The debate about the 'reconstruction of the social state' was more fraught against this background, but also given the context of the economic position of Germany. It was linked to criticism from employers that the social welfare system was no longer financially viable and had to be privatized and reduced. The CDU/CSU-FDP coalition supported this view and attempted to direct legislation along those lines. The opposition and the trade unions, however, were against this. Cuts would not bring about a reduction in unemployment and the maintenance of economic production but would be a threat to social harmony and political stability. While the government went ahead with reductions in pension, sickness and unemployment insurance payments, in the new healthcare insurance established in 1995 the principle of its being financed 50 per cent by employees' contributions and 50 per cent by employers' contributions was abandoned. The employers' contribution was made up for by losing one public holiday. Fixed elements of the welfare state such as social security benefits came under pressure from powerful economic forces. Changes in the labour law followed. In relation to periods of notice the prevailing regulations for employees were worse and in the case of businesses with under ten employees the legal protection against dismissal was no longer in place.

The automobile industry had to take on board large losses in sales. Economic setbacks and the pressure of competition meant a reduction of car production of around 25 per cent. In 1993 car manufacturing reduced the number of employees by tens of thousands. Volkswagen chose another alternative. The firm proposed a four-day week or laying off 30,000 workers at the VW plants. In view of high unemployment the supporters of the four-day week saw, in the reduction of individual working time by 20 per cent and the resulting sharing-out of work, a means of securing jobs and the unemployed being taken on again. Here the question of wage compensation was controversial. While the employers demanded a relative cut in wages of around 20 per cent, the trade unions demanded full compensation for the wages. The union responsible for the VW workforce reacted positively to the proposal by the Volkswagen management, leading to an agreement on the four-day week from 1994: the working week provided for 28.8 hours and a loss of 10 per cent of one's annual income. VW saved around 2 billion DM in staff costs, and at the same time it was possible to prevent redundancies. Elsewhere comparable settlements were the exception. Periods of reduced working hours with reductions in wages were nevertheless introduced to a limited extent in several collective agreements as a means of securing jobs.

Right-wing and Left-wing Extremism: Attacks on Foreigners and RAF Attacks on the 'Establishment'

Following German unification in 1989–90 there was also an outbreak of violence against foreigners in the form of brutal attacks by right-wing extremists. At first this seemed to be a feature of the former GDR. Sociological studies pointed to the 'losers of unity', people uprooted from the highly controlled social system of the GDR and those without a political home and without future prospects due to mass unemployment, giving rise to discontent, despair and anger directed at foreigners. There was a manageable group of people belonging to minorities from former 'fraternal socialist states' such as Angola, Cuba, Mozambique and Vietnam, which had been brought in by the SED regime to be employed as cheap labour in the ex-GDR; they numbered approximately 80,000 people, about 0.5 per cent of the population. Because of the 'friendship between peoples' discredited by association with the SED, these people lived a life isolated from the GDR population. Foreigners were seen to be faceless, on the margins of society, cut off from integration.

After 1989–90 a campaign of violence against these 'foreigners' in a few towns in the new Federal Länder began. Violent and mindlessly aggressive types went on the rampage while people looked on in silence. These acts of violence caused by xenophobia were not just, however, limited to the new Federal Länder. Right-wing extremism was also sparked off in the old Federal Republic. There were repeated night-time arson attacks and assaults on asylum seekers' hostels and accommodation occupied by foreigners. Rowdy scenes lasting for days by fanatical and right-wing extremist youths outside hostels in Hoyerswerda in Saxony in 1991 or in Rostock-Lichtenhagen in August 1992 were not only a cause for shame but affected the image of the united Germany. The foreign media eagerly highlighted the terrible events. These horrible attacks made it all too easy to play on the image of the 'bad German'. The authorities added to this with their unfortunate response. The uncoordinated and hasty measure of moving the foreigners to other places did not help very much, particularly since those being attacked were only protected for the time being. These measures just added fuel to the fire of the extremists' attacks and demands. The outburst of violence in some cases got out of control and the authorities and police failed to deal with it. What was clear about this was the lack of sympathy and the limited amount of tolerance shown towards foreign fellow citizens. A low point was reached when there were arson attacks on housing occupied by foreigners in the towns of the old Federal Republic, in Mölln in November 1992 and in Solingen in May 1993, in which ten Turkish citizens, including five children, lost their lives.

Throughout the Federal Republic opposition to these malicious attacks and inhuman outbreaks of violence was organized to express the outrage and anger of the majority of the German population. Millions went onto the streets to show solidarity with the victims by means of large-scale demonstrations. Mass events in the form of candlelit parades underlined the determined rejection of xenophobia and extreme right-wing violence on the part of the overwhelming majority of the population and countered the image of the 'bad German'. Together with Federal President Weizsäcker they called on politicians to carry out a reform of the right to citizenship that did not come in until 1 January 2000. In the meantime there were repeated attacks and assaults, such as the arson attack on the synagogue in Lübeck in March 1994 or the desecration of the concentration camp memorial at Buchenwald in July 1994. Public interest faded for a while until a broader public movement against violence from the right formed once again following serious criminal acts. The definite stance of the overwhelming majority of the German population was also illustrated by the rejection of extreme right-wing parties who were shunned by the electorate in 1990 as well as 1994. Only in the Landtag elections in Baden-Württemberg were the 'Republikaner' (Republicans) able to repeat any success, gaining 9.1 per cent of the vote by 2001; the German People's Union ('Deutsche Volksunion', DVU) in Saxony-Anhalt nevertheless got 12.9 per cent in 1998.

In the united Germany, politically motivated violence not only originated with right-wing extremists. Despite a number of arrests and sentences, the danger from left-wing extremists was still not averted, as was shown by the RAF's assassination attempts on Karl-Heinz Beckurts, the manager of Siemens and his chauffeur, as on the highest official at the Foreign Office in Bonn, Gerold von Braunmühl, four years before unification in 1986.

The RAF, still in operation and with logistic capability, was not persuaded to give up their terrorism by the political changes in Germany in 1989/90. A few weeks after the fall of the Wall, a fatal attack was carried out on Alfred Herrhausen, the CEO of the Deutsche Bank and the most influential German business manager on 30 November 1989.

The RAF, following their anti-fascist and anti-capitalist logic, was also opposed to German unity, which they were bound to see as a defeat of their efforts. The head of the 'Treuhand' body, Detlev Karsten Rohwedder, fell victim to an assassination just seven months into his period of office on 1 April 1991. He was killed in his Düsseldorf flat by gunshots aimed through the window-panes. The RAF also claimed responsibility for this attack. It was years before this left-wing terrorist organization was wound up after the belated recognition of the hopelessness of its struggle against the 'system of the Federal Republic'.

Preparation for the Introduction of the 'Euro' and Stronger International Involvement: The Controversy over the Role of Germany in Europe and the World

The new role of the united Germany in Europe and the world was a continual subject of public debate in the years following unification. On the basis of the revolutionary events of the turbulent years 1989–91 (NATO, for one Germany, abolition of COMECON and the Warsaw Pact, collapse of the USSR) as well as the fact that the enlarged Germany with 82 million inhabitants was the most populous country in Europe after Russia, different conclusions were drawn: this new Federal Republic would pursue foreign policy and international commitments more strongly than before and at the same time also loosen its traditional and exclusive ties to its Western partners, particularly France and the USA. It would follow a more independent policy more in line with German interests and this would go for its relations to Eastern and South-Eastern European states, and for Russia as well. The opposing position was that the unification of Germany gave no cause for changing anything as regards its role up until now defined in terms of integration within the EU and NATO. On the one hand, this meant being the 'financial and economic powerhouse' within the framework of the EU and, on the other, maintaining military abstinence within NATO.

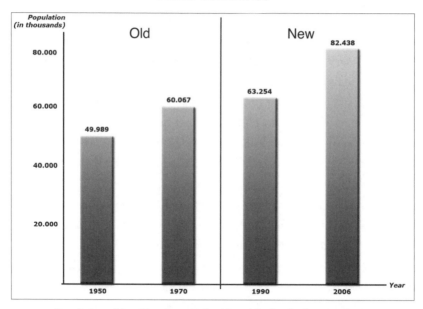

Population of the old and new Federal Republic (in absolute numbers).

If one looks at the development of the population in absolute numbers from the founding of the Federal Republic up to the first year of the Grand Coalition of Merkel/Steinmeier, it shows that it had about 50 million inhabitants one year after its foundation. The number increased to 80 million inhabitants by the time of unification. This population increase frightened many politicians in the neighbouring countries, while their people took it in a more relaxed fashion. The governments of Helmut Kohl and Hans-Dietrich Genscher, as well as those of Kohl and Foreign Minister Genscher's successor, Klaus Kinkel (FDP), were never tired of emphasizing that the new Federal Republic was also closely tied to the West and in particular remained committed to the policy of European integration. This, however, still had to be conceived on a new basis, which was to happen from the middle of the 1990s with the Organization for Security and Cooperation in Europe (OSCE).

After the collapse of the Communist regime the CSCE as the only all-European institution initially formed the framework for a new order in Europe, particularly since the EU up until then only consisted of Western and Southern European states. With the signing of the Paris Charter for a New Europe on 21 November 1990 by the 35 CSCE states, the Cold War was officially declared to be over. The Charter for a New Europe, which was signed by all the members of NATO and of the Warsaw Pact, promised a peaceful future for Europe: never again should there be war and hostility in Europe. Within the framework of the Helsinki conference of 1992, the CSCE was reorganized as an institution of the United Nations with a new institutional structure.

The building of political trust and laying the basis for further economic development of the dynamics of integration – despite the burdens of German unity – remained essential continuities of German policy on Europe and integration in the 1990s. Federal Chancellor Kohl declared to US Secretary of State James Baker 'that the development of Germany has to be built into a European architecture'. In order to diminish unease on the part of EU partners at Germany's economic potential, Kohl was all the more prepared to share in the formation, agreed to before 1989, of an economic and monetary union, even against German national interests (above all, in relation to the retention of the DM).

The German economic and monetary union between the Federal Republic and the GDR, in force from 1 July 1990 and making possible a short-term customs union between the EU and the GDR, marked the start of the economic unification of Germany. It was also to be a pointer in the direction of European unity. This admittedly had first to be pursued in the Western part of the continent before one could think of an 'enlargement to the East'.

There were unavoidable warning signs: the financial consequences of German unity, the collapse of the rouble zone, the stalling of economic dynamism in Europe, the recession in the EU states becoming more and more noticeable with the growth in unemployment, turbulence in the European monetary system caused by large-scale international speculation (such as by the stock-market guru George Soros, which caused the pound sterling and the Italian lira to leave the EMS), along with the failure of a European security policy in face of the crises and wars in the Balkans, all illustrated the 'lack of action', an expression frequently used by Chancellor Kohl.

Against this background the treaty negotiated at Maastricht for a European Union (EU) was a common effort to pool all the resources. On 9 and 10 December 1991 the EC heads of state and government, at this summit conference, agreed on a treaty to create an economic, monetary and political union by upgrading the Western European Union (WEU) and the creation of a Common Foreign and Security Policy (CFSP) as well as an intensification of cooperation in internal and judicial policy, which was signed on 7 February 1992. Compared with previous efforts at integration, the treaty was to be a great success. Above all, it acted as an enhanced framework for integration and a control mechanism on the new Germany. The 'treaty on the foundation of the European Union' provided for citizenship of the European Union as well as a strengthening of the European

Parliament. It was given greater rights to be involved in the appointment of the Commission and in European legislation. Under Commission President Jacques Delors the deepening of the community took priority over new accessions. The debates within states over the Maastricht Union Treaty therefore also produced a sharp polarization of public opinion. With the exception of Ireland, whose population voted 68.7 per cent for the new union in June 1992, intense controversy had developed on the continent. The ratification process therefore extended over the years 1992–3. France decided in favour on 20 September 1992 with only a narrow majority of 51.05 per cent and Denmark only on the second go on 18 May 1993 with 56.8 per cent. The Maastricht decision of the German Constitutional Court in Karlsruhe was a milestone in German legal history when a decision was made on its compatibility with the 'Grundgesetz' and a green light was given for the Union Treaty. Thus the Treaty was able to come finally into effect on 1 November 1993.

The internal market had already come into effect following the guideline of the Single European Act (1987) on 1 January 1993. The free movement of people, goods, services and capital within the community was thus guaranteed. The EU with a 25 per cent share of world imports (in 1991, without internal trade) was the largest market in the world and was on the point of also drawing more closely together politically. This was made easier still by the planned single currency, the Euro, the introduction and the procedural stages of which had already been predetermined by Maastricht and the EU treaty of Amsterdam in 1997 (which came into effect in 1999). Kohl came out decidedly in favour of the European currency and thus, clearly against the will of the Germans, for giving up the DM. He acted in line with representative democracy and was decisively responsible for this political decision making it possible for the necessary preparations for this historic step to be made in the 1990s. Maastricht provided for a precise timetable for the introduction of the European single currency. Common criteria to be fulfilled for participation in the monetary union were worked out to ensure the necessary adjustment and conformity of the economies participating in the Euro. The achievement or maintenance of these 'convergence criteria' (low inflation rate, continuing price stability, no excessive budget deficit, two years without variations in the exchange rate in the EMS, limitation on public debt) for the creation of an Economic and Monetary Union (EMU) necessitated budget adjustments, economies in expenditure and tax increases, not just in Germany but in all European states.

In 1998 the European Central Bank was founded in Frankfurt am Main on the model of the Deutsche Bundesbank. It was to function as an independent institution, ensuring price stability. As a result of the monetary union aimed for, there emerged a tension between a common monetary policy and national economic policy, since exchange rates as a means of guaranteeing different economic developments were now a thing of the past. The greater transparency of the price mechanism would stimulate competition, which would work to the benefit of consumers due to falling prices, as well as boosting innovation on the part of business and strengthening the position of the Euro countries in the global market. The export-led economy of the states belonging to the Eurozone would profit from the lower exchange rate of the euro against the US dollar; above all, however, the opportunity of international speculators such as George Soros to play European currencies off against one another would be taken away. These were the motivations behind the introduction of the euro.

On 1 January 1999 the DM was no longer an autonomous currency. The introduction of the Euro as money in account signalled its demise. The citizens of the Federal Republic were still able to pay with DM up to 31 December 2001. The exchange of banknotes and coins from 1 January 2002 represented the final end for this currency that had been so important for Germans and their self-image. In its place there was now the euro, a common and supranational currency of twelve EU countries with the exception of Denmark, Great Britain and Sweden, who stuck to their own national currencies.

Going back to the 1990s, with the large-scale achievement of the internal market (1 January 1993), the main requirement for a deepening of integration had been fulfilled and the way ahead was free for new negotiations: on 1 January 1995 Sweden, Austria and Finland joined the newly formed EU. The 'community of fifteen' was a reality while the Norwegian population again rejected joining. Within the new EU, Germany became the main partner in the dialogue with Central, Eastern and South-Eastern European states who, likewise, aimed to become EU members soon.

Following the decision at the successor conference in Budapest on 5–6 December 1994, from 1 January 1995 the CSCE was renamed the Organization for Security and Cooperation in Europe (OSCE) and enlarged. It now included 53 member states in Europe, Central Asia and North America. Its main aim was to prevent conflict and deal with crises. How far Germany would be involved in international crisis management, however, was still undecided.

Already shortly after German unification the Gulf War of 1991 against Saddam Hussein after his invasion of Kuwait led to renewed debates, in which modifications of the positions in place hitherto were revealed. In view of the threat to Israel from Iraq, a military involvement of Germany on the side of the coalition led by the USA was requested. This remained at the level of logistical support, however, because of the absence of military aid at the same time as a massive German financial contribution followed to what the USA spent on the war. Military engagement outside of the territory of NATO, which was at that time still conceived of as a defence alliance, continued to be highly controversial in the Federal Republic. The deployment of the Bundeswehr in Somalia and in the context of air surveillance in Bosnia were examined by the Federal Constitutional Court in Karlsruhe and declared legal on the basis of the carrying out of democratic political responsibilities (i.e. a decision of the Bundestag in accordance with the constitution). In respect to the question of the participation of the Bundeswehr in a peacekeeping force, the Implementation Force (IFOR), in Bosnia-Herzegovina, there was a greater readiness on the part of the government coalition with its large majority in the Bundestag. German foreign policy remained closely coordinated with EU and NATO members. The Bundeswehr, reduced from around 500,000 to 340,000 soldiers, was to be engaged in the context of the United Nations or other alliance partners on a temporary basis and was to be targeted at peacekeeping.

Fundamental Changes: The First All-German President and the Politically Relevant Role of the Federal Constitutional Court

In the light of the difficult situation as regards the labour market and economic policy in the Federal Republic in the 1990s, the problem of the increasing immigration of people and families from other countries led to a modification of the 'Grundgesetz' of 1949, considered up until this time to be sancrosanct. After heated public debates a serious change to the law on asylum was introduced in 1993, to be essentially confirmed three years later by the Federal Constitutional Court. This involved a limitation and a stemming of the continually growing tide of asylum seekers. While in the year before unification there were just over 100,000 asylum seekers, the figure in 1992 amounted to well over 400,000. The right of asylum for political refugees remained sacrosanct. What was new was that people from so-called politically 'safe third countries' or countries of origin without the threat of political persecution were no longer able to claim asylum. Key to this was the supposition that political persecution could not be presumed in such cases. The change in legislation had become necessary as cases of abuse in relation to asylum applications were increasing. Added to this was the difficult situation of the labour market but also a greater challenge to the achievement of a multicultural society, which was coming in for increasing criticism. In addition there arose questions of limits and

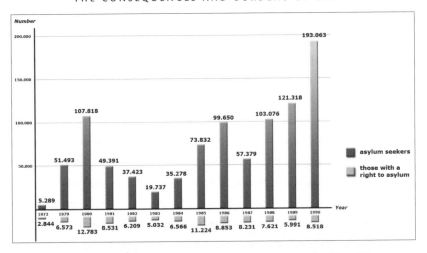

Asylum seekers and those with a right to asylum in the Federal Republic
of Germany between 1972 and 1990.

practicality in relation to the integration of foreign nationals and their families both
with respect to the readiness of the immigrants to integrate and also the ability of
German society to integrate them.

In the case of asylum seekers and those with the right to asylum in the Federal
Republic between 1972 and 1990, including German reunification, one can make out
very marked variations in the illustration above. Jumps to over 100,000 in 1980, to
just under 100,000 in 1986, over 100,000 again in 1988 and 120,000 in 1989 can be
explained in terms of refugee movements from overseas, but also the migration of
people of German origin from abroad (from the Baltic states, Russia, Hungary and
Romania). A strong trend is recorded in 1990 in the context of German unification
with approximately 200,000 people in which case one can distinguish between
those with a right to asylum and those seeking it. At the bottom those with a right
to asylum are listed, clearly making up a smaller number than the asylum seekers. A
stagnation is recorded in the number of those with a right to asylum, which bears
no relation to the number of immigrants. It is unclear whether those with a right to
asylum were actually given asylum or whether their applications were rejected.

Further amendments to the law followed in the wake of the changing social
values: in 1994 the Bundestag passed supplementary legislation aimed at the
promotion of true equality of men and women as well as a ban on discrimination
against disabled people. An additional aim of the state was to ensure the 'protection
of the natural environment', as well as giving local authorities their own responsibility for finance. Added to this was also the shift in responsibilities between the
state and the Federal Länder. The Federal government was given the responsibility

for legislation in the areas of gene technology, reproductive medicine and organ transplantation. The fact that the changes in the constitution were also becoming a matter of public debate, in which elements of direct democracy were seen as worth introducing (e.g. plebiscite and referendum) was also significant for the status quo of German representative democracy. They did not get the necessary two-thirds majority in the constitutional commission responsible. It therefore remained the case that no referendums were allowed in the Federal Republic over fundamental and vital questions involving the policy of the state such as the intro-duction of the Euro or the EU treaties of Maastricht or Amsterdam. The Treaty of Amsterdam provided for further steps towards integration, including a right of veto on the part of the European Parliament whenever the Council decided by a majority. This made it possible for co-operation in the areas of justice and internal policy to be included in the EU Treaty and laid the basis for a unified right of asylum. The ability of the EU to deal with foreign policy was extended and a common defence system envisaged.

The first President of the united Germany was the CDU/CSU candidate, Roman Herzog, who received more votes than the fellow SPD candidate and Minister-President of North Rhine-Westphalia, Johannes Rau. As a qualified lawyer, he was professor of Constitutional Law and Politics at the Hochschule for Administrative Sciences in Speyer, a state secretary under Kohl, when he was still Minister-President of Rhineland-Palatinate, as well as President of the Federal Constitutional Court. In his accession speech on 1 July 1994 Herzog promised to continue the policy of his predecessor Weizsäcker. This statement was combined with a clear denial of Germany's going its own way in Europe and the world as well as a rejec-tion of a relativization of German responsibility for the wrongs committed by the Nazis. These points were part of the broad consensus anyway in the political culture of the Federal Republic, but Herzog obviously felt the need to make them clear. He acted as a president whose words were unmistakeable. The introduction of an annual day of remembrance for the victims of National Socialism on 27 January was at his request. It was the date of the liberation of the last surviving inmates of Auschwitz concentration camp by the Red Army. With the annual 'Berlin speech', each time on a specific subject, he founded a tradition that his successor Rau continued. Herzog was only available for one period of office and retired from office in 1999.

Jutta Limbach, Senator for Justice in Berlin, was, in 1994, the first woman to become President of the Federal Constitutional Court. A qualified lawyer and professor at the Free University, Berlin, until her election to this office she was a judge and Deputy President of the Federal Constitutional Court. In the history of the Federal Republic, norm-checking procedures in particular by this institution were highly significant. In such a procedure the Federal Constitutional Court checks whether a norm (i.e. a law or a treaty) is also compatible with the 'Grundgesetz'. This also led to a tendency towards the politicization of constitutional justice. Many politically and socially relevant controversies have been brought before the Federal Constitutional Court and discussed in proceedings checking them from the point of view of constitutional law. The CDU/CSU opposition, for example, challenged the 'Grundlagen-Vertrag' with the GDR and this was rejected on the grounds that, the Court held, the German Reich still existed in law and that the GDR was therefore not a foreign country.

Norm-checking procedures were also instituted in relation to Article 218 (termination of pregnancy), the right of asylum, the right to conscientious objection to military service and the free expression of opinion. Conflicts between branches of the constitution (i.e. the Federal Government and the Länder or between the Länder) likewise have had to be resolved. This was the case for the challenges by the SPD and FDP groupings in the Bundestag in 1994 against the deployment of the Bundeswehr in humanitarian missions taking place outside of NATO territory such as in Somalia and Yugoslavia. Here a trend was established of pushing decisions unpopular with the public onto the Federal Constitutional Court, washing one's hands of the responsibility and relieving the Bundestag of the burden, in the vague hope that the relevant decisions would be better received by the population if they took the form of a legal ruling than if the Bundestag had made a decision. The way the Federal Constitutional Court dealt with the argument over the NATO deployment of Bundewehr soldiers 'out of area' is an example of this.

Bundestag Election, Victory of the SPD and the Greens, Kohl's Removal in 1998

After the triumph in the Landtag elections in Lower Saxony in spring 1998, Minister-President Gerhard Schröder of the SPD was unanimously proposed as the candidate for Chancellor. His considerable lead in the polls over the CDU/CSU-FDP coalition under Kohl and Kinkel, which was still in office, nevertheless steadily decreased the nearer it came to the election date, so that the result again appeared very uncertain. Already in 1994 the SPD had not been able to take advantage of a comparable lead under their candidate for Chancellor Rudolf Scharping and Kohl was able to achieve a victory.

On 27 September 1998 the SPD in the end won the election with 40.9 per cent of the votes. For the first time a government coalition was completely voted out by a Bundestag election. The CDU/CSU obtained only 35.1 per cent, their worst result since the founding of the Federal Republic. Only in the first Bundestag election in 1949 had they achieved a worse result. Alliance 90/the 'Greens', with 6.7 per cent, came out as the third largest party ahead of the FDP (6.2 per cent). The successor party to the SED, the Party of Democratic Socialism (Partei des Demokratischen Sozialismus, PDS), with 5.1 per cent just managed to overcome the 5 per cent hurdle and got into the Bundestag. The right-wing extremist parties again failed to get into parliament as they had done in 1990 and 1994.

The victory of the SPD, which was again the largest grouping in the Bundestag after 1972, can be explained above all by the desire of the electorate for a new chancellor. If it is not an exaggeration, it may be partly the case that in this context over the future government policy of the Federal Republic it was more a matter of voting Kohl out than voting Schröder in. A decisive reason for this election result was the widespread desire of the population for a change. Kohl had pushed through his renewed candidature against the chairman of the grouping, Wolfgang Schäuble. The Germans wanted a new sort of politics. It was not clear which coalition would provide this change. The political climate was rather against a Red and Green coalition. A Grand Coalition led by the SPD was the general wish. Evidently the population had more hope and expectation of the SPD than of the CDU/CSU as regards reducing the high unemployment. In the judgement of the electors, the SPD were able to ensure a greater capacity to solve problems than the Christian Democrats. Schröder enjoyed growing support over his demand for social justice and innovation. With the slogan of the 'new centre', in contrast to the chairman of the SPD, Oskar Lafontaine, he successfully appealed to dissatisfied CDU supporters as well as open-minded younger voters and floating voters. After the SPD victory in the Bundestag election in 1998, Schröder brought to an end Kohl's 16-year chancellorship and formed a coalition with Alliance 90/the 'Greens'.

The Bundestag election ended not just with a total defeat for Kohl. Angela Merkel's share of the first votes dropped by 11 per cent to 37.3 per cent. Wolfgang Schäuble, Kohl's 'eternal crown prince', had repeatedly raised the 'question about the Chancellor' since 1996–7 (i.e. the question of who should stand as the candidate for Chancellor in the Bundestag election). He had not been able to win out against Kohl, the 'eternal Chancellor'. Even before the decision on the candidate, Schäuble had hinted at criticism over Kohl's candidature. After his defeat, Schäuble was elected as the new chairman of the Federal party. At his suggestion, Merkel became the General Secretary of the CDU, one of the most important positions within their new role as the opposition party. Kohl was elected honorary chairman, with a seat in the party presidium and the executive committee of the Federal party.

The end of the Kohl era was brought about by a number of things, mostly to do with domestic policy and within the party. As the 'Chancellor of unity' he could point to a large number of achievements. After two successfully fought elections (1990, 1994), admittedly, this bonus was used up. The euphoria of the policy of the German unification of 1989–90 had also rapidly faded. The aftermath and consequences of unity were far more painful than had been envisaged.

The massive financial burdens for the 'construction of the East' and the associated material costs were blamed on Kohl in retrospect and he was accused of a misjudgement of the situation and an underestimate of the true economic scale of unification. The burdens of German unification for Germans in both East and West were more painful than had originally been envisaged, overshadowing the events of 1989–90 and the associated achievements in German policy on the part of Kohl. Managing the crisis of the aftermath and dealing with the enormous financial and economic challenges of German unification pushed strongly into the background the need for a redirection of the economic policy of the Federal Republic towards an innovative and future-oriented economy based on information and technology. This area was considerably neglected in the second half of the Kohl era (1990–98).

Added to this were the growing insoluble social and economic problems of the Federal Republic. The reduction of unemployment was a great concern. The Christian Democrat–Liberal government failed in dealing with this – the number of those out of work continued to rise in the second half of the 1990s from 1.8 to 3 million people.

The unemployment figures in the Federal Republic between 1970 and 1997 show a clear trend for the old Federal territory. From just under 150,000 people out of work at the start of the 1970s there followed a dramatic rise in 1980 to 900,000. The number doubled and against the background of German unification reached nearly 2 million and that only included those registered as unemployed. The real figure was even higher. The number of those registered as unemployed then rose to over 3 million by the end of the Kohl era. Unemployment rates were not given. In 1970 this was 0.7 per cent, in 1980 3.8 per cent, in 1990 7.2 per cent and in 1997 11 per cent. The years of the Economic Miracle accordingly did not have such a deep and long-lasting effect as is often thought. Things were already starting to go downhill economically in the 1970s. After 1990 the unemployment figures went up considerably, making the economic backwardness of the new Federal Länder painfully obvious. The absolute numbers thus would increase by another 1.5 to 2 million, resulting in migration (i.e. people moving from the new Federal Länder into the old ones).

Looking at economic growth from 1982 (the year of the so-called conservative 'change') to 1997 and the percentage changes in GDP it becomes clear that between 1983 and 1992 increasing growth was able to be achieved (i.e. more than 2 per cent; in 1990 there was even economic growth of 5.7 per cent). In 1993 a short dip into recession is noticeable, leading to negative values. The year 1992, with the collapse of the European Monetary System, the withdrawal of the pound sterling and of the Italian lira from the EMS, was a turning point. The DM had to come to the aid and provide support, but also the consequences and burdens of German unification had a serious effect. Germans had not participated in the second Gulf War, which the alliance partners had called for. In addition, Bonn had to make enormous payments for its non-participation in 1991–2.

Radical renewal of the health, social security and economic systems was lacking. The 'bottleneck in reform' in the Kohl era was regrettable, particularly the lack of the necessary shift in the wake of globalization to a more modern and competitive social and organizational policy. German academics and intellectuals preferred to go abroad. Industries and businesses moved their production abroad. Kohl's policy in Germany was therefore less along the lines of a 'reorientation and continuity' (as Andreas Rödder argues), more a matter of the 'status quo and stagnation'. It was rather a blocking mechanism than a reorganization. The 'change' was not successful as regards social policy. Unemployment remained a permanent theme. Within the party, confidence in and commitment to his person plummeted. No-one from his close political circle dared even to suggest the slightest criticism of him. Kohl gave the impression in the last years of his government's policy of being more focused on policy towards the formation of the European Union and being increasingly detached. The desire for the required changes in his own country increasingly passed him by. He was not open to a change of course in time or an early departure from the political stage. Kohl had not encouraged any likely successor. His relation to possible crown princes such as Schäuble became more difficult. Kohl left no doubt about his candidature at the head of the party for the Bundestag election of 1998. He was totally confident of being re-elected and underestimated the change of political climate in the meantime and the changed mood in the country. He was portrayed as a dinosaur on the SPD election posters, summing up the feelings of the voters. To elect Schröder it was enough not to want Kohl any more.

He had lost the power to be effective and carry conviction in the last years of being in office as Federal Chancellor. Within the party no-one was able to challenge his position of almost unlimited power, let alone topple him. The electors had the last word in the end and contributed to his removal by their votes. After the election defeat Kohl also resigned from the chairmanship of the CDU.

Kohl was not just the longest serving Federal Chancellor (1982–98) but also one of the most influential political personalities in the history of the Federal Republic, which he, along with Konrad Adenauer (1949–63), decisively shaped, above all by the achievement of German unification. Kohl was no intellectual, but a pragmatist. As a result of his simple manner and, frankly, at times crude way of expressing himself he was not always taken seriously; indeed, he was underestimated by his opponents (Helmut Schmidt of the SPD or Franz Josef Strauß of the CSU). His strengths consisted in 'sitting problems out', doggedness and determination. His flexible and open attitude to the German question led to a rapid solution for the unification. He accepted the economic difficulties as part of the bargain. In his German policy he was primarily concerned with people, above all those in the East of the country, for whose suffering and fate he had a lot of sympathy, unlike Adenauer. On the European stage Kohl was a valued and recognized politician who contributed to the reputation of the Federal Republic.

9

The 'Red–Green' Coalition as a Half-way Experiment, 1998–2005

The Main Characters: Gerhard Schröder and Joschka Fischer

After the election success of the SPD in the Bundestag election of 1998, on 27 October 1998 Gerhard Schröder was elected by the Bundestag with 351 of the 666 votes cast, making him the seventh head of government of the Federal Republic. He was the first chancellor who made the oath without swearing by any religion. The son of a war widow, Schröder grew up in poor circumstances. He went to a *Volksschule*, did a commercial apprenticeship and, following evening classes where he did the equivalent to A-levels as a mature student, he studied law. He practised as a lawyer from 1978 until 1990, in the process defending amongst others the RAF terrorist Horst Mahler. From 1963 he was a member of the SPD, later, Federal chairman of the Young Socialists (1978–80), also a member of the Bundestag (1980–86), and then chairman of the SPD local branch in Hanover from 1983 to 1993, member of the Landtag of Lower Saxony, chairman of the SPD grouping and member of the party executive committee from 1986 as well as of the SPD presidium from 1989. Schröder immediately made a name for himself in the party. From 1990 to 1998, as Minister-President, he governed a Red–Green coalition and following that a solely SPD government. Schröder was the first Social Democratic Chancellor initially against the will of his own party. After an unsuccessful attempt to gain hold of the Federal party executive committee and the candidature for Chancellor in 1993, at a special party conference five years later he managed to push forward the idea of a 'policy of the New Centre' and became the candidate for Chancellor. This new direction was controversial up to the last minute and set off conflicts within the party.

After the start of his period of office, Schröder was supposed to have said in February 1999 that, in order to govern in Germany, he only needed *Bild* – the most popular tabloid newspaper in Germany – along with *Bild am Sonntag* and television.

Like no other of his predecessors he was concerned about how he was portrayed in the media and thus achieved great popularity. He always came way ahead of his party in opinion polls. Soon after his election as Federal Chancellor, Schröder – somewhat unusually for an SPD politician – made a show of luxury in the form of expensive suits and cigars. He appeared in the popular TV series *Wetten dass?* ('Do you want to bet?'). His decidedly close relationship with the business world also brought him the nickname 'the bosses' comrade'. While his charisma attracted people to him, critics complained that Schröder only used clichés like 'the New Centre' or a 'softly softly' policy and expressions like 'Basta!' ('that'll do!') in order to boost his image with the public.

Joschka (actually Joseph Martin) Fischer was born the third child of a butcher. His parents were Germans from Hungary who had to leave their home at Budakeszi near Budapest in 1946 and emigrate to Germany. The Christian name used by Fischer came from Jóska, a diminutive of the Hungarian József. Fischer practised various professions. He had been, for example, a casual labourer, taxi driver and a book-salesman. In 1967 he became involved in the student movement and the extra-parliamentary opposition (APO). Later he admitted to the acts of violence he had committed, but did not distance himself from them. In 1976 he had been arrested, after a demonstration following the death of Ulrike Meinhof, in connection with an attack on the police using Molotov cocktails in which two policemen were seriously wounded, but he only remained in custody for two days. Before joining the party in 1982, along with Daniel Cohn-Bendit and others, he had also founded the Workers' Circle for Realpolitik in Frankfurt am Main, which worked on 'realpolitical' positions for the 'Greens'. Elected to the Bundestag in 1983, he belonged to the first grouping of the 'Greens' in the Bundestag, acting as parliamentary spokesman for them. Fischer made a name for himself somewhat controversially and was excluded from a session for insulting the Deputy President of the Bundestag, Richard Stücklen.

He held office twice as Environment Minister of Hesse. In 1985 the formation of the first Red–Green coalition came about in Hesse under Minister-President Holger Börner. Fischer became Minister of State for Environment and Energy. The oath-taking ceremony caused a stir as he appeared dressed in a jacket, jeans and sports shoes, giving rise to the nickname 'Minister of Trainers'. In 1987 he was dismissed from office because the 'Greens' had given an ultimatum on the continuation of the coalition based on the cancellation of planning permission for a nuclear plant. In 1991 there was a reformation of the Red–Green coalition under Minister-President Hans Eichel (SPD). Fischer again became Environment Minister.

At the same time he was the deputy of the Minister-President and Minister of State for Federal Affairs. In 1994 he resigned from all his positions in Hesse and after the return of the 'Greens' to the Bundestag became along with Kerstin Müller spokesman for the grouping of Alliance 90/the 'Greens' in the Bundestag.

In 1995 Fischer set off heated criticism within the party because he broke with the pacifist tendency of the 'Greens' and supported the military measures for the protection of the UN safe havens in Bosnia-Herzegovina. Orientation towards the market economy turned the 'Greens' under Fischer into a 'realpolitical' party. Critics increasingly accused him of supporting positions as Foreign Minister that he had rejected before the Red–Green takeover of government.

In the course of the formation of the Red–Green government agreement was reached on three ministerial posts for the 'Greens'. The most important departments were occupied by Fischer as Foreign Minister and deputy Chancellor, Otto Schily (SPD, formerly with the 'Greens') as Minister of the Interior and Rudolf Scharping (SPD) as Defence Minister. The chairman of the SPD, Oskar Lafontaine, took over the Finance Ministry enlarged to include the functions of the Economics Ministry.

Schröder's 'New Centre', Lafontaine's Resignation and Losses by the 'Greens'

Schröder's slogan, the 'New Centre', by which his claim to government was legitimated, was synonymous with a new political and economic programme designed to serve classical Social Democratic needs (i.e. union-led as well as new modern societal interests). The idea was based on the view that the SPD would only achieve government majorities if it was successful in appealing not just to traditional working-class sections of the population, but also to young, socially mobile voters, or rather non-voters, professionals and those employed within the service sector who could be identified with the new left-wing-oriented centre. In the election campaign the slogan 'New Centre' was used. By this Schröder proclaimed full employment even though this goal had not been achievable since the 1970s. Taking as a model the British Labour politician Tony Blair, who reformed his party and achieved impressive election successes in 1997 and 2001, Schröder and the SPD attempted to follow on and open up a 'third way', forming the basis for the so-called 'Schröder-Blair paper' of 1999. In terms of the economy the course of the 'New Centre' involved an orientation towards a liberal market economy, a ratcheting up of employment policy at the expense of a redistribution, improvement of the context for economic growth and the creation of a new stimulus for education and training. Increased self-reliance was promoted along with a reduction of welfare and care by the state, which would lessen the differences with the economic and social programme of the CDU/CSU. Schröder targeted a policy of the 'New Centre' primarily at the area of finance and pensions, immediately giving rise to conflicts with Finance Minister, Lafontaine. The government policy was initially unconvincing, particularly since the argument between the Federal Chancellor and Party chairman, Lafontaine, in the wake of discontent with the way the party was going, led to a string of serious losses by the SPD in the Landtag elections in 1999. Lafontaine was unwilling to go along with Schröder's neo-liberal policy directed towards supply. The power struggle between him and Schröder would damage their public images, particularly since Lafontaine (as party chairman since 1995) had welded the SPD together and had considerable share in the election victory. Following Lafontaine's surprise resignation from all of his political positions, Schröder also became party chairman of the SPD in April 1999. He was re-elected to this office in 2001 and 2003. The new Finance Minister was Hans Eichel, who had been voted out of office as the Minister-President of Hesse shortly before.

The 'Alliance Greens' also had problems adapting and transforming themselves. On becoming part of a Federal government for the first time, there was a heated debate between the 'fundamentalists' and the 'realists'. The change of profile to that of a liberal party resulted in conflicts with potential voters who were environmentally oriented. Dissatisfaction with the Red–Green government brought success to the CDU in the West and the PDS in the East in the Landtag elections of 1999.

New and Controversial Foreign Policy: The 'Kosovo War' of 1999 and the Peace Mission in Macedonia

The foreign policy of the Federal Republic changed fundamentally under the Red–Green coalition. The government argued that the position of Germany in the world had to be 'normalized'. Accordingly in past years it had not been normal. The Federal Republic had to 'bear responsibility' for security in the world.

The euphoria after the fall of the Wall in 1989 at first gave the impression that peace had broken out for ever in Europe. However, in 1991 bloody conflicts took place within the territory of Yugoslavia in view of the tendencies towards secession of the partial republics making up the country. The rivalries between Serbs, Slovenes, Croats and Bosnian Muslims blew up in a horrific manner, leading to 'ethnic cleansing'. International intervention prevented worse from happening. In the Dayton Agreement of 21 November 1995 (signed in Paris on 14 December 1995) the conflicts were resolved for the time being. The Serbian President Slobodan Milošević directed his attention at Kosovo where, already at the start of his period in office, he had expressed Serbian nationalism and prejudice against the Albanian majority. The autonomy of Kosovo, guaranteed under Tito within the framework of the Republic of Serbia, was abolished step by step in 1989–90, the use of the Albanian language prohibited and the Albanian majority subjected to acts of repression. The activities of the Serbian army and police units caused tens of thousands of Albanians to become refugees while the Albanian underground army, the UCK, carried out acts of violence.

The Western media and Western politics gave the impression that there was a threatening genocide that had to be averted. In February 1999 the Bundestag agreed to participation in military measures on the part of the Bundeswehr. An attempt at a diplomatic agreement at the Château of Rambouillet failed. Milošević seemed to be manoeuvring the Western alliance into a split and not to be prepared to give in. Following the failure of the efforts towards a settlement, NATO began the war on 24 March 1999 and carried out the threatened air raids against Yugoslavia. Federal Chancellor Schröder, Foreign Minister Fischer and Defence Minister Scharping hardly hesitated and were ready for a military confrontation. They justi-fied the war and thus the engagement of German soldiers. Above all, the enraged Fischer, without consulting his own party's base on his decision in favour of entry into the war, operated on the basis of the exaggerated argument that a new Auschwitz had to be prevented. On 7 April 1999 he said: 'I have not only been taught: never again war. I have also been taught: never again Auschwitz.' In answer to the question from the magazine *Newsweek* as to whether he saw a direct parallel between the events in Kosovo and the policy of the Nazis, he said: 'I see a parallel with that brutal Fascism. Evidently the 1930s have returned and we cannot accept that.' Using the subject of the Holocaust as an argument only partly silenced critics in Germany of the military action.

Fischer was sharply criticized for his campaign as German Foreign Minister for NATO intervention and called a 'war criminal' by supporters of the peace move-ment. The Higher Regional Court in Berlin nevertheless ruled that this term was illegal. In May 1999 at the conference of the Greens at Bielefeld, Fischer had a bag of red dye thrown at him in protest at NATO intervention and suffered a punctured eardrum in the process.

Despite the criticism the German public agreed with Germany carrying out the war against Serbia. It was called a 'humanitarian intervention', according to the current questionable reasoning, which sought to mask the breach in international law. Even supporters of the peace movement went along with the one-sided anti-Serb media campaign and the targeted propaganda on the part of NATO and its leading member states and were for the military action. The champions of pacifism lost their innocence in the process. Of course they gave reasons for their decision, which with hindsight seem rather insubstantial and problematic. What was important for the supporters of the war was to actually prevent Milošević from playing Western states off against one another and dividing NATO. The alliance used the controversy over Kosovo in the end to show their strength, to present themselves as an intervention force and thus to act against the alleged miscreant. In fact the problem could not be reduced to a simple black-and-white position but was much more complex.

The German Bundeswehr participated for the first time in an 'out of area' operation by NATO, which had changed from a defensive to an intervention alliance. According to the international principles of justice the engagement was illegal because there was no unanimous UN mandate and its charter was violated. The action represented a serious blow to prevailing international law because the charter of the United Nations of 1945 had prohibited forever the use of force between states (except in the case of defence, which was not the case here). China and Russia, among others, were therefore opposed to military intervention against Belgrade.

The consequences of the decision to go to war were unfortunate: the situation in Kosovo was not improved by the NATO bombardment, referred to euphemistically as 'air strikes', but became worse. Serbian units began systematically destroying villages and forcing their inhabitants to flee. The number of refugees from Kosovo further multiplied in the wake of the NATO attacks on Serbia. There was insufficient provision of humanitarian aid for tens of thousands of people. NATO's war, disguised as humanitarian intervention, aggravated the situation and led to an actual humanitarian catastrophe.

The bombardment lasted for weeks. On the basis of five conditions made by NATO to Serbia (immediate cessation of violence and evictions, withdrawal of all forces from Kosovo, agreement to an international peace mission, return of all refugees, and a start to political negotiations), a political solution was forced through by the involvement of Russia, leading to a cessation of hostilities on 9 June 1999.

Starting on 12 July 1999, American, European and Russian soldiers, acting as Kosovo Force (KFOR) peacekeeping troops, supervised the implementation of the agreements under the umbrella of the United Nations. The internationally composed force acted in the service of the UN and with the participation of German soldiers.

However much of the engagement in Kosovo was subsequently sanctioned by the UN, through the NATO deployment of its airforce Germany was part of a military operation that involved fighting for the first time since the Second World War. What was wrongly referred to as the 'Kosovo War' against Serbia was a test case for a NATO that was newly constituted as an intervention alliance, as well as for international acceptance and a test for further 'international engagements' on the part of the Federal Republic.

Milošević seemed to survive the war politically. In October 2000, however, protests against his policy built up and led to a shift of power. He was voted out and in 2001 he was handed over by the Serbian government to the International War Crimes Tribunal in The Hague where a trial was conducted against him that lasted a number of years. He died in custody on 11 March 2006.

In 2001 violent acts increased in Macedonia between the Slavic population and the Albanian minority. Following diplomatic pressure and mediation a peace agreement was reached in Skopje in the very same year. It led, along with demilitarization and a guarantee of freedom from prosecution for the UCK (except for war criminals), to a change in the Macedonian constitution extending the rights of minorities. The UCK and NATO agreed to a process of demobilization and disarming in which over 400 German Bundeswehr soldiers were involved. In line with the 'Grundgesetz' the Federal government had proposed a vote in the Bundestag on 29 August 2001 on the participation of the Bundeswehr in this engagement, which was limited to 30 days outside of the territory of the alliance. The decision led to a clear majority with the exception of the PDS (528 in favour and 40 against with ten abstentions). Sections of the SPD grouping, however, voted against it and for the first time the coalition had to get by without its own majority. The engagement of the Bundeswehr was no longer referred to by the Red–Green coalition as a 'peace enforcement' measure as in the case of Kosovo but as a measure towards the stabilizing of Macedonia within the framework of the EU.

The 'Kosovo War' clearly illustrated the shortcomings in the 'common' European foreign and security policy, and above all the strong military dependence of the EU on the USA, and resulted in the EU states reinforcing their capabilities in these areas. As a result of the conflict in Kosovo more emphasis was put on the prevention of civil conflict in order to avoid war as in 1999. The EU and the OSCE went in more for measures of pacification, democratization and aid. The Bundeswehr took over the military leadership of the NATO contingent for the protection of the OSCE observers.

Some of the most outstanding foreign policy activities in the period of the Red–Green coalition included the setting up of the International Court of Justice, the introduction of a national plan of action on human rights, the debt relief initiative started at the G7 summit in 1999 in Cologne and the worldwide build-up of development aid, with an agreement at the G8 in London on the increase of development aid by US$50 billion annually by 2010. Other foreign policy measures were the increase in funds for the fight against AIDS of US$20 million per year in 1998 to US$300 million per year in 2004, as well as the granting of US$500 million aid to the tsunami catastrophe of 2005.

Upsurge and Setback of the CDU Caused by the Party Donations Scandal

In the Federal Republic elections at the Länder level often resulted in losses for the parties in government, which were the winners at the Federal level. This continuity was confirmed in 1998–9. With the exception of Hesse and Bremen, the SPD lost strongly in the Saarland, Brandenburg, Thuringia, Saxony and Berlin. In 1999 Alliance 90/the 'Greens' lost without exception while the CDU strongly gained except in Saxony. In the Saarland and Thuringia they won the absolute majority of seats in the Landtag and in Saxony they were able to keep it, causing the Red–Green majority to be lost in the Bundesrat. The results are proof of the stability of the CDU vote as well as a readiness to vote differently according to the situation. In the elections for the European Parliament the SPD clearly lost out in June 1999 to the CDU/CSU. Kohl's level of popularity picked up again and even extended to members of the government. Public appearances mounted. He was given recognition as the honorary chairman of the CDU and reservations about his period in government declined. The party donations scandal, which became publicly known from November 1999 then, however, paralysed the CDU.

In December 1999 a Bundestag committee of enquiry was appointed to establish whether decisions by Kohl's government had been influenced by payments of money from interested parties. The way Kohl and the former treasurer, Walther Leisler Kiep, had conducted the financial affairs of the CDU looked questionable, paralysing the party and to some extent causing it to lose its credibility as an opposition. The situation was murky but, following investigations, a number of serious facts came to light.

The arms dealer Karl-Heinz Schreiber had handed over 1 million DM in cash to the former tax adviser to the CDU, Horst Weyrauch, in the presence of Leisler Kiep. Schreiber claimed that the money was intended for the CDU but it never reached it. The suspicion of bribery was in the air. The question was raised as to whether this money was a payment for the previously approved delivery of 'Fuchs reconnaissance armoured vehicles' to Saudi Arabia. Kohl admitted that he had personally accepted donations of about 2 million DM between 1993 and 1998 and had passed them on to the CDU. These amounts, however, did not appear in the party's accounts.

Kohl refused to divulge the names of the donors, claiming his 'word of honour'. In the wake of this scandal his government and party policy was revealed as the 'Kohl system', which consisted of a network of personal relationships and political connections. This is how the 'Bimbeskanzler' (the Chancellor of Cash) managed to secure his power and beat or eliminate any potential rivals (Kurt Biedenkopf, Heiner Geißler, Lothar Späth, Rita Süssmuth). The extent to which financial favours, not within the statutes of the party, were carried out for individual persons or organizations was an open question.

In the case of the sale of the refinery at Leuna (in the former GDR) to the French oil company, Elf Aquitaine, following German unification, according to investigations by French and Swiss public prosecutors, bribes in the millions had been paid to Germany. This was confirmed by the former CEO of the company, Alfred Sirven. The files of the Federal Criminal Bureau on the sale of the Leuna refinery had disappeared at the end of Kohl's government, becoming the subject of investigations by the Public Prosecutor.

The former treasurer of the CDU, Brigitte Baumeister, and the former chairman of the Federal party, Wolfgang Schäuble, produced contradictory versions of what had happened to a 100,000 DM donation by the arms dealer Schreiber, of which there was no sign in the party accounts. The secret Swiss bank accounts of the CDU going back to the 1960s in Zurich and money-laundering facilities in Vaduz (the Norfolk Foundation) formed an additional controversial consideration. In 1989 and 1992 Kohl is said to have handed over to the agent responsible for the treasury of the CDU 2–3 million DM for these accounts. These amounts also only appeared to some extent in the CDU accounts.

In 1983 the Frankfurt Metallbank paid around 21 million DM into three Swiss bank accounts at the request of the general secretary of the CDU in Hesse, Manfred Kanther. Disguised as 'Jewish legacies', the money came straight back to Hesse in order to help pay for the Landtag election campaign there in 1999.

The Public Prosecutor in Bonn instituted in the context of this affair a series of proceedings for the misappropriation of funds (e.g. the judicial enquiry against Kohl for breach of trust to the detriment of the CDU which resulted in a fine of 300,000 DM). A total of 84 judgements were handed out but only in eight cases were there any charges brought. Even now there has been no overall clarification of what happened. The party drew the consequences as regards its organization. Donations of more than 3,000 DM could only be made via domestic accounts. Kohl's reputation badly suffered as a result of these accusations and misdemeanours. The fame of the 'Chancellor of Unity' declined. The CDU donation scandal became the 'Kohl scandal'. Schäuble also lost out as regards office and reputation. The disaffection with Kohl was complete. The scandal opened up the way for the rise of Angela Merkel as the new party chair, clearly distancing herself from the 'Kohl system'.

Deregulation and Internationalization: Germany's Role in the Wake of Globalization and the Enlargement of the EU

The term 'globalization' only entered into public consciousness in the 1980s. At first glance it meant worldwide markets open to products, capital and services. This phenomenon was in no way reducible just to the economy but rather was a process on several levels. The concentration of finance capital and the emergence of regions of world trade indicated an economic dimension. The ubiquity of new media also draws attention to a communications-technological extension of mass culture onto a social dimension. Increasingly the characteristics of globalization include the international distribution of labour and interconnections, cooperation between states, cultural change and supranational environmental protection. Globalization was carried out by national states that, along with international organizations such as the European Union, promoted the reduction of customs duties and non-tariff obstacles to trade, deregulation within states, the reduction of bureaucracy, the liberalization of the flow of capital, the development of a dense information network, reduced transport costs and the homogenization of technical norms. This development was given a further boost by the collapse of the socialist system in the states of Central and Eastern Europe in 1989–90. Both of these were greeted prematurely as a triumph of capitalism and the market economy, added to which was the gradual opening up of the People's Republic of China in its economic and trading policy.

For the Federal Republic the consequences of globalization resulted in a number of pressures on internal and external policy. In the wake of the liberalization of various branches of the economy, Germany, whose economy and production are export-led in a country with few raw materials, was in competition with other aspiring economic powers such as Brazil, China and India. The high social standards and heavy taxes along with the laws regulating labour and relating to the environment came increasingly under critical scrutiny in internal political debates in the light of international competition. In the Kohl era there were only limited reactions to these challenges. The Red–Green coalition was therefore forced, through an active policy of reforms in the area of taxes and old-age provision, to create a framework of favourable conditions in relation to globalization. Part of the reform policy was also an increased tendency towards deregulation and privatization, going hand in hand with the reduction of jobs in the public services.

The development of employees in the public services, covering the period from the start of the 1990s up to 2006, shows two things: starting at 6.7 million in 1991 the number was reduced to 5 million in 2006. Over half a million civil servants were employed by the Federal government, over 2 million by the Länder, over 1 million in the area of local government and well over half a million indirectly related to public service. The fall between 1993–4 and 1995 was a result, among other things, of the separation of the Federal Postal Service. The tendency towards the reduction of civil service posts and the limitation on public positions is evident. The image of Germany changed, not just in internal affairs.

The new external position of the Federal Republic emerged from the overcoming of the division of Germany and thus also of the division of Europe. Because of its so-called full sovereignty, Germany became an equal partner in the structure of international relations. Expectations on the part of other states increased correspondingly. Germany was called upon more than ever, for example in relation to peacekeeping measures in South East Europe, but also in relation to military engagements enforcing peace (e.g. on behalf of NATO).

The conflict over Kosovo and the war against Yugoslavia also changed the attitude of the German government towards the 'enlargement eastwards' of the EU. Initially rather reserved, Germany saw a strategic priority of its European policy in a rapid enlargement of the EU as a means towards the stabilization of the political and economic situation in the neighbouring states of Central and Eastern Europe. Within the framework of the EU the Federal Republic, therefore, played an increasingly important role in the integration of the accession applicant countries in Central and Southeastern Europe. As a country committed to the United Nations Organization, Germany repeatedly stood up for human rights and the rights of minorities, aided in the alleviation of poverty, promoted a global policy on the environment by supporting the Kyoto Protocol, propagated the protection of natural resources and, under Foreign Minister Fischer, even offered to be a negotiating partner and mediator in the Middle East conflict. The policy of positive European integration, maintained under Schröder despite initial and occasionally voiced reservations, proved to be an element of continuity in foreign policy.

With strong German support the EU entered into accession negotiations with twelve applicant states, these being Bulgaria, Estonia, Malta, Latvia, Lithuania, Poland, the Czech Republic, Romania, Slovakia, Slovenia, Hungary and Cyprus. As the thirteenth country, Turkey was also given the status of an applicant state in 1999 due to particular support from the Red–Green coalition and in the light of good relations between Schröder and the Turkish Prime Minister Recep Tayyip Erdoğan.

Schröder was committed to the admission of Turkey into the EU, arguing, amongst other things, that Turkey occupied a peacekeeping position as a bridge between East and West. Critics saw in the possible EU entry of Turkey an overextension and overburdening of the European Union. The leader of the opposition, Angela Merkel, paid a three-day visit to Turkey in February 2004 and there committed herself to the model of a 'privileged partnership', in other words as an alternative to the full EU membership sought by the government. In a speech on 20 November 2004, speaking of the internal political situation of Germany as regards the problem of integrating the Muslim, largely Turkish population, she referred to the 'multicultural society' as a 'failure'. She brought up the question of the majority German culture and criticized Muslims' lack of readiness to integrate.

During Schröder's period in office, relations between Germany and Russia improved considerably, particularly since he personally got on well with President Vladimir Putin. Relations with France also improved as a result of the good personal relationship with the French President. Thus, Schröder was represented by Chirac at the EU summit in Brussels on 20 September 2003, allowing him to attend the voting on his reform proposals in the Bundestag. This was a gesture of trust unique in the history of the EU and highlighted the agreement between the political leadership of the two countries.

Fischer won recognition as Foreign Minister and was considered to be a likely candidate for the post of EU foreign minister planned in the Constitutional Treaty. He laid the basis for this in his speech 'From Association of States to Federation' at the Humboldt University in Berlin on 17 May 2000 in which he underlined the finality of European unification and called for European Federalism.

The enlargement of the EU by 100 million people in 2004–7 brought into being an economic area of 500 million inhabitants, representing remarkable growth in the context of global competition. The biggest enlargement in its history enabled preparations to be made, expressed for example in the Copenhagen Criteria in

1993: to be eligible for admission each applicant state had to guarantee democracy, the rule of constitutional law, stability of institutions, a market economy, human rights and the rights of minorities as well as the fulfilment of the common legal and political obligations ('*acquis communautaire*'). Membership was only possible with exceptions (opt-outs) and transition periods. To be capable of admitting these states, the EU itself also had to be prepared to reform its institutions, which was called for by the Germans in particular. In December 2000 the European Council in Nice attempted to create a basis for the institutional arrangements of the EU in view of the coming enlargement. The extension of majority voting and the new weighting of votes in the Council, the increase in parliamentary seats as well as the composition of the Commission played a role in this. Structural aid for the poorer, new EU members was necessary. The previous costly EU Agricultural Policy had to be reformed. In the area of the liberalization of the EU labour market the Federal Republic had to take countermeasures and argued for a time extension.

Tax and Pension Reform, Move Away from Nuclear Power, Erosion of Society and Conflict over Bio-technology

As early as November 1998 the Red–Green coalition agreed on an ecological tax reform with the intention of discouraging energy consumption. The legislation came into effect from 1 April 1999. The 'eco-tax' aimed to make mineral oil and the consumption of energy more expensive. The tax revenue was to be used to lower pension insurance contributions, reduce working costs and promote employment. The environmental benefit was questioned by critics because neither an efficient tax system nor a corresponding stimulus were in place for reducing emissions of damaging substances. However, fuel was made more expensive, although manufacturing was less affected than domestic households, as opponents argued. Energy intensive companies were also exempt from the taxation. Experts, however, advised against dropping the eco-tax.

Structural characteristics of domestic arrangements covering the years at the beginning of the 1950s up to the start of the Grand Coalition of the CDU/SPD (2005) show that, in the case of marriages, viewed in relation to the overall development, there was a general trend downwards, with occasional small rallies at the start of the 1980s and of the 1990s. Afterwards it went sharply downwards. Divorces, initially at a moderate level, clearly increased in the 1980s. The figure of 96,200 in 1980 doubled within 25 years. The world of stable values characterizing the post-war generation hardly existed any more. In this context the argument was also that, in particular, marriages that had started during the war were (more) durable, those of the generation after the war by contrast were (more) unstable, with partners tending to separate in search of advantages or a simpler or better life. It is also worth noting here that the average age on first marriage rose continuously from 28 for men and 25 for women on average by a good three years (by 2006). In other words, people spent longer thinking over whether they should marry at all. This aspect is also, to a certain extent, reflected in the higher divorce rates. If in many cases the marriage 'goes wrong', people think it over for longer and more carefully.

In the area of family policy there was therefore a lack of action. Particularly in the case of East Germany, a dramatic potential for social disintegration as regards marriage and the family was noticeable. After 2000 the share of births outside of marriage in the new Federal Länder continued to be around 50 per cent together with a sharp decline in births, going hand in hand with a drastically reduced number of marriages after 1989 and an increase in the age of people who did get married. New forms of cohabitation, the pressure of job mobility and the move of young people to the West and the generally insecure socio-economic circumstances contributed to this. The higher level of unemployment in the East relative to the West represented a greater problem than demographic change.

A further fundamental tax reform was passed by the Bundestag ('Federal Parliament') on 18 May and also on 14 July 2000 by the Bundesrat ('Federal Council') – in opposition to what the leaders of the Christian Democrats intended. By this the Red–Green coalition aimed for a perceptible easing of the burden on families and on businesses with the declared goal of creating new jobs and promoting economic growth, as well as a strengthening of the position of the Federal Republic in the global market and the maintenance of new investment. Between 2000 and 2005 the basic tax rate was lowered from 23 per cent to 15 per cent. The top tax rate was reduced at the same time from 51 to 41 per cent, which was a concession to the opposition, who nevertheless called for a further lowering to 35 per cent and had criticized discrimination against the middle classes. The Red–Green coalition fixed the degree of relief provided by the tax reform through tax concessions at 87 billion DM.

An extremely ambitious goal was to reach a balanced budget by 2006 without incurring any new debts. Furthermore, by 2020 the total debt of the Federal government, amounting in 2001 to about 1,450 billion, was to be repaid. Schröder and Eichel proved to have the required ability to assert themselves and leadership qualities over the use of the proceeds of the sale of UMTS licences, amounting to approximately 99 billion DM, by the Finance Minister for repaying the debts.

The pension reform passed in 2001 had the following features: despite the increasing age of society, contributions would be reduced to below 20 per cent by 2020, curbs would be put on this for adjustment and a state-subsidized private pension would compensate for the lower increases in the official pension. Allowances for normal and low earners would rise to 300 DM, and women would receive improved child benefits according to the number of children they had. Surviving dependants' pensions were reduced, allowing for an age limit. Pension contributions saved could be used to finance property before starting to claim the pension.

In energy policy the governments of the Federal Republic up until 1998 backed a mixture of gas, coal, nuclear and regenerative sources of energy. After the horrific reactor accident at Chernobyl in 1986 the SPD had called for a 'move away from nuclear energy' in the following ten years. The SPD and the 'Greens' were in agreement as government partners to end the use of nuclear power stations in consultation with those in control of them. The danger of accidents, radioactive fallout and the problem of the disposal of nuclear waste were the reasons given. On 14 June 2000 the Red–Green coalition and the energy suppliers agreed on an orderly end to the production of nuclear energy: the nuclear power stations would only continue to operate within certain time limits, the recycling of waste would only be permitted up until 1 July 2005, interim storage facilities would be set up at the sites of the nuclear power stations and transport of nuclear waste would be reduced by up to two-thirds. Construction of the disposal site at Gorleben was stopped. The signing of the agreement on 11 June 2001 laid the foundation for the change in the legislation on nuclear power. A total of 19 nuclear power stations were running on average for only another 13 years. Older nuclear power stations could be closed down earlier, more recent ones could still continue to function. The German nuclear waste for recycling in France and Great Britain could be stored for the time being at Gorleben.

The controversy between the Federal Chancellor and the Federal President over the use of scientific knowledge about human genes illustrated a difference of perspective. Schröder was in favour of non-ideological research pointing to the economic possibilities of bio-technology, while Johannes Rau voiced ethical concerns.

Compensation for Forced Labour and the Holocaust Memorial

As previously the new Federal Republic also showed a readiness to shoulder its responsibilities in relation to the history of the Third Reich and to provide material compensation for acts of injustice that had been carried out in the name of Germany during the Second World War. At the same time, however, there was also a very clear desire for a 'line to be drawn underneath it' (i.e. a definitive, political closure). The new Germany had, in the meantime, reached the twenty-first century, but the responsibility for the history of Nazi crimes would remain and the German state should take these seriously, also on a personal level.

In the so-called Third Reich after 1939, particularly from 1942, forced labour had been introduced to ensure production. In 1944 this involved over 7.5 million people. Working and living conditions were at times below average, at times inhumane. Approximately 1.7 million Polish and 2.8 million Russian forced labourers were employed, including prisoners of war and concentration camp inmates. They were forced to work for some world-famous firms and some medium-sized businesses, but mostly in agriculture. A third of the workforce was made up of forced labourers, as much as 50 per cent in armaments factories. For decades there was talk of them receiving compensation but not until the new Federal government took office in 1998 did negotiations get underway, concluding in 2001.

According to special legislation, those affected received compensation for the loss of freedom associated with forced labour. At the same time, claims against their former employers could not be brought. Individual German firms had been making payments voluntarily since the end of the 1980s. When proceedings for additional demands were instituted in the us courts, there was the threat of damage to the international reputation and also to the business of German firms. Negotiations immediately took place between the Federal Republic and the USA as well as with representatives of Israel and Eastern European states, leading to the formation in 1999 of a compensation fund of 10 billion DM. This was paid for half and half by business and the public purse. In the same year a number of large German businesses set up a foundation called Remembrance, Responsibility and the Future, receiving money from German firms, the distribution of which was, however, linked to a renunciation of any future claims for compensation.

After July 2000, when the legal basis was established, it was possible to sign a German-American treaty on the 'legal security' of German firms in the USA. On 31 May 2001 the Bundestag authorized the payment of compensation.

As the new capital, Berlin was not free of the historic associations around the decisions that had been made in this city during the Second World War, such as those taken at the Wannsee conference in 1942 at which the mass murder of European Jews had been decided and organized. In the 1990s a debate got underway about the creation of a symbol of remembrance: 'lest we forget', a 'sign of German mourning' for the victims of the Holocaust and the erection of a 'memorial to the murdered Jews of Europe'.

In late summer 2001, under the Red–Green coalition, work was started on this: 2,700 columns, each over 2 metres long and just under 1 metre thick, each one sloping at an angle of up to 2 degrees and sunk into the ground to various depths, giving the appearance of an undulating wave. They are positioned above an underground information centre, the 'House of Remembrance', containing a register with the names of the 4.4 million murdered Jews.

The Bundestag not only agreed to the controversial building in June 1999 but also declared the memorial to be a national memorial. Thus the Holocaust and its memory were pronounced part of the national identity of Germany, but also acted as an aid to self-reflection and self-discipline, something that was asserted at times by politicians but that was not completely shared by the German population.

The creator of this large work of art was the American architect Peter Eisenman. The installation, costing over 50 million euros, did not refer to other Nazi victims such as the Sinti and the Roma, homosexuals or the victims of political persecution. It was dedicated exclusively to Jews, which caused some objections. Critics saw in it the symbol of a uniquely German burden, but also a 'typically German' exaggerated expression of guilt, particularly in light of the fact that other European countries had collaborated with the Nazis and their citizens had aided and abetted the arrest and transportation of Jews to the extermination camps in Eastern Europe. Its supporters saw the memorial as an opportunity for a necessary and permanent reminder of the wrong done to the Jews.

The Argument about the Right to Citizenship – Germany as a Country of Immigration

The population of the Federal Republic from the 1960s consisted of an increasing number of foreigners. In 1960 there were around 700,000 foreigners. As a result of targeted recruitment from foreign and distant countries on the part of employers the number increased to roughly three million by 1970. In the following three decades the number more than doubled (i.e. to over seven million). By the time of the unification of Germany they made up 9 per cent of the resident population. This growth in the foreign population was not specific to Germany. A glance over the borders clearly showed that the number of immigrants in the last decades had risen sharply in other European countries as well as a result of the success of the European Community as regards growth and prosperity.

Data on foreigners within the territory of the Federal Republic covering the period from 1968 to 1998 (i.e. the 30 years between the first Grand Coalition and the end of the Helmut Kohl era), show that the foreign population grew from just under 2 to 7.5 million. It is worth noting that the number of these who were liable to pay social insurance contributions only doubled rather than quadrupled. If one considers the period from 1978 to 1998, there is a stagnation related to this. The arrival of foreigners on the labour market was not so strongly represented, or rather their integration was not yet so far advanced that foreigners could enjoy equal rights to Germans. Nevertheless, the data show that foreigners (i.e. fellow citizens with an 'immigrant background'), did not seek or find employment with a liability to pay social insurance contributions but instead occupied limited niches in the labour market.

In view of widespread fears that Germany's society was ageing and shrinking, with all the consequences this would have for the economy, the political debate led to a review of the significance of immigration. As a result of the 'enlargement of the EU to the East' taking place, a renewed increase in the number of foreign immigrants was expected. The controversy over the reform passed in 1999 of the right to citizenship, speeding up and simplifying the process of gaining citizenship, as well as dual nationality for children initially took place along ideological and party political lines. The initiative launched by Federal Chancellor Schröder to recruit foreign IT specialists gave impetus to the debate. The lack of computer experts brought about the issue of a 'Green Card' for such workers from abroad. In 2000–2001, the CDU, SPD and Alliance 90/the 'Greens' cooperated together on behalf of the Federal government to set up a commission that worked out the principles for an immigration policy, headed by the former Bundestag President Rita Süssmuth.

There was a consensus that, unlike the current practice, there was the need for an active and targeted policy of integration. During the rest of the debate it became clear that, along with human rights issues, German interests also had to be given greater consideration. A speeding-up of the asylum process was likewise welcomed along with specific contributions to integration such as a comprehensive system of language teaching. The Süssmuth commission set concrete immigration figures and the associated costs of integration. The 'Greens' opposed an overall limit on immigrants. In their view, there was no objectively measurable limit to the possibility of social integration. They called for the extension of the prevailing right to asylum also to victims of non-state and socially specific persecution. The SPD did not see a lack of immigrants until after 2010 and argued for keeping the basic right to grant asylum without serious modifications.

The Fight Against Terrorism Following 9/11 and the Vote of Confidence in the Bundestag

On 11 September 2001 the world changed when two US passenger aircraft crashed into the two 420-metre-high towers of the World Trade Center (WTC) in New York, another into the Pentagon in Washington and a fourth in a field in Pennsylvania. The images of these targeted, concerted acts of terrorism, the largest in human history, sent out a shockwave all over the world. Thousands of innocent civilians fell victim to the hitherto unimaginable attacks. Now for the first time, modern terrorist attacks had changed into post-modern mass terrorism and revealed its extremely ugly face. The origin of the terrorist attacks was taken to be Osama bin Laden's Al-Qaeda network. Seeing the WTC on fire and collapsing in clouds of smoke produced horror all over the world. The USA, for the first time in the history of NATO, declared a case for the alliance and thus also called upon the aid of their allies. US President George W. Bush called for a comprehensive alliance against terrorism.

The broad German public and the parties, except for the PDS, supported military retaliation taking place on the part of the USA. The Taliban regime in Afghanistan was publicly identified as harbouring Bin Laden's Al-Qaeda terrorists, but already immediately after the attacks, internally within the top circles around Bush, Iraq under the leadership of Saddam Hussein was identified as the chief future target of war preparations.

The terrorist attack on the USA was classed as an attack on the whole NATO alliance, The individual members had to decide what aid they would provide. Federal Chancellor Schröder, in the name of his government, assured his 'unlimited solidarity', which did not mean very much. Many considered this declaration went too far, others mere rhetoric. Supporters were of the view that Schröder intended to express international shock and the feelings of the Germans. Anyhow, the Bundeswehr (the Federal armed forces) sent AWACS airspace-surveillance planes to the USA to replace the US aircraft there that were ear-marked for engagement in Afghanistan. The Anglo-American air raids starting on 7 October 2001 and the engagement of special ground troops in Afghanistan two weeks later were supported by the majority of the German public – despite the regrettable loss of civilian lives. Of the parties only the PDS opposed military intervention. Foreign Minister Fischer repeatedly and insistently called for the overthrow of the Taliban in power there. Without this, help could not be delivered to the people. These radical Islamic forces had brought large parts of the country under their control since the middle of the 1990s. The Saudi Arabian multi-millionaire bin Laden was able to use Afghanistan as the base for his terrorist operations. China and Russia joined the 'alliance against terror' proclaimed by Bush.

When it came to the question of German military engagement, 'solidarity' was no longer so 'unlimited'. On 16 November 2001 the Bundestag agreed, by a narrow majority of the government parties but supported by the CDU/CSU and the FDP, to the provision of just under 4,000 Bundeswehr soldiers for the 'war on terror'. Schröder had linked the voting to a vote of confidence, so as to demonstrate the capability for action on the part of the Red–Green coalition, but this would not be certain. An engagement of the Bundeswehr against the Taliban in Afghanistan was rejected by sections of the government parties in the Bundestag. Even though the Federal Chancellor could be certain of the agreement of the opposition, he asked for a vote of confidence to gain a majority for himself in favour of participation by the Bundeswehr in the international operation Enduring Freedom.

Internal and external security now also had the highest priority in the Federal Republic since partly innocent, partly naive citizens of the Federal Republic, as in Max Frisch's play *Biedermann and the Fire Raisers*, had sheltered the 9/11 terrorists in their houses and apartments. The terrorists had pretended to be well-behaved foreign students, but had in fact led a double life, preparing terrorist attacks and at the same time carrying out their financial transactions. In the Federal Republic they found an ideal place as a haven of peace and seclusion that they made full use of, as was soon proved in the case of three of the suicide pilots. An intensification of the fight against terrorists now seemed to be required.

Following 9/11 the Federal Republic was transformed from a haven for 'sleepers' (people living unobtrusively, in fact terrorists living secluded in German towns) into a more strictly controlled surveillance state. The former defence lawyer chosen by the RAF terrorists who had gone over from the Greens to the SPD, Minister of the Interior Otto Schily worked out a string of measures for fighting terrorists: the privileging of religion was removed from the right of assembly, which had previously made the prosecution of fanatical fundamentalists and radical Muslims impossible. A new law in the criminal code allowed for the prosecution of foreign terrorists even if no branch of this organization existed in the Federal Republic, something the previous legislation had prevented. Now on the insistence of the 'Bundesverfassungsschutz' ('the Federal Office for the Protection of the Constitution'), banks had to provide information about all account transfers made by suspects. A few weeks after the attacks, over 200 accounts with a total of 8 million DM were blocked. In October/November 2001 the Red–Green coalition passed a second anti-terrorism package following the above mentioned 'security package' put forward by the Minister of the Interior a few days after the attacks.

The 'anti-terrorism package II', which went much further, contained measures that severely disturbed the original agreement within the Red–Green coalition on internal security. Objections were raised by the 'Greens', but also by the Federal Ministry of Justice. A 30-hour negotiation produced a series of amendments. The main aim was to apprehend terrorists living in the Federal Republic, or at least to prevent new fundamentalists from arriving in the country. Measures for recognition were introduced so as to be able to rapidly establish the identity of individuals. Official passports had to include biometric data, fingerprints, the shape of the hand or iris identification. Encoded details could be stored on computers. Schily's plans to extend the powers of the Federal Criminal Bureau (Bundeskriminalamt, BKA) were, in the end, watered down by the 'Greens'. Nevertheless, the BKA was able to gather information independently of the police forces of the Länder. The Federal Office for the Protection of the Constitution was able to demand information from banks, airlines and postal services about their customers and the Federal Intelligence Service was able to pursue investigations more intensively in its own country. Employees of institutions such as energy producers, hospitals or radio and TV organizations were subject to security checks. The new regulations were initially limited to five years. The pinpointing of suspects by means of computer analysis of data and telephone surveillance by the Federal Criminal Bureau, the Office for the Protection of the Constitution and the police began on 'sleepers' and Al-Qaeda cells. The interrogation without warning of suspect witnesses and the surveillance of financial transactions followed. Amongst the arrested were Arab business people, as well as illegal asylum seekers and students with connections to Al-Qaeda.

The Euro, Flood Disaster and Opposition to the Iraq War: The Close Victory of the Red–Greens in 2002

The monetary union already agreed upon in the 1990s had provided for a deepening of the policy of European integration. The euro, which Schröder, when he was Minister-President of Lower Saxony, had been dismissive about, calling it an 'abortion', replaced the Deutsche Mark as money in account in 1999 and from 1 January 2002 the new currency was in circulation. The task associated with the introduction of the Euro involving the sovereignty of monetary policy was heavily criticized in the Federal Republic. This move towards even stronger integration of Germany was due to political necessities and was for France an important compensation for the increased weight that Germany had gained through unification. As Federal Chancellor Schröder had more sympathy with this.

In the Bundestag elections on 22 September 2002 the SPD and the 'Greens' won a mandate by a narrow majority, and continued the coalition under Schröder. A few months before the election the CDU/CSU with Edmund Stoiber, together with the FDP under the leadership of Guido Westerwelle, had been clearly ahead of the Red–Green coalition. Two unforeseen factors were decisive for the election: a flood disaster in Eastern Germany, which brought about the sight of the Federal Chancellor in a helmet and rubber boots right at the scene along with other members of the government demonstrating their competence at crisis management. The decisive rejection of the Iraq War planned by the USA – unlike the CDU/CSU opposition under Merkel and Stoiber – played a further significant role. The German public very much appreciated both these stances. In addition to this was a third factor: above all Fischer was to thank for the fact that the 'Greens' had improved on their 1998 result from 1.9 per cent to 8.6 per cent, winning eight extra seats despite the reduced Bundestag and thus helping the government coalition to a close victory.

Schröder's election victory was therefore explained by his popularity in coming to the aid of those affected by the flooding of the river Elbe. More important, however, was his disapproving attitude to the Iraq War; the rival candidate, the Minister-President of Bavaria Edmund Stoiber, could not get non-participation accepted. In the run-up to the war Merkel had made known her sympathies towards the Iraq policy of the USA and the 'coalition of the willing'. As leader of the German opposition, she even criticized the foreign policy of the Federal government on American soil, bringing her a sharp rebuke from Berlin. The head of the SPD faction of the Bundestag, Müntefering, described Merkel's remarks as 'kowtowing to the US administration'. In the Shrove Tuesday Carnival procession in Cologne she was portrayed on a float as a doll crawling up George W. Bush's backside. In a speech to the Bundestag on 19 March 2003 Merkel declared the support by the Christian Democrats for the ultimatum to Saddam Hussein to be the 'last chance for peace' and called upon the government to do likewise in order 'really to prevent war in Iraq'. The clear 'No' on the part of the Federal government in office contrasted with Merkel's commitment to Bush's policy of confrontation that had been dubbed by her a 'backdrop of threat' (against Saddam Hussein). As soon became clear, this led to a horrendous war with counterproductive consequences for the Western alliance and the USA.

The government under Schröder and Fischer consistently opposed a possible attack on Iraq in the third Gulf War – even in the event of a possible UN resolution. The refusal to participate in the war was also not just based on the absence of a UN mandate but also on the lack of any connection to 9/11. Regarding the decision taken at the critical phase in the election campaign of 2002, critics insinuated that Schröder had used it as a strategy, particularly since the government alliance was behind the CDU/CSU and the FDP in the opinion polls. Schröder's anti-war policy was more than just domestic politics, however. He was concerned with a new and independent German foreign policy. As a result also of the lack of information from the partners in the NATO alliance, the position of the Federal Republic led to considerable tensions with the Bush administration and to criticism of the Federal Republic allegedly coming into its own. However, Berlin continued to honour its commitments to the transatlantic alliance, limiting itself to the personnel who permanently guaranteed air security in AWACS aircraft. Bundeswehr units were also of service, supplying information to the powers involved in the war in the forefront of the attack on Iraq and in the context of the airstrikes. Nevertheless, the Federal government stuck firmly to their anti-intervention position, supported by a clear majority of the German population, as reflected in a number of demonstrations.

Limits to Reform, New Elections and the End of the Red–Green Coalition in 2005

After his re-election as Federal Chancellor, Schröder went ahead with renewed plans for reform, admittedly also coming up against stiff resistance from his own party ranks. On 14 March 2003 he put forward the Agenda 2010 reform project, which would create economic growth and higher employment against the background of globalized competition. Industrial groups supported the programme as a step in the right direction, but for critics it proved to be an unpopular measure, particularly since it only appeared to guarantee the changes that were lacking. Apart from the CDU and the FDP, criticism also came from the trade unions and the left wing of the SPD. The talk was of cutbacks in the social services, but in the Bundestag debates criticism was only voiced by a minority.

Schröder was only able to push through the reform project with difficulty and sometimes more through veiled hints or open threats of resignation and was therefore also still able to hold the coalition together. He had made it his personal concern to halve unemployment. Plainly speaking, it went down in 1998 and 2002 but not at all by as much as had been predicted. To deflect personal criticism as a result of attempts at profound reform, Schröder set up advisory bodies and commissions working effectively in the public sphere. They were designed to secure a broad consensus of experts for the agreed reforms, which was in turn criticized on the grounds that this would undermine the mechanisms of democracy. Against this it was argued that these commissions would only be involved in the run-up to the introduction of bills and would have no influence on the legislation taking place according to the usual procedures. There were various commissions. In February 2002 the Red–Green coalition instituted the commission on the 'modern service industries in the labour market' chaired by the manager of vw, Peter Hartz, the Weizsäcker Commission on the future of the Bundeswehr, the Süssmuth Commission on the subject of immigration and the Rürup Commission on the future of the social sector. On 27 July 2005 another commission, chaired by Kurt Biedenkopf, was to start work on proposals for a reform of worker co-determination within companies. Schröder often preferred former CDU politicians to chair these commissions in order to gain as much agreement as possible amongst the opposition. The freedom of manoeuvre of the Red–Green coalition was already limited as a result of the voting majority of the CDU and the FDP in the Bundesrat. By means of concessions Schröder was at times able to gain the support for his government policy in the Bundesrat of individual Länder with the CDU participating in their governments. But this did not do away with the internal party oppositions.

On 6 February 2004 Schröder announced that he would resign from the chairmanship of the party at an extraordinary SPD party conference in March. The head of the SPD grouping in parliament up until then and the head of the SPD in North Rhine-Westphalia, Franz Müntefering, was elected as the new Federal chairman of the SPD. Schröder justified his decision on the grounds that he 'could spend more time on government business' when, in fact, it was more of an attempt to put a stop to his diminishing popularity and the agreement arising from the reforms.

At the start of 2005 Joschka Fischer, as the responsible minister, was summoned before an investigating committee to answer questions on the 'visa affair'. He had to appear as a witness before the cameras, admitting to his own failures and accepting full political responsibility. There had been considerable irregularities in the issuing of visas by the German representative authorities (e.g. in Kiev, by means of which a large number of immigrants came to Germany illegally). Fischer rejected demands for his resignation. One consequence of the visa affair was also the loss of his hitherto high rating on the popularity scale.

After the severe defeat of the SPD in the Landtag elections in North Rhine-Westphalia on 22 May 2005, followed by a series of defeats in Landtag elections in 2003 and 2004, the SPD party boss Müntefering and, shortly after that, Federal Chancellor Schröder announced, half an hour after the closing of the polls and without consulting the leadership of the Green Party, that they would press for the bringing forward of new elections for Autumn 2005. Schröder could foresee a challenge to the basis of his policy.

On 1 July 2005 he asked for a vote of confidence in the Bundestag and got 151 'Yes' votes and 296 'No' votes with 148 abstentions; he did not therefore get the required majority to be chancellor, but this was the intention. It was seen by the public to be a problem from the legal and constitutional perspective that Schröder – similar to Kohl at the change of circumstances in 1982 – intended to lose in the vote in order to achieve his goal. After consultation with Federal President Horst Köhler, Schröder called for the dissolution of the 15th legislative period of the Bundestag. Köhler agreed to the motion on 21 July and ordered new elections for the 18 September 2005. On 25 August 2005 the Federal Constitutional Court in Karlsruhe rejected objections by two members of the Bundestag to the premature dissolution of the Bundestag and the calling of new elections.

On 9 July 2005 a conference of SPD delegates from the Land of Lower Saxony, by 99.5 per cent of the votes (191 out of 192), elected Schröder to be the chief candidate on the SPD list for the Land in the forthcoming Bundestag elections.

The election campaign was extremely exciting right up to the last minute. In the end the SPD, after rallying dramatically, got 34.5 per cent of the votes and thus 222 of the 614 seats. It therefore emerged from the elections as the strongest party but, as a result of the partnership of the CDU and CSU grouping, it was only the second most powerful grouping in the Bundestag's 16th legislative period. The results of the Bundestag election of 18 September 2005 – a historic outcome in which Schröder had embarked on a spectacular rally, once more seriously threatening Merkel's comfortable position in the opinion polls – show that of the 614 seats available in the Bundestag there were only 226 for the coalition of the CDU/CSU, with a small lead of 4 seats over the SPD following closely behind. It clearly shows that the CDU/CSU had achieved 35.2 per cent and the SPD were only just 1 per cent behind. It was a very close outcome that called for a Grand Coalition and the end of the Red–Green, Schröder/Fischer government. A 'rainbow coalition' of Black (CDU/CSU), Yellow (FDP) and Green might have been mathematically possible – the Free Democrats had won 61 seats and the 'Greens' 51 – but after the protracted coming and going and Schröder's refusal to give up office prematurely, a Grand Coalition consisting of the CDU, the CSU and the SPD was formed.

With the prospect of a possible Grand Coalition, in a TV discussion immediately following the election, Schröder, in an outburst of emotion as he clung onto power, initially continued to claim the office of Federal Chancellor – totally in contrast to the tradition by which the strongest grouping always appoints the head of government. Only weeks later did he indirectly declare his readiness to give up his role as leader in a new government. Since then, Schröder has become active once more as a lawyer and freelance adviser for, among others, the pipeline consortium NEGP, the company formed from the Russian gas company Gazprom, which controls the Baltic pipeline linking Russia and Germany. This project had been supported by him as Federal Chancellor and by Russian President Vladimir Putin. As Schröder had paved the way for this project as Federal Chancellor, there was public criticism of the fact that he was given this lucrative position as head of the advisory board after completing his period in office.

After the Bundestag election of 2005 Fischer announced that, if it was a case of going into opposition, he was no longer available for the office of chairman of the party grouping in the Bundestag or any other posts in the party as it was time for a new generation to take the positions of power. In 2006 he resigned from his seat in the Bundestag.

The Red–Green Coalition as a Project: The Mixed Record of a Unique Government

For the first time in the history of the Federal Republic representatives of the new social movements were included within a government that embodied a change in German political culture. Under the heading of Red–Green it was not just a government coalition that had been elected, but a new social project in which those belonging to the 1968 generation, such as Joschka Fischer, were able to start the long wished-for 'march through the institutions' in order to bring about more acceptance for the emancipation of men and women and more tolerance towards minorities as well as more respect for the environment.

The fact that in the process Fischer as Foreign Minister would support and approve of the first war of aggression since the Second World War on the part of the Federal Republic was unacceptable for many conscientious objectors and pacifists. The decision on the first German military engagement since the Second World War was made by the Bundestag while Bonn was still the capital and not Berlin. How the Minister of the Interior, Schily, a former sympathizer and defender of the members of the RAF, became one of the strongest supporters of the anti-terrorism package, was a mystery to those who remembered the scene as it was earlier, but in the end the seduction of power and the force of political circumstances made this change explicable, if not excusable, in the cases of both Fischer and Schily.

On the negative side, under the Red–Green coalition utopianism and impotence also came together, as in the problems of integrating immigrants. Above all, the unemployed were disappointed by the Red–Green coalition as it was not possible to reduce unemployment at a stroke. However, one area of success was pension reform, guaranteeing provision for old age in spite of the demographic changes. The official pension was supplemented by private provision backed by capital and easing the burden. Private pension contributions by employees were also encouraged by the state in order to offset the predicted drop in value of the pension level. Child care was to be more closely reflected in the provision of benefits. The tax reform carried out under the overall control of Finance Minister Eichel, with a volume of tax relief amounting to over 62 billion DM, met with broad acceptance and contributed to the reputation of the Red–Green coalition. The revenue obtained from the auction of the UMTS licences for mobile telephony in August 2000, amounting to nearly 100 billion DM, helped in the reorganization of the state finances. Despite criticism from the CDU/CSU that the middle classes were being neglected, there was an important structural reform, particularly as regards the consolidation of the budget.

On the domestic political front the Schröder government put into effect its so-called election manifesto of 'innovation and justice' along with tax and pension reform: a conclusion to the negotiations lasting many years over compensation for forced labourers under the Nazis, amendment in agreement with the FDP to the right to citizenship in place since 1913, the introduction of the Green Card, civil partnerships for gays and lesbians and various initiatives on education and training (linking schools up to the Internet, reform of the terms of service for university lecturers) along with reforms in agricultural policy.

Mad-cow disease (bovine spongiform encephalopathy) did not result in an adverse effect on the government. A high-profile Green politician, Renate Künast, was given the top responsibility for agriculture, which was reorganized as the Ministry of Consumer Protection and Agriculture.

After initial teething problems the government proved itself to be capable of acting. In the case of relevant reforms, it was possible to overcome opposition from the ranks of the CDU/CSU and the FDP. The Red–Green coalition also managed to push through a reform of the Industrial Constitution Act in the face of opposition from business.

Some personal triumphs on the part of Schröder, such as the appointment of Müntefering as SPD general secretary, along with well-targeted projects like the 'Schröder-Blair paper', a vision for a new Europe and a national council on ethics, helped to restore his profile during the crisis of the CDU over its party donations scandal in the second half of Schröder's term in office. In the end the SPD failed more because of opposition internally within the party and from the trade unions and because of the decline in support amongst the public than because of the opposition in parliament.

10

New Beginnings and Tradition: The Grand Coalition under Angela Merkel, 2005–9

Angela Merkel: The Road to Becoming the First Female Federal Chancellor

After seven male predecessors, Angela Merkel was the first female Federal Chancellor in the history of the Federal Republic. She was also, at the age of 51, the youngest holder of the position, and the first from the new Federal Länder to do so, as well as the first scientist in this office. Angela Dorothea Merkel is the daughter of a theologian and a teacher. Shortly after the birth of their daughter in Hamburg in 1954 the family then moved to the GDR, where the father was appointed as a pastor of the Lutheran Church for a parish in Berlin-Brandenburg. After passing the Abitur, the equivalent to A-levels, with top grades in 1973, she went on to study physics at Leipzig. She became a member of the Ernst Thälmann Young Pioneers and the FDJ Youth movement. As a qualified physicist she obtained a position at the Central Institute for Physical Chemistry of the Academy of Sciences in Berlin-Adlershof. After getting her PhD Merkel switched to the field of analytical chemistry. During her time at the Academy she was active in the local leadership of the FDJ and as the secretary for Agitation and Propaganda, which she later referred to as 'cultural activities' that she 'found fun'. Merkel was neither a member of the SED or in one of the Bloc parties, but she did not belong to the opposition in the GDR either.

At the time of the so-called 'Wende' ('turning point' or 'change'), she was involved with the organization for Democratic Change (Demokratischer Aufbruch, DA), initially unpaid as a provisional administrator working on electronic data processing, then full-time as an expert and a sort of press spokesperson on behalf of the chairman, Wolfgang Schnur, who formerly worked for the Stasi. Friends and acquaintances were surprised that Merkel became a CDU politician. They had expected her to be closer to the Greens.

The election for the Volkskammer of 18 March 1990 resulted in a severe defeat for the DA (0.9 per cent). Following the 41 per cent for the Eastern CDU as an alliance partner, the 'Alliance for Germany' was the de facto winner of the election. The bad result for the DA led to its support for the CDU, which Merkel accepted. In line with the 'coalition arithmetic', she became a spokesperson representing the government in the first and at the same time last freely elected government of the GDR.

On 4 August 1990 an extraordinary conference of the DA agreed to joining the West German CDU after the preceding merger with the Eastern CDU. After unification Merkel became a ministerial advisor in the Federal Press and Information Office (Bundespresse- und Informationsamt, BPA). Through the influence of her sponsor Günther Krause, the Land chairman of the CDU in Mecklenburg-West Pomerania, she stood for a seat in the Bundestag and was successfully elected to parliament for her constituency. Kohl, the victor in the elections, then surprisingly appointed her to ministerial office. Merkel's rapid rise was largely boosted by support from the Federal Chancellor. The nickname 'Kohl's girl' dates back to this time.

In 1991 Merkel became deputy Federal chairwoman of the CDU, following Lothar de Maizière. After he and Krause resigned, she succeeded in becoming the CDU Land chairwoman of Mecklenburg-West Pomerania. Between 1990 and 1994 she was Federal Minister for Women and Young People and between 1994 and 1998 Minister for the Environment, the Protection of Natural Resources and Reactor Safety in Kohl's cabinet. After 1998 she also rose to general secretary of the party. In this position she criticized Kohl's role in connection with the party donations scandal and called for links to be severed with him. The party then demanded that he suspend his honorary chairmanship until such time as the donors were named. Kohl refused and replied by resigning. Schäuble, likewise as a result of the party donations scandal, could not remain as the Federal chairman of the CDU. Thus, Merkel was elected as the new Federal chairwoman of the CDU on 10 April 2000.

In the Bundestag election of 2002 she loyally accepted the unsuccessful candidature for Federal Chancellor of the Minister-President of Bavaria, Edmund Stoiber. Following this, Merkel was re-elected CDU chairwoman, winning out against Friedrich Merz, the chairman of the CDU/CSU parliamentary grouping, with whom her relations were marked by conflict and tension.

The end of the period in office of Federal President Johannes Rau made a new appointment necessary. Opponents of Merkel within the party favoured Schäuble. Horst Köhler was Merkel's candidate, however, and his election success in the

Bundesversammlung (the Federal Assembly whose job it is to elect the President) of 2004 could be seen as a consolidation of his position of power. After the elections that were brought forward the CDU and the CSU appointed Merkel their candidate for Chancellor on 30 May 2005. She was initially uncontested as it had been possible to marginalize opponents within the party. Merkel's shadow cabinet was presented as a 'competent team' because of the coalition with the FDP favoured by her. The model put forward by the Heidelberg University professor Paul Kirchhof, along with the CDU's ideas on sickness insurance ('flat rate per head'), were 'difficult to put over' to the public, however, and were among other things responsible for their growing decline in popularity with the voters. Even the short-term reactivation of their rival Friedrich Merz could not reverse this downward trend. Schröder embarked on a spectacular rally with which he only quite narrowly missed winning against a CDU/CSU majority.

In the Bundestag election of 18 September 2005 the Christian Democrats clearly fell short of their predictions and were unable to achieve their election goal, an absolute majority of Bundestag seats for the CDU/CSU and the FDP. In her own constituency No. 15 (Stralsund, the region of North Pomerania and the island of Rügen) Merkel won 41.3 per cent of the first votes. Along with the Christian Democrats, the SPD had to suffer losses so that the previous government coalition made up of the SPD and the Greens lost their majority in parliament.

The Building of the Grand Coalition

In the television discussion on the eve of the election, despite the loss of his Red–Green majority, Schröder claimed for himself the right to form a government in such a high-handed manner that it led to vehement criticism. He himself later on referred to his conduct as 'sub-optimal'. The critics of Merkel within the CDU were forced by Schröder's arrogant behaviour to back their candidate even though she had suffered some losses.

In the next few days all the talk was about whether the office of Federal Chancellor would go to the SPD as the largest single parliamentary party grouping in the Bundestag or to the CDU/CSU as the largest combination of parliamentary party groupings. The shape of the coalition was still undecided. Merkel was then re-elected chairwoman of the party grouping by the Bundestag grouping of the Christian Democrats, meeting for the first time since the election, in a secret ballot with 219 of the 222 votes – a vote of confidence after the disappointing election result and significant backing for the coalition talks. Schröder at first continued in office after the constitutive session of the 16th Bundestag on 18 October 2005 at the request of the Federal President.

Merkel and Stoiber had not ruled out explanatory talks on a possible Black–Yellow–Green 'rainbow coalition' with Alliance 90/The Greens together with the FDP. It was not possible, however, to form either a Black–Yellow coalition made up of the CDU/CSU and the FDP or a Red–Green coalition made up of the SPD and Alliance 90/The Greens. Thus, an absolute majority of Bundestag seats could not be achieved, also owing to the arrival of the left-wing Linkspartei/PDS (bringing together Oskar Lafontaine and Gregor Gysi) that was able to gain 8.7 per cent of the votes and which none of the other parties were prepared to go into a coalition with. After short exploratory talks, the categorical refusal on the part of the FDP of what is referred to as a 'traffic-light coalition' (between the SPD, the FDP and the Greens), and on the part of the SPD and of Alliance 90/the 'Greens' of a coalition tolerated by Die Linke–PDS, all signs were pointing towards a Black–Red coalition. The members of the last named party were dubbed 'inheritors of Honecker' by one of their sharpest critics, Hubertus Knabe.

On 10 October the SPD, CDU and the CSU published a common agreement, including the planned election of Merkel as Federal Chancellor by the 16th Bundestag. On 12 November, after five weeks of negotiations, she presented the coalition contract between the CDU/CSU and the SPD. On 18 November it was signed by the chairmen of the three parties. Considerable influence in the coalition negotiations was attributed to the SPD chairman, Müntefering. The SPD was able to gain a few important ministries by renouncing the office of Chancellor. After the defeat in the vote in the Federal party executive over the new general secretary Müntefering nevertheless resigned as party chairman, being succeeded by Matthias Platzeck, who therefore also signed the coalition contract for the SPD on 18 November.

On 22 November 2005 Merkel was elected by the members of the 16th Bundestag as Federal Chancellor with 397 of the 611 valid votes (votes against: 202; abstentions: 12). This was 51 fewer votes than the coalition parties had seats. In the next few days Schröder resigned his seat. In her government declaration of 29 November 2005 Merkel praised Schröder for the measures of his government within the context of the Agenda 2010 programme. Merkel's policy was able to follow on seamlessly from the Red–Green reform policy.

Even before the start of the legislative period, Merkel's longstanding rival Stoiber surprisingly declined the position of Economics Minister for which he was intended, according to his own statement because of Müntefering's resignation from the party chairmanship of the SPD with whom he had imagined he would be

'We elect the Chancellor – Encourage Merkel: Both votes CDU.'

in tandem, but this argument did not sound very convincing. As head of the Federal Chancellery Merkel chose Thomas de Maizière, the cousin of the last Prime Minister of the GDR, Lothar de Maizière. Matthias Platzeck as successor only led the SPD in the Grand Coalition for a short time, as he had to resign from office on 10 April 2006 on health grounds. His successor was the Minister-President of the Rhineland-Palatinate, Kurt Beck, who had an equally unfortunate experience in office.

In March 2006 Merkel put forward an eight-point programme for the second phase of the legislative period, setting out the goals in relation to Federal reform, reduction in bureaucracy, research and innovation, energy policy, budgetary and financial policy, policy on the family, policy on the labour market and particularly health reforms. Even though there was a lack of radical measures, Merkel's decidedly down-to-earth style of government went down well with the population as well as with those in control of the economy and people abroad. On 27 November 2006 she was re-elected by 93 per cent of the votes as chairwoman of the party at the CDU party conference.

Active Foreign Policy, Presidency of the EU Council
and the Connection to Israel

Angela Merkel soon surprised everybody by putting emphasis on the area of foreign policy. She criticized George W. Bush over the resemblance of the US internment camp at Guantanamo Bay to a concentration camp. The reception of the Dalai Lama at the Federal Chancellery in 2007 upset the People's Republic of China. Merkel also publicly criticized Pope Benedict XVI for his highly controversial attempt in January 2009 to rehabilitate Bishop Richard Williamson, who had denied the Holocaust. The Pope had already caused controversy. On 19 April 2005 the former German Cardinal Josef Ratzinger had been elected as successor to John Paul II by the largest ever conclave. After nearly 500 years, once again the Pope was a German. The media hailed this, the *Bild* newspaper headline 'We are a Pope!' catching the mood of the moment. The 78-year-old, born in Bavaria and a former member of the Hitler Youth, achieved the approval ratings of a pop star and astonished people all over the world with his friendliness, sincerity and commitment. Behind this facade, however, there lurked a convinced dogmatist and orthodox Catholic with correspondingly fundamentalist views.

The Pope came in for rejection and criticism following his lecture in Regensburg on 12 September 2006 after using a quotation without comment from the Byzantine Emperor Manuel II Palaiologos (who had referred to Islam in derogatory terms). Benedict besides, in a document published on 10 July 2007 on the 'Congregation for the Doctrine of the Faith', emphasized the uniqueness of the Roman Catholic Church and in so doing denied the Protestant Church 'in the true sense' the status of a church, something that according to the chairman of the Council of the Lutheran Church in Germany, Bishop Wolfgang Huber, meant a setback for ecumenism. This papal dictum would also have affected Federal Chancellor Merkel as a Protestant.

In the middle of 2006 the country was gripped by football World Cup fever – *Deutschland. Ein Sommermärchen* ('Germany: A Summer Fairytale') was the title of a film by Sönke Wortmann, even expressing a new acceptable and laid-back German 'flag-waving patriotism'.

The culmination of Merkel's period governing in the Grand Coalition was her term as President of the EU Council along with Foreign Minister Frank-Walter Steinmeier (SPD) between 1 January and 30 June 2007. The chairmanship was assumed in turn within the framework of the 'troika' with Portugal and Slovenia. Merkel referred to the 'EU Constitutional Treaty', the 'policy on climate and energy', the 'deepening of the transatlantic economic partnership' and a 'policy of neighbourliness in the Black Sea region and Central Asia' as the most important goals. The German Presidency of the European Council was to be a success in as much as it was possible for the substance of the EU Constitutional Treaty – rejected in 2005 by the populations of France and the Netherlands – to be salvaged as a reform treaty and eventually to be signed. The crucial leadership of Merkel and Steinmeier during the German Presidency managed to build on the momentum developed by the Austrian Presidency of the Council in 2006 and continued by the Finns and steer the controversial issue towards a solution.

In the context of the German Presidency of the Council, the EU had formally committed itself to large-scale reforms. Federal Chancellor Merkel, EU Commission President José Manuel Barroso and the President of the European Parliament Hans-Gert Pöttering (European People's Party) signed the Berlin Declaration at an act of celebration on 25 March 2007. With Bulgaria and Romania joining on 1 January 2007 the union, which had grown to encompass 27 states and 490 million citizens, would be made more capable of action and brought closer to the citizens. A modern treaty would be drawn up for this purpose by 2009. The Berlin Declaration placed the people at the centre of its concerns.

The history of the EU from the signing of the two Treaties of Rome on 25 March 1957 up to today has been described as a successful model. Its achievements have been said to include peace and freedom, the European model of society, solidarity and equal rights, the common market and the Euro. Challenges for the future have been recognized in relation to globalization, in the fight against international terrorism, against racism and xenophobia as well as in relation to protection of the climate. In the Berlin Declaration the EU committed itself to internal reforms by the time of the next European elections in the middle of 2009. The controversial word 'constitution' was not mentioned.

In her speech Merkel pressed for a solution to the crisis. 'Failure would be a historic omission', she said in her role as President of the EU Council. It was therefore necessary that the EU was united in its aim of putting the Community on a renewed common basis by the time of the elections to the European Parliament in 2009. The German Federal Chancellor emphasized that she wanted to issue a timetable for the constitution at the end of the German chairmanship of the Council in June 2007. In this she relied on the support of all the heads of state and government. Barroso agreed with her and spoke in favour of strong institutions. Pöttering underlined the fact that the 'substance' of the Constitutional Treaty had to be legally binding including the common values. In her formal address Merkel expressed a persuasive commitment to Europe. In this she was speaking from her experience as a citizen of the GDR, having suffered at close hand the division of Germany, the Berlin Wall and the overcoming of the split in Europe. She pointed out her personal conviction regarding the Judeo-Christian roots of Europe. Here the Federal Chancellor was reacting once again to the criticism by the Pope. The head of the Catholic Church, with his tendency towards right-wing conservative, fundamentalist ideas, had accused the EU of turning its back on faith. The Berlin Declaration even lacked a reference to a Christian heritage. Merkel had pressed for the reference to God and Christian faith to be included in the EU constitution, something which, despite support from Poland, Ireland and Italy, was not possible to push through. In the Treaty of Lisbon there was only a reference to the 'cultural, religious and humanistic heritage of Europe'. The Czech President Václav Klaus criticized Merkel, declaring: 'There is a lack of democratic debate, of a democratic discussion.' Individual governments had not been sufficiently involved or informed.

In parallel with the meeting of the heads of government, a European festival was organized around the Brandenburg Gate. At the party for the fiftieth anniversary of the signing of the Treaties of Rome the 27 member states put themselves on display to the public. Information on the 'EU family', and also on other organizations such as the Franco-German youth exchange movement and the equivalent German-Polish one, was available in more than 75 tents. At the close there were fireworks shooting up into the Berlin night sky with the blue and gold of the EU colours. Thus, the new Germany put itself on display as a European Germany open to the world.

The German Presidency of the Council turned out a success, particularly since essential compromises on the preparation of a new treaty were achieved. The Federal Chancellor was recognized for her commitment to European policy. On 1 May 2008 she received the Charlemagne Prize from the city of Aachen 'for her services towards the further development of the European Union'. The award speech was given by the French president Nicolas Sarkozy.

One month later to the day the heads of state and of government signed the new Treaty of Union during a summit in the Portuguese capital at the Hieronymite Monastery. The purpose of the Treaty was to improve the decision-making process in the enlarged EU by reforming the voting rights in the Council, reducing the power of the Commission and strengthening the role of the European Parliament and the national parliaments. In addition it created the new posts of President of the Council and High Representative for Foreign and Security Policy. To come into effect, the treaty had to be ratified by all 27 member states.

Eventually the Federal Constitutional Court had to deal with the subject. Constitutional challenges to the legislation on agreement to the Lisbon Treaty as well as to the corresponding associated pieces of legislation were instituted (particularly for being contrary to the principle of democracy), and proceedings were also initiated by the csu member of the Bundestag, Peter Gauweiler and the Bundestag grouping of the left-wing Linkspartei. The challenges were successful in that the Federal Constitutional Court ruled one of the relevant associated pieces of legislation to be unconstitutional. However, the Treaty of Lisbon itself was on the other hand judged to be in conformity with the constitution, even though the ratification process could not be concluded until the amended associated legislation had been passed. The Grand Coalition therefore still planned to pass the legislation in a revised form before the end of the election term. In the meantime the Lisbon Treaty had gained the force of law, which had a lot to do with the involvement of the Federal Chancellor.

In her policy towards Turkey, when still in opposition, Merkel had spoken about a 'privileged partnership'. During her time as Chancellor and as president of the EU Council she was silent on that. When the Turkish Prime Minister Recep Tayyip Erdoğan, on a visit to Germany in February 2008, warned the Turks in Germany against assimilation, she criticized his 'understanding of integration'.

International crisis management was extended by the Grand Coalition to include the Middle and the Far East. German soldiers continued to be engaged within the framework of the ISAF mission in Afghanistan, despite severe setbacks and losses. Merkel was initially reserved as regards German participation in a UN peacekeeping force in South Lebanon for a settlement of the Israel–Lebanon conflict. Israeli Premier Ehud Olmert, however, called for the participation of German troops. 'I have informed Angela Merkel that we have absolutely no problem over German soldiers in South Lebanon', he said, adding that there is no nation that Israel behaves towards in such a friendly manner as Germany. On 18 March 2008 Merkel gave a speech to the Knesset beginning in Hebrew. She underlined Germany's historical responsibility for Israel; the security of the Jewish state was one of Germany's national priorities and never in question. Merkel was the first foreign head of government to be invited to deliver a speech to the Knesset.

Continued Policy of Reform Showing Successes and Failures

Quite unlike Austria, the Grand Coalition in the Federal Republic continued to be seen as a special case of political democracy. The large majority that such a government could rely upon in parliament was automatically interpreted as a danger for democracy; it was argued that the opposition was too weak and that the political fringes would be radicalized. This ambivalent feeling was further strengthened by the expectation that only a coalition consisting of both large parties was capable of carrying out the necessary structural reforms.

Merkel in her first government declaration had called the Grand Coalition a 'coalition of new possibilities', which was apt: she certainly managed a series of reforms, even some far-reaching ones. The second Grand Coalition in the history of the Federal Republic, like the first one between 1966 and 1969, set itself important tasks. The absolute majorities in the Bundestag and the Bundesrat were also to be used to that end. A pressing concern was balancing the budget, i.e. the presentation of a budget without net borrowing by 2011.

The first measure was the raising of VAT to 19 per cent and a reduction in expenditure, particularly in the area of education, requiring the introduction of tuition fees for students in the Länder. As regards Federal reform, the relation between the Federal government and the Länder was to be reorganized. Reforms were undertaken on family policy in relation to child benefits and the development of child-care centres. These reforms had already been sought by the Red–Green ministers of family affairs but the breakthrough only came about under Merkel's government. The same goes for the raising of the statutory pension age and the reform of the taxes on business: after 20 years of discussion, the tax burden of German companies was lowered to come into line with the average in those states that had been EU members for 15 years. One success that can also be marked up to the coalition is the consolidation of the budget up until the financial crisis of summer 2008. Its committed engagement in confronting this crisis was likewise remarkable (see below).

The Grand Coalition was able to achieve a symbolic success in relation to social insurance contributions, lowering these to below the level of 40 per cent of gross salary. Many reforms remained patchwork, were contradictory or ended in failure: the 'unplanned' pension increases of 2008 and 2009 were incompatible with the raising of the statutory pension age. The attempts to lower contributions to unemployment insurance were undermined by the lengthening of the period of eligibility for unemployment pay on the part of older workers. The reforms in health care for the old and sick were not successful. Both of these actually led to a rise in contributions. The minimum wage was controversial by being introduced without covering the whole area of employment as the spd had called for. The liberalization of the labour market demanded by the cdu/csu did not come about. The engagement of the Bundeswehr in the homeland called for by the Christian Democrats did not become reality. A legal code on the environment was something else that failed, along with key privatization projects (railways and air traffic control). The reasons are plain to see: the Grand Coalition had a majority in the Bundestag, but not uncontrolled power. It was, however, not so much other institutions and organizations that were the big opponents to large-scale reforms, but rather the partners in the Grand Coalition itself. The standpoints of the coalition partners were diametrically opposed over essential questions. The spd and the cdu had fought one another in the election campaign of 2005 over health policy, with contradictory ideas, involving social insurance as opposed to flat rates per head, that could not be reconciled into a common project. This was also the case for reform in health care for old people and the labour market. The spd rejected the liberalization of the labour market demanded by the cdu. The cdu prevented the introduction of the minimum wage across the board but nevertheless had to accept an increase in broad support for it. In the battle for the electors' votes, both parties hesitated to push through reforms that were too radical.

Despite all the efforts as regards policy on the labour market and the economy, there still remained an East–West divide in real economic standards. The economic data comparing East and West clearly indicate that the most populous Federal Länder are also the most economically powerful Länder in Germany: North Rhine-Westphalia, Bavaria and Baden-Württemberg. The new Länder such as Brandenburg, Saxony-Anhalt, Thuringia and Mecklenburg-West Pomerania, which were and are also affected by the migration of population, are at the same time at the bottom as regards economic production in the new Federal Republic.

The Financial and Economic Crisis, Campaign of Exclusions, Elections and the End of the Grand Coalition, 2008–9

In 2008 the property bubble burst in the usa, bringing about the crash of the renowned banking concern Lehman Brothers. In the autumn the historic scale of the unfolding financial crisis became clear due to the insolvency of numerous large financial institutions. A number of German Länder banks (Landesbanken) as well as private institutions had to write off considerable sums. The Bundestag initially reacted by bringing in legislation limiting risk. On 8 October 2008

Merkel's government issued a declaration guaranteeing savings deposits in Germany – there was in fact no serious basis for this promise any more. This guarantee should be valid for every institution and every depositor of every institution that is part of German banking security. Previously the Federal Chancellor had sharply criticized the Irish government for its own state guarantee, which in any case only affected internal banks. Merkel's action was criticized by other European finance ministers as a nation going it alone but something which the EU commission did not consider distorting to competition and therefore not likely to be a problem with regard to integration. The Grand Coalition showed ability to act in the securing of economic rescue packages, the development of environmental premiums and the current solution to the Opel crisis. 2009 continued to be dominated by dealing with the financial crisis, which had developed into a worldwide crisis. The obligations of the state to save the banking system and stimulate the economy rocketed. A further rise in the deficit and indebtedness was expected by experts in the case of Germany for the period up until 2011. Rising unemployment figures and falls in prosperity were thought to be inevitable.

The approaching election campaign indicated that Merkel's preference was not for the SPD as a coalition partner but for the FDP. As the first party the SPD had appointed Foreign Minister Steinmeier as their leading candidate. Merkel again ran as the candidate for Chancellor for the CDU/CSU and Guido Westerwelle as leading candidate for the FDP. In the case of Alliance 90/The Greens, Renate Künast, the head of the grouping, and her deputy Jürgen Trittin were nominated. In the case of the left-wing Die Linke, the head of the party, Lothar Bisky, had indicated that he would not be a candidate again for the Bundestag. In 2009 the chairmen of the grouping, Gregor Gysi and Oskar Lafontaine, led the party election campaign. In parallel to this, Lafontaine ran as the candidate for Die Linke to be Minister-President of the Saarland.

The CDU/CSU and the FDP on the one hand, and Die Linke on the other, fundamentally rejected a coalition with either of the other sides at a level above the regional. Steinmeier ruled out the positions on foreign and domestic policy of the left-wing party and made it clear that he did not wish to be elected by the votes of the left-wing. A Red–Red–Green coalition was therefore ruled out. Die Linke for their part ruled out a coalition with the SPD at Federal level because of differences on foreign policy (opposition to the involvement of the Bundeswehr in Afghanistan) and on domestic policy (opposition to the Hartz IV employment programme). The Christian Democrat parties (CDU/CSU) favoured a Black–Yellow coalition over the existing Grand Coalition. One week before the election, the FDP,

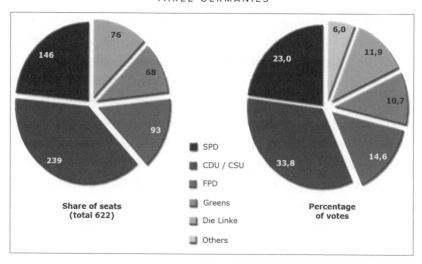

Bundestag elections of 27 September 2009 (preliminary official result given the next day).

after pressure from the CDU, ruled out a coalition with the Greens and the SPD (i.e. a 'traffic-light coalition'). The Greens ruled out a 'rainbow coalition'. As a result of all these things being ruled out the only options left were a Black–Yellow coalition and a Grand Coalition.

The election for the 17th Bundestag took place on 27 September 2009 and – as the two pie charts show – resulted in the necessary majority for the Christian Democrat parties and the FDP, making it possible for them to form a Black–Yellow coalition. Though the opposition parties, the FDP, Die Linke and Alliance 90/The Greens in places won considerable numbers of extra votes and achieved the best results in the history of any of their parties, the parties in the governing Grand Coalition hit an all-time low in popularity with the electorate. The SPD had their worst ever result in a Bundestag election, the CDU and the CSU their worst results since the first Bundestag election in 1949. The turn-out of 70.78 per cent was the lowest in the history of the Federal Republic. The following findings were particularly remarkable: the largest section of the country consisted of non-voters at the same time as there was an increased interest in politics on the part of the population! The political landscape in the Federal Republic became more fragmented. There were no 'people's parties' any more, and Die Linke had now arrived for good even in the West of Germany. Merkel was confirmed again as Federal Chancellor despite recent losses in popularity with the electorate. The former FDP opposition politician Westerwelle became deputy Chancellor and Foreign Minister.

Results of a 'Forced Marriage'

The impression given to the public of a stalemate and stagnation in the policy of the Grand Coalition does not totally correspond to reality. Admittedly, it did not manage to forge a harmonious policy, and nor was its record one long success story. The Grand Coalition, however, was far from being as unsuccessful as has been portrayed in the media. It achieved notable successes in the area of Federal reform, business taxation and family policy. There were no structural reforms, however. Differences in programme between the coalition partners as well as considerations of election tactics held up large-scale reforms. The models of developments in domestic policy and of the formation of parliamentary will changed only a little in the Federal Republic under the Grand Coalition.

Empirical analysis has nevertheless shown that fears and expectations were exaggerated. The Grand Coalition, with its broad parliamentary base and its participation in all of the Länder governments, did not have unlimited power. At the end of the legislative period it had even lost its majority in the Bundesrat, illustrated by a rise in the number of challenges to bills. The Federal President exercised his constitutional control extremely strongly. One could not speak of an uncontrolled exercise of power on the part of the Grand Coalition.

The second Grand Coalition has been seen as a 'forced marriage'. Characterized by delusory expectations, great disappointments and the ordeal of finding the lowest common denominator and agreeing to it, it could not be summed up as a success story. Forced together by the electorate on 18 September 2005, this partnership soon proved not to be up to solving the most pressing problems of the country. The two parties were in a state of mutual stalemate. They were more concerned with not losing their image than with seeing through the job of government to a successful conclusion. The hopeless state of the SPD obscured the profound problems of the CDU and even more of the CSU. Despite all the obstacles, between the individual characters there were alliances and partnerships going beyond party boundaries. No friendship emerged between the CDU/CSU and the SPD politicians. Following the 'wedding' there was a troublesome period lasting right up to the end of the forced partnership, which could be described as a failed 'marriage' (as Eckart Lohse and Mark Wehner called it).

11

From Europe's Troubleshooter to the Continent's Lame Duck: The Merkel Era and the Berlin Republic at a Crossroads

Social Upheavals

Germany's unification came hand in hand with a huge financial burden that pushed the West German economy and social system to the limit. The solidarity surcharge introduced for this purpose is a direct tax levied by the Federal Government, which had raised €16.85 billion by 2016. Despite the 'reconstruction of the East' (Aufbau Ost), Germany held on to its position as a global export power reaching far beyond the EU's internal market. The value of exports in 2015 stood at 1,193.6 billion euros, with an export surplus of 244 billion euros. This includes the export of armaments. In 2018, 11,142 individual permits were issued for the export of armaments to a value of 4.82 billion euros, representing a drop of 23 per cent on the previous year, when such exports stood at 6.24 billion euros. Although the bulk of these exports went to EU and NATO countries, there were also sales to Algeria, Israel and Saudi Arabia. In view of the unpopularity of these exports, the Grand Coalition Federal Government had to go to great lengths to defend its stated intention to 'pursue a restrictive and responsible policy of armaments exports'. Despite this fall in arms sales the state continued to register record tax surpluses. In 2019 the Federal government, states, municipalities and social insurance took in 58 billion euros; prospects for the future are said to be not encouraging owing to the coronavirus pandemic.

Its political role as the custodian of European integration and economic power assigned the Berlin Republic under Merkel a leading role in Europe between 2005 and 2015. Within the EU, the balanced-budget amendment made Germany the poster girl for precisely that – a balanced budget – and the mainstay of a stable eurozone. Germany was seen as the initiator of a shared European asylum policy and an advocate for energy transition. Its export prowess, tax surplus and economic clout gave Germany the wherewithal to shape policies in Europe and beyond and to contribute significantly to internal and external integration.

After reunification, priorities were shifted to the fresh opportunities it offered and, above all, to the great challenge inherent in steering Germany as a whole towards rebirth as a more European, modern and cosmopolitan state, capable of offering its citizens a framework in which their lives would be more worth living in spite of a spate of serious problems: comparatively high unemployment, a rapidly expanding low-wage sector, low birth rates and a widening divide between rich and poor. At the beginning of the twenty-first century, German society had entered into a phase of transition.

At the same time, and rather belatedly, there came the official admission that Germany was an 'immigration country'. Berlin's former SPD finance senator, Thilo Sarrazin, took umbrage at this admission, laying out his views in 2010 in a controversial book entitled *Deutschland schafft sich ab* (Germany Abolishes Itself). Focusing his critique on the steadily rising percentage of people from abroad, especially of Muslims, he ignited a broad public discussion. While reactions to the book concentrated on a number of rather questionable assumptions, the facts it listed tended to be talked down or even ignored altogether, so Sarrazin had the mantle of the lonely prophet in the wilderness thrust upon him. The book proved a bestseller: by early 2012 more than 1.5 million copies had been sold. For weeks on end it occupied the number 1 slot on *Der Spiegel*'s list of bestsellers.

Another major talking point was the resignation of Pope Benedict XVI in 2013, once he had 'obtained absolute certainty' that his powers, diminished as they were by old age, were no longer 'sufficient to do justice to the Petrine ministry'. His pontificate was overshadowed by revelations of a substantive amount of sexual and other abuse committed within the Roman Catholic Church in the past; several cases were native to the German episcopate, where attempts had been made to sweep them under the carpet. These were and still are a great source of public indignation.

Tasks relevant to Germany's future as pursued by the CDU/CSU-FDP coalition (2009–13) and the Grand Coalition (2013–20) were a move towards higher qualification requirements for migrants, the introduction of a minimum wage (8.50 euros gross per hour from 1 January 2015) and investment in information technology and the general modernization of industry.

The digitization of the economy was promoted under the slogan 'Industry 4.0', a comprehensive strategy aimed at upgrading Germany's industrial production through wholesale digitization. It was based on a project of the same name in the high-tech sector of the Federal government's strategic planning. The point was to link industrial production to state-of-the-art information and communication technology. A prerequisite for this was intelligent, digitally networked systems that would make the self-organization of production possible: key elements as diverse as plant, logistics, machines, human resources and production would communicate and collaborate directly with one another, optimizing value-added chains all the way, from the conception of a new product to its development, production and use and on to its maintenance and recycling. For all its promise, this miraculous magical world lacked indispensable requirements: in 2012 not all Germans had Internet access (even though 85 per cent did, against the EU average of 76 per cent) and roughly 82 per cent had access to broadband (EU average: 72 per cent). The Berlin Republic had set itself the goal of a nationwide data transfer speed of at least 50 Mbps, a goal it failed to achieve. Of Germany's 62,000 businesses only one-third had access to high-speed Internet in June 2019; the fact that two-thirds had to make do without was viewed by industry representatives as a serious obstacle to innovation. As far as digitization is concerned, Berlin is lagging behind. An investment package for schools worth billions, known as the *Digitalpakt*, was passed but there are still dead zones in rural areas. A lack of qualified personnel meant that much of the necessary work never got beyond the planning stage. While it is obvious that the Federal government is aware of the importance of speeding up the development of AI – several billions have been set aside for a relevant funding programme – Germany nevertheless falls far behind the United States and China in this area.

Political and private communication underwent dramatic changes through the establishment of social networks such as Facebook, Instagram and WhatsApp. One way younger generations used these forums was to voice their objections to what they saw as censorship of the Internet when upload filters were installed as a consequence of the Directive on Copyright in the Single Market by the EU. Between March and June 2019 networks for the new generation of cellular network technology, 5G, were auctioned off, generating revenue totalling 6.5 billion euros. What bidders criticized about the process was that not enough funds were made available for the nationwide installation of the network.

Facebook was given a comparatively large fine for passing on user data to Cambridge Analytica, which was held to have potentially interfered in the outcome of the 2016 presidential elections in the United States. In addition to this infringement of data protection regulations, social media also have a significant problem with online hate speech, which is uploaded and either not deleted at all by their operators or deleted only after intolerable delays. Facebook was sentenced to pay 2 million euros to the Federal Office of Justice in Bonn for infringing the Network Enforcement Act by failing to delete hate speech content in reasonable time. On 11 July 2019 the French government passed a resolution in favour of a national digital tax, requiring internationally active IT corporations to pay a tax of 3 per cent on advertising revenue generated through their online operations. Whether Germany will follow in France's footsteps is still a moot point, since the United States might retaliate by imposing tariffs on cars and mechanical engineering products.

Germany suffered from a pronounced lack of personnel in the low-wage sector of nursing care for the elderly in 2019. The minimum wage in this sector was 11 euros per hour. Only 20 per cent of those working in nursing care are covered by collective agreements. The situation was so precarious that Health Minister Jens Spahn was forced to use a visit to Kosovo to canvass for nursing personnel.

Germany was still a nation of car manufacturers and motorists, but in view of the climate debate the motorcar was increasingly seen as problematic, a state of affairs encapsulated in the ban on diesel cars in German cities in response to EU directives. The recently privatized Deutsche Bahn was unable to muster the funds for urgently required investments, with its trains only rarely running on time. On average, only one ICE in five was fully operational. One of the excuses for trains not running to schedule was 'delays in operating procedures' (*Verzögerungen im Betriebsablauf*).

Another great challenge alongside climate change was transformations in environmental technology and their consequences. Energy transition had already been initiated by the Red–Green government (1998–2005), targeting measures such as the construction of windmills, the promotion of photovoltaics and the provision of thermal insulation. Merkel had put forward a medium-term withdrawal from atomic energy as early as 2011 but there was still a great deal to be done.

Following the inexorable trend towards social change, same-sex marriage was declared legal on 1 October 2017. Even though the women's movement was becoming steadily more mainstream, the wage gap between women and men was higher in Germany than in most other European countries. Taking all other factors into account, men in 2017 earned an average of 21 euros an hour, with women lagging behind at about 17 euros.

The service society was expanding and becoming more of an entertainment society. Privatization of TV multiplied the number of channels. In the spirit of post-modernity, an event- and fun-fixated society was becoming more and more dismissive of the crises of the day. Referring to private TV as 'shallowland' (*Seichtgebiete*, a neologism offering a dig at Charlotte Roche's *Feuchtgebiete*), journalist Michael Jürgs pondered the question of why audiences were allowing television to be radically dumbed down; the answer proved elusive. TV audiences increasingly forsook state channels in favour of ad-pushing private ones, thereby upping the heat on print media with their traditional dependence on advertising and forcing them to intensify their presence on the Internet. A similar trend made itself felt in a prurient interest in political scandals. In 2011 overwhelming evidence of plagiarism in Federal Defence Minister Karl Theodor von und zu Guttenberg's doctoral thesis made the author a sitting duck for the investigative Internet platform VroniPlag, leading to the spectacle of an up-and-coming political star being exposed as a fraudster as more and more copy-and-paste passages in his thesis were discovered every minute. Von Guttenberg had already been viewed as a candidate for the chancellorship and as Angela Merkel's successor. He evinced no sense of wrongdoing, blamed media pressure for his enforced resignation and published a book defiantly entitled *Vorerst gescheitert* (Rebuffed for Now). Guttenberg's legacy as Defence Minister was a reform of the German Armed Forces that never got off the ground and, on the assets side of the balance sheet, the 2010 suspension of compulsory military service.

A massive media scandal blew up at the turn of 2018/19 when Claas Relotius, a top prize-winning *Spiegel* journalist widely admired by insiders, was shown to have duped his readers with attractively written, politically correct stories that were utterly devoid of any factual basis. Relotius had supplied various highly respected German and international print media with copy in addition to *Der Spiegel*, but they, and indeed the entire journalistic community, went back to business as usual after what had never been more than a brief self-examination, wrapping themselves in a shroud of collective silence over the case.

Continuation of 'Agenda 2010' and Troubleshooting in the European Debt Crisis

The Grand Coalition (2005–9) gave priority to a balanced budget and the presentation of a budget that dispensed with net borrowing until 2011. A reform of Germany's federal structure was to redefine the relationship between the Federal government and the governments of the individual states, the Länder. Reforms in the area of family policy were tackled, especially as regards parental benefit and care centres (Kindertagesstätten, KITAS); a persistent shortage of personnel made sure this agenda was never put into practice. The reforms had already been mooted by Red–Green family ministers but the first real breakthroughs were achieved only under Merkel. Another feather in the coalition's cap was the consolidation of the budget before the advent of the 2008 financial crisis.

On 28 October 2009, Merkel was given a second term as Chancellor. After April 2010, the European debt crisis dominated this second term. In the banking, finance and sovereign debt crisis Merkel earned universal acclaim as a deft troubleshooter.

During Merkel's coalition with the FDP's Guido Westerwelle (2009–13), the members of the eurozone voted in favour of an emergency rescue plan for Greece, which was facing sovereign default. The Chancellor felt compelled to sound the alarm. On the occasion of the Charlemagne Prize award to EU Council President Donald Tusk in Aachen on 13 May 2010, she said in her laudation: 'Should the euro fail, much more is at stake than just a currency. In that event what fails is Europe, the very idea of European unification,' a warning she was to repeat in a speech at the Bundestag on 19 May. This dramatic claim, however, did not in itself contribute to building confidence in European unification, given the fact that Merkel was reducing the EU to a monetary community. Merkel found the euro already laden with a great deal of historical baggage and she made it quite clear that the currency was closely associated with the future of the entire European project. Its failure was something the EU should not be prepared even to consider and there could be no question of any country leaving the eurozone. There was no legal basis for the expulsion of any individual country and the interest of the entire EU was best served, according to Merkel, by the continued existence of the eurozone in its present form. Its disintegration threatened the very foundations of the Union. The collapse of the Lehman Brothers investment bank in September 2008 and the close global interdependence of the international banking and financial markets, which led to European credit institutes being saddled with bucketloads of bad loans and worthless derivatives, resulted in these institutes having to undertake substantial value adjustments and to ask for state help. This was a matter of concern for all EU member states and especially so for the structurally weak countries in Europe's south, which had already been mired in debt before the advent of the crisis. The inevitable downgrading of the credit rating of these countries pushed up borrowing rates. The sovereign debt crisis had required a first aid package in a nominal total of 107.3 billion euros for Athens as early as April 2010; the final transfer had amounted to 73 billion euros. Since Greece's economy had contracted by 20 per cent since 2008, more aid was needed and more was provided. Created in June 2010 and designed to serve as a mechanism of interim stabilization, the European Financial Stability Facility (EFSF) proved inadequate to coping with the fallout of the crisis in the eurozone. The 'leverage effect' could not guarantee decisive success, and nor was the European Central Bank (ECB) up to settling all the state deficits. In addition to Greece, Ireland, Portugal and Spain had become dependent on aid. In view of the EFSF programme's lifespan coming to an end in 2013, demands to install a long-term mechanism for warding off actual and future crises were voiced. Angela Merkel, who had still been nursing doubts about how to proceed in the first half of 2010, at last joined French President Nicolas Sarkozy in an effort to tackle the crisis. On the agenda of the EU summit on 23 July 2010 were the reform of the financial sector, an increase of capital reserves, the reduction of manager bonuses and stress tests for financial institutions. At Germany's instigation, on 29 October a European Council addressed the question of how the eurozone could be made more resistant to crises. Having rejected, at the initiative of several EU member states such as Germany, the idea of Eurobonds as a tool to regulate sovereign debt defaults, the heads of states and governments of the Euro Group reached an agreement proposed by Germany at the European Council on 16–17 December 2010 to rephrase Article 136 and provide further details on the provisions of the EU Treaty to give the stability mechanism a legal basis. The unbundling and downsizing of banking conglomerates and the creation of new fiscal authorities were measures that were felt to be necessary. On 1 January 2011 three new European financial supervisory authorities went on stream for banks, insurance, company pensions and securities. On 25 March the Euro-Plus Pact was adopted with a view to strengthening economic and fiscal discipline in the Economic and Monetary Union of the EU. It provided the basis for a eurozone agreement designed to call into being a long-term European Stability Mechanism (ESM). Klaus Regling, blooded at the International Monetary Fund (IMF) and the EU Commission, took on the role of crisis manager at the ESM in Luxembourg with a war chest filled with several billion euros, which allowed it to pull Greece back from the brink again and again.

It did not take long for criticism of this fiscal strategy to be voiced: with their policy of rescuing the euro, 'Merkozy' (Merkel in tandem with Sarkozy) were driving a wedge into the continent. The allegations of the portmanteau term for the Franco-German crisis management (2008–12) missed their mark. 'Two-speed Europe' in the fields of trade, trade balance, growth and export was a long-established reality, but it was generally ignored. There was, however, another point of criticism that was more pertinent: Germany had become a crisis profiteer. Steadily improving economic data had resulted in zero or even negative rates of interest on newly issued government bonds. In contrast to this, other countries of the eurozone such as Italy, which had been in the habit of reacting to economic crises by devaluing their currency, now found themselves caught in a euro trap. The charge was therefore raised repeatedly that, by ensuring the stability of the euro and enforcing fiscal restraint, Germany was fanning the crisis in Europe's south and splitting the continent in order to cement its dominance.

The ESM and a fiscal pact tied granting credits to countries mired in debt to conditions that satisfied the German demand for 'conditionality'. This was a necessary precondition to ensure the German public would play ball. The point the afflicted countries were making was that austerity alone, without programmes to stimulate the economy, was only going to make matters worse. Rising unemployment figures, violent rioting and the increasing impoverishment of broad sectors of society were the inevitable result. More than 18 million were unemployed across the EU by July 2012. All of this was especially salient for Greece, regardless of the fact that in November 2012 the country had received renewed assurances of aid totalling 43.7 billion euros. For Germany, as Europe's financial and economic powerhouse, the euro was a highly effective device for enforcing discipline and cohesion at the EU level. In concert with the heads of state and government of the powerful eurozone countries, Germany did everything in its power to ensure the euro's stability. On 26 July 2012 the President of the ECB Mario Draghi undertook, in view of the ECB's government bond purchasing scheme, 'to do whatever it takes' to defend the euro. 'And believe me – it will be enough.' In September 2012 this architect of the EU's fiscal U-turn, reputedly in hock to the taskmaster Germany, overruled critics who maintained that the ECB was not entitled to meddle in economic policy, declaring there was going to be no limit to the ECB's purchases of government bonds. He cited the independence of the ECB, which did not make his zero-interest policy any more palatable to German savers.

All this gave the ECB, bolstered by the ESM, the role of a political actor in the containment of the euro crisis. In the eyes of some, the ECB was a veritable white knight selflessly committed to buying up government bonds issued by the countries in crisis; for others, it had overstepped its mandate and was ignoring the dangers of inflation, much to the chagrin of the President of the German Federal Bank, Jens Weidmann, and other exponents of the German culture of stability. While initially charging the ECB with having broken a taboo with its government bond purchasing scheme, these critics fell silent when the emergency measures to calm the financial markets began to yield a measure of success.

Success in the containment of the euro crisis depended to a large extent on Germany's capacity for compromise. The country had been the Community's largest net payer from the very beginning. German contributions were actually often higher than was required by the size of the country's population and economy. According to the Berlin political scientist Herfried Münkler, Germany had to remain committed to bolstering Brussels' compromise-finding process financially, thus in effect continuing Kohl's 'politics of the cheque book'. Given the increase in political clout this entailed, the German government knew better than to translate this into a claim for political influence and to communicate any such ambitions to its own population. Merkel consistently avoided taking on a high profile, which would have come with the risk of conjuring up memories of Germany's past and of the Second World War. This had to be avoided at all costs. It was only logical for a third aid package for Greece to follow in 2015. Regardless of this, the Greek parliament passed a resolution in 2019 requiring the two countries to enter into negotiations on outstanding reparations for crimes committed by the Wehrmacht in the Second World War. The claims concerned looted gold and forced loans that had never been repaid and added up to a sum of between 250 and 300 billion euros. Berlin considered these claims to be void in view of the Two-Plus-Four Treaty of 1991 and refused to countenance pressure from claims couched in the terms of the politics of the past, let alone allow itself to be blackmailed. Similar claims were voiced by Poland and were met with the same response. In any such calculations, Germany's cession of territory to Poland and the millions of Germans expelled by Warsaw after the Second World War were conspicuous through their absence. The unconditional rejection of the Greek and the Polish reparation claims by Germany in 2018/19, based on legal international law treaties, marks a significant difference between the Bonn and the Berlin Republics.

Ongoing 'Reconstruction of the East'; Abrupt Repudiation of Atomic Energy; the Neo-Nazi and Right-wing Underground

'Flourishing landscapes' of the sort predicted for East Germany by Helmut Kohl in the 1990 electoral campaign were never going to be easy to realize in the new Länder. By 2010 almost 3 million East Germans had voted with their feet against the viability of that prospect. The chief obstacles were the depopulation of entire regions, the shortage of human resources in the professions and in medical care, and the absence of a productive industrial base and of a middle class, hounded to extinction by more than 40 years of Communist rule. While the former East Germany has made a great deal of economic progress since reunification, this is largely the result of the support it has received from its Western counterpart. This has led to many 'Ossis', as East Germans were dubbed with more than a touch of condescension, regarding themselves as second-class citizens. The deficit in lived equality resulting from four decades of separation and a socialist planned economy did not lend itself to quick fixes. Inequality persisted, breeding feelings of inferiority. This, however, did not have any effect on government policy, not at first anyway.

On 22 September 2013 the CDU, led by Merkel, came to within touching distance of an absolute majority. Forty per cent of votes for the CDU put her at the zenith of her power – but this did not alter the fact that the nation was confronted with a host of problems. The most urgent issue to be dealt with by the newly formed CDU-SPD coalition was the migration crisis, which rapidly escalated towards the end of the summer of 2015. This crisis had grave repercussions for the political atmosphere and the party-specific mix of interests in the East. Large sectors of the population there were about to succumb to change fatigue after what they had felt was an extremely demanding transformation process in the wake of reunification. People had the feeling that they had been exposed to a surfeit of finger-wagging from the West, whether of the paternalistic and friendly or of the condescending and unfriendly kind. Both attitudes were seen as arrogant, as the former Federal Minister of the Interior Thomas de Maizière, a resident of Dresden, noted.

In 2014 Thüringen elected Bodo Ramelow as its minister president, a premier, in view of the fact that Ramelow belongs to Die Linke, a party supported to a significant extent by former SED members and sympathizers. In September 2017 Merkel managed to hold on to a majority, which allowed her to continue as Federal Chancellor. However, as these Bundestag elections made quite clear (see below) with the comparatively strong showing of the 'Alternative für Deutschland' (AfD) especially in the 'new Länder', what was still missing in Germany, more than 25 years after reunification, was a unification of hearts and minds. 'Ossis' and 'Wessis' accepted one another, but there was little genuine understanding on either side. Thinking also continued to be channelled in the old categories by the older generation. The 'reconstruction of the East' and West German transfer payments, funded through the Solidarity Surcharge, the 'Soli', secured the continuity and stability of the new Berlin Republic, but did not give the East enough manoeuvring space, an urge for innovation or self-confidence. A mindset that mirrors 40 years of SED rule, which is widespread among the middle and the older generations, is not helpful either.

After the disaster in Japan's Fukushima Daiichi nuclear power plant on 11 March 2011, caused by major earthquakes and a tsunami hitting the power station and followed by multiple meltdowns, explosions and a catastrophic release of radioactivity resulting in a spike of cancer deaths, Merkel announced only three days later, on 14 March, an abrupt U-turn in Germany's energy policy. This was done without her having previously informed her own party and without consulting the Bundestag or having put the matter to the vote. The Federal Cabinet subsequently decided on 6 June 2011 to put eight nuclear power stations out of service immediately and to bring in a gradual withdrawal from nuclear energy, to be completed by 2022. It was unclear at this stage how these decisions were going to be implemented, given their far-reaching implications for investments and energy costs. However, the proposal for Germany to withdraw from nuclear energy altogether found a solid Bundestag majority on 30 June. On 8 July 2011 the Federal Council (Bundesrat) passed the requisite legislative package.

Somehow Merkel never got round to explaining the reasons for her change of mind, nor was an internal party debate on the topic forthcoming in either the CDU or the CSU. The nuclear catastrophe in the Far East had made the Federal Chancellor change her energy-related political course practically overnight. Having given the green light to the lifetime extension of German nuclear power plants in 2010 in the wake of the Bundestag elections, thereby cancelling the anti-nuclear energy consensus, she now embarked almost singlehandedly on a course that would put renewable energy centre stage.

After the MCA (maximum credible accident) on Fukushima, the Ethics Commission was convened for the sole purpose of rubber-stamping a political decision that had already been taken and of officially certifying what society more or less as a whole agreed upon. One of the consequences of this headlong flight from nuclear energy was that power-plant operators took the government to court, suing for compensation for their lost investments, which they had made on the assurance that the reactors would remain in operation for much longer. They won their case.

In addition, the German energy industry had to cope with the decommissioning of brown-coal-fired power stations and with what was called the Hard Coal Pact, which attempted to rein in coal-based power generation in general. The energy transition project, in which Germany was supposed to play a pioneering role and serve as a model for other countries, was aimed at stopping global warming. Closer to home, tens of thousands of jobs were lost, especially in the car and the brown coal industries.

Fukushima and the controversy surrounding the railway project 'Stuttgart 21' put Winfried Kretschmann into Baden-Württemberg's driver's seat as that state's first Green minister president, spelling an end to the CDU's decades-long monopoly on government in the 'Ländle'. Since the state elections in Mecklenburg-Vorpommern in 2016 the Greens have been represented in all state parliaments as well as in the Bundestag. Buoyed by a wave of sympathy, their two leaders, Robert Habeck and Annalena Baerbock, make a point of hobnobbing with voters and sympathizers, enhancing their reputation for tactile warmth and their popular appeal.

On 4 November 2011 the ignominious past cast its shadows on the young Berlin republic. A group calling itself 'Nationalsozialistischer Untergrund' (NSU) was charged with the murders of persons of Turkish and/or Greek origin. The NSU was a neo-Nazi terror organization that had been active since the end of the 1990s, motivated by xenophobic and racist ideas of killing citizens who were immigrants. Between 2000 and 2007 Jena-born Uwe Mundlos, Uwe Böhnhardt and Beate Zschäpe, leading a secretive existence in Chemnitz and Zwickau, killed nine migrants and a policewoman, made attempts on the lives of 40 other people, orchestrated three bomb attacks in Nürnberg (1999) and in Cologne (2001, 2004), and committed fifteen robberies. The total number of those in the know, of sympathizers, accomplices and supporters and their networks, has remained unclear to this day, with estimates that include right-wing extremist sympathizers and confidential informants on the payroll of the Office for the Protection of the Constitution (Bundesamt für Verfassungsschutz, BfV) going into three figures. The NSU was brought to public attention when the bodies of Mundlos and Böhnhardt were discovered in a burnt-out camper and Zschäpe set fire to her apartment in Zwickau to destroy evidence and started mailing confessional videos. For far too long police investigations had remained focused on the personal environments of the victims, nonplussing and embittering their relatives. The protracted underperformance of the police force led to a breakdown of trust in internal security policy. People on the staff of the Office for the Protection of the Constitution destroyed decisive evidence after the three people at the centre of the NSU had their cover blown. In 2012 the heads of the Federal Office for the Protection of the Constitution and of the corresponding state authorities in Thüringen, Sachsen and Berlin were forced to resign. Fact-finding commissions in the Bundestag and in eight state parliaments sought to screen the questionable use of confidential informants. Flaws in investigative procedures, administrative shortcomings and the names of putative and actual supporters came to light. It was only in the context of the NSU trial, which went on for years, that more details about the milieu in which those crimes were planned and perpetrated started to emerge. The trial of Beate Zschäpe and four alleged accomplices at the Munich

Higher Regional Court faced a slow start in May 2013 owing to the main defendant's protracted refusal to testify. Having been found guilty of complicity in the murders, the bomb attacks and one case of first-degree arson, she was given a life sentence on 11 July 2018. Four accomplices were sentenced to several years in prison. Especially repulsive was the behaviour shown by her sympathizers during the trial and sentencing.

These alarming events again elicited public statements by top representatives of the Federal Republic reaffirming continued commitment to atoning for the crimes committed during the Third Reich. Neo-Nazi terror as exemplified by the NSU made this necessary. Nor was this the only case in which right-wing extremism reared its head. It had even infiltrated the Bundeswehr.

A special case in point are the so-called 'Reichsbürger', 20,000 or so partly armed people who view the Federal Republic as the 'FRG dictatorship' and consider themselves to be citizens of the German Reich. The group includes members of the security services. 'Reichsbürger' Wolfgang P. shot and killed a special forces policeman in an attempt to keep intruders out of his one-man state.

In the summer of 2019 another right-wing Neo-Nazi underground emerged, a network called 'Nordkreuz', based in Brandenburg and Mecklenburg-Vorpommern, with affiliated groups 'West-' and 'Südkreuz'. These groups had compiled a hit list with the names and addresses of 25,000 people all over Germany whom they regard as their political enemies, people belonging to the left half of the political spectrum with a special focus on those who had expressed sympathy for refugees.

How serious this threat is became apparent when Walter Lübcke, a former CDU member of Hessen's Landtag and from 2009 to his death district president of Kassel, was shot and killed in front of his house on 2 June 2019. Public engagement for refugees and his critical attitude towards the supporters of PEGIDA (see below) had given Lübcke prominence across Germany. A right-wing extremist was arrested on 15 June 2019 as the prime suspect and confessed to the murder, but later withdrew his confession.

On 9 October 2019 an armed right-wing extremist tried to break into the synagogue in Halle an der Saale with a view to causing carnage among the Jews assembled there for Yom Kippur. When he failed to burst through the fortified door, the professed anti-Semite shot and killed a woman who happened to be passing the synagogue and a man in a kebab shop. On the run he shot another two people, badly injuring them, before being arrested by two police officers on patrol. Causing a shock that engulfed all of Germany, the crime was called 'previously unthinkable' by Federal President Frank-Walter Steinmeier. Realizing that they had underestimated the intensity of anti-Semitic feeling in certain pockets of society, the police subsequently stepped up the protection given to Jewish institutions.

At the beginning of 2020, the Berlin Republic was in shock. On 19 February several people were murdered in the Hesse city of Hanau. The perpetrator shot eight men and one woman with an immigrant background in and in front of two shisha bars as well as his 72-year-old mother and then himself. Five of the victims had German citizenship, two Turkish and one each Afghan, Bosnian, Bulgarian and Romanian. Because of strong suspicions of a terrorist act, the Federal General Prosecutor immediately took charge of the investigation, as 'there were serious indications of a racist background'. The perpetrator had an Islamophobic, anti-Semitic and xenophobic world view, influenced by various conspiracy theories, and called for violent struggle and the annihilation of the population of entire states. Accusations were made that German authorities were doing too little to combat right-wing extremism and right-wing terrorism, which were described as the greatest potential threat in Germany at present.

Two weeks after the racist attack in Hanau, the city commemorated the victims with a central memorial service. Steinmeier called the act an 'attack on the basic understanding of our living together'. However, the grief and anger was mixed with determination: 'We stand together. We stick together. Because we want to live together,' he said.

NSA Wikileaks, the 'Refugee Crisis' and 'Wir schaffen das!'

The disclosures of the former CIA employee and whistleblower Edward Snowden made clear the extent of the global surveillance and espionage practices of the US foreign intelligence service. The ensuing upheaval centring on the National Security Agency (NSA) had repercussions in Germany. While initially the Federal government tried to restore calm by asserting that German citizens and authorities were not affected, this soon turned out to be manifestly untrue when it became known that Merkel's telephone had been hacked before she became chancellor. Spying among friends was a no go, Merkel told Washington, a message that presumably had little effect. Furthermore, the Federal Intelligence Service (Bundesnachrichtendienst; BND) and the NSA continued to make common cause. The indignation shown by Berlin felt like tokenism. German top politicians had to be aware that they were at least occasionally on the radar of foreign secret services, since after German reunification the United States and Great Britain had insisted on keeping their existing competences in Germany, which included spying on

German citizens and companies. It is widely assumed that the United States and Great Britain tied their consent to German unification to the new entity forgoing the exercise of certain sovereignty rights. This is why the British and the US secret services are legally permitted to engage in espionage unhindered. Germany did not attain full sovereignty after reunification and the Two-Plus-Four treaty, and the former occupation forces were not fully withdrawn. They were now the forces of 'friendly' allies, who continued to be stationed on German soil as partners with undiminished rights.

In trying to understand this change, the following facts may be helpful: since the 1990s the relationship between the United States and the EU, with its constantly growing economic clout, had become increasingly overshadowed by competition and conflict. The intensification of Germany's economic collaboration with China, Iran and Russia and the aforementioned export of armaments made Anglo-American economic espionage imperative from the point of view of their respective countries. Close communication between the NSA and the US business sector was evident. Anglo-American interest in eavesdropping on Germany and the German export industry had acquired an altogether new significance and urgency compared with the time of the Cold War, when the Federal Republic, kept on a short leash, was much easier to control.

Given this background, the hacking of Merkel's mobile phone comes as no surprise. The sovereignty of the Federal Republic has always had its limits, a fact Wolfgang Schäuble for one made quite clear when, as early as 2011, he publicly declared that 'in Germany we have been fully sovereign at no time since 8 May 1945' – an assertion to the effect that the post-war state has outlasted 1990, the year of German unification. 'German-American friendship' presupposed a relationship of trust, which was quite simply no longer possible, particularly after it became clear that the United States was determined to pursue its own interests ruthlessly at the expense of other countries it called its allies. Upon the breaking of the NSA scandal President Obama's ratings in Germany dropped temporarily to the same depths as those of his warmongering predecessor, George W. Bush. A majority of Germans felt that the United States was no longer trustworthy and raised Snowden to the status of a hero who had been reduced to seeking refuge in Moscow. Snowden's application for asylum in Germany and the debate this triggered in the country led Washington to demand that this not even be considered; the German government promptly complied. Snowden then publicly criticized the Federal Chancellor for denying him asylum. In 2017 the Federal Prosecutor dropped all proceedings in the NSA scandal. This was a politically opportune move aimed at staving off further harassment.

The rapid economic development seen in the Bonn Republic since the 1950s had led to a steep decline in unemployment, soon accompanied by shortages in the construction sector, in agriculture and in small businesses in general. Setting up liaison offices in Southern Europe and in Turkey, the Federal government began canvassing for labourers. In 1964 the one-millionth *Gastarbeiter*, someone from Portugal, was welcomed in a ceremony that included the gift of a motorbike; in the early 1970s the 2 million mark was reached. In many cases these economic migrants were joined by family members. Rapidly arising questions concerning social integration both in the school system and in the world of employment were left unanswered and attracted little public attention, mainly because it was generally assumed that the migrant labourers were only here to help out during the boom and would sooner or later return to their native countries. That Germany was increasingly becoming an immigration society was a fact the government either did not recognize or simply refused to see and admit.

When in August and September 2015 hundreds of thousands of people fled countries torn by civil war such as Syria and sought refuge in Germany, where Merkel welcomed them, it became painfully obvious that the Federal government, having been remiss for decades in the integration of *Gastarbeiter*, had no tried and proven strategy to handle new waves of immigration. Integration deficits owed above all to cultural differences resulted in barriers arising between the migrant labourers and the German population. Since the 1980s, and maybe even earlier, it had been evident that parallel societies were emerging.

In 2015 war refugees from the Middle and Near East were added to this mix on a massive scale: more than a million people, Egyptians, Afghans, Algerians, Iraqis, Jordanians, Libyans, Tunisians and Syrians, having made their way across the Mediterranean, were attempting to gain a foothold in the EU and start a new life. In Germany this development was referred to as the 'refugee crisis', a term that is obviously misleading. It would be more to the point to refer to this intra-European problem as a crisis of solidarity. The massive rise in the numbers of new arrivals in the second half of 2015 posed insurmountable problems for Italy and Greece, which led to tranches of refugees simply being waved through in the direction of their preferred destinations, Austria and Germany.

The rapidly deteriorating situation and its dramatic consequences were insufficiently understood by the German government. There was no genuine expertise in the Office of the Federal Chancellor or in the Ministry of the Interior, nor was there any regular involvement or consultation of experts on migration. The wake-up call inherent in the arrival of thousands of refugees on the Italian island of

Lampedusa had not been heeded and no relevant joint initiatives had been pursued at EU level.

There had been prior warning in the first half of 2015: on 7 May the Federal Agency of Migration and Refugees (Bundesamt für Migrationsfragen; BAMF) announced that 450,000 refugees were expected to arrive in Germany. On 19 August Federal Minister of the Interior Thomas de Maizière had to almost double that figure to 800,000. On 31 August, when Budapest and Vienna signalled their wish to send what was felt to be an unmanageable stream of refugees to Germany on 4/5 September, Merkel used words at a press conference that were soon to return to haunt her. On that occasion, the Chancellor declared herself ready to welcome the refugees, noting that Germany was a 'powerful country': 'The attitude with which we approach these matters must be: We've accomplished so much, we can do this. We can do it (*Wir schaffen das*), and wherever something blocks the way, it needs to be overcome.' Sounding almost like an ultimatum in the ears of some sectors of German society, what remained unclear in this statement was just who constituted the first-person plural used by Merkel in her declaration: did 'we' refer to Germans only or did she include all other Europeans?

Furthermore, the crucial question, whose complexity made an unequivocal answer elusive for years to come, was *how* a solution was to be found. Having over-ruled the reservations of her Minister of the Interior, the Federal Chancellor decided not to stop or turn back the influx of refugees. At Budapest's Keleti railway station Albanians, Iraqis and Syrians were chanting 'Deutschland, Deutschland!' and 'Merkel, Merkel!' When the Hungarian authorities refused to give the green light to the departure of the massively overcrowded trains, the refugees set off on foot along motorways and railway tracks and across fields, woods and meadows in the direction of Germany. On 5 September Merkel spoke on the phone with Hungary's Fidesz Party Prime Minister Viktor Orbán and Austrian Federal Chancellor Werner Faymann (SPÖ). Orbán declared the situation was out of control. Merkel and Faymann decided to waive border checks. Merkel's government spokesperson announced that Germany would not turn the refugees away. On 13 September de Maizière reasserted himself by announcing the reintroduction of border checks, a step he had agreed in advance with the SPD leadership. The Office of the Federal Chancellor reacted to this development by declaring that 'orderly procedure' had to be reinstated. This was not yet exactly a U-turn but it did signal to its European partners that Germany was going to reintroduce border checks. While this did not solve the underlying problem, it at least put it on a to-do list. When asked on 15 September 2015 whether she thought she herself had contributed to the escalation of the refugee crisis, Merkel replied that there were situations where one could not possibly 'deliberate for twelve hours'; a decision had to be taken then and there. Putting aside this argument from imminent necessity for the moment, she moved on to express her appreciation of the Germans' readiness to help, which had done wonders for the country's image abroad. Other members of the EU saw this differently, viewing the Chancellor's generosity and her candour alike with scepticism. They worried about what all this was going to mean for their own countries.

What remained largely unsaid was that the head of the German government did not get to choose – in the face of international obligations and treaties such as the Geneva Conventions, the Universal Declaration of Human Rights, the European Convention on Human Rights of the Council of Europe and the German Constitution – between whether she was going to receive politically persecuted asylum seekers or not. Nor was there any serious consideration of the question of what the international response and the political verdict would have been if the Chancellor had decided otherwise; if she had cold-shouldered the refugees and turned them away at the German border. Appealing to the conscience of the other EU member states with the same ultimatum-like, rather flat rhetoric she had used in the euro crisis and claiming there was no viable alternative, she said, 'if Europe fails on the refugee crisis, if this close link to universal human rights is broken, then we will lose one of the crucial founding incentives of a united Europe – one that has defined us since the very beginning. We must take care that such impulses never cease to bind us.'

Herfried Münkler has interpreted Merkel's decision not to close the German border to refugees in the late summer of 2015 in the light of Germany's role as the dominant power at the heart of the continent: if the German border had been closed on the night of 4/5 September 2015, this would have meant the definitive end of the Schengen Area. It would have led to a tremendous tailback of hundreds of thousands of refugees on the Balkan route, which would have been a burden the weak states in that area could not possibly have borne and which would have subjected the fragile ethnic-religious balance of these states after the wars of the disintegration of Yugoslavia to a dramatic stress test. The German decision to receive these people, if only to prevent a feared collapse of order in the Balkans between Bosnia-Herzegovina and Greece, had demonstrated, according to Münkler, that the Federal government was acting in its role of steward of a collective good, namely stability in the Balkans, and remained committed to its European responsibility. A heavy price had to be paid for this, again according to the German professor, in the rise of the AfD (see below). Vicious infighting had seemed to spell a steep downward trend for this right-wing party in the summer of 2015. What became known as the refugee crisis reversed that trend so that the party was again polling in the double-digit range by the beginning of 2016.

That said, there was more. Merkel's decision on 5 September 2015, taken in agreement with Budapest and Vienna, to allow the refugees who were massing at the Austro-Hungarian border to cross into Germany – without prior registration in either Hungary or in any of the other countries they had crossed on their way and therefore in flagrant contravention of the Dublin Accord – broke applicable EU regulations. This led to controversies in public – and published – opinion, while a temporary state of emergency descended on those German cities and municipalities that bore the brunt of Merkel's policy. She soon turned to stressing the need for a joint, uniform European asylum und refugee policy, which was to give priority to integration. Part of that policy was the streamlining of asylum procedures and the expeditious deportation of economic migrants. However, neither of these two measures could be implemented to the extent envisaged under the policy; they were therefore unrealistic. Also on Merkel's agenda were warnings against the formation of parallel societies and an assurance that xenophobic attacks would be met with criminal prosecution. In fact, such societies were already in existence in Germany, and further attacks of the kind that had already taken place in the town of Freital in Saxony since 2015 were extremely likely. On 22 June these attacks escalated, with demonstrators ready to use violence pouring in from outside, resulting in regular sieges being laid to asylum seekers' homes. Protest had engendered the formation of vigilante groups. There were bomb attacks on refugee centres and on refugee-friendly politicians, followed by counter demonstrations and campaigns of solidarity with refugees.

The massive, uncontrolled and undocumented influx of refugees was followed on 13 September 2015 by the reintroduction of border checks, which were now widely believed to be necessary. According to the Schengen Agreement, such checks were permissible in the eponymous area only in exceptional situations and limited to a maximum of six months. Shortly afterwards, Austria, Slovakia and the Netherlands similarly announced the reintroduction of border checks. This de facto suspension of the Dublin Accord put the refugees in a situation where they had to decide in what country to apply for asylum, a decision inevitably influenced by an appraisal of the quality of life in the respective country and the availability of social benefits.

On 1 September 2015 Merkel had insisted that there was no 'upper limit' to the basic right of asylum for the victims of political persecution, a principle especially valid for war refugees. Her position provoked criticism even in her own party and in the CSU, the CDU's sister party. Horst Seehofer, Bavarian minister president since 2008 and leader of the CSU, repeatedly demanded that an upper limit should be set to new arrivals. After a prolonged struggle with the political establishment and the Chancellor, he succeeded in creating what became known as 'anchor centres' (*Ankerzentren*). These are designed to accommodate refugees from their arrival through the asylum procedure and to its conclusion, whether that be acceptance or deportation.

The CDU Party Conference on 13 December 2015 in Karlsruhe succeeded in formulating a compromise, which avoided the mention of an absolute limit while committing to a 'palpable reduction of the number of refugees' in the country. Merkel doggedly reiterated her 'We can do it', adding that 'I am entitled to say that because it is part of our country's identity that we succeed in our most ambitious objectives.'

At the turn of the year a change in the German immigration policy was in the wind: in a government declaration on asylum policy delivered to the Bundestag on 16 December, Merkel declared her support for the EU's stated intention to step up securing its external border by means of an EU agency such as Warsaw-based FRONTEX, even in cases where the countries in question felt this was not needed.

In 2015 Germany had 890,000 registered asylum seekers. The government passed two legislative packages concerning asylum and migration but the Federal Office of Migration and Refugees kept attracting hostile headlines because of systems overload and irregularities in registration.

Merkel's seemingly off-the-cuff announcement in early September on the distribution of refugees among EU member states, which had not been voted on in the Bundestag, elicited very little in the way of positive response from the countries concerned. At the same time, she clarified her own approach to the issue by saying that for Germany the 'opportunities' created by migrants 'outweighed the risks', with, admittedly, the caveat that integration was an indispensable prerequisite. With this remark Merkel put her finger on the sore point, the decades-old, seemingly intractable problem of integration. A comprehensive solution for the refugee issue was not forthcoming from Merkel, and neither was a keynote speech on Germany, Europe and Islam, which the population felt was urgently needed, all the more so when terrorist attacks began hitting Germany. Merkel preferred to sit the problem out and to shroud it in silence, even though it was apparent that an excessively liberal refugee policy was at odds with providing internal security. The German population was at risk from terrorists smuggled into the country by the

Islamic State, the terrorist militia whose Middle East caliphate had been defeated militarily in March 2019. The number of officially identified Salafists in Germany, people who reject values such as democracy and gender equality and are intolerant of other religions, rose between 2017 and 2019 from 10,800 to 11,500.

Islamist Terrorism, Merkel's Sinking Star and Germany's Loss of its Leadership Capacity in Europe

Europe has repeatedly been struck by terrorist attacks committed by perpetrators belonging to a wide range of ideological camps. In Germany, too, terrorists claimed victims. Against the backdrop of a partly clueless, partly naive 'culture of welcome', the omission of security political precautions and a disregard for warnings about potential terrorism planted the seeds for a bloody harvest. In the wake of massive crowd-groping incidents and other sexual assaults against women near Cologne's main railway station on New Year's Eve 2015/16, which were at first swept under the carpet by the media and only investigated hesitantly after persistent complaints, an Islamist-inspired terrorist act took place on 18 July 2016 in Würzburg-Heidingsfeld, committed by a seemingly well-integrated, inconspicuous underage Afghan refugee, who used an axe and a knife to assault five passengers on a regional train, causing critical injuries. He tried to escape but was shot and killed by a special police unit who had rushed to the crime scene. The unit was then criticized by Green politicians and a sector of the public, who wondered whether the perpetrator's motif had been 'helplessness' or, in what can only be called a bizarre attempt to shift responsibility away from him, society's unwillingness to integrate him.

Acting in the name of the Islamic State, a Syrian refugee carried out a bomb attack in Ansbach near Nuremberg on 24 July 2016, which injured fifteen people and killed the attacker. It was the first suicide attack on German soil. In December 2018 four inebriated refugees aged between seventeen and nineteen launched indiscriminate attacks on defenceless citizens, injuring twelve. The media at first attempted to tone down the incident, but subsequent investigation revealed its seriousness. The charge of causing grievous bodily harm landed an Iranian refugee and his accomplices from Afghanistan in prison and marked them for subsequent deportation.

The climax of Islamist terrorism was an attack that took place on 19 December 2016 towards 8 p.m. at Breitscheid Platz near Berlin's Gedächtniskirche, where an Islamist terrorist, Anis Amri, crashed a trailer, whose Polish driver he had previously shot and killed, into a Christmas market, killing eleven people and injuring 55 others, some of them critically. Amri managed to flee from the scene and it was only after two days that he was revealed to be the prime suspect, even though he had been on the authorities' radar and tabs had been kept on him for more than a year owing to information obtained from a confidential informant. It was known that he was planning an attack and to kill as many people as possible in the 'name of Allah'. On 23 December the 24-year-old Tunisian was shot and killed by a police patrol during a routine check in Italy's Sesto San Giovanni. The Islamic State posted a message on its website that Amri, who had resided for years in various places in Germany under a number of different identities, had been acting on their behalf.

In August 2018 the Saxon city Chemnitz hit national and international headlines. The death of a 35-year-old Cuban German, Daniel Hillig, unleashed massive protests by the citizens, followed by xenophobic, right-wing rioting and days of demonstrations and counter-demonstrations by different political groupings. On the fringe of a *Stadtfest* squabbles had broken out on 26/27 August and again on 1 September 2018, which saw Hillig stabbed to death and two others critically injured. When the news broke that the presumed culprits were migrants and refugees, right-wing and extreme right-wing groups organized a series of major demonstrations meant as a show of force. The ugly mood spread to other parts of Germany, where extremists and Neo-Nazis targeted actual or presumed migrants, policemen, journalists, passers-by and a Jewish restaurant. Throwing warnings of the Office for the Protection of the Constitution to the wind, the police grossly miscalculated the size of the demonstrations and the readiness of the demonstrators to use violence. This resulted in the police being hopelessly outnumbered on the ground. The city's reaction to the ensuing mayhem was to organize a free rock and pop concert to protest against right-wing extremism under the motto 'Wir sind mehr' (There are more of us). The concert attracted a crowd of 65,000.

European crisis management on the migration question remained patchy at best. Member states proved clueless and helpless in their attempts to regulate the stream of refugees. The increase in the number of new arrivals was partly blamed on the German Chancellor's refugee-friendly attitude and on the 'culture of welcome', which had predominated in the early days. Shared immediately on modern communications networks, some of Merkel's statements decidedly lent themselves to being interpreted as a standing invitation to migrants of all stripes to come to Europe, which had ultimately led to a suspension of the Schengen Agreement. Otherwise known for her balanced judgement and cool rationality, the Chancellor had pushed up refugee numbers in Germany by her emotional and bracing but insufficiently considered 'We can do it!' On top of this, she had also caused a great deal of irritation in other EU member states. She was quickly made aware of the limits of European support and solidarity especially by Central and East European member states, which had reacted in 2015/16 by putting up barbed wire fences several metres high, unmistakably marking the end of the 'Refugees welcome' path.

The Southern Europeans' rejection of Merkel's generous migration policy was motivated not least by the grudge they bore her for the austerity policy she had imposed on them as part of her efforts to contain the 'euro crisis' back in 2008. The 'refugee crisis' quickly expanded into a solidarity crisis and then into a governmental crisis in Berlin, with support for Merkel's leadership beginning to crumble. Europe's troubleshooter was showing signs of fatigue. By the autumn of 2015 the only course that remained open for her and her team was to backpedal to prevent any further erosion of trust. A fundamental insight that is still far from generally appreciated even today opened up: without the collaboration of other EU countries Germany would always struggle to get its way within the Community. For crisis management to be effective there needs to be a joint effort, with most, if not all, EU members pooling their forces. By 2015 Merkel had been forced to switch from action to reaction at the European level. The liability of the 'refugee crisis' was exploited by other EU politicians intent on weakening Merkel's position. As the Berlin Republic sought to cope with the previously underestimated influx of refugees in 2015, it learnt the hard way that unquestioning European loyalty could not be taken for granted, as Merkel had originally assumed. Her nemesis, Hungary's anti-migrant Prime Minister Viktor Orbán, called this out as 'moral imperialism'.

Closing the Balkan Route, the Refugee Agreement Struck with Turkey, Rising Tensions between Brussels and Ankara, and the Establishment of the AfD

The failure to protect the EU's external border and disagreement among member states regarding the introduction of a quota system for the distribution of refugees were grist to the mill of the EU's opponents, critics and sceptics, who failed to realize, let alone admit, that the member states were at the root of the problem. In the UK, where criticism of anything coming out of the EU was fomented by the tabloids' one-sided coverage, Merkel's attitude in the refugee question was equated with a failure of nerve at a critical juncture and as the breakdown of state authority: Berlin had unilaterally suspended the Schengen Agreement, sown discord among EU member states and divided the EU. By not returning the refugees to Syria, even though they had first made landfall in the EU in some other member state, Germany had infringed the Dublin Accord. 'Take back control' was the message distilled from this critique, which was as simplistic as the political plans of the Brexit advocates.

Nevertheless, this critique could not easily be refuted. A quota system for the distribution of refugees to individual states had long been debated without success. The Dublin Accord with its regulation concerning first-reception states had been designed for a relatively low number of refugees and proved unworkable in the face of so massive an influx, all the more so since its implementation was largely left to Southern European EU member states still reeling from the banking, finance and sovereign debt crisis. Germany, Austria and Sweden, the three countries that had taken in the bulk of the refugees, pleaded for a quota regulation, with the Visegrád Group – Poland, Czechia, Slovakia and Hungary – most vociferously opposed. They were joined by the UK, which in the years after EU enlargement to the east had seen a significant influx of Central and Eastern Europeans in areas of the service industry, such as the culinary sector. Hundreds of thousands of Polish immigrants had moved to the United Kingdom. Unlike Germany, France and Austria, which had insisted on the introduction of transition periods before the concession of free movement of workers, Great Britain had waived such a restriction in 2004, giving labour migrants from Central and Eastern Europe unlimited access to its labour market. In the context of the Brexit debate this encouraged xenophobia, nationalism and racism to run wild in the UK, especially in England, to the benefit of right-leaning populists.

On 24 February 2016, Austria hosted a conference in Vienna whose explicit agenda was the reduction of the number of refugees using the Balkans route on the way to the EU. Sebastian Kurz, Austria's foreign minister at the time, played a leading role in closing this route, stopping the influx of refugees to Germany and bringing some relief to the beleaguered Merkel.

Even more important for the continued closure of that route was an agreement struck on 18 March 2016 between the EU and Turkey, in which Brussels committed to the payment of 3 billion euros, earmarked for the construction of refugee camps in Turkey. The agreement comprised in addition the deepening of Turkey's customs union with the EU, the re-opening of accession negotiations and an improvement of humanitarian conditions in Syria. The visa freedom for Turkish citizens demanded by Ankara was made contingent by Brussels on the readiness of Recep Tayyip Erdoğan, the Turkish AKP politician in office as State President since 2014, to substantially modify Turkish anti-terror legislation, a demand Erdoğan refused to countenance. Croatia, Slovenia, Serbia and Macedonia closed their borders for visaless transit travellers, rendering it next to impossible for them to reach Central Europe by the Balkans route. In addition to the financial aid committed to Turkey for the reception of refugees, the EU gave an undertaking that it would improve the protection of its borders and step up its sea rescue operations and its measures against people smugglers. By 2016 a significant reduction in the number of asylum applications was evident.

Instead of the agreed amount of 3 billion euros Ankara soon demanded double that amount, repeatedly threatening the suspension of the refugee agreement if the EU did not comply. In the wake of the attempted military coup on 15 July 2016 and the subsequent persecution of persons actually or supposedly involved in it, orchestrated by an increasingly authoritarian Erdoğan, tensions between the EU and Turkey were steadily on the rise. Here, too, Germany soon reached the limits of its capacity for crisis management and was even forced to turn a blind eye to developments in Turkey that were highly questionable in democratic terms. Erdoğan, combining open threats and the unrelenting persecution of real or imaginary rebels and 'terrorists' with a self-congratulatory show of abiding by his commitment not to unleash another massive wave of refugees, forced the EU, open to blackmail as it was, to be at its most lenient towards Ankara.

Restrictions of the freedom of the press and the imprisonment of foreign correspondents caused the climate between the EU and Turkey to deteriorate even further. The German-Turkish journalist Deniz Yücel and the human rights advocate Peter Steudtner had to stand trial in 2017, charged with belonging to a terrorist organization. Yücel, editor of the *taz* between 2007 and 2015 and the Turkey correspondent of the *WeltN24*-Gruppe since 2015, was remanded in Turkish custody for a year on the charge of having engaged in terrorist propaganda. In February 2018 he was discharged after the public prosecutor had brought charges against him, demanding an eighteen-year prison sentence if he were convicted. Steudtner was arrested during a workshop in Turkey. He too was charged with supporting 'terrorist organizations' and remanded in custody. He was then released unconditionally but the proceedings against him continued. Steudtner was the tenth German citizen to be arrested after the attempted coup in July 2016. Cem Özdemir, a leading member of the Bündnis 90/Die Grünen, noted that in Turkey there was 'no legal security, not for anyone'.

By undertaking the care, supply and restraint of millions of refugees from Iraq, Jordan and Syria in Turkey, Erdoğan had given himself a means of exerting pressure on the EU, which had no option but to assure him it would continue accession negotiations. Relations between Germany and Turkey were further strained by the intra-Turkish conflict between Erdoğan and Gülen supporters on the one hand and between the Turkish government and Kurds on the other, all of which had repercussions on Germany.

Founded in Cologne in 1984, the Turkish-Islamic Union of the Office for Religion (Diyanet İşleri Türk İslam Birliği; DİTİB) with its approximately 900 Turkish-Islamic associations in Germany, representing 70 per cent of Muslims resident in the country, had always declared itself a 'non-partisan organization', officially professing loyalty to the German constitution. It is active in the areas of integration and the training of imams, who are posted to Germany by Turkey and are on Ankara's payroll. DİTİB was headed at the time by the theologian Nevzat Yaşar Aşikoğlu, the representative in Germany of the state-run Presidium for Religious Matters in Turkey (Diyanet İşleri Başkanlığı; Diyanet), which answers directly to the Turkish prime minister. In 2015 the suspicion arose that DİTİB was not only close to President Erdoğan but was actually his agent, in that it spied on his critics and reported its findings to the authorities in Turkey. The Attorney General opened investigations against the Turkish secret service Millî İstihbarat Teşkilâtı (MİT) for its targeted eavesdropping on German Turkish and Turkish citizens.

While the leadership of the Berlin Republic bent over backwards in its attempts to contain damage and to exercise restraint regardless of the problems created by its appeasement of an increasingly authoritarian-dictatorial regime in Turkey, the Austrian government demanded a freeze on accession negotiations with Turkey. The German-Turkish relations were dented significantly when Turkish politicians were banned from public appearances in the Federal Republic in the run-up to the 2017 referendum on constitutional amendment. No longer certain how this would play out, Erdoğan was becoming increasingly nervous. He poured oil on to the fire by accusing Germany of using 'Nazi methods' and by calling Europeans 'Nazi remnants'. Branding the EU a 'crusader alliance', he evoked the manifold suffering inflicted on Muslims by Christians during the Crusades.

The two million Turks resident in Germany were a political asset for the Turkish potentate. Of the 58.2 million Turkish citizens eligible to vote, 1.4 million were resident in Germany. They were, as experience had shown, traditionally more positively inclined towards the AKP and towards Erdoğan himself than the average citizen in Turkey. In the presidential elections he had received 17 per cent more votes from

Turkish voters in Germany than in Turkey; in parliamentary elections in November 2015 the AKP share of votes had been 10 per cent higher than in the total result in Turkey.

The referendum in Turkey on 16 April 2017 resulted in a scant majority of 51.4 per cent voting 'Evet' (Yes) to the planned constitutional amendment, a victory for Erdoğan, but a Pyrrhic victory at best, given that he had declared in his election campaign that he wanted a majority of at least 60 per cent. The opening and consecration of the huge Central Mosque in Köln-Ehrenfeld in 2018 was not helpful either, since German guests were pointedly excluded and Erdoğan garnished his appearance with the Islamist salute of the Grey Wolves, a Turkish far-right ultra-nationalist organization.

One thing had become clear in the meantime to all refugee-receiving countries in the EU was that for a refugee policy to be successful, it needed to be backed up by a common immigration and integration policy. However, the majority of EU members were not prepared to face up to this – due to historically motivated differences in their political culture and/or the rise of populist, far-right nationalist parties. As early as 2016 a partly rigid, partly self-defeating and erratic deportation practice had set in in Germany, the result of polls showing that the AfD, a right-wing conservative party, was rapidly gaining support among German voters. The party had been founded in February 2013 by eurosceptic economists. The liberal conservative founders around Konrad Adam, Olaf Henkel and Bernd Lucke having soon departed, the party, under its new leaders Alexander Gauland and Frauke Petry, developed into an anti-EU and anti-globalization outfit focused on the refugee question and opposed to freedom of movement, Germany's fiscal policy, *multikulti* and immigration. Gauland called the 'refugee crisis' a gift to his party.

More than a year after Merkel had unilaterally proclaimed a culture of welcome, the Chancellor reacted to the change in public opinion by admitting that a breaking point had been reached and that a fair distribution of refugees within the EU was imperative. Her new version of 'We can do it' had a different priority: 'What is now needed above all rather than the reception of a great number of additional refugees is the integration of those already in the country.'

The pent-up discontent of the losers in East Germany's 'Wende' made the AfD the mouthpiece of malcontents. Many citizens of the former GDR had never had anything but low expectations of the Federal Republic's political system. In earlier elections, the extreme right Nationaldemokratische Partei Deutschlands (NPD) and the Deutsche Volksunion (DVU) had carried off a substantial share of the votes, a potential that now switched to the AfD. In Dresden the AfD now rubbed shoulders with a protest movement calling itself Europe's 'Patriots against the Islamization of the Occident' (Patrioten Europas gegen die Islamisierung des Abendlandes') or PEGIDA for short. The group organized its first demonstration against alleged Islamization and against German and European immigration and asylum policy as early as 20 October 2014, even before the beginning of the refugee crisis. All its demonstrations provoked counter-demonstrations, which sometimes outnumbered the adherents of PEGIDA. Having spread across Germany from its origins in the east, PEGIDA saw its appeal drop again in line with the subsidence of the refugee crisis. In the eyes of sociologist Holger Lengfeld, AfD voters are not so much economic losers as cultural malcontents lacking any experience of migrants. In his view, the AfD's 'cultural modernization deficit' was what made it tick. Refusing to engage its members in a dialogue could only be counterproductive.

This, however, was more easily said than done. Mutual recriminations – 'Nazi party' and 'fake news' (*Lügenpresse*) – barred the path to a fact-centred debate and were evidence for how polarized the mood had become. It was unacceptable both for the AfD as a whole to be painted as a Nazi party and for all print media to be accused of being purveyors of fake news. The AfD is a German national and conservative right-leaning protest party with right-wing exponents and groupings, which is frequently given selective and tendentious coverage that tends to partly ignore, suppress or downplay negative aspects of the refugee issue. The AfD accuses its opponents of defaming it and of threatening its members, while presenting itself as the only party prepared to stand up for the constitution.

In view of the recalcitrant attitude of EU members east of the old Iron Curtain on the question of immigration, Merkel expressed her disappointment in June 2017 at the EU's inability to accommodate refugee numbers from Syria that were significantly lower than those hosted by Turkey. 'It is sad, when you have in mind the idea of a common world, that so many countries remain stuck in denial and in fear of others or of other religious persuasions or are afraid of having something taken away from them.' In the EU it was especially Central and Eastern European countries that refused to accept the quota regulation for the distribution of Syrian refugees.

Sanctions against Russia, Dieselgate and the Brexit Referendum in the UK

With newly Europeanized Germany's traditional special relationship and close economic ties to Russia, the country found itself at the centre of the action when a pan-European peace and security order was demanded. Having taken up a new position at the heart of Europe following the Eastern enlargement of the EU and NATO, the German government was soon made aware that these geo-economic and geopolitical shifts in influence and power were increasingly creating problems with Moscow, especially since it could not – and was certainly not prepared to – cast off the tow rope that bound it to US politics. In spite of the obligations arising from its membership of US-dominated NATO, considerations of trade, investment and economic policy in general compelled Germany to seek an understanding with Russia, to play the moderator and, in conflict situations, to act as an honest broker, as far as it could. This proved difficult at times. Berlin was in a double bind owing to its involvement with NATO. Rejecting the 'Austrian' model, it not only consistently eschewed neutrality as a tool of foreign policy in the Cold War, but lambasted the concept to the point of stigmatization. When protests against the decision of Viktor Fedorovych Yanukovych's pro-Russian government to position itself against Ukraine's association agreement with the EU escalated at Kiev's Euromaidan around the turn of 2013/14, German Foreign Minister Frank-Walter Steinmeier and his French and Polish counterparts tried to intervene, offering mediation, but could not prevent further escalation. Rioting and state-sponsored and other violence followed, resulting in hundreds of casualties. Yanukovych fled to Russia. On 21 March 2014 Russia annexed the Crimean peninsula and from 2015 began covert military operations in the Donetsk and Luhansk areas of east Ukraine. OSCE observer missions were designed to calm the situation down but had little effect. The Minsk Protocols (I and II) are considered to have created the preconditions for normalization in the region. The Ukraine crisis, Russia's annexation of the Crimea and the war in east Ukraine strained relations between the West and Moscow. Steinmeier had another go at pacification under the aegis of the German OSCE presidency and was foiled yet again. In reaction to the annexation of the Crimea ordered by Putin, which was condemned by Berlin as a violation of international law, and to the war Russia had unleashed in Eastern Ukraine, the EU imposed sanctions on Russia, which Germany had no way of avoiding. The German-Russian relationship is now decidedly strained.

At roughly the same time a totally different topic moved to the top both of the domestic agenda and of international media interest: the German car industry was hit by a hitherto unparalleled scandal sometimes referred to as Dieselgate. On 18 September 2015, when the US Environmental Protection Agency (EPA) served the Volkswagen Corporation with a Notice of Violation, the news broke that Volkswagen AG had installed an illegal defeat device in the emission management system of its diesel cars. It had been shown that Volkswagen, in order to comply with US emissions regulations, had chosen to programme the engine control unit in its cars to switch from good fuel economy and high NOX emissions to low-emission-compliant mode when it detected an emissions test. What added to the damage to the car maker's image was that cars fitted with the defeat device had been marketed in the United States in a high-profile campaign as 'clean diesels'. While Volkswagen was not alone in engaging in these criminal practices, the company's name was more closely associated with them than those of its competitors and VW was made to bear the brunt of the litigation costs.

The repercussions of Dieselgate were felt throughout the German car industry. It turned out that a sizeable number of people had been in the know for years. Many have since been fired or forced to resign, including VW CEO Martin Winterkorn, who was charged with fraud and conspiracy in the United States (2018) and with fraud in Germany (2019). To no avail had political and scientific bodies, government agencies and interest associations been flagging irregularities in emission testing for years before the scandal broke, with dire warnings of the consequences.

At the Nationales Forum Diesel, a diesel 'summit' involving the Federal government and German car makers held on 2 August 2017, a benefit from the scandal arose in that basic agreements were reached that paved the road to a 'Verkehrswende', a new approach to transport.

In one of the crucial questions discussed at the forum – the relative merits of e-mobility versus hybrid technologies – VW announced its decision in November 2018 to opt for battery-powered, digitally networked vehicles. The car-industry-friendly government of Lower Saxony announced its willingness to chip in, for the simple reason, as Minister President Stefan Weil put it, that according to one study as many as 114,000 jobs in the car and automotive supply industry would be at stake by 2035 because of the shift from combustion engines to electric vehicles. For VW to meet the EU's climate and environment parameters demanding a reduction of the CO_2 emissions of its fleet by 37.5 per cent, the company needs to push the overall share of electric cars in new car registrations to 40 per cent by 2021. It is hoped that by that time the present shortage of charging stations will be a thing of the past.

A related point was the debate on a CO_2 tax which polarized the Grand Coalition: while the SPD advocated a 'socially acceptable' solution, the CDU/CSU was vehemently opposed to making any new demands on the taxpayer.

Finally, Brexit. The welcome Merkel gave to war refugees from Syria in the late summer of 2015 was another boost to the anti-EU mood then prevailing in the UK. Immigration was one of the most hotly touted issues in the run-up to the referendum on whether the UK should leave the EU. The Brexiteers made it clear – something that had never occurred to Merkel where Germany was concerned – that they wanted to regain control of the UK's borders and stop immigration from EU countries. Since freedom of movement is one of the EU's basic principles, once the UK left the EU it could no longer be a member of the European Single Market. On 23 June 2016 a small majority of 51.89 per cent voted leave. Prime Minister David Cameron submitted his resignation and was replaced by Theresa May, who presided for more than two and a half years over hapless negotiations with the EU. The negative consequences Brexit would have for Germany and for the EU were plain to see: it amounted to the loss of the second-largest net contributor to the EU budget with the second largest industry and the third largest population. In 2015 Germany contributed 14.3, the UK 11.5 and France 5.5 billion euros to the Community's budget. Brexit would necessarily lead to an increase in the burden on the remaining net payers. Germany's contribution to the EU household would, according to Minister of Finance Wolfgang Schäuble (2009–17), have to rise by roughly 4.5 billion euros for 2019 and 2020. The British shares in the European Investment Bank (EIB) of 16 per cent (3.4 billion euros) would likewise have to be discounted.

Brexit turned out to be much more complex than the Brexiteers had claimed. A full three years after the referendum there was still no solution in sight. All deals submitted to Parliament by May were rejected, leading to her resignation in June 2019. Since then, her successor Boris Johnson has led the country into one constitutional crisis after the other. In the end, he was able to win new elections in 2019 and emerged as the clear winner with 43.6 per cent of the vote. It was the Conservatives' biggest election success since the 1980s under Margaret Thatcher. Thus Brexit was decided, though it is still unclear how it will be carried out.

The 2017 Bundestag Elections as a Political Earthquake and the AfD's Arrival

The question hanging over the outcome of parliamentary elections in 2017 was whether it would lead to another mandate for a Grand Coalition. Early in that year, the President of the European Parliament, Martin Schulz, was unanimously elected leader of the SPD and candidate for the office of chancellor by the party conference. Almost immediately afterwards, a media hype set in of a kind no one had been expecting, least of all Schulz himself. The print media portrayed him as the saviour of his party. The CDU and the CSU were getting cold feet. Having been unable to agree on a common candidate for the post of federal president, they had had the SPD candidate, Frank-Walter Steinmeier, crammed down their throats. The controversy about the 'ceiling' in the refugee question still exercised the Christian Democrat sister parties. When Seehofer publicly disavowed and humiliated Merkel at the CSU conference in Munich on 20/21 November 2015, she kept her cool despite visible irritation, but that cool was misleading; it was not indicative of what was going on in the country. At first, though, the victory of the CDU led by Annegret Kramp-Karrenbauer in the Landtag elections in Saarland seemed to signal business as usual, followed as it was by the 'crashing' defeat (Schulz) of 'Landesmutter' Hannelore Kraft in the heartland of Social Democracy, North Rhine-Westphalia; the SPD is yet to recover from this debacle. Schulz himself was off to a gutsy start, banking on a general desire for change. Slogans like 'It's time' (Es ist Zeit) and 'For more justice' (Für mehr Gerechtigkeit) were designed to hammer home Schulz's message about many key themes (the sorry state of education; shortage of daycare centres; high rents; deficits in the care system and in the infrastructure in the western half of Germany; pensions). He presented himself as the architect of a great future, while Merkel seemed to be content with presiding over the status quo. The Chancellor made a point of ignoring her challenger.

In view of the uncertainties besetting the international situation and the crisis-ridden EU, many Germans felt more comfortable committing themselves to Merkel's safe pair of hands. Schulz countered Merkel's slogan 'Germany is OK' with 'Germany is OK, that is true. But not all Germans feel OK.' This fell on deaf ears. The CDU programme adopted several SPD positions and appropriated them, while Merkel seemed confident that she could cling on to her lead. All she had to say about her coalition partner in view of the bogeyman of a Red–Red–Green coalition, which never looked like a serious contender, was, 'You may ask the SPD what they want and when they want it – you won't get an answer.' A TV confrontation was the last straw the SPD candidate could cling to – but the duel developed into a duet where the moderators did not allow enough room for the really pressing topics, such as care for senior citizens and nursing.

The refugee issue dominated the election campaign to a greater extent than had been anticipated by Merkel, from which benefited the AfD. They polled 12.6 per cent, which made them the third strongest party at Federal level. The massive losses for the governing parties repeated themselves in the Landtag elections in Bavaria and in Hesse in 2018. Merkel the troubleshooter appeared exhausted and overstretched. What made the AfD so strong was the weakness of the main parties, their organizational ineptitude and their inability to get to the bottom of the problem of mass immigration. In the election campaign, fundamental policy debates were noticeable by their absence. This included the challenge of digitization, which was not yet taken seriously in political circles. What proved a liability for Merkel was above all the immigration question. Her hope that Germans would let bygones be bygones was mistaken; the pictures of the onslaught of refugees in 2015 had been engraved in people's memories, all the more so since it had remained unclear all along how Merkel's 'We can do it' was to be worked through. There were hundreds of thousands who had not been granted asylum, yet they had not been issued with a notification of deportation either. In most cases where such a notification was served, the individuals in question took the Republic to court. Justified worries of citizens were belittled in the political debate and criticism of migration policy was sometimes attributed to racist phobias. A comprehensive immigration law to end endemic asylum abuse and legal provisions to give asylum seekers access to the job market were lacking. The 'refugee crisis' was the top election issue for the AfD, which had scored its first successes during the euro crisis of 2010 to 2014. In May 2016 the party launched its slogan 'Islam has no place in Germany' (Der Islam gehört nicht zu Deutschland), in open contradiction to a

AfD poster for the local elections in Halstenbek, Schleswig-Holstein, 2018.

statement made by former Federal President Christian Wulff on 3 October 2010. The AfD slogan implied banning minarets, muezzin calls and the full-face veil. The AfD functioned as a protest party channelling deep-seated frustration with political parties and a widespread disenchantment with politics. It met its nemesis in the shape of its own ideological 'brown' dregs, sowing discord. A case in point is the story of one of the party's first spokespersons, Frauke Petry. When Petry found she could not bring the AfD's extreme right wing to heel, she left the party, citing her dissatisfaction with the radicals in its ranks destroying the party's prospects of governing. She subsequently founded Blaue Wende (the Blue Party), a splinter party that never really got off the ground. Her place in the party was taken up by Alice Weidel, who has since become notorious for her radicalism.

In spite of its continued internal squabbles and ideological-political controversies the AfD continued to grow by leaps and bounds, and not exclusively at the expense of the CDU. Soon it was represented in the parliaments of ten *Länder* (Baden-Württemberg, Berlin, Brandenburg, Bremen, Hamburg, Mecklenburg-Western Pomerania, Rhineland-Palatinate, Saxony, Saxony-Anhalt und Thuringia).

The AfD benefited from the quarrel the two Christian Democrat sister parties had been fighting out before an uncomprehending public since 2016, tarnishing both their brands for the 2017 parliamentary elections. Horst Seehofer made a name for himself as a contrarian, steering whatever course he felt was expedient, even if it involved repeated U-turns. Having long criticized Merkel harshly to the point of humiliating her, he pulled her from his hat as 'the best candidate' immediately before the elections. By that time Seehofer had lost it completely in the eyes of many CSU supporters, who now voted for the FDP or the AfD. The latter brazenly proclaimed on its posters: 'We keep the promises the CSU makes.' Appealing predominantly to male voters, the AfD emerged from the 2017 elections in the eastern *Länder* as the second strongest party and as the strongest in Saxony, where it polled 27 per cent of the vote. Things looked rather different in the western parts of Germany.

While the AfD made it to the Bundestag, the SPD was in retreat. The moment the election results were in, the SPD announced the end of the Grand Coalition ('Groko') and its own future role in opposition. Having called Merkel 'unprincipled' (*prinzipienlos*) and the 'world champion of imprecision' (*Weltmeisterin des Ungefähren*) in the run-up to the elections, Schulz had reserved his pent-up frustration with the Chancellor for a post-election TV talk-round in Berlin, where he declared that Merkel had behaved 'scandalously' in the election campaign and that the SPD refused even to consider a continuation of the coalition.

It is not too much to say that by now the depoliticization of public debate had become a method. Indecisiveness, procrastination and the refusal to enter into a political debate on such questions as raising the retirement age and allowing family reunions for refugees created a political vacuum that was quickly filled with verbal rhetoric by the AfD. The obsessive focus on that party kept up by the media and politicians led to a blockage of the capacity for balanced, adversatorial debate. The Left's Sahra Wagenknecht kept lambasting the AfD as the Nazi party, which had little effect. Politologist Karl-Rudolf Korte understandably called the Groko a 'moratorium on addressing a mine field' ('Stillhalteabkommen über ein Minenfeld') and a 'huggers' democracy' ('Umarmungsdemokratie'). The debating culture that had gone AWOL in the Bundestag resurfaced in TV talk-shows. Unexciting as the election campaign had been as far as the top slot was concerned, the race for third place more than made up for it, as was made quite clear by the rise in voter turn-out to 76 per cent. Korte called the election result an 'ex-post referendum on the refugee question' and therefore also on the Chancellor. *Der Spiegel* journalist Jakob Augstein went even further, calling Merkel the 'mother of the AfD'. She deserved to be voted out since it was she who was responsible 'for Nazis taking up their place in the Bundestag'. As Merkel was sure to remain in office, the question was, according to Augstein, whether casting one's vote was worth the bother.

There was indeed little doubt that Merkel's role in the reception of the bulk of refugees and her misjudgement of the consequences had a decisive influence on the election result. Thirty-seven per cent of the population agreed that it was a good thing for the AfD to strive to reduce the influence of Islam on Germany. However, the party continued to be at loggerheads with itself. Its leader, Alexander Gauland, a disappointed former CDU politician from Hesse, called the AfD 'that bunch of agitators'. Strong internal tensions remained, leading to the hive-off of groups and splinter groups. Petry was followed by the nationalist and right-wing conservative André Poggenburg. It is astonishing that the radical German nationalist Björn Höcke, on the radar of – and flagged by – the Office for the Protection of the constitution, has been able to keep his position on the party's so-called 'Flügel', a group generally considered to be located on the extreme right, where he provides opponents and critics of the party with a target. A moderate 'Alternative Mitte' was formed to provide a counterpoint. In January 2019 the AfD was prematurely classified as being on the Office's blacklist ('Prüf-Fall'), a decision that soon had to be revoked. The agency may investigate the AfD, but it is not entitled to classify it as a 'Prüf-Fall'.

AfD exponents have a knack of hitting the headlines and of pandering to their German nationalist and right-wing clienteles at one and the same time. Having explicitly accepted Germany's responsibility for the twelve years of its history from 1933 to 1945, Alexander Gauland, speaking at the Federal Conference of the 'Junge Alternative für Deutschland' in early June 2018, in the same breath called that period 'no more than bird shit when set against more than a thousand years of successful German history' ('nur als ein Vogelschiss in über tausend Jahre erfolgreicher deutscher Geschichte'). By thus minimizing and relativizing, the AfD appeared to give proof both of his limited intellectual capacity and of his irresponsible treatment of National Socialism. As Gauland is a highly educated historian with a raft of books on German history to his credit, this was no mere verbal aberration but a deliberate transgression and breach of taboos. Prior to this, on 17 January 2017, the aforementioned Björn Höcke had this to say about Berlin's Holocaust Memorial: 'We are the only people in the world to plant a monument of shame in the heart of their capital.' The former history teacher called for 'a 180° U-turn in the German culture of remembrance', making it clear that he completely rejected the culture of remembrance currently practised. AfD representatives cultivate links to internationally networked xenophobic groups. In 2018 they declared the AfD completely compatible with PEGIDA. Similarly, the radical right conservative youth movement Die Identitären is one of the AfD's recruiting grounds for young adults in pre-political space.

One of the continuities linking the Bonn and the Berlin Republics was the high-profile demarcation line drawn under Germany's Nazi history. This repeatedly led to political debate excessively referencing the past, weakened critical analysis of the SED dictatorship and occasionally blocked the view of current political tasks, of urgently required solutions to pressing problems (reform of the education system and the Bundeswehr, the pension and tax systems, tackling problems in infrastructure and the housing sector) and of dealing with issues vital for the country's future (demography, digitization, energy security, climate change and migration).

In the wake of the elections intensive negotiations were scheduled between top representatives of the CDU/CSU, FDP and the Green Party to try and hammer out a so-called 'Jamaica' coalition: with the SPD ostensibly out of the race, a black-yellow-green government pact seemed to be on the cards. The Green veteran Jürgen Trittin put the required squaring of the circle in a nutshell: the CDU had to become more 'ecological', the CSU more 'liberal' and the FDP 'more social'. The FDP's leader Christian Lindner, who had run the election campaign virtually as a one-man show, demanded more than just a domestic sea change. He also insisted that Germany distance itself from the offer of a closer Franco-German partnership proposed by French President Emmanuel Macron, given that this offer entailed an increase in German transfer payments. A somewhat muted Seehofer demanded 'No more of the same!' (*Kein weiter so*) to stop the CSU bleeding votes to the AfD. The question was whether under these auspices Merkel would be able to hold the 'progressive centre'. On her watch, the CDU had developed into a party that was opposed to nuclear energy, had abolished national service, had come to the rescue of Greece and was taking a favourable view of refugees; it had, in other words, come a long way from its previous centre-right position. The coalition negotiations dragged on without Merkel taking a particularly active part. In charge at the negotiating table was the head of the Federal Chancellery, Peter Altmeier, who went out of his way to accommodate the Greens, presuming that the FDP was safely on board already. The negotiations foundered when the Liberals walked out; they felt they had not been paid enough attention.

The last thing the losers of the ballot seemed to be concerned with was learning a lesson from the consequences. Seehofer refused to resign and Merkel showed herself completely intransigent: 'I fail to see what we should do differently now', was how, to widespread bafflement, she reacted to the lost elections. She continued to bank on the docility of the Germans, even though they had just punished both 'people's parties' at the ballot box. Unsurprisingly, personnel debates dominated the agenda in both parties. With Seehofer and Merkel remaining in office, they came to represent a politically divided Germany, a state of affairs that was being normalized in Europe. The election result made it clear that they were office holders only until further notice. When further elections brought further losses at the *Länder* level, both had to resign from the leadership of their respective parties. At a special CDU party conference on 7 December 2018 in Hamburg, Saarland Prime Minister Annegret Kramp-Karrenbauer beat Friedrich Merz to the post by the smallest of margins. Seehofer was followed in his role of leader of the CSU by Markus Söder in January 2019.

Necessary though these personnel changes were, they did not strengthen Germany's position in Europe. Germany threatened to become its own nemesis and to succumb to domestic self-paralysis. It was unable to provide new stimuli to tide the EU over its internal and external crises. Those weeks lost in negotiations about the formation of a Black–Yellow–Green 'Jamaica' coalition between CDU/CSU, FDP and Greens in 2017 that led nowhere; the initially negative and then indecisive, hesitant attitude towards joint governing in 2017/18 on the part of an SPD leadership in visible disarray; the long protracted birth of another Grand

Coalition (2017–18), with the CDU and CSU caught up in a quarrel fuelled by the differences between Seehofer and Merkel on the migration question: all this was toxic for Germany's role in the EU. The drop in domestic and intraparty support for Merkel's policy and the public's increasing dissatisfaction with it made the Federal Chancellor Europe's lame duck. The year 2017 had begun on an upbeat note with the election of Macron in France; 2018 turned out to be a lost year for German-French cooperation in Europe. Merkel failed again to provide a substantive, timely answer to the proposals for the political reform of integration put forward by the French President. The end of the Merkel era seemed to be close once she had resigned from the party leadership she had maintained for eighteen years. It seemed a mere question of time before she was replaced as head of government, particularly when her health was seen in public as deteriorating. In this last ditch battle she scored a notable success on the immigration front: on 7 June 2019 the Bundestag passed a legislative package on migration that substantially improved prospects for foreign skilled workers and gave people in the helping professions reason to hope that they would be allowed to remain in the country. Financial support for asylum seekers was to be upgraded. A rise in the number of deportations was unlikely, since some countries of origin were dragging their feet over the identification and repatriation of their citizens. Anyone holding down a job, earning their livelihood and reasonably fluent in German was to be 'tolerated' and allowed to stay in the country. These seven pieces of legislation were supplemented by an eighth on changes in the law of citizenship, aimed at dual-nationality individuals who had joined a terrorist association. They were to be deprived of their German passports. Individuals living in polygamous relationships were to be denied naturalization and anyone who had obtained citizenship on the basis of false claims was to be stripped of it again.

The Aachen Treaty – Hardly a Promising Relaunch

In view of Germany's domestic self-paralysis in 2017/18 it was obvious that renewing the German-French Elysée Treaty originally concluded on 22 January 1963, a project desired by both sides, would require a concerted effort. In a first reaction to the German parliamentary elections, Macron proposed a renewal of this treaty in an address he delivered at the Sorbonne on 26 September 2017. The date he envisaged for signing, 22 January 2018, fell through because of the delay in the formation of the German government. Where the 1963 treaty had been controversial even in the original community of the six, the renewal project was bound to be

Macron and Merkel signing the Aachen Treaty in 2019.

met with even greater opposition in a community with four times as many members
and a unified, enlarged Germany. Objections were raised against the 'avant-garde'
and the alleged establishment of a duopoly. The left party spectrum in both countries was united in its opposition. Macron's proposal to transform the eurozone to
accommodate nineteen euro countries was impossible to implement in a bilateral
pact, quite apart from the fact that it ran afoul of the more well-heeled euro partners. Adjourned for one year, the reaffirmation of friendship between the two
nations took place on 22 January 2019 in the Coronation Hall of Aachen's Town
Hall, where Macron had earlier been awarded the Charlemagne Prize. The update
of the Elysée Treaty took the form of 28 supplementary articles in which Berlin
and Paris assured each other of the closest possible collaboration in all questions
concerning Europe and of their mutual commitment to deepening their cooperation in foreign and security policies, invoking the need for joint action whenever
and wherever possible. Special emphasis was put on the EU's autonomy, after
Macron had stressed the need for 'Europe's full-fledged sovereignty' in his celebrated Sorbonne address. Berlin and Paris assured each other of mutual assistance
in case of an armed attack on either country, as was already provided for by Article
52 of the NATO treaty and Article 42 of the EU Treaty. Military and armaments
cooperation was to be streamlined, a goal that would be achieved by a regularly
convened security and defence commission staffed with ministers from both countries. Macron had been advocating joint rapid deployment forces for quite some

time and had elicited a positive response from the then German Defence Minister, Ursula von der Leyen. The creation of such a force was now considered a done deal. Politically precarious third countries were to be stabilized not by military means but by cooperation in the fields of the secret services, the judiciary and the police. This was to be followed by a closer European partnership with countries in Africa.

In 2019/20 Germany, a non-permanent member of the UN Security Council, assumed the presidency, with France as the next in line for that role. The German request to be given a permanent seat in the Security Council met with support, which put paid to the project of transforming the French permanent seat into a seat for the EU, which would have given the EU a voice in the world community. Other measures to improve German-French cooperation concerned making common cause in border regions for infrastructure projects such as bilingual vocational schools, trade zones and hospitals; the border regions were thereby given a status that differed in some respects from the applicable law in each respective country. This was, as it were, a down payment for the much more ambitious goals of establishing a joint German-French trade area and of moving the science and research establishments of the two countries closer together to study social change and work out solutions. Another proposal in the pipeline was for mutual recognition of school leaving exams ('Abibac') in line with what was already the case with academic degrees.

Of more immediate importance than these high-minded plans were the deficits and incompatibilities hampering German-French relations. What was badly needed was a mandatory joint energy policy and a binding German-French immigration law to serve as a catalyst for pan-European legislation. How – and indeed whether – Europe was to benefit from the newly formed German-French alliance was unclear, given the social turmoil in France and Germany's divided, parlous state. The sharp French reaction to the German proposal to transform the French UN Security Council seat into an EU seat bodes little good for the EU. Nor was Kramp-Karrenbauer's inadequate answer to Macron's proposals for a sweeping reform of the EU helpful. She suggested relocating the European Parliament from Strasbourg to Brussels and a German-French armament joint venture, the construction of an aircraft carrier. In light of the manifest deficits of much of the Bundeswehr's hardware, this proposal was greeted in Paris, if not with downright mirth, then at least by raised eyebrows. Differences and incompatibilities between Germany and France continued unabated at the most elementary level, such as the German withdrawal from nuclear energy against its prioritization in France; German budgetary discipline versus the French flirtation with sovereign debt; and

Germany's parliamentary army versus the French strike force. Another case of Germany and France locking horns that proved more amenable to resolution arose in connection with the Nord Stream II gas pipeline project. The first version of this project designed to channel natural gas from Russia to Mecklenburg-West-Pomerania was vetoed by France. However, a compromise was soon reached. The pipeline system was to be diversified but not rejected altogether. The solution was a new gas directive and a broadening of the supply system to include third states. But serious American threats of sanctions for participating companies threatened to delay the project.

Quite apart from these obstacles, it was obvious that for the EU to show cohesion neither the challenge posed by Brexit nor the Berlin-Paris axis were sufficient by themselves. What was needed was winning over hearts and minds in the EU's Central and Southeast European member states, where the toxic legacy of Soviet socialism remained virulent for much longer than had been allowed for the continent's west. It was clear that a bilateral axis would never work as a substitute for pan-European cohesion. Reservations against the avant-garde airs flaunted by Berlin and Paris were soon voiced by Central and Eastern European countries. With France deeply divided domestically and a unified, enlarged Germany infuriating Budapest, Prague and Warsaw by throwing its weight around in the EU much more than the Bonn Republic had ever done in the days of the EEC and the EC, an EU relaunch had become that much more difficult.

While the Aachen Treaty provided some hope that Germany would be able to overcome its self-imposed weakness, the EU perspective clearly depended on whether a significant number of states could be brought to support the project of an EU relaunch.

After the European elections on 26 May, Merkel was unable to install the top candidate of the European People's Party, the Bavarian CSU politician Manfred Weber, as president of the Commission. Instead, Ursula von der Leyen was elected to the post on 16 July and, in a closely related development, the head of the IMF, Christine Lagarde, was appointed the new president of the ECB. These appointments – neither of the two women had initially been candidates – represented a compromise. Macron had proposed von der Leyen as this move enabled him to push through Lagarde as the leader of the ECB. Decisive arguments in favour of von der Leyen, at least in Macron's eyes, were her ambitions in the field of European defence policy and the fact that she is fluent in French. On this occasion, Macron and Merkel had shifted decision-making from the level of the supranational community to the intergovernmental platform for the heads of states and governments.

Elected by the European Parliament with an extremely thin majority – only nine votes more than the needed quorum, with a total of 383 in favour, 327 against, 22 abstentions and one non-valid vote – von der Leyen is the second German president of the Commission after Walter Hallstein (1958–67). Before the vote she had announced her resignation from her post as defence minister. She was succeeded in this by the leader of the CDU, Annegret Kramp-Karrenbauer.

The Landtag elections in Brandenburg and Saxony on 1 September 2019 were the prelude to tension-fraught domestic times. There were several losers and one winner: in the Free State of Saxony, the AfD polled 27.5 per cent (a gain of 17.8 per cent); all other parties lost votes, with the exception of the Freie Wähler and the Greens. In Brandenburg the AfD polled 23.5 per cent (a gain of 11.3 per cent). While in Saxony a Black–Red–Green 'Kenya' coalition of CDU, SPD and the Greens was considered as an emergency solution, Brandenburg was looking to form a Red–Red–Green government. The AfD was especially successful with voters in economically backward, depopulated and structurally weak regions and with former non-voters in urban areas. The CDU was left to lick its wounds and the SPD suffered even worse losses in Saxony. The Grand Coalition had run out of road there and the same was true of the Red–Red government in Brandenburg.

In the state elections in Thuringia Prime Minister Bodo Ramelow's party, Die Linken, gained vote share, emerging as the leading party for the first time in state elections in the reunited Germany with 31 per cent of the vote. The AfD registered the largest gain in vote share of all parties, 12.8 per cent, polling 23.4 per cent overall, making it the second largest party, followed at 21.7 per cent by the CDU, the clear loser, as they recorded their worst result ever in the Free State. The SPD and the Greens also suffered losses. No possible coalition could command a majority. Were the FDP and the CDU supposed to support a Red–Red–Green coalition, with the sole purpose of keeping the AfD out of power?

In the election of the Thuringian Minister President on 5 February 2020, Thomas Kemmerich (FDP) ran for office in the third round of voting. He did so in order to offer a 'civic alternative' to the two candidates from the far left and far right. Previously, in two rounds of voting, neither former Prime Minister Ramelow (Die Linke) nor Christoph Kindervater (AfD) had achieved an absolute majority. In the third round of voting, Kemmerich received 45 of 90 votes with one abstention and thus became the new Prime Minister. This was only possible with the consent of the AfD, which had put up its candidate merely for the purpose of deception. In fact, to the surprise of everyone, the AfD voted for Kemmerich, together with the FDP and most members of the CDU. This was followed by massive social and public protests. Kemmerich announced his withdrawal one day later and resigned on 8 February 2020.

On 4 March in a new election Ramelow received the necessary majority with 42 votes in favour in the third round of voting. He held all the votes of the Red–Red–Green coalition. He was thus once again Prime Minister of Thuringia and formed a minority government. The AfD has 22 mandates. The four FDP members of parliament present in the plenary hall did not vote and remained seated. The Liberals had previously announced a boycott of the election. Ramelow's opponent, Thuringia's AfD party and faction leader Björn Höcke, had also failed in two previous attempts. Ramelow would not shake his hand as he would not clearly declare his support for democracy.

The government crisis in Thuringia did not remain without repercussions for Berlin. FDP leader Lindner had to ask his party the question of confidence and remained in office. On 10 February 2020 CDU chairwoman Kramp-Karrenbauer announced her withdrawal and her renunciation of her candidacy for chancellor for 2021. She had already been weakened and had virtually asked for a vote of confidence at the Leipzig CDU party conference in 2019. Although she was able to settle the dispute with the CSU under Markus Söder on the refugee issue, she was unable to overcome her own party's dissent on the issue of clearly distinguishing itself from the Left and clearly distancing itself from the AfD. A so-called 'union of values' ('Werte-Union') of about 4,000 CDU members rejected the exclusion of the AfD and had welcomed Kemmerich's election with the support of the AfD. Kramp-Karrenbauer could not prevail against this.

In 2018/19 the Grand Coalition was often burdened with internal party personnel debates. Andrea Nahles saw herself forced to resign from the Social Democratic Party leadership due to internal party criticism. For months, the SPD busied itself in order to clarify the question of succession in interviews. In the election, the duo Norbert Walter-Borjans and Saskia Esken, who had repeatedly questioned the Groko, prevailed.

In February 2020 the CDU was also threatened by the scenario of an internal dispute after Annegret Kramp-Karrenbauer announced her withdrawal from the party chairmanship and rival wings had different preferences for her succession. Therefore the CDU thus found itself in an internal party crisis. A party conference was to bring programmatic clarity and determine a successor as party leader and a candidate for chancellor. Possible successors were North Rhine-Westphalia's Premier Armin Laschet, former CDU/CSU faction leader Friedrich Merz and the former CDU minister for environmental policy Norbert Röttgen. More than ever it seemed that the Merkel era was coming to an end, as her favourite for her successor, Kramp-Karrenbauer, was unable to assert herself within the party.

The Berlin Republic was confronted with the coronavirus pandemic, Covid-19, which originated in China and since January 2020 had taken only a few weeks to spread throughout the world. After initially leaving political communication to Health Minister Jens Spahn, Merkel announced comprehensive government measures for crisis management on 11 March. She saw that Germany was in a good position to protect its economy because it had sufficient financial reserves. The commitment to help companies affected by the crisis with unlimited credit programmes was quickly taken up by Finance Minister Olaf Scholz and Economics Minister Peter Altmaier. Half a trillion euros were to be made available through an increased guarantee framework with the state bank Kreditanstalt für Wiederaufbau (KfW). The extent of the consequences of the crisis subsequently made it necessary to make several improvements to various government aid and support measures.

The crisis was a major political challenge and at the same time a political opportunity, not only for the Federal Chancellor but for the party political system. Together with the often criticized Grand Coalition, Merkel was able to limit the consequences of the pandemic through crisis management, which led to a renewed increase in her popularity. The supposedly negative image of the 'refugee chancellor' was to fade away. If, however, the crisis management was not successful, the measures taken were insufficient for the economy and the population reacted to the restrictions with incomprehension, the government and its bosses could once again expect a loss of image. As a result of the public debate on the appropriateness of the restrictive measures, new forms of social division in Germany became apparent through controversial demonstrations.

On 3 June 2020, after 21 hours of negotiations to deal with the consequences of the coronavirus crisis, the Grand Coalition reached a consensus on a large, comprehensive and prudent economic stimulus package of 130 billion euros for that and the following year. In doing so, it once again demonstrated its ability to act and to manage crises, and Merkel's leadership and moderation skills. These qualities will once again be necessary under the German EU Council Presidency in the second half of 2020 and the categorical integration imperative will be the sine qua non when it comes to holding Europe's united states together with money.

12

Three Different Republics:
Bonn – Pankow – Berlin,
Attempt at a Summary

The Weimar Republic was a democracy with too few democrats; the Federal Republic a democracy of those who were growing to be and gradually became convinced democrats; while the GDR remained a state of democrats who were prevented from practising democracy, repressed and persecuted.

While the Weimar Republic was an incomplete democracy, the Bonn Republic was one that was controlled from outside and largely developed from inside, as such a 'successful democracy' (as Edgar Wolfrum puts it), even if it was strongly oriented towards consensus and only partly pluralist in its political parties. That was precisely what guaranteed its continuity and stability.

Whereas the GDR went through integration with the East in line with the Sovietization of its society, culture and economy, in the Federal Republic integration with the West and Americanization were the order of the day. The striking difference between the orientations of the two partial states in two different directions consisted in the fact that the Federal Republic, through its Europeanization in the form of integration with Europe, still possessed an alternative scenario below the transatlantic level, an equivalent that the GDR lacked. 'Europe' acted as a 'magic spell' (as Eckart Conze calls it) for the Western state, 'Europe' was entirely missing as a point of reference and an object of identification for the East German partial state – at least in the 1950s and '60s.

Despite all the serious differences between Prussia and the old Federal Republic there was one surprising parallel: the accounts of their respective histories. Their contemporary historians sang the praises of both states. In both cases, more critical aspects, charges and hypotheses about the actual basis of the two German states were lost from view during their time and even beyond: both Prussia and the

Federal Republic emerged as the creations of partial states and each one claimed to be the 'better' and 'more progressive' Germany for its time, but in fact they did not reflect the whole reality of German culture and language. One of these creations (Prussia) resulted in the exclusion of Austria from the formation of the Reich and the need for a concept of a 'third Germany'; the other (the Federal Republic) the renunciation to Europe as a 'third force', the detachment of Central and Eastern Germans beyond the Elbe and leaving them to their fate behind the Iron Curtain, and ultimately the responsibility for the division of Germany and thus the division of Europe. A clear recognition and an open discussion of these serious circumstances and consequences of the creations of the German state in the nineteenth and twentieth centuries is hardly forthcoming from West German historians educated in the old Federal Republic, not even from younger ones. This is probably not just a specifically (West) German problem but a wider (West) European one.

While the Federal Republic, seen from the historical perspective, has been characterized as a 'happy story' (as Wolfrum calls it), this can hardly be said of the GDR. Whereas people in the Western state were able to rate their prospects as 'happy', this was much less or only partially the case in the Eastern state. The East Germans had to adapt to the orders, directives and guidelines of that 'unity party' and its state in many areas and thus bow to their fate. No doubt life in the 'free West' was a lot more pleasant and comfortable than in East Germany. If the old Federal Republic stood for happiness, development and self-fulfillment, then the GDR stood for fate, restriction and coercion.

The 'Bundesliga' (football league), West German victories in the Football World Championship in 1954, 1974 and 1990, as well as of course above all the Deutsche Mark and Volkswagen, came to sum up the identity of the Western state and its people. The GDR could not seriously compete, either with its football premier league or with the 'people's own' vehicle, the Trabant ('Trabi') – one had to wait for years before a 'Trabi' could be owned – let alone with the much weaker Ost-Mark. It is true that the GDR population also experienced prosperity, but this was based on credit and from the middle or at the latest the end of the 1980s this was getting out of control.

The Germans and their alleged ambitions for unity were viewed with suspicion and scepticism abroad. In fact the Germans were not really that interested and were above all much less aggressive and dangerous than they were perceived to be in the East or in Western Europe. In the cabaret 'Die Distel' ('The Thistle') this was stated out loud in 1990: 'What a great unity it was when we were still divided!' As late as the 1970s most Germans accepted the division of their country as a fact, even if they had not yet made themselves at home as much as possible in their partial states. On both sides of the Iron Curtain, the division of Germany was taken to be an unalterable 'normality', something which, however, proved to be a mistake and self-delusion. As a result of the circumstances, described in this book, surrounding the crumbling power position of the Soviet Union in the context of the failed invasion of Afghanistan as well as in the context of the intensification of the Cold War in the first half of the 1980s along with the prevailing dire economic circumstances in the GDR, the collapse of the Eastern Bloc and thus of the East German state too was only a matter of time. By 1990 – when its economic statistics and liabilities became known – nobody was interested in maintaining and supporting it any more. Thus, the position of Germany as two states and the separation were no longer sustainable. The GDR – a state whose citizens were trying to become refugees – had virtually ceased to be viable.

After the period of confrontation under Adenauer and Ulbricht in the 1950s and 1960s, the two German states grew closer in the 1970s, admittedly on the political level this became a certain keeping one another at a distance, but the Germans in East and West grew more and more estranged to one another. Above and beyond this, the Federal Republic and the GDR deepened the division of Europe and continued to cement the structures of the Cold War in place. German historians are strangely silent about this, hardly mentioning the responsibility of the two German states over this, whereas the suffering and the victims of the East German population are highlighted.

The GDR, largely dependent on the will of the USSR, was a chance result of Stalin's failed German policy. It was a product of the involuntary forced circumstance of the Cold War. Then again, the integration of the Federal Republic with the West was the result of a more or less free decision of the will with the necessary tie to the United States. If, however, the GDR was a 'satrap of the Soviet colonial empire' (as Hans-Ulrich Wehler calls it), then the same can be said of the Federal Republic, i.e. that it had acted as it were a sort of satellite of the US empire. The old Federal Republic had also been a child of the Cold War, with all its associated biases, fixations, stereotypes and dislocations.

The pursuit of security from the threat from the East in the arms of the USA on the part of the Federal Republic (NATO, the EEC and the EU) as well as the pursuit of the continued existence of the GDR under the protective umbrella of the USSR in the East (COMECON and the Warsaw Pact) were both self-evident and delusory in the apparent stability of the Cold War. The GDR as a republic that was not democratically legitimated was to a large extent dependent on the will of Moscow, in the end also on the existence of the USSR itself. That was not so starkly the case when it comes to the Federal Republic and the USA. It had far more, indeed considerable potential for freedom at its disposal, making possible an emancipation and a departure from US policy without in the process endangering its survival. Signs of weakness and reform measures in the Soviet Union, on the contrary, had to affect the survival of the GDR sooner or later and bring about fatal consequences for it. The 'pursuit of security' (as Eckart Conze calls it) in the case of the Federal Republic initially developed in an opposite, equally unbalanced, direction but there seemed to be no alternative. Despite everything it was not just extremely cost-intensive but also an expression of short-sightedness together with a disregard for and underestimate of its own possibilities in the centre of Europe, amounting to a self-disregard, even a self-denial. This remarkable pursuit of security also barred the way to the pursuit of oneself. A concern with German interests was for a long time looked down upon and considered old-fashioned. Federal Chancellor Kohl, like his predecessors, Schmidt and Brandt, avoided the term 'reunification'.

Not until 1989–90 did unity take off as a concrete possibility and still now it has not worked itself out, particularly since people were not really focused on it, let alone prepared for it. At the same time another factor also played a role: again and again the Germans were in pursuit of self-assurance after the political and moral catastrophe of the Nazi period and were still living, as it were, under the shadow of the National Socialist past.

The fact that Germany consisted of partial states, politically accepted as part of the bargain involving the 'pursuit of security', and the faith in its permanence in the end represented a dead end as well as a misjudgement. The idea that the burden of the Nazi past and the resulting responsibility for Auschwitz did not allow Germans their unity was misguided wishful thinking on the part of intellectuals as regards both political morality and popular education. It was also at the same time a blatant underestimate of the historically enduring power of the tendency towards the nation state in Europe, which surfaced again and again in the history of the nineteenth and twentieth centuries, and was not commensurate with the artificial position of a Germany consisting of two separate states either.

The Federal Republic in the period between 1949 and 1989, looked at in the round, made considerable – even above average – financial, economic and political efforts to lay the groundwork for European integration. It was the largest net contributor to the EC, helping to finance for example France's agriculture, its overseas territories and its nuclear forces, and put the question of German unity on the back burner (which is not to say that its founding father consciously renounced it). It needs to be further investigated, however, to what extent such a policy could always be called 'European': on the contrary, it was motivated above all by national politics, and this was also noted by third parties. The current suspicion and residual scepticism towards Germany and its reliability were revealed to all the world in 1989–90. So much for the efforts at laying the groundwork for Europe as a basis for trust. Following this critical line, one could also argue that the forms of integration from the European Coal and Steel Community (in 1952) to the EEC (in 1958) simply represented the temporary replacement of peace treaties for the provisional West German state. Instead of signing a peace treaty with Germany, the increased integration of the Federal Republic within the framework of the EC or EU was pushed ahead. One could with full justification argue that the Federal Republic, a trading nation which from the economic point of view is more than averagely dependent on exports, also benefited from European integration and had created a considerable economic bias in favour of ultimate German unity thanks to the integration of domestic German trade and thus of the GDR within the EEC Customs Union of the Common Market.

By the end of the Cold War in Europe the relic of Germany as two partial states – the Berlin Wall – had to fall, having in its day saved the GDR from a mass exodus. Nikita Khrushchev had seen it as a compromise in the confrontation over Germany. Uninterrupted German responsibility for the past and the resolute realization of national unity combined together without any problem and did not contradict one another, just as the German writer Günter Grass had postulated.

In 1989 history went into a different gear. The unity of the German national state was held up and drawn out over decades, representing the policy of Adenauer and Ulbricht, but it could not be prevented in the end. Both post-war politicians came into their own as ideal types in their Cold War thinking. The Federal Chancellor was concerned about the goals of any relaxation of US policy in Europe. He needed confrontation with 'Soviet Communism' and stoked up exaggerated fears over neutrality just as Walter Ulbricht required the 'Fascist' and 'Imperialist' Federal Republic to distinguish from his 'democratic' and 'peace-loving' republic. In a different and yet similar way, both of them personified and embodied vassal republics. The actual feudal lords resided in Washington and Moscow, their minions in Bonn and Pankow.

The Ostpolitik of the Federal Republic was a logical consequence of the one-way street of the West German policy of integration with the West. This was to surface for the first time in the course of the 1970s and '80s, when both Helmut Schmidt and Erich Honecker tried to emancipate from the protecting powers and not only defined internal German interests in their own way but even fulfilled them. But would the Germans have to remain divided?

Peter Bender has described the development of the two German states as curves. At the start there were still things in common, remaining from the unity of the Reich. In the 1950s they began to grow apart, in the 1960s they became alienated from one another. Against the background of the Basic Treaty ('Grundlagen-Vertrag') the lines of development came together again and grew close without coinciding. The ways of dealing with the Nazi legacy did not follow the same path, whereas emancipation from the protecting powers evolved in similar directions, if not simultaneously and from the same motives. The question of unity divided them, but there was a recognition of the fact 'that they have to stay separate in order to reach the possible degree of unity'. In Berlin this enmity was at its sharpest. It was not just the battleground of the Big Powers but also an obstacle for the GDR and a burden for the Federal Republic. In the 1970s 'Europe' was at a crossroads: It determined their fate and in this way they also made progress along the road to fulfilling their ambitions as Germans. 'Change through rapprochement' (as Egon Bahr and Willy Brandt called it) meant a brightening up of the dark period of the 1950s and '60s.

Germany had represented many different states in its earlier history and a complete national unified state was the exception. Would the situation of Germany being made up of partial states be continued by the Federal Republic and the GDR? For forty years it looked like it. In the end, however, the Germans returned to 'European normality', to the Europe of nations that produced new forms of states after 1919 and again after 1989. Germany would discover its continuing future as a national state within the EU. There was obviously no other way.

In the wake of the decolonization taking place through the 1950s and '60s, and against the background of the collapse of the larger and smaller multi-ethnic political units in the 1990s, there emerged a large number of new states. After the fall of the Soviet Union and Yugoslavia there were 26 new states. In this context the dramatically rapid development towards the creation of a German national state seems to be a perfectly logical and natural process. It was not an especially German path embarked upon in 1989–90. This development was embedded within the creation of new states in Central and Eastern Europe and as such it was a part of European 'normality'.

The GDR population emancipated itself from being a puppet regime of the USSR originally installed at Moscow's behest. The Federal Republic freed itself step by step, if less dramatically, from its one-sided dependency on the USA.

The year 1989 highlighted the difference between the two German states: democracy and constitutional state on the one hand, dictatorship and illegitimate

Some of the last surviving parts of the Wall.

state on the other. That democracy of the Western type would win out was the decision of the mutinous East German population that chose to follow the path of personal freedom and unity. 'The Germans were already united, the politicians had to follow them', as Peter Bender puts it. The East Germans had kept more national consciousness compared with their Western compatriots. They were doubtless the 'more German Germans', who had read more Goethe and Schiller and listened to more Bach and Händel, as was argued by the former West German politician Bernhard Vogel, who held the office of Minister-President of Thuringia for a number of years after the *Wende* ('turning point' or 'change') and knew what he was talking about.

Despite the 'dual foundation of states' (as Christoph Kleßmann calls it) and the situation of Germany as two states there still remained one German nation. All attempts to create a 'socialist nation' as in the GDR or else ideas of a West German nation along the lines of 'constitutional patriotism' (as Dolf Sternberger calls it) were doomed to failure. The German nation in the tradition of the bourgeois freedom movement (the *Vormärz*) of 1848 surfaced once again.

That the Federal Republic made the framework for a peaceful and rapid incorporation of the ex-GDR into the economic and political system of Western democracy possible was no accident but already prepared for by the Basic Law ('Grundgesetz') and the Treaty of Rome. Thus, in the new and enlarged Federal Republic the history of repression, persecution and breach of trust in the former

East German partial state could also systematically have a line drawn under it and be overcome.

The German revolution of autumn 1989 differed from all the freedom movements in Central and Eastern Europe in that it was able to combine the ideas of freedom and nation. A united and German national state immediately and directly emerged from it. Nevertheless, even now 30 years after the non-violent revolution in the GDR and the peaceful unification with the Federal Republic, the Germans – apart from the younger generation – still lack an internal unity, a unity of hearts and minds. Germans in East and West still do not fully understand and love one another.

The incorporation of the former GDR as 'new Federal Länder' into the system of the Federal Republic took place under the slogan 'construction of the East'. The process of transition into becoming West German guaranteed a certain degree of continuity and stability to the new Federal Republic but it did not allow enough room for active involvement and innovation on the part of the East Germans.

The basic pillars of the post-war West German state were largely uncontested between the major parties, the CDU and the SPD: links to the USA, large-scale integration with Western Europe, agreement and reconciliation with France, responsibility for the legacy of the Third Reich and compensation to Israel. The basic pillars of the post-war East German state were a one-party dictatorship with a virtual pluralism involving pseudo-parties with a highly developed surveillance state and apparatus of persecution: dependence on the USSR, only partial integration with Central and Eastern Europe, unacknowledged agreement and reconciliation with Poland, and neither readiness to accept responsibility for National Socialism nor reparations to the Jewish state characterized this second German state of a different kind.

The Berlin Republic was essentially built up on the basic pillars of the West German state. It was in addition to enjoy freedom of action at home and abroad, i.e. to achieve 'full sovereignty'. In the war against what remained of Yugoslavia over Kosovo in 1999 German 'Luftwaffe' (air force) units were engaged for the first time since the Second World War within the framework of the NATO offensive. The close tie to the USA was put in question during the Iraq crisis of 2003 at the latest and became looser through the autonomous decision of Federal Chancellor Gerhard Schröder not to take part in that Anglo-American war with the so-called coalition of the willing.

European integration was now to encompass Central and Eastern Europe as well, over which the new Federal Republic – unlike France – could claim a special 'competence' and 'responsibility'. Social and cultural relations with France stagnated and threatened to become dormant. The attitude of responsibility towards history and support for Israel remained in place, even stronger: under Foreign Minister Fischer the Berlin Republic was actively involved in diplomatic efforts towards a solution of the Middle East conflict and the Federal navy was engaged in the Lebanon War against the attacks from Hezbollah against Israel in 2008. Both events would have been totally unimaginable before 1989.

Just as the emphasis shifted in foreign policy, in domestic policy too there were remarkable shifts in the power relations. The party-political heir to the GDR was now called not the SED, but the Party of Democratic Socialism (Partei des demokratischen Sozialismus, PDS) which contributed later on under the leadership of Gregor Gysi and Oskar Lafontaine to a further broadening of the party spectrum, rechristened as the Neue Linke ('New Left'), or Die Linke/PDS, and following in the footsteps of The Greens in the old Federal Republic.

The move from Bonn to Berlin initially changed very little as regards the orientation of German domestic and foreign policy. With the construction of the Holocaust Memorial near the Brandenburg Gate the Federal Republic put on record its continued condemnation of Nazi atrocities and its sympathy for the victims and, going beyond that, the special relationship with the state of Israel.

The location of the capital in the East of the country had a favourable effect on the relations between West and East Germans – an alternative scenario with Bonn as the Federal capital would have been far less beneficial, but the city of Berlin as such continued to remain divided.

How much the political culture has been changed by the Berlin Republic can be clearly seen from the fact that the daughter of a Protestant pastor from Mark Brandenburg in the East holds the office of Federal Chancellor, something that would have been unimaginable in the CDU in the days of the Catholic Rhinelander Adenauer.

The transformation of the East German to the West German economy and society led to high unemployment and a number of social problems in the East of the country and at the same time increased the alienation brought about by 40 years of division between East and West. 'A flourishing landscape', such as Helmut Kohl had prophesied in 1990, did not come about so quickly, more a kind of 'German Mezzogiorno without the mafia', as Helmut Schmidt had soberly put it. 2.7 million East Germans had migrated to the West. The depopulation of whole areas of the country, the lack of industrial hubs and of a broad middle class (a legacy of Socialism) still remain the main problems in the 'new Federal Länder'.

East Germany has nevertheless caught up enormously since unification, even if this has been paid for at a high price by the West. The policy of division in the 1950s now took its toll. West Germans had to share their prosperity enjoyed for decades with East Germans, or rather pay them back. Before 1989 every East German produced a third of what a West German contributed to the GNP. Productivity in the East of Germany has nonetheless reached 70 per cent of the GNP in the meantime. The engine of development has been the manufacturing sector: VW built a factory in Zwickau, Opel in Eisenach and BMW in Leipzig. Nevertheless, there remained differences: while industry in Thuringia eventually increased its creation of wealth by 10 per cent annually, in Mecklenburg-West Pomerania it was only 5 per cent. The unemployment figures in the East came down steeply from a high of 21 per cent to 12 per cent. The East German economy makes up just under 6 million employees but their number is not sufficient to pay for their unemployed and pensioners themselves. Correspondingly high transfers of finance continued to flow from West to East, 35 billion annually to pay for pensions and the unemployed alone.

The history of the unification of Germany has been by and large successful in spite of, or because of, all the financial strains and burdens when one considers the following question: what have the Germans made out of their recent history and their continued existence as a nation? In 1989, after the political setback of 1918 and the catastrophe of 1945, they were given a third chance to reposition themselves and take on a new image. This was primarily owing to the geo-strategically important, i.e. central, location of their country on the continent. Germany was and remained – even during the period of division – in the middle of Europe. There was a chance after 1918–19 and after 1945. The third chance in the twentieth century came after 1989–90, after two grave errors in the course of history consisting of the Nazi dictatorship (1933–45) and the SED dictatorship (1949–89). After a long period dominated by the 'fear of power', the Berlin Republic has at last managed a 'return to the world stage', as Gregor Schöllgen described it. Berlin no longer dances to every American tune: it acts as an intermediary in the Middle East conflict and can speak directly to Moscow.

The Germans have used their chance to continue the development of a European and modern state open to the world, which, despite all the problems as regards rising unemployment, the declining birthrate, the growing gap between rich and poor, increased indebtedness and lower economic growth, still continues to provide its citizens with (many) chances in life – far more than other states in the world do. The Federal Republic survived the economic crises of the 1970s and '80s better than its European neighbours. This leaves hope for the future of this country and therefore for the European Union as well.

The metaphor Ian Kershaw used for Europe's history in the latter part of the twentieth and the first part of the twenty-first century, the roller coaster, is equally applicable to the history of Germany in that period. Harking back to Fritz Stern's *Five Germanys I Have Known*, the book in which the well-known historian (1926–2016) describes his experience of the Weimar Republic, the Third Reich, the GDR, the FRG and the Berlin Republic, the title of the present book, *Three Germanies*, refers to post-1945 Germany. Predicated on demagoguery, popular assent and aggression, the Nazi state (1933–45) was followed by the compliance-, repression- and surveillance-based SED dictatorship (1949–89). If one puts aside for a moment the many profound differences that kept the two dictatorships apart, especially the Nazis' murderous effectiveness, both were characteristically German in that they were equally single-minded, totalitarian and all-pervasive. The GDR's western contemporary was the FRG. Unification in 1990 resulted in the Berlin Republic. What marked the definitive break with the Bonn Republic was not the decision on the capital of Germany passed by the Bundestag on 20 June 1991 – six federal ministries (Defence, Food and Agriculture, Economic Cooperation and Development, Environment, Nature Conservation and Nuclear Safety, Health and Education and Research) retained their main seats in Bonn anyway – but German involvement in the war against Serbia from 24 March 1999, when NATO switched from being a defensive alliance and embraced interventionism.

'The German question is back', Mainz historian Andreas Rödder wrote in *Wer hat Angst vor Deutschland?* (2018). Yet in a way the German question has never gone away ever since it was first raised at the Vienna Congress in 1814–15. It remained virulent throughout the nineteenth century and was pushed to the fore by the attempts at containment and control that marked the 1919 Versailles 'peace' treaty and the conferences at Yalta and Potsdam in 1945. Time and again Europe tried to come to grips with the problem that was Germany; success was never more than temporary. After the Second World War Germany was subjected to a division with assistance from a non-European power, the United States, and with active German cooperation in both the East and the West. This arrangement, too, lasted for only a limited time. Aiming to bring about the 'final settlement with respect to Germany', the Two-Plus-Four Treaty (the Federal Republic and GDR plus the four Allies: the USSR, United States, UK and France), which was signed on 12 September 1990 and entered into force on 15 March 1991, brought international recognition for German unification. While in official parlance the German side claimed to have obtained 'full sovereignty', the reality on the ground looked different. The German question was still urgent, as appears from the way the Maastricht Treaty aimed to tie Germany closer to Europe than ever before, with the German government apparently playing along.

The European dilemma of being unable to achieve permanent control of Germany has a counterpart in Germany in what the historian Ludwig Dehio referred to as Germany's 'semi-hegemony'. The country had never been powerful enough to dominate the whole of Europe but it was powerful enough to make others feel ill at ease.

What does that mean in terms of Germany's role in the EU in the twenty-first century? Germany was – and still is – Europe's leading power in terms of trade, economy, currency and finance. While its leading role in the EU is indisputable, Germany is at the same time dependent on the export markets of the other EU members, on their assent to its integration policy, on majority decisions and other countries' readiness to forego the exercise of their veto rights in the EU Council. The situation in which the Berlin Republic finds itself can be summed up neatly in what might be called the *categorical integration imperative*, a variation on Kant's iconic dictum: 'Act only according to that maxim whereby you can, at the same time, be content that it should become a universal *community* law.'

Given Germany's dependence on assistance from its European partners, the threat of cutting back subsidies for those EU countries that withheld their solidarity in the migration question proved counterproductive by exacerbating already existing tensions between old and new member states. This was the lesson seemingly all-powerful Germany had to learn between 2015 and 2019, forcing it to eat its demands for unconditional acceptance of refugee contingents.

When fears of a resurgence of German power are voiced by outside observers, one factor is usually overlooked: what remains paramount for the foreseeable future are the social fragmentation and the predominance of domestic dissent over consensus, the legacy of German 'unification'. Short-lived euphoria lasting only from November 1989 to the spring of 1990 was followed by massive disillusionment when the new Länder were visited by those emissaries of the not-so-social market economy, de-industrialization and mass unemployment. Attempts to mitigate transformation by systematically comparing experiences and giving a voice to trauma in public were in short supply. The mania for material gratification is not a climate in which mutual understanding can flourish. While unification was easy for the West to enact, its implementation in what was East Germany was beset by grave social and economic problems. The East German run on the D-mark and the speedy 1–1 exchange of ostmark to D-mark caused the former GDR's internal and export economies to collapse, unable as they were to compete with Western products. The Treuhand then quickly disposed of what remained after the rash adoption of the deutschmark. This East German malaise created a fertile breeding ground for 'eastalgia' and an idealization of the past. Many East Germans only ever became committed GDR cititzens after the 'Wende', which served as a prism through which they became aware of some of the specificities of their East German existence.

In 2019 the Berlin Republic was still a country with two souls whose incompatibility surfaces in different political attitudes and different mentalities. The 'Jugendweihe', a ceremony introduced by the Communist regime as a replacement for Protestant and Catholic confirmation, is still being practised. De-christianization is proving the most potent legacy of the Ulbricht-Honecker era. Russia is considered an ally in spirit and a fellow victim of transformation. The majority of East Germans (55 per cent) are opposed to the sanctions imposed on Moscow. Forty-two per cent of East Germans still saw themselves in 2019 as second-class citizens, left to fend for themselves by West German politicians. Taking up their cause, the AfD, a protest party under West German leadership, received the lion's share of its vote from former East Germany. With 89 MPs, a third of whom are from East Germany, the party maintains a powerful presence in the Bundestag.

In power at the federal level since 2017, the Grand Coalition of CDU/CSU and SPD largely failed to gain recognition for its considerable achievements. In 2019 Germany was more divided in social terms and in terms of party politics than ever, which has serious implications for the country's room for manoeuvre in European politics. Merkel's repeated calls for European unity fell mostly on deaf ears. In the elections to the European parliament on 26 May 2019, the majority of votes in the West went to the Greens and in the East to the AfD, with the Greens also scoring successes in the major cities in the East. The German electorate was clearly on a path towards increasing polarization.

While committed to the categorical integration imperative mentioned above, continued diversification of the party political spectrum, leading to a loss of domestic stability and a split into a cosmopolitan left-liberal and a national-conservative bourgeois camp, may bring about a situation where that imperative can no longer be heeded. The self-deprecating hegemonial power of European politics is at times immobilized by a self-inflicted paralysis whose spell no one can break, if not Germany itself.

In the new Berlin Republic, concurrent declarations of German national statehood and of German historical guilt were no longer regarded as mutually contradictory. The Nazi past remained a live issue and moved centre stage during the controversy surrounding the construction of a Holocaust memorial. Charged with powerful symbolism, the large-scale monument near the Brandenburg Gate has become a key statement of the new republic's acceptance of moral responsibility for the crimes of the Nazi regime. Alongside the controversy centring on the Holocaust Memorial, a debate unfolded about the Zentrum für Flucht und Vertreibung, the Centre for Flight and Expulsion. Erected in Berlin at a cost of 60 million euros, the documentation centre of the Foundation Flight, Expulsion, Reconciliation was completed in the summer of 2019, ready for inauguration in February 2020. The extent to which the suffering of the 12 to 14 million German deportees can legitimately be the focus of this permanent exhibition remains a highly controversial issue.

Since 1989 a great deal has changed in Germany: the euphoria about the reputedly vanishing Cold War patterns of confrontation and the putative victory of liberal democracy (Francis Fukuyama) gave way to a development that totally belied expectations. While giving democracy a shot in the arm, this break brought with it a renaissance of nationalism, which many had thought dead and buried. The opening up of the East and the implosion of the Soviet empire created the preconditions for NATO enlargement, which received powerful support from Federal Chancellor Helmut Kohl and Defence Minister Volker Rühe, soon to be followed by the EU.

While in the run-up to the Iraq war in 2003 the United States succeeded under Secretary of Defense Donald Rumsfeld in splitting increasingly unified Europe into its 'old' and 'new' components, the nation-building project of the war coalition ended by plunging Iraq into total chaos. The Federal Republic under Schröder and Fischer had rejected the request by the United States to join the war coalition. The Red–Green government's refusal to take part in George W. Bush's Iraq war provides a reminder that under Chancellor Ludwig Erhard (1963–6) the Federal Republic had declined the role of the United States' ally in the Vietnam war. Instead, only the German hospital ship *Helgoland* was sent to that theatre of war.

In Afghanistan allied NATO troops were on the retreat. On the global stage, the hyper-dominance of the United States marking unipolarity since 1991 was replaced after 2001 by a multipolar world order beyond the remit of the Berlin Republic. Germany was a long way off spending the minimum 2 per cent of its GDP on its military until 2024 as its contribution to NATO. To the very last it showed itself loath to yield to American requests to increase its defence spending. This amounted to a refusal to give the United States the allegiance it felt it was owed. Between 2017 and 2019, the number of Germans in favour of membership of the

North Atlantic Treaty Organisation dropped from 68 per cent to 54 per cent, mirroring the dwindling of German support.

Barack Obama's re-election on 4 November 2012 promised a further improvement in transatlantic relations, compared to the irritations and frustrations that had marked those relations during the two terms George W. Bush (2000–2008) had held office. The election on 8 November 2016 of a real-estate tycoon, the multi-billionaire Donald Trump, came as a shock to the leadership of the Berlin Republic. Cancellation of the Transatlantic Trade and Investment Partnership (TTIP), the United States' withdrawal from the Paris Agreement under the United Nations Framework Convention on Climate Change and from the Iran nuclear deal framework and the repeated threat of the imposition of so-called punitive tariffs on German and European products – especially on motor vehicles – to correct the trade balance deficits of the United States pushed open the door to a hitherto inconceivable deterioration in transatlantic relations, signalling the sun setting on the traditional pro-American German political culture.

Nor was this confined to the political establishment. It was obvious that public trust in the United States was being rapidly eroded. Trump scored higher than Putin when it came to assessing the danger they spelt for Germany and the world. The decidedly one-sided, partisan US Middle East policy was called into question, without the familiar knock-out argument that what was being voiced was pure anti-Americanism or increasing anti-Semitism. Unlike Trump, Merkel mounted a clear criticism of Israel's settlement policy, advocating a two-state solution for Israelis and Palestinians in unison with the EU. In the controversy surrounding the nuclear deal with Iran, Berlin again took a stand against Washington and Tel Aviv, which led to Israel's Prime Minister Benjamin Netanyahu accusing Merkel of being too soft on Teheran.

Compared to Kohl's world, the world Merkel had to deal with was much more complex, conflict-ridden and obscure. In the Cold War the Iron Curtain had drawn a demarcation line straight down the middle of the continent. Now the conflict zones tended to be located at Europe's periphery. When after the stellar investment into the Aufbau Ost Germany had reasserted itself as Europe's key economic and monetary power, its trade and other economic interests did not allow it any longer to pursue the one-sided transatlantic or exclusively West European orientation that had predominated in the Cold War. Germany's foreign policy now had to attach more weight than had traditionally been the case to the continent's north-south dimension and it had to play its own role on the world stage. This had already been anticipated by Joschka Fischer's active Middle East policy and was taken up Frank-Walter Steinmeier's mediation diplomacy in the Iran question and in the Ukraine conflict.

The new capital represented a new, colourful and multicultural Germany at the heart of an enlarged EU. During the German EU presidency in 2007, the Berlin Declaration was passed. After the ratification of the European constitution had foundered on the negative referenda in France and the Netherlands, this Declaration was designed to breathe new life into the process of EU reform. It succeeded in paving the way for what was to become known as the Treaty of Lisbon.

While Berlin was successful in dealing with the banking and financial market crisis in 2008/9, the Black–Yellow Merkel–Westerwelle coalition initially dithered over the Greek question, the sovereign debt crisis and the euro crisis (2009/10) and only hesitantly reached for 'rescue packages', for which, as the Chancellor famously declared, 'there was no alternative'. It was in reaction to this repeatedly used dictum that the new party called itself 'Alternative für Deutschland'. Initially a single-issue party fixated on its opposition to the euro, the AfD then made itself the first port of call for voters who had become politically homeless during the refugee crisis. Though always wary in her calculation of political consequences, this time the Chancellor was taken by surprise.

Environmental politics was another area where the coalition parties failed to impress. Having made the environment part of her special agenda as early as 2007, the Chancellor allowed the goals she had set for 2020 to slip from sight, which caused the young generations to turn away from her in disappointment. The

Angela Merkel and Donald Tusk at the European People's Party Congress in Bucharest, 2012.

climate protection movement reached Germany in the spring and summer of 2019, when sixteen-year-old Swedish environmental activist Greta Thunberg captured the hearts and minds of young people, especially of schoolchildren and students, with her demand for a radical climate agenda. In the run-up to the EU elections activists canvassed for a 'global climate strike', moving the environment to the top of the agenda. Adopting the name 'Fridays for Future', the 'school strike for the climate' rapidly turned into a movement demanding that governments abide by the Paris Climate Accord. All of this caused a spike in approval for the Greens under Robert Habeck and Annalena Baerbock, where the polls seemed to justify speculation about a future Green federal chancellor.

At the end of September 2019 the grand coalition passed a climate package, albeit one that has been criticized by environmentalists and Green politicians as lightweight and much too weak to achieve the desired climate goals. Nevertheless the coalition government has given itself something to shout about by achieving what the SPD had set as its goal when it entered into the coalition.

What are the characteristics that define Angela Merkel as a politician and as the Federal chancellor? While reputedly viewing her fellow beings with a certain degree of scepticism, she rewarded trustworthiness with trust, demanding unconditional loyalty from the people around her. True to her character as the daughter of a Protestant pastor from the Uckermark, she remained completely untouched by political affairs and scandals. She may be said to have lived up to her declared intention of serving Germany without compromising her integrity, upholding what might be called the Prussian values of discipline and straightforwardness.

Her critics wanted to know where the chancellor wanted to lead the Berlin Republic. The question as such was ill conceived. The only course open to Merkel was to try and navigate her country through the stormy weather of international politics into calmer waters and to keep the secessionist tendencies in the EU at bay. She approached the latter task with an attitude that came from cool reasoning rather than from the heart. In 2016 President Obama won her over when he asked her to stand for the chancellorship one more time to ensure Europe's political stability. Having taken some time over this decision, she stood by it, once it was made, without ifs and buts and in the face of a creeping loss of power that had already set in a year earlier.

What was the basis of Merkel's successes and of her failures? Her greatest strength was her resolve not to commit herself as long as a public debate was still brewing and not to make any decision until all the pros and cons were on the table and could be properly assessed. The long periods of her silence and hesitancy were often lambasted as attempts to sit out crises, as symptoms of weakness and as a lack of vision. However, when a quick decision was needed, she was capable of making it, as in the withdrawal from nuclear energy and in the reception of the refugees.

While Merkel was often seen as an anti-populist, she in fact took a keen interest in public opinion, regularly commissioning polls from the Bundespresseamt and other polling institutes that asked very specific questions. Knowing the direction the wind was blowing among the populace, Merkel then made her decisions in a way that reflected a broad consensus. This was the case on 14 March 2011 both with the withdrawal from nuclear energy and with her readiness to welcome the refugees ('Wir schaffen das!') on 31 August 2015 at a time when a solid majority of the population backed those decisions. Her decisions were therefore not as untainted by populism as might appear at first sight.

In the last analysis, Merkel was a chancellor full of contradictions, as becomes clear when the period of her chancellorship is seen as a succession of five different phases:

(1) Between 2005 and 2007, she and Vice Chancellor and Foreign Minister Frank-Walter Steinmeier (SPD) jointly salvaged the European constitution after its rejection by France and the Netherlands in 2005 by transforming it during Germany's EU presidency (2007) into the Basic or Reform Treaty; it entered into force in 2009 as the Treaty of Lisbon. This achievement was the first proof of Merkel's skill in dealing with crises affecting European

'Fridays for Future' in Germany: Dresden in spring 2019.

integration.

(2) In close rapport with French presidents Nicolas Sarkozy (2007–12) and the politically much weaker François Hollande (2012–17), Merkel gave further proof of her skill as a troubleshooter between 2008–9 and 2014–15. Together with the head of the ECB, Mario Draghi (2014–19), the EU's heads of states and governments and the president of the Commission, José Manuel Barroso (2004–14), she played a leading role in protecting the eurozone and the cohesion of the European Union.

(3) In the refugee crisis in 2015, Merkel increasingly courted controversy. She initially insisted on all EU member states jointly receiving proportionate contingents of refugees from war- and disaster-torn areas in the Middle East. This led to objections from Czechia, Slovakia, Hungary and Poland, sowing the seeds of discord. It took Merkel until 2016–17 to adopt a more concilia-tory tone while she continued, admittedly with mixed results, to conjure up a spirit of cooperation among Europe's heads of states and governments.

(4) In the final years of her chancellorship (2017–19) Merkel has largely failed to come up with a timely, concrete and substantive response to the proposals made by Emmanuel Macron, most notably to those put forward in the famous speech he delivered at the Sorbonne on 26 September 2017. This meant she was losing out on a unique opportunity for Germany to team up with France in pursuit of a new dynamism for the EU's halting inte-gration process that would define new goals shared by all members and advance specific projects. In this way she not only weakened Macron's domestic position, where he had been pushed into defensive mode by the months-old strike of the 'gilets jaunes', but made him turn against her preferred candidate for the post of Commission president at the European parliament elections in May 2019, Manfred Weber. Nor was criticism of Merkel confined to France: quite a few Germans, including people in her own party with impeccable European credentials, begged to differ with her.

(5) The final phase of the Merkel era (2019–20) was marked by a loss of power, moderation and damage limitation on the domestic political level. Confidential figures withdrew one after the other: Health Minister Hermann Gröhe had to step aside for Jens Spahn. CDU-CSU faction spokesman Volker Kauder did not get a majority and was replaced by Ralph Brinkhaus. Finally, party leader Annegret Kramp-Karrenbauer, in view of the differences of opinion with the CDU in the East German states on how to deal with the AfD, surrendered and withdrew. In view of the creeping loss

of power and trust in her own party, Merkel was a significantly weakened partner among her EU partners and left Macron almost entirely in charge of the opinion leader on the future of the EU. After the outbreak of the Covid-19 pandemic, Merkel showed strength in leadership and moderation both at the German level through aid and economic stimulus programmes within the Grand Coalition and at the European level with multi-billion-euro programmes to support weaker EU partners in a duo with Macron and in cooperation with the Commission.

German historian Andreas Rödder offered a critical balance in 2018: Merkel's legacy includes manifold divisions, in her own party, in East and West Germany and in the EU. On the other side of the coin are polls taken in July 2019, in which 70 per cent of Germans declared themselves satisfied with Merkel's government. This seems to suggest that there is a limit to any tendencies for division. Question marks remain, however, about the continuation of the Grand Coalition.

What is the future for Germany and the EU? Can the EU make further progress in its integration? The answer gives us little confidence. Merkel and Macron are not community Europeans, but government Europeans. The dilemma of Germany's ailing and therefore weak European policy remains to be feared in the year 2020. It resembles a duck that has been lame since 2017 and has taken refuge on the global stage. Merkel's intended successor was unable to hold her own. The political discourse has shifted to the right as a result of a right-wing bourgeois protest party with almost 90 members of parliament in the German *Bundestag*, which tends towards German nationalism and even right-wing extremism. Starting from a small Federal state like Thuringia, the AfD can already shake the party political system.

If Germany's European political backing for the EU continues to fail, it will be all the more difficult for Ursula von der Leyen's EU Commission to succeed. Jacques Delors as president of the Commission (1985–95) with twelve member states could only be so successful with his integration policy in his time because Kohl and Mitterrand were behind him. Both statesmen were more than just government Europeans and had strong domestic support.

As time goes on the German question will still be with us – topical, acute and open at all levels. To a strong degree Germany's commitment provides the guarantee that together with France and all the other member states the next chapter of the EU's history can be written, and that the continent's and the world's all-decisive anchor of stability will survive.

Abbreviations

ACC	Allied Consultation Committee
ADN	Allgemeiner Deutscher Nachrichtendienst
AfD	Alternative für Deutschland
AKP	Adalet ve Kalkınma Partisi
APO	Außerparlamentarische Opposition
ARD	Arbeitsgemeinschaft der öffentlich-rechtlichen Rundfunkanstalten
BAMF	Bundesamt für Migrationsfragen
BDM	Bund Deutscher Mädel
BfV	Bundesamt für Verfassungsschutz
BKA	Bundeskanzleramt
BMW	Bayerische Motorenwerke
BND	Bundesnachrichtendienst
BPA	Bundespresseamt
BVG	Bundesverfassungsgericht
CC	Central Committee
CDU	Christlich-Demokratische Union
CDUD	Christlich-Demokratische Union Deutschlands
CEO	Chief Executive Officer
CFE	Conventional Forces in Europe
CFLN	Committee for French Liberation
CFSP	Common and Foreign Security Policy
COMECON	Council of Mutual Economic Cooperation
CPSU	Communist Party of the Soviet Union
CSCE	Conference of Security and Cooperation in Europe
CSU	Christlich-Soziale Union
DA	Demokratischer Aufbruch
DDP	Deutsche Demokratische Partei
DGB	Deutscher Gewerkschaftsbund
DİTİB	Diyanet İşleri Türk İslam Birliği

DKP	Deutsche Kommunistische Partei
DM	Deutsche Mark
DP	Demokratische Partei
DPA	Deutsche Presseagentur
DRP	Deutsche Reichspartei
DSU	Deutsche Soziale Union
DVP	Deutsche Volkspartei
DVU	Deutsche Volksunion
EAC	European Advisory Commission
EC	European Communities
ECB	European Central Bank
ECSC	European Coal and Steel Community
ECU	European Currency Unit
EDC	European Defence Community
EEA	European Economic Area
EEC	European Economic Community
EFSF	European Financial Stability Facility
EFTA	European Free Trade Association
EMS	European Monetary System
EMU	European Monetary Union
EPA	Environmental Protection Agency
ESA	European Stability Mechanism
EU	European Union
EURATOM	European Atomic Energy Community
FAZ	Frankfurter Allgemeine Zeitung
FDGB	Freier Deutscher Gewerkschaftsbund
FDJ	Freie Deutsche Jugend
FDP	Freie Demokratische Partei
FRG	Federal Republic of Germany
G8	Group of Eight
GDP	Gross Domestic Product
GDR	German Democratic Republic
Gestapo	Geheime Staatspolizei
GG	Grundgesetz
GNP	Gross National Product
IFOR	Implementation Force
IMF	International Monetary Fund
IM	Inoffizieller Mitarbeiter (GDR)
IMS	International Monetary System
IMT	International Military Tribunal
INF	Intermediate Range Nuclear Force
ISAF	International Security Assistance Force
IT	Information Technology

KB	Kulturbund (GDR)
KFOR	Kosovo Force
KFW	Kreditanstalt für Wiederaufbau
KITA	Kindestagesstätten
KOMINFORM	Kommunistisches Informationsbüro
KPD	Kommunistische Partei Deutschlands
KVP	Kasernierte Volkspolizei (GDR)
LDPD	Liberaldemokratische Partei Deutschlands
LPG	Landwirtschaftliche Produktionsgenossenschaft
MCA	Maximum Credible Accident
MERCOSUR	Mercado Común del Cono Sur
Mfs	Ministerium für Staatssicherheit (GDR)
MIT	Millî İstihbarat Teşkilâtı
MRP	Mouvement Républicain Populaire
NAFTA	North American Free Trade Association
NATO	North Atlantic Treaty Organization
NDR	Norddeutscher Rundfunk
NKWD	Ministry of Interior of the USSR
NPD	Nationaldemokratische Partei Deutschlands
NSA	National Security Agency
NSU	Nationalsozialistischer Untergrund
NVA	Nationale Volksarmee (GDR)
NWDR	Nordwestdeutscher Rundfunk
OEEC	Organization of European Economic Cooperation
OKW	Oberkommando der Wehrmacht
OMGUS	Office of Military Government of the United States
OPEC	Organization of Petroleum Exporting Countries
ORF	Österreichischer Rundfunk
OSCE	Organization of Security and Cooperation in Europe
ÖVP	Österreichische Volkspartei
PDS	Partei des Demokratischen Sozialismus
PEGIDA	Patrioten Europas gegen die Islamisierung des Abendlandes
RAF	Rote Armee Fraktion
SA	Stormtroopers
SALT	Strategic Arms Limitation Talks
SD	Security Service
SDP	Sozialdemokratische Partei in der DDR
SEA	Single European Act
SED	Sozialistische Einheitspartei Deutschlands
SMAD	Soviet Military Administration
SPD	Sozialdemokratische Partei Deutschlands
SPO	Sozialistische Partei Österreichs
SS	Schutzstaffel

SRG	Schweizer Rundfunk- und Fernsehgesellschaft
SRP	Sozialistische Reichspartei
SZ	Süddeutsche Zeitung
TTIP	Transatlantic Trade and Investment Partnership
UÇK	Ushtria Çlirimtare e Kosovës
UMTS	Universal Mobile Telecommunications Systems
UNO	United Nations Organizations
USSR	Union of Socialist Soviet Republics
VAT	Value Added Tax
VEB	Volkseigener Betrieb
VOPO	Volkspolizei (GDR)
VVN	Verein der Verfolgten des Naziregimes
VW	Volkswagen
WDR	Westdeutscher Rundfunk
WEU	Westeuropäische Union
ZDF	Zweites Deutsches Fernsehen
ZESt	Zentrale Erfassungsstelle Salzgitter

Bibliography

Abelshauser, Werner, *Deutsche Wirtschaftsgeschichte seit 1945* (Munich, 2004)

Aretz, Jürgen, Günter Buchstab and Jörg-Dieter Gauger, eds, *Geschichtsbilder.*
   Weichenstellungen deutscher Geschichte nach 1945 (Freiburg, Basel, Vienna, 2003)

Auerbach, Lore, 'Emigration und Remigration – Ein Lebensbericht', lecture given
   under the supervision of Dr. h.c. Lore Auerbach at the 'Europagespräche' at the
   Institut für Geschichte der Universität Hildesheim, 24 November 2008, at
   www.uni-hildesheim.de/de/36240.htm (10 April 2010).

Bahr, Egon, *Zu meiner Zeit* (Munich, 1996)

Bald, Detlef and Wolfram Wette, eds, *Alternativen zur Wiederbewaffnung in*
   Westdeutschland 1945–1955 (Frieden und Krieg. Beiträge zur Historischen
   Friedensforschung 11) (Essen, 2008)

Baring, Arnulf, *Im Anfang war Adenauer. Die Entstehung der Kanzlerdemokratie*
   (Munich, 2nd edn 1982)

Bauer, Fritz, *Botschafter in zwei deutschen Staaten. Die DDR zwischen Anerkennung*
   und Auflösung (1973–1990). Die aktive österreichische Neutralitätspolitik
   (Vienna, n.p.)

Becker, Jörg, 'Destabilisierungsversuche der BRD im deutsch-deutschen Kalten
   Krieg. Bizim Radyo – türkische Radiosendungen aus der DDR von 1959 bis 1989',
   paper given at the 'Europagespräche' at the Institut für Geschichte der Universität
   Hildesheim, 20 January 2010, at www.uni-hildesheim.de/de/ 43813.htm (29
   January 2010).

Bender, Peter, *Deutsche Parallelen. Anmerkungen zu einer gemeinsamen Geschichte zweier*
   getrennter Staaten (Berlin, 1989)

—, *Episode oder Epoche? Zur Geschichte des geteilten Deutschland* (Munich, 2nd edn 1996)

—, *Deutschlands Wiederkehr. Eine ungeteilte Nachkriegsgeschichte 1945–1990* (Stuttgart,
   2007).

Benz, Wolfgang, with Edelgard Bially, Gisela Gerdes, Jana Richter, Angelima Schardt
   and Juliane Wetzel, *Deutschland seit 1945. Entwicklungen in der Bundesrepublik und*
   in der DDR. Chronik – Dokumente – Bilder (Munich, 1990)

Berndt, Burkhard, 'Die Treuhandanstalt im Kontext der deutschen Einigung, Bericht über den Vortrag in den Europagesprächen des Instituts für Geschichte der Universität Hildesheim', 2 July 2007, at www.uni-hildesheim.de/de/29224.htm (15 April 2010)

Bertelsmann Stiftung, ed., *Woran glaubt die Welt? Analysen und Kommentare zum Religionsmonitor 2008* (Gütersloh, 2009); see the contributions by Karl Gabriel, Matthias Petzoldt and Monika Wohlrab-Sahr, pp. 99–124; 125–50; 151–68

Bitsch, Marie-Thérèse, Wilfried Loth and Raymond Poidevin, eds, *Institutions Européennes et Identités Européennes (Organisation Internationale et Relations Internationales 41)* (Brussels, 1998); see the contribution by Wolf D. Gruner, '"Les Europe des Européens": The Perceptions of Europe in the Debates of the Consultative Assembly of the Council of Europe 1949–1951', pp. 89–121

Böick, Marcus, *Die Treuhand. Idee – Praxis – Erfahrung 1990–1994* (Göttingen, 2018)

Bösch, Frank, ed., *Geteilte Geschichte. Ost- und Westdeutschland 1970–2000* (Göttingen, 2015); (Bonn: Bundeszentrale für politische Bildung, Schriftenreihe 1636).

Boysen, Jacqueline, *Angela Merkel. Eine Karriere* (Berlin, 2005)

—, *Das 'weiße Haus' in Ost-Berlin. Die Ständige Vertretung der Bundesrepublik bei der DDR* (Berlin, 2010)

Bracher, Karl-Dietrich, Wolfgang Jäger and Werner Link, *Republik im Wandel 1969–1974. Die Ära Brandt (Geschichte der Bundesrepublik Deutschland*, vol. V/1 (Stuttgart and Mannheim, 1986)

Bruck, Elke, *François Mitterrands Deutschlandbild* (Frankfurt am Main, 2003)

Bulmer, Simon, 'Deutschland in der EU: Europas unverzichtbarer Hegemon?', in *Integration*, 42 (2019), pp. 1, 3–20 (Baden-Baden: Nomos)

Burrichter, Clemens, Detlef Nakath and Gerd-Rüdiger Stephan, eds, *Deutsche Zeit-geschichte von 1945 bis 2000. Gesellschaft – Staat – Politik. Ein Handbuch* (Berlin, 2006)

Conze, Eckart, *Die Suche nach Sicherheit. Eine Geschichte der Bundesrepublik Deutschland von 1949 bis in die Gegenwart* (Munich, 2009)

Creuzberger, Stefan, *Westintegration und Neue Ostpolitik. Die Außenpolitik der Bundesrepublik* (Berlin, 2009)

—, Dominik Geppert and Dierk Hoffmann, 'How to Write the History of a Divided Nation: Germany, 1945–1990', in *German Historical Institute London Bulletin*, XLI (May 2019), no. 1, pp, 3–18.

Dokumente zur Deutschlandpolitik, ed. Bundesministerium des Inneren und vom Bundesarchiv. *I. Reihe/vol. V: Europäische Beratende Kommission 15. Dezember 1943 bis 31. August 1945, Erster und Zweiter Halbband, bearbeitet von Herbert Elzer* (Munich, 2003)

Dokumente zur Deutschlandpolitik, ed. Bundesministerium des Inneren u. vom Bundesarchiv. *Rh. VI, vol. II: 1. Januar 1971 bis 31. Dezember 1972; Die Bahr-Kohl-Gespräche 1970–1973.* Bearb. v. Hanns Jürgen Küsters, Monika Kaiser, Hans-Heinrich Jansen and Daniel Hofmann, 2 vols (Munich, 2004)

Dokumente zur Deutschlandpolitik, ed. Bundesministerium des Inneren u. vom Bundesarchiv. VI. Reihe, vol. IV: 1. Januar 1975 bis 31. Dezember 1976. Bearb. v.

Hans-Heinrich Jansen, Monika Kaiser in Verbindung mit Daniel Hofmann (Munich, 2007)

Ehlert, Hans, Christian Greiner, Georg Meyer and Bruno Thoß, eds, *Die NATO-Option (Anfänge westdeutscher Sicherheitspolitik 1945–1956*, vol. III) (Munich, 1993)

Engler, Wolfgang, *Die Ostdeutschen. Kunde von einem verlorenen Land* (Berlin, 1999)

—, and Jana Hensel,*Wer wir sind. Die Erfahrung ostdeutsch zu sein* (Berlin, 2018)

Eschenburg, Theodor, *Jahre der Besatzung 1945–1949* (*Geschichte der Bundesrepublik Deutschland*, vol. 1) (Stuttgart and Wiesbaden, 1983)

Foschepoth, Josef, 'Antikommunismus in der politischen Kultur der USA und der Bundesrepublik', Bericht über den Vortrag in den Europagesprächen des Instituts für Geschichte der Universität Hildesheim und 10 Thesen zum Thema, 14 December 2009, at www.uni-hildesheim.de/de/43489.htm (15 April 2010)

—, ed., *Kalter Krieg und Deutsche Frage. Deutschland im Widerstreit der Mächte 1945–1952* (Göttingen, 1985)

—, ed., *Adenauer und die Deutsche Frage* (Göttingen, 2nd edn 1990)

François, Etienne, and Hagen Schulze, eds, *Deutsche Erinnerungsorte. Eine Auswahl* (*Schriftenreihe der Bundeszentrale für politische Bildung 475*) (Bonn, 2005)

Friedrich, Jörg, *Der Brand. Deutschland im Bombenkrieg 1940–1945* (*Spiegel* edn 45) (Hamburg, 2002)

Fuhr, Eckhard, with Nicola Kuhn, Hans-Ulrich Ronnger and Wolfram Weimer, *Geschichte der Deutschen 1949–1990. Eine Chronik zu Politik, Wirtschaft und Kultur* (Frankfurt am Main, 1990)

Fulbrook, Mary, *A Concise History of Germany,* 3rd edn (Cambridge, 2019)

Galkin, Aleksandr/Tschernjajew, Anatoli, eds, *Michail Gorbatschow und die deutsche Frage. Sowjetische Dokumente 1986–1991*, Quellen und Darstellungen zur Zeitgeschichte, vol. LXXXIII (Munich, 2011)

Gallus, Alexander, *Die Neutralisten. Verfechter eines vereinten Deutschland zwischen Ost und West 1945–1990* (Düsseldorf, 2001)

Gehler, Michael, *Europa. Ideen – Institutionen – Vereinigung* (Munich, 2005, 2nd extended edn 2010, 3rd extended edn 2018)

—, *Modellfall für Deutschland? Die Österreichlösung mit Staatsvertrag und Neutralität 1945–1955* (Innsbruck, Vienna and Bozen, 2015)

—, ed., *Vom gemeinsamen Markt zur europäischen Unionsbildung. 50 Jahre Römische Verträge 1957–2007. From Common Market to European Union Building./50 years of the Rome Treaties 1957–2007* (Institut für Geschichte der Universität Hildesheim, Arbeitskreis Europäische Integration, Historische Forschungen, Veröffentlichungen 5), unter Mitarbeit von Andreas Pudlat (Vienna, Cologne and Weimar, 2009) (see the contribution by Andreas Pudlat, pp. 521–40)

—, Rainer F. Schmidt, Harm-Hinrich Brandt and Rolf Steininger, eds, *Ungleiche Partner? Österreich und Deutschland in ihrer gegenseitigen Wahrnehmung. Historische Analysen und Vergleiche aus dem 19. und 20. Jahrhundert* (Beiheft 15 of the *Historischen Mitteilungen of Leopold von Ranke-Gesellschaft*) (Stuttgart, 1996; Innsbruck and Vienna, 2009)

—, and Ingrid Böhler, eds, *Verschiedene europäische Wege im Vergleich. Österreich und die Bundesrepublik Deutschland 1945/49 bis zur Gegenwart. Festschrift für Rolf Steininger zum 65. Geburtstag* (Innsbruck, Vienna, Bozen, 2007)

—, and Andreas Pudlat, eds, with Imke Scharlemann, *Grenzen in Europa* (*Historische Europa-Studien* 2) (Hildesheim, Zürich and New York, 2009); see the interview with Hans-Jürgen Grasemann, 'Die deutsch-deutsche Grenze aus juristischer Hinsicht', pp. 195–207

Geiger, Tim, and Amos Heike, eds, *Die Einheit. Das Auswärtige Amt, das DDR-Außenministerium und der Zwei-plus Vier-Prozess*, ed. Auftrag des Instituts für Zeitgeschichte München – Berlin (Göttingen, 2015)

Geppert, Dominik, *Die Ära Adenauer* (*Geschichte kompakt*) (Darmstadt, 2nd edn 2007)

—, and Udo Wengst, eds, *Neutralität – Chance oder Chimäre? Konzepte des Dritten Weges für Deutschland und die Welt 1945–1990* (Munich, 2005)

Gerhards, Jürgen, and Holger Lengfeld, *European Citizenship and Social Integration in the European Union* (London, 2015)

—, and —, *Wir, ein europäisches Volk? Sozialintegration Europas und die Idee der Gleichheit aller europäischen Bürger* (Wiesbaden,2013).

Görtemaker, Manfred, *Geschichte der Bundesrepublik Deutschland. Von der Gründung bis zur Gegenwart* (Munich, 1999)

—, *Die Berliner Republik. Wiedervereinigung und Neuorientierung* (*Deutsche Geschichte im 20. Jahrhundert 16*) (Berlin, 2009)

—, *Kleine Geschichte der Bundesrepublik Deutschland* (Munich, 2002)

Graf, Maximilian, *Österreich und die DDR 1949–1990. Politik und Wirtschaft im Schatten der deutschen Teilung* (Internationale Geschichte 3) (Vienna, 2016)

Gräf, Heinz, *Grenze durch Deutschland/ Frontier through Germany/ Frontière à travers l'Allemagne* (Düsseldorf, 1961)

Grafe, Roman, *Die Grenze durch Deutschland. Eine Chronik von 1945 bis 1990* (Berlin, 2002)

Grasemann, Hans-Jürgen, 'Eine Unrechtsgrenze in Europa. Die Zentrale Erfassungs-stelle in Salzgitter', at www.uni-hildesheim.de/de/35576.htm (10 May 2010)

Gritsch, Kurt, *Inszenierung eines gerechten Krieges? Intellektuelle, Medien und 'Kosovo-Krieg'* (*Historische Europastudien* 3) (Hildesheim, Zürich and New York, 2010)

Der Grosse Ploetz, *Die Enzyklopädie der Weltgeschichte* (Göttingen, 35th revised and expanded edn 2008)

Grosser, Alfred, *Die Bonner Demokratie. Deutschland von draußen gesehen* (Düsseldorf, 1960)

Grosser, Dieter, *Das Wagnis der Währungs-, Wirtschafts- und Sozialunion. Politische Zwänge im Konflikt mit ökonomischen Regeln* (*Geschichte der Deutschen Einheit in vier Bänden*, Bd. 2) (Stuttgart, 1998)

Gruner, Wolf D., *Deutschland in Europa 1750 bis 2007: Vom deutschen Mitteleuropa zum europäischen Deutschland* (Presa Universitarä Clujeana, 2009)

Guérin-Sendelbach, Valérie, *Frankreich und das vereinigte Deutschland. Interessen und Perzeptionen im Spannungsfeld* (Opladen, 1999)

Hacke, Christian, *Die Außenpolitik der Bundesrepublik Deutschland. Weltmacht wider Willen?* (Berlin, new and expanded edn 1997)

—, *Die Außenpolitik der Bundesrepublik Deutschland. Von Konrad Adenauer bis Gerhard Schröder* (Frankfurt am Main and Berlin, 2003)

Haftendorn, Helga, *Deutsche Außenpolitik seit dem Zweiten Weltkrieg. Zwischen Selbstbeschränkung und Selbstbehauptung* (Munich, 2001)

Hardtwig, Wolfgang, and Heinrich August Winkler, eds, *Deutsche Entfremdung. Zum Befinden in Ost und West* (Munich, 1994)

Hawel, Marcus, *Die normalisierte Nation. Vergangenheitsbewältigung und Außenpolitik in Deutschland* (Hannover, 2007)

Henrich-Franke, Christian, *70 Jahre Bundesrepublik Deutschland. Nationale Staatlichkeit im förderalen Europa* (Wiesbaden, 2019)

Helwig, Gisela, ed., *Rückblicke auf die DDR. Festschrift für Ilse Spittmann-Rühle* (Cologne, 1995)

Herbst, Ludolf, *Option für den Westen. Vom Marshallplan bis zum deutsch-französischen Vertrag* (Munich, 1989)

—, ed., *Unterwerfung, Kontrolle, Integration* (Munich, 1986)

Hertle, Hans-Hermann, *Chronik des Mauerfalls. Die dramatischen Ereignisse um den 9. November 1989* (Berlin, 11th expanded edn 2009)

Heydemann, Günther, and Heinrich Oberreuter, eds, *Diktaturen in Deutschland – Vergleichsaspekte. Strukturen, Institutionen und Verhaltensweisen* (Bonn, *Schriftenreihe der Bundeszentrale für politische Bildung*, vol. CCCXCVIII) (Bonn, 2003)

Hildebrand, Klaus, *Von Erhard zur Großen Koalition 1963–1969* (*Geschichte der Bundesrepublik Deutschland*, vol. IV) (Stuttgart, Wiesbaden, 1984)

Hilger, Andreas, Mike Schmeitzner and Clemens Vollnhals, eds, *Sowjetisierung oder Neutralität? Optionen sowjetischer Besatzungspolitik in Deutschland und Österreich 1945–1955* (*Schriften des Hannah-Arendt-Instituts für Totalitarismusforschung*, 32) (Göttingen, 2006)

Hockerts, Hans-Günter, with Elisabeth Müller-Luckner, *Koordinaten deutscher Geschichte in der Epoche des Ost-West-Konflikts* (*Schriften des Historischen Kollegs Kolloquien*, 55) (Munich, 2004)

Hoffmann, Dierk, and Michael Schwartz, eds, *Sozialstaatlichkeit in der DDR. Sozialpolitische Entwicklungen im Spannungsfeld von Diktatur und Gesellschaft 1945/49–1989* (*Schriftenreihe der Vierteljahrshefte für Zeitgeschichte Sondernummer*) (Munich, 2005)

Holtmann, Everhard, and Anne Köhler, *Wiedervereinigung vor dem Mauerfall. Einstellung der Bevölkerung der DDR im Spiegel geheimer westlicher Meinungsumfragen* (Bonn, 2016)

Ihme-Tuchel, Beate, *Die DDR: Kontroversen um die Geschichte* (Darmstadt, 2nd edn 2007)

Jäger, Wolfgang, and Werner Link, *Republik im Wandel 1974–1982. Die Ära Schmidt* (*Geschichte der Bundesrepublik Deutschland*, vol. V/2) (Stuttgart and Mannheim, 1987)

—, *Die Überwindung der Teilung. Der innerdeutsche Prozeß der Vereinigung 1989/90* (*Geschichte der Deutschen Einheit in vier Bänden*, vol. III) (Stuttgart, 1998)

Jansen, Thomas, *Die Entstehung einer Europäischen Partei. Vorgeschichte, Gründung und Entwicklung der EVP* (Bonn, 1996)

Jarausch, Konrad, *Die Umkehr. Deutsche Wandlungen 1945–1995* (*Schriftenreihe der Bundeszentrale für politische Bildung*, vol. DCLVII) (Bonn, 2004)

Jesse, Eckhard, *Die Demokratie der Bundesrepublik Deutschland. Eine Einführung in das politische System* (Berlin, 6th edn 1982)

Kagan, Robert, 'The New Question. What Happens When Europe Comes Apart?', in *Foreign Affairs*, vol. 98/3 (May/June 2019), pp. 108–120

Klessmann, Christoph, *Zwei Staaten, eine Nation. Deutsche Geschichte 1955–1970* (*Schriftenreihe der Bundeszentrale für politische Bildung*, vol. CCCXLIII (Bonn, 2nd expanded edn 1997)

—, *Die doppelte Staatsgründung. Deutsche Geschichte 1945–1955* (Göttingen, 5th expanded edn 1991)

—, and Peter Lautzas, eds, *Teilung und Integration. Die doppelte deutsche Nachkriegsgeschichte* (Schriftenreihe der Bundeszentrale für politische Bildung, vol. 482) (Bonn, 2005)

Knabe, Hubertus, *17. Juni 1953. Ein deutscher Aufstand* (Berlin, 2004)

—, *Die Täter sind unter uns. Über das Schönreden der SED-Diktatur* (Berlin, 2007)

—, *Honeckers Erben. Die Wahrheit über die Linke* (Berlin, 2009)

Kohl, Helmut, *Erinnerungen 1930–1982* (Munich, 2004)

—, *Erinnerungen 1982–1990* (Munich, 2005)

Köhler, Henning, *Adenauer. Eine politische Biographie* (Frankfurt am Main and Berlin, 1994)

Korte, Karl-Rudolf, *Deutschlandpolitik in Helmut Kohls Kanzlerschaft. Regierungsstil und Entscheidungen 1982–1989* (*Geschichte der Deutschen Einheit in vier Bänden*, vol. 1) (Stuttgart, 1998)

—, and Manuel Fröhlich, *Politik und Regieren in Deutschland, Strukturen, Prozesse, Entscheidungen*, 3rd edition (Paderborn, 2009)

—, *Die Bundestagswahl 2017. Analysen der Wahl-, Parteien-, Kommunikations- und Regierungsforschung*, ed. Jan Schoofs (Wiesbaden, 2019)

Kossert, Andreas, *Kalte Heimat. Die Geschichte der Deutschen Vertriebenen nach 1945* (Berlin, 2009)

Kowalczuk, Ilko-Sascha, *Endspiel. Die Revolution von 1989 in der DDR* (Munich, 2009)

Kraushaar, Wolfgang, ed., *Die RAF. Entmythologisierung einer terroristischen Organisation*, Bonn (Schriftenreihe der Bundeszentrale für politische Bildung, vol. 657) (2008)

Küsters, Hanns Jürgen, and Daniel Hofmann, *Dokumente zur Deutschlandpolitik. Deutsche Einheit. Sonderedition aus den Akten des Bundeskanzleramtes 1989/90* (Munich, 1998)

—, *Die Gründung der Europäischen Wirtschaftsgemeinschaft* (Baden-Baden, 1982)

—, *Der Integrationsfriede. Viermächte-Verhandlungen über die Friedensregelung mit Deutschland 1945–1990* (*Dokumente zur Deutschlandpolitik Studien*, 9) (Munich, 2000)

Lappenküper, Ulrich, *Die Außenpolitik der Bundesrepublik Deutschland 1949 bis 1990* (*Enzyklopädie Deutscher Geschichte*, 83) (Munich, 2008)

—, *Die deutsch-französischen Beziehungen 1949–1963. Von der Erbfeindschaft zur 'Entente élémentaire'*, 2 vols (Munich, 2001)

Lehmann, Hans Georg, *Deutschland-Chronik 1945 bis 2000 (Schriftenreihe der Bundeszentrale für politische Bildung*, vol. 366) (Bonn, 2000)

Lehmann, Ines, *Die Außenpolitik der DDR 1989/90. Eine dokumentierte Rekonstruktion* (Baden-Baden, 2010)

Lemke, Christiane, *Die Ursachen des Umbruchs 1989. Politische Sozialisation in der ehemaligen DDR* (Darmstadt, 1991)

Leonhard, Nina, *Integration und Gedächtnis. NVA-Offiziere im vereinigten Deutschland* (Konstanz, 2016)

Lever, Paul, *Berlin Rules: Europe and the German Way* (London and New York, 2018)

Lohse, Eckart, and Mark Wehner, *Rosenkrieg. Die große Koalition 2005–2009* (Cologne, 2009)

Loth, Wilfried, *Helsinki, 1. August 1975. Entspannung und Abrüstung (20 Tage im 20. Jahrhundert)* (Munich, 1998)

—, *Stalins ungeliebtes Kind. Warum Moskau die DDR nicht wollte* (Berlin, 1994)

—, *Die Teilung der Welt. Geschichte des Kalten Krieges 1941–1955* (Munich, 2000)

Maelstaf, Geneviève, *Que faire de l'Allemagne? Les responsables français, le statut international de l'Allemagne et le problème de l'unité allemande (1945–1955) (Direction des Archives Ministère des Affaires Étrangères)* (Paris, 1998)

Mann, Golo, *Deutsche Geschichte des 19. und 20. Jahrhunderts* (Frankfurt am Main, 1958)

Mastny, Vojtech, and Gustav Schmidt, *Konfrontationsmuster des Kalten Krieges 1946 bis 1956* (Munich, 2003)

Mau, Steffen, *Lütten Klein. Leben in der ostdeutschen Transformationsgesellschaft* (Berlin, 2019)

Mayer, Tilman, ed., *20 Jahre Deutsche Einheit. Erfolge, Ambivalenzen, Probleme (Schriftenreihe der Gesellschaft für Deutschlandforschung 97)* (Berlin, 2010)

Mertens, Lothar, *Bilanz und Perspektiven des deutschen Vereinigungsprozesses (Schriftenreihe der Gesellschaft für Deutschlandforschung*, vol. xc) (Berlin, 2006)

Metz, Andreas, *Die ungleichen Gründerväter. Adenauers und Erhards langer Weg an die Spitze der Bundesrepublik* (Konstanz, 1998)

Morsey, Rudolf, *Die Bundesrepublik Deutschland. Entstehung und Entwicklung bis 1969 (Oldenbourg Grundriss*, 19) (Munich, 5th expanded edn 2007)

Mueller, Wolfgang, Michael Gehler and Arnold Suppan, eds, *The Revolutions of 1989: A Handbook* (Vienna, 2015)

Müller, Helmut M., with Karl Friedrich Krieger, Hanna Vollrath and Meyers Lexikonredaktion, *Schlaglichter der deutschen Geschichte (Schriftenreihe der Bundeszentrale für politische Bildung*, 615) (Bonn, 1990, 1993, 2002, 2009)

Müller, Uwe, and Grit Hartmann, *Vorwärts und Vergessen! Kader, Spitzel und Komplizen: Das gefährliche Erbe der SED-Diktatur* (Berlin, 2009)

Neubert, Ehrhart, *Geschichte der Opposition in der DDR 1949–1989* (Berlin, 1997)

Oplatka, Andreas, *Der erste Riss in der Mauer. September 1989 – Ungarn öffnet die Grenze* (Vienna, 2009)

Osterroth, Franz, and Dieter Schuster, *Chronik der deutschen Sozialdemokratie,*
Band III: Nach dem Zweiten Weltkrieg (Berlin, 1975)

Overesch, Manfred, *Buchenwald und die DDR oder die Suche nach Selbstlegitimation*
(*Sammlung Vandenhoeck*) (Göttingen, 1995)

Pfetsch, Frank R., *Die Außenpolitik der Bundesrepublik 1949–1992* (Munich, 2nd
expanded edn 1993)

Port, Andrew I., *Conflict and Stability in the German Democratic Republic* (New York, 2007)

—, *Die rätselhafte Stabilität der DDR. Arbeit und Alltag im sozialistischen Deutschland*
(Berlin, 2nd edn 2010)

Pötzl, Norbert F., *Der Treuhandkomplex. Legenden. Fakten. Emotionen* (Hamburg, 2019)

Rathgeb, Eberhard, *Deutschland kontrovers. Debatten 1945 bis 2005* (*Schriftenreihe der*
Bundeszentrale für politische Bildung, vol. 494) (Bonn, 2005)

Recker, Marie-Luise, *Geschichte der Bundesrepublik Deutschland* (Munich, 3rd extended
edn 2009)

Reutter, Werner, ed., *Germany on the Road to 'Normalcy': Policies and Politics of the*
Red-Green Federal Government (1998–2002) (New York, 2004)

Rittberger, Volker, ed., *German Foreign Policy since Unification: Theories and Case*
Studies (Manchester and New York, 2001)

Ritter, Gerhard, *Der Preis der deutschen Einheit. Die Wiedervereinigung und die Krise des*
Sozialstaats (Munich, 2006)

Rödder, Andreas, *Deutschland einig Vaterland. Die Geschichte der Wiedervereinigung*
(Munich, 2009)

—, *Die Bundesrepublik Deutschland 1969–1990* (*Oldenbourg Grundriss der Geschichte,*
vol. 19A) (Munich, 2004)

Ruggenthaler, Peter, ed., *Stalins großer Bluff. Die Geschichte der Stalin-Note in*
Dokumenten der sowjetischen Führung (*Schriftenreihe der Vierteljahrshefte für*
Zeitgeschichte, 95) (Munich, 2007)

Rupieper, Hermann-Josef, *Der besetzte Verbündete. Die amerikanische*
Deutschlandpolitik 1949–1955 (Opladen, 1991)

Sabrow, Martin, *Erinnerungsorte der DDR* (Munich, 2009)

—, *Wohin treibt die DDR-Erinnerung? Dokumentation einer Debatte* (Göttingen, 2007)

Schabert, Tilo, *Wie Weltgeschichte gemacht wird. Frankreich und die deutsche Einheit*
(Stuttgart, 2002)

Schildt, Axel, and Arnold Sywottek, eds, *Modernisierung im Wiederaufbau. Die*
westdeutsche Gesellschaft der 50er Jahre (*Politik- und Gesellschaftsgeschichte,*
Forschungsinstitut der Friedrich-Ebert-Stiftung, vol. XXXIII, ed. Dieter Dowe und
Michael Schneider) (Bonn, 1993)

Schöllgen, Gregor, *Angst vor der Macht. Die Deutschen und ihre Außenpolitik* (Berlin, 1993)

—, *Der Auftritt. Deutschlands Rückkehr auf die Weltbühne* (Munich, 2004)

—, *Die Außenpolitik der Bundesrepublik Deutschland* (Munich, 3rd edn 2004)

Schröder, Hans-Jürgen, ed., *Marshallplan und westdeutscher Wiederaufstieg. Positionen*
– Kontroversen (Stuttgart, 1990); see the contributions by Werner Abelshauser,
pp. 97–113; 150–78.

Schroeder, Klaus, *Der SED-Staat. Geschichte und Strukturen der DDR* (*Bayerische Landeszentrale für politische Bildungsarbeit*) (Munich, 2nd edn 1999)

Schumacher, Joerg, *Das Ende der kulturellen Doppelrepräsentation. Die Auswärtige Kulturpolitik der Bundesrepublik Deutschland und der DDR am Beispiel ihrer Kulturinstitute 1989/90*, Dissertation, University of Hildesheim 2010.

Schwan, Heribert, and Rolf Steininger, *Die Bonner Republik 1949–1998* (Berlin, 2009)

Schwarz, Hans-Peter, *Die Ära Adenauer. Gründerjahre der Republik 1949–1957* (*Geschichte der Bundesrepublik Deutschland*, vol. II) (Stuttgart and Wiesbaden, 1981)

—, *Die Ära Adenauer. Epochenwechsel 1957–1963* (*Geschichte der Bundesrepublik Deutschland*, vol. III) (Stuttgart and Wiesbaden, 1983)

—, ed., *Die Bundesrepublik Deutschland. Eine Bilanz nach 60 Jahren* (Cologne, Vienna and Weimar, 2008)

Seidendorf, Stefan, 'Frankreich, Deutschland und die europäische Integration im Aachener Vertrag', in *Integration*, 42 (2019), 3, 187–204

Sieker, Ekkehard, Wolfgang Landgraeber and Gerhard Wisnewski, *Das RAF-Phantom* (Frankfurt am Main, 2008)

Sietz, Henning, *Attentat auf Adenauer. Die geheime Geschichte eines politischen Anschlags* (Berlin, 2003)

Staadt, Jochen, and Klaus Schroeder, *Die Todesopfer des DDR-Grenzregimes an der innerdeutschen Grenze 1949–1989. Ein biografisches Handbuch* (Frankfurt/Main, 2017)

Staritz, Dietrich, *Die Gründung der DDR. Von der sowjetischen Besatzungsherrschaft zum sozialistischen Staat* (Munich, 3rd edn 1995)

Steininger, Rolf, *Deutsche Geschichte. Darstellung und Dokumente in vier Bänden*, vol. I: *1945–1947*, vol. II: *1948–1955*, vol. III: *1955–1974*, vol. IV: *1974 bis zur Gegenwart* (Frankfurt am Main, 2002)

—, *Berlinkrise und Mauerbau 1958 bis 1963* (Munich, 4th expanded edn 2009)

—, *Eine Chance zur Wiedervereinigung? Die Stalin-Note vom 10. März 1952. Darstellung und Dokumentation auf der Grundlage unveröffentlichter britischer und amerikanischer Akten* (Archiv für Sozialgeschichte Beiheft 12) (Bonn, 2nd edn 1986)

—, *Wiederbewaffnung. Die Entscheidung für einen westdeutschen Verteidigungsbeitrag: Adenauer und die Westmächte 1950* (Erlangen, 1989)

—, *17. Juni 1953. Der Anfang vom langen Ende der DDR* (Munich, 2003)

—, *Berlinkrise und Mauerbau 1958 bis 1963. Mit einem Kapitel zum Mauerfall 1989* (Munich, 4th extended edn 2009)

—, *Der Kalte Krieg* (Frankfurt am Main, 2003)

—, and Heribert Schwan, *Helmut Kohl. Virtuose der Macht* (Mannheim, 2009)

Stern, Carola, and Heinrich August Winkler, eds, *Wendepunkte deutscher Geschichte 1848–1990* (Frankfurt am Main, 7th edn 1998)

Stern, Fritz, *Fünf Deutschland und ein Leben* (Munich, 2007)

Stickler, Matthias, 'Ostdeutsch heißt Gesamtdeutsch'. *Organisation, Selbstverständnis und heimatpolitische Zielsetzungen der deutschen Vertriebenenverbände 1949–1972* (Düsseldorf, 2004)

Stiftung Haus der Geschichte der Bundesrepublik Deutschland – Zeitgeschichtliches
 Forum Leipzig, ed., *Einsichten. Diktatur und Widerstand in der DDR* (Leipzig, 2001)

Stöver, Bernd, *Die Bundesrepublik Deutschland: Kontroversen um die Geschichte*
 (Darmstadt, 2002)

—, *Der Kalte Krieg. Geschichte eines radikalen Zeitalters 1947–1991* (Munich, 2007)

—, *Zuflucht DDR. Spione und andere Übersiedler* (Munich, 2009)

Stuhler, Ed, *Die letzten Monate der DDR. Die Regierung de Maizière und ihr Weg zur
 deutschen Einheit* (Berlin, 2010)

Suppan, Arnold, and Wolfgang Mueller, eds, *Peaceful Coexistence or Iron Curtain?
 Austria, Neutrality, and Eastern Europe in the Cold War and Détente, 1955–1989*
 (Europa Orientalis, ed. Institut für Osteuropäische Geschichte at the University
 of Vienna 7) (Vienna and Berlin, 2009)

Ther, Philipp, *Das andere Ende der Geschichte. Über die Große Transformation* (Berlin,
 2019)

Thiemeyer, Guido, *Die Geschichte der Bundesrepublik Deutschland. Zwischen
 Westbindung und europäischer Hegemonie* (Stuttgart, 2016)

Thränhardt, Dietrich, *Geschichte der Bundesrepublik Deutschland* (Frankfurt
 am Main, 1986)

Thoß, Bruno, *NATO-Strategie und nationale Verteidigungsplanung. Planung und Aufbau
 der Bundeswehr unter den Bedingungen einer massiven Vergeltungsstrategie 1952–1960*
 (Sicherheitspolitik und Streitkräfte der Bundesrepublik, vol. 1) (Munich, 2006)

Uhl, Matthias, *Die Teilung Deutschlands. Niederlage, Ost-West-Spaltung und Wiederaufbau
 1945–1949* (Deutsche Geschichte im 20. Jahrhundert 11) (Berlin, 2009)

Vinke, Hermann, *Die Bundesrepublik. Eine Dokumentation mit zahlreichen Biographien
 und Abbildungen* (Ravensburg, 2009)

Weber, Hermann, *Die DDR 1949–1990* (Munich, 3rd edn 2000)

Weber, Jürgen, *Deutsche Geschichte 1945 bis 1990* (Munich, 2004)

Wehler, Hans-Ulrich, *Eine lebhafte Kampfsituation. Ein Gespräch mit Manfred Hettling
 und Cornelius Torp* (Munich, 2006)

—, *Deutsche Gesellschaftsgeschichte*, vol. V: *Bundesrepublik und DDR 1949–1990*
 (Munich, 2008)

Weidenfeld, Werner, with Peter M. Wagner and Elke Bruck, *Außenpolitik für die
 deutsche Einheit. Die Entscheidungsjahre 1989/90* (Geschichte der Deutschen Einheit in
 vier Bänden, vol. IV) (Stuttgart, 1998)

Wengst, Udo, and Hermann Wentker, eds, *Das doppelte Deutschland. 40 Jahre
 Systemkonkurrenz* (Berlin, 2008)

Wensierski, Peter, *Die unheimliche Leichtigkeit der Revolution. Wie eine Gruppe junger
 Leipziger die Rebellion in der DDR wagte* (Bonn, 2017)

Wettig, Gerhard, *Bereitschaft zu Einheit in Freiheit? Die sowjetische Deutschland-Politik
 1945–1955* (Munich, 1999)

Winkler, Heinrich-August, *Der lange Weg nach Westen*, 2 vols (Munich, 3rd edn 2001)

—, *Geschichte des Westens. Von den Anfängen in der Antike bis zum 20. Jahrhundert*
 (Munich, 2009)

Wirsching, Andreas, *Abschied vom Provisorium. Geschichte der Bundesrepublik Deutschland 1982–1990* (*Geschichte der Bundesrepublik Deutschland*, vol. VI) (Munich, 2006)

Wolfrum, Edgar, *Die geglückte Demokratie. Geschichte der Bundesrepublik Deutschland von ihren Anfängen bis zur Gegenwart* (Stuttgart, 2007)

—, *Die Mauer. Geschichte einer Teilung* (Munich, 2009)

Zelikow, Philip, and Condoleezza Rice, Sternstunde der Diplomatie. Die deutsche Einheit und das Ende der Spaltung Europas (Munich, 2nd edn 2001)

Zentrum für Zeithistorische Forschung Potsdam/Stiftung Berliner Mauer, ed., with Hans-Hermann Hertle and Maria Nooke as project leaders, *Die Todesopfer an der Berliner Mauer 1961–1989. Ein biographisches Handbuch* (Berlin, 2009)

Acknowledgements

For the translation of the last new chapters I thank Otmar Binder, and for proof-reading the first edition I thank both him and Tjark Strich. Frank Binkowski supported me with additional information in completing the new chapter and finishing the indexes, for which I would also like to thank him.

Photo Acknowledgements

The author and publishers wish to express their thanks to the below sources of illustrative material and/or permission to reproduce it:

After Burrichter Clemens, Nakath Detlef and Stephan Gerd-Rüdiger, eds, *Deutsche Zeitgeschichte von 1945 bis 2000: Gesellschaft – Staat – Politik. Ein Handbuch* (Berlin, 2006): p. 59; after Hans Dollinger, ed., *Die Bundesrepublik in der Ära Adenauer 1949–1963: Ihre Geschichte in Texten, Bildern und Dokumenten* (Munich, 1966): pp. 13, 18, 47; photos Michael Gehler: pp. 42, 123, 206 (Deutsches Historisches Museum, Berlin), 210 (Miniatur Wunderland, Hamburg), 215, 292, 352; after Dieter Geiß, ed., *Der Große Ploetz: Die Enzyklopädie der Weltgeschichte*, 35th new and expanded edn (Göttingen, 2008): pp. 55, 104, 220; after Frank Grube and Gerhard Richter, *Die Grunderjahre der Bundesrepublik: Deutschland zwischen 1945 und 1955* (Hamburg, 1981): p. 90; photo Ludovic Marin/AFP via Getty Images: p. 340; Dr Otto May Collection, Hildesheim: pp. 56, 117, 152, 211, 242; after Andreas Rödder, *Die Bundesrepublik Deutschland 1969–1990* (Munich, 2004)/ *Statistisches Jahrbuch 2006 für die Bundesrepublik Deutschland* (Wiesbaden, 2006): p. 248; after *Statistisches Jahrbuch 2009 für die Bundesrepublik Deutschland* (Wiesbaden, 2009): p. 300; after Andreas Wirsching, *Abschied vom Provisorium: Geschichte der Bundesrepublik Deutschland 1982–1990* (Munich, 2006): pp. 161, 253.

European People's Party (EPP), the copyright holder of the image on p. 361, has published it online under conditions imposed by a Creative Commons Attribution 2.0

Index

Institutions

Adalet ve Kalkınma Partisi (AKP) 326–8

Alternative für Deutschland (AfD) 8, 311, 319, 324, 328, 329, 333–8, 343, 344, 358, 361, 365

artificial intelligence (AI) 304

Allgemeiner Deutscher Nachrichtendienst (ADN) 129, 201, 205

Allied Consultation Committee (ACC) 11

Arbeitsgemeinschaft der öffentlich-rechtlichen Rundfunkanstalten (ARD) 128, 129

Außerparlamentarische Opposition (APO) 136, 139, 140, 261

Bayerische Motorenwerke (BMW) 355

Brexit 8, 325, 329, 331, 332, 342

Bund Deutscher Mädel (BDM) 34

Bundesamt für Migrationsfragen (BAMF) 318

Bundesamt für Verfassungsschutz (BfV) 313

Bundeskriminalamt (BKA) 280

Bundesnachrichtendienst (BND) 315

Bundespresseamt (BPA) 289

Bundesverfassungsgericht (BVG) 84

Central Committee (CC)
    CPSU 175, 192
    KPD 89, 91
    SED 90, 91, 101, 155, 243
    SPD 89

Chief Executive Officer (CEO)
    Herrhausen, Alfred 247
    Sirven, Alfred 268
    Winterkorn, Martin 331

Christlich-Demokratische Union (CDU) 8, 21–3, 35–7, 49, 50–58, 64, 78, 79, 82, 84–7, 127, 129, 132–6, 140, 141, 147–9, 153, 155, 156, 165–7, 174, 177–82, 187, 190, 191, 211, 220, 221, 230, 233, 244, 254–6, 259, 263, 267, 268, 269, 272, 277, 279, 281–92, 298, 299–301, 303, 311, 312, 321, 331, 332, 333, 335–9, 343, 344, 353, 354, 358, 364

Christlich-Soziale Union (CSU) 8, 21, 22, 37, 49, 50, 57, 78, 79, 85, 87, 127, 129, 132–6, 140, 141, 146, 147, 148, 149, 153, 156, 165, 166, 177, 178, 179, 181, 182, 187, 188, 190, 191, 220, 230, 233, 244, 254–6, 259, 263, 267, 279, 281, 282, 284–7, 289–91, 298, 299–303, 312, 321, 331–33, 335, 337, 338, 339, 342, 344, 358, 364

Central Intelligence Agency (CIA) 116, 315

Committee for French Liberation (CFLN) 12

Common and Foreign Security Policy (CFSP) 249

Communist Party of the Soviet Union (CPSU) 175, 182, 192, 195, 196, 197, 204

Conference of Security and Cooperation in Europe (CSCE) 145, 150, 151, 156, 175, 195, 197, 201, 215, 223, 248, 249, 251

Conventional Forces in Europe (CFE) 176

Coronavirus 2019 (Covid-19) 365

Council of Mutual Economic Cooperation (Comecon) 41, 61, 76, 101, 120, 188, 238, 247, 348

Demokratischer Aufbruch (DA) 213, 220, 288, 289
Demokratische Partei (DP) 49, 50, 57, 79, 81, 85
Deutsche Demokratische Partei (DDP) 23
Deutsche Kommunistische Partei (DKP) 84, 140, 176
Deutsche Mark (DM) 41, 45, 60, 113, 162, 163, 199, 221, 231, 234, 235–6, 249–51, 258
Deutsche Presseagentur (DPA) 128
Deutsche Reichspartei (DRP) 137
Deutsche Soziale Union (DSU) 220
Deutsche Volkspartei (DVP) 23, 79
Deutsche Volksunion (DVU) 138, 246, 328
Deutscher Gewerkschaftsbund (DGB) 80
Die Tageszeitung (TAZ) 326
Diyanet İşleri Türk İslam Birliği (DITIB) 327
Diyanet İşleri Başkanlığı 327

Environmental Protection Agency (EPA) 330
European Advisory Commission (EAC), 11, 12, 46
European Atomic Energy Community (EURATOM) 108, 109, 111, 112, 150
European Central Bank (ECB) 308, 309, 342, 364
European Coal and Steel Community (ECSC) 68, 76, 108, 109, 150
European Communities (EC) 150, 187, 188, 198, 223, 249, 342, 349, 350
European Currency Unit (ECU) 156
European Defense Community (EDC) 70, 71, 95
European Economic Area (EEA) 1968
European Economic Community (EEC) 76, 108, 109, 111–13, 126, 150, 187, 198, 228, 342, 348, 350
European Financial Stability Mechanism (EFSF) 308

European Free Trade Association (EFTA) 150, 198
European Investment Bank (EIB) 332
European Monetary System (EMS) 156, 249, 250, 258
European Monetary Union (EMU) 250
European Stability Mechanism (ESM) 308, 309
European Union (EU) 8, 42, 72, 150, 223, 229, 247–50, 254, 266, 269, 270, 271, 272, 277, 293–6, 299, 302, 304, 307–9, 316–21, 324–33, 338, 339, 340–42, 345, 348, 350, 351, 357, 359, 360–65

Frankfurter Allgemeine Zeitung (FAZ) 128
Freie Demokratische Partei (FDP) 23, 36, 49, 51, 57, 78, 79, 81, 107, 118, 132, 134, 135, 136, 139–42, 146, 148, 155, 156, 158, 165, 166, 173, 177–82, 187–91, 212, 220, 230, 233, 244, 248, 255, 256, 279, 281–3, 285, 286, 286, 287, 290, 291, 299, 300, 303, 335, 337, 338, 343, 344
Freie Deutsche Jugend (FDJ) 78, 91, 92, 102, 124, 288
Freier Deutscher Gewerkschaftsbund (FDGB) 124, 237
French Liberation Committee (CFLN) 12
Frontierès Extérieures (FRONTEX) 321

Geheime Staatspolizei (Gestapo) 29, 30, 91, 100, 218
German Democratic Republic (GDR) 7–9, 24–8, 32, 42, 44, 48, 52–4, 58, 60, 61, 62, 63, 66, 67, 76–8, 80, 81, 83, 86, 87, 88, 89–107, 110–25, 127, 129–32, 135, 138, 142, 143–6, 150, 151, 153, 154–6, 160, 161, 162, 163–5, 170, 175, 177, 181–3, 186, 191, 192, 193, 194–226, 228–32, 234–41, 243–5, 255, 268, 282, 292, 295, 328, 346, 347, 348–54, 356, 358
Gross Domestic Product (GDP) 198, 235, 258, 359
Gross National Product (GNP) 189, 236, 355

Hezbollah 354

Implementation Force (IFOR) 252

information technology (IT) 257, 269, 303, 304

Intermediate Range Nuclear Force (INF) 181–3

International Military Tribunal (IMT) 28, 30, 34

International Monetary Fund (IMF) 308, 342

International Secutity Assistance Force (ISAF) 296

Islamic State (IS) 279, 322, 323

Kasernierte Volkspolizei (KVP), (GDR) 77

Kommunistisches Informationsbüro (KOMINFORM) 21

Kommunistische Partei Deutschlands (KPD) 19–21, 25, 43, 49, 50, 83, 84, 89, 91, 93, 100, 101, 213

Kosovo Force (KFOR) 265

Kreditanstalt für Wiederaufbau (Kfw) 354

Kulturbund (GDR) 124

Landwirtschaftliche Produktionsgenossenschaft (LPG) 92, 93, 237

Liberaldemokratische Partei Deutschlands (LDPD) 23

Mercado Común de Cono Sur (MERCOSUR) 198

Millî İstihbarat Teşkilâtı (MIT) 327

Ministerium für Staatssicherheit/ Ministry of State Security (Mfs) (GDR) 165, 218, 219, 237

Ministry of Interior of the USSR (NKVD, NKWD) 25, 30

Mouvement Républicain Populaire (MRP) 88

Narodnij Komissariat Wnutrennych Del (NKVD, NKWD) *see* Ministry of Interior of the USSR

National Security Agency (NSA) 315, 316

Nationaldemokratische Partei Deutschlands (NPD) 133, 135, 137, 138, 328

Nationale Volksarmee/ National People's Army (NVA) (GDR) 77, 78, 116, 153,205, 206, 218, 237

Norddeutscher Rundfunk (NDR) 128

Nordwestdeutscher Rundfunk (NWDR) 128, 130

North American Free Trade Association (NAFTA) 198

North Atlantic Treaty Organization (NATO) 71–6, 78, 85, 86, 109, 111, 112, 114, 115, 118, 125, 127, 151, 170, 174–6, 180, 181, 187, 191, 195, 223–5, 247, 248, 252, 255, 264–6, 270, 278, 282, 302, 330, 340, 348, 353, 356, 359

Oberkommando der Wehrmacht (OKW) 29

Office of Military Government of the United States (OMGUS) 18, 32

Organization of European Economic Cooperation (OEEC) 40, 41, 59

Organization of Petroleum Exporting Countries (OPEC) 157

Organization of Security and Cooperation in Europe (OSCE) 248, 251, 266, 330

Österreichische Volkspartei /Austrian People's Party (ÖVP) 44

Österreichischer Rundfunk (ORF) 130

Partei des Demokratischen Sozialismus (PDS) 217, 220, 221, 243, 256, 266, 278, 279, 291, 354

Patrioten Europas gegen die Islamisierung des Abendlandes (PEGIDA) 314, 329, 337

Rote Armee Fraktion (RAF) 141, 166–170, 247, 260, 279, 286

Schutzstaffel (SS) 26, 29, 30, 84, 138, 184, 222

Schweizer Rundfunk- und Fernsehgesellschaft (SRG) 130

Security Service (SD) 29, 30

Single European Act (SEA) 188

Soviet Military Administration (MAD) 20, 21, 25, 32, 46, 129, 131

Sozialdemokratische Partei in der DDR (SDP) 213, 220, 221

Sozialdemokratische Partei Deutschlands (SPD) 8, 19–21, 33, 35–7, 43, 49, 50, 53, 57, 65, 68, 78, 79, 81, 82, 85, 86, 89, 93, 95, 107, 109, 110, 129, 132–6, 139, 140–42, 146–9, 153, 155, 156, 158, 165, 166, 173, 176–82, 184, 187, 190, 191, 213, 219–22, 230, 233, 234, 241, 254–6, 258, 259, 260–63, 266, 267, 272, 274, 277, 278, 279, 281–5, 287, 290, 291, 292, 293, 298–301, 303, 311, 318, 331–3, 335, 337, 338, 343, 344, 353, 358, 362, 363

Sozialdemokratische Partei Österreichs (SPÖ) 43, 44, 318

Sozialistische Einheitspartei/ Social Unity Party (SED) 8, 20, 21, 23, 25, 28, 32, 37, 48, 49, 53, 54, 60, 61, 62, 67, 77, 78, 83, 88–96, 99, 100–105, 110–112, 115, 116, 118–25, 129–32, 152–5, 161, 162–165, 170, 177, 191–4, 196, 199, 200, 203–10, 212, 213, 214, 217–22, 234, 235, 237–41, 243, 245, 256, 288, 311, 337, 354, 355

Sozialistische Reichspartei (SRP) 84, 137

Stormtroopers (SA) 29, 30

Strategic Arms Limitation Talks (SALT) 151

Süddeutsche Zeitung (SZ) 128

Union of Socialist Soviet Republics (USSR) 12, 15–17, 35, 39–42, 44, 47–9, 54, 60, 61, 63, 66, 76, 77, 85, 86, 92, 94, 95, 101, 106, 111, 113–17, 120, 135, 142, 145, 151, 154, 175, 176, 181–3, 186, 192, 193, 196, 204, 208, 210, 216, 219, 224, 225, 228, 238, 247, 348, 349, 351, 353, 356

United Kingdom (UK) 17, 49, 126, 324, 325, 329, 331, 332, 356

United Nations Organization (UNO) 110, 146, 150, 262, 265, 266, 282, 341

United States of America (USA) 12, 16, 17, 35, 36, 39–42, 46–9, 54, 57, 59, 63–5, 68, 70, 71, 73, 75–7, 84–6, 102, 110, 112, 113, 125–7, 140, 142, 148, 151, 157–9, 166, 176, 182, 184, 196, 198, 225, 247, 252, 266, 75, 278, 281, 282, 298, 348, 349, 351, 353

Universal Mobile Telecommunications Systems (UMTS) 274, 286

Ushtria Çlirimtare e Kosovës (UÇK) 264, 266

Value Added Tax (VAT) 295

Volkseigener Betrieb (VEB) 61, 119, 131

Volkspolizei (VOPO) 77, 115, 116

Volkswagen (VW) 41, 85, 169, 245, 331

Waffen-SS 138, 184, 222

WeltN24-Gruppe 326

Westeuropäische Union/ Westeuropean Union (WEU) 71–4, 76, 114, 249

Westdeutscher Rundfunk (WDR) 130

Zweites Deutsches Fernsehen (ZDF) 64, 129, 130, 210

Zentrale Erfassungsstelle Salzgitter (ZEST) 164, 165

Persons

Abelshauser, Werner 60

Adam, Konrad 328

Adenauer, Konrad 20, 22, 31, 36, 38, 42, 44, 50, 52, 54–9, 63–5, 68, 70, 71, 74, 76, 78, 79, 81–8, 94–6, 98, 106–12, 114, 116–18, 121, 125–7, 129, 132, 135, 136, 139, 141, 142, 148, 151, 156, 160, 176, 184, 223, 225, 227–9, 241, 259, 348, 350, 354

Adorno, Theodor 100, 139

Agartz, Viktor 56

Ahlers, Conrad 118

Aichinger, Ilse 131

Albrecht, Susanne 168, 170

Altmeier, Peter 338

Amri, Anis 322, 323

Andreotti, Giulio 223

Andropov, Yuri 192, 196

Anlauf, Paul 218

Arnold, Karl 22

Attlee, Clement 16

Augstein, Jakob 336
Augstein, Rudolf 118

Baader, Andreas 166, 167, 169
Bachmann, Josef 140
Baerbock, Annalena 362
Bahr, Egon 117, 121, 143, 145–7, 165, 179, 351
Bahro, Rudolf 101, 154
Baker, James 224, 249
Barraclough, John 22
Barroso, José Manuel 294, 364
Barschel, Uwe 188, 190, 191
Barzel, Rainer 148, 156, 179, 190
Baum, Gerhart 178
Baumeister, Brigitte 268
Becher, Johannes R. 131
Beck, Kurt 292
Beckurts, Karl-Heinz 247
Begin, Menachem 64
Behrens, Fritz 100
Benary, Arne 100
Bender, Peter 7, 8, 351, 352
Benedict XVI, Pope 293, 303
Berbuer, Karl 39
Berghofer, Wolfgang 206
Bergmann-Pohl, Sabine 221
Bidault, Georges 88
Biedenkopf, Kurt 202, 268, 283
Biermann, Wolf 100, 132, 154
Bin Laden, Osama 278
Birthler, Marianne 219
Bisky, Lothar 299
Bismarck, Otto von 65, 240
Blair, Tony 262, 287
Blank, Theodor 74, 75
Bloch, Ernst 99, 100
Blücher, Franz 56
Böckler, Hans 81
Bohley, Bärbel 213
Böhme, Ibrahim 213
Böhnhardt, Uwe 313
Böll, Heinrich 131
Boock, Peter-Jürgen 169, 170
Borchert, Wolfgang 131
Bormann, Martin 29
Börner, Holger 261

Brandt, Willy 103, 109, 116, 117, 121, 133, 135, 141–4, 146–57, 160, 164, 166, 178, 180, 181, 211
Brauchitsch, Eberhard von 18, 190
Brauer, Max 49
Braunmühl, Gerold von 247
Brecht, Bertolt, 99, 131
Breuel, Birgit 238
Brezhnev, Leonid 101, 120, 192, 196, 197, 206
Brinkhaus, Ralph 364
Broz, Josip, Tito 21, 122, 264
Buback, Siegfried 167
Bush, George Sr 193, 214, 222
Bush, George W. Jr 278, 279, 281, 282, 293, 316, 359, 360
Byrnes, James F. 48

Cameron, David 332
Chernenko, Konstantin 192, 196
Chirac, Jacques 271
Chnoupek, Bohuslav 147
Churchill, Winston S. 15, 16, 39, 70, 96, 97
Clay, Lucius D. 23, 46, 49, 63
Cohn-Bendit, Daniel 261
Conze, Eckart 31, 86, 142, 182, 346, 349
Cyrankiewicz, József 144

Dalai Lama 293
De Gaulle, Charles 86, 108, 109, 117, 125–7, 184
De Maizière, Lothar 221, 226, 230, 289, 292
De Maizière, Thomas 292, 311, 318
Deckert, Günter 138
Dehler, Thomas 56
Delors, Jacques 223, 250, 365
Döblin, Alfred 131
Draghi, Mario 309, 364
Drenkmann, Günther 167
Dubček, Alexander 97
Dulles, John Foster 96, 181
Dutschke, Rudi 140

Ebert, Friedrich 48
Ehard, Hans 37
Ehrmann, Riccardo 209

Eichel, Hans 261, 263, 273, 286
Eichmann, Adolf 27
Eisenhower, Dwight D. 31, 96, 116, 125, 181
Eisenmann, Peter 276
Engholm, Björn 190, 191
Ensslin, Gudrun 166, 167, 169
Eppelmann, Reiner 100
Erdoğan, Recep Tayyip 271, 296, 326
Erhard, Ludwig 54–7, 78, 83, 88, 118, 121, 127,
    132, 133, 139, 141, 142, 359
Ertl, Josef 178

Falin, Valentin 224
Fechner, Max 99
Fischer, Joschka 260, 262, 264, 270, 271, 279,
    281–6, 354, 359, 361
Flick, Friedrich 188–91
Foschepoth, Josef 31, 52, 84
Frederick the Great 183
Frey, Gerhard 138
Frick, Wilhelm 29
Friderichs, Hans 189, 190
Friedrichs, Hanns-Joachim 210
Frisch, Max 279
Führer, Christian 207
Fukuyama, Francis 195, 359
Fürnberg, Louis 90

Gauck, Joachim 219
Gaudian, Christian 200
Gauland, Alexander 328, 336, 337
Gauweiler, Peter 296
Genscher, Hans-Dietrich 178–181, 153, 155,
    156, 202, 212, 226, 248
Gerassimov, Gennadi 204
Giscard D'Estaing 156, 158
Globke, Hans 115
Goebbels, Joseph 29, 196
Goethe, Johann-Wolfgang 352
Gorbachev, Mikhail 173, 180, 189, 190, 193,
    194, 195, 202, 214, 215, 220, 222, 223
Göring, Hermann 29
Graml, Hermann 52
Grass, Günter 131, 222, 350
Grewe, Wilhelm Georg 107
Gröhe, Hermann 364

Gromyko, Andrei 115, 143, 144
Grotewohl, Otto 20, 21, 53, 101, 110
Gruner, Wolf D. 69
Gueffroy, Chris 200
Guillaume, Günter 153
Gülen, Fethullah 327
Gurion, Ben 64
Gysi, Gregor 291, 299, 354

Habeck, Robert 313, 362
Habermas, Jürgen 185
Habsburg, Otto von 201
Haig, Alexander 170
Hallstein, Walter 106–9, 114, 122, 127, 135,
    343
Harich, Wolfgang 61, 99
Härtling, Peter 131
Hartz, Peter 283, 299
Havemann, Robert 99, 100, 154
Heer, Friedrich 159
Heinemann, Gustav 87, 109, 135, 155
Heinrich, Ingolf 200
Helbing, Monika 170
Helms, Wilhelm 148
Henkel, Olaf 328
Henselmann, Hermann 25
Hermann, Joachim 207
Hermlin, Stephan 131
Herrhausen, Alfred 247
Herrnstadt, Rudolf 96
Herter, Christian A. 116
Hertle, Hermann 210
Herzog, Roman 254
Hess, Rudolf 30
Heuss, Theodor 23, 51, 78
Heym, Stefan 131
Himmler, Heinrich 29
Hitler, Adolf 11, 12, 14, 22, 27–30, 33, 138, 216,
    224, 231, 293
Höcherl, Hermann 118
Höcke, Björn 336, 344
Hofmann, Sieglinde 169, 170
Hoffmann, Dierk 7
Hoffmann, Karl-Heinz 138
Hollande, François 364
Honecker, Erich 42, 89, 91, 102, 120, 125, 153,

154, 160, 161, 162, 163, 165, 182, 191, 193, 195, 198, 201, 203–5, 207, 212, 214, 215, 219, 291, 358

Horkheimer, Max 100, 139

Horn, Gyula 201

Huchel, Peter 132

Hüber, Sven 200

Huber, Wolfgang 293

Hupka, Herbert 148

Hussein, Saddam 251, 278, 281, 282

Ismay, Hastings, Lionel, 1st Baron 73

Jahn, Roland 219

Jedrychowski, Stefan 144

Jessup, Philip 48

John Paul II 293

Johnson, Boris 332

Jürgs, Michael 306

Kaiser, Jakob 19, 33, 34

Kant, Hermann 130

Kant, Immanuel 357

Kanther, Manfred 266

Kauder, Volker 364

Keitel, Wilhelm 29

Kemmerich, Thomas 343, 344

Kennedy, John F. 117, 118

Khrushchev, Nikita 61, 101, 102, 106 114, 116, 350

Kiechle, Ignaz 217

Kiesinger, Kurt-Georg 121, 132, 133, 135, 136, 142

Kindervater, Christoph 343

Kinkel, Klaus 248, 255

Kirchhof, Paul 290

Kirkpatrick, Ivonne 94

Kirsch, Sarah 101, 132

Kissinger, Henry 148

Klar, Christian 168

Klaus, Václáv 295

Kleßmann, Christoph 352

Klier, Freya 194

Knabe, Hubertus 240, 291

Koenig, Pierre 49

Koerfer, Daniel 56

Kohl, Helmut 42, 156, 177–82, 184, 187, 188, 191, 193, 196, 201, 202, 207–9, 211, 212, 214–17, 221–30, 232, 233, 242, 244, 248–50, 254–9, 267–9, 270, 277, 284, 289, 310, 349, 354, 359, 360, 365

Kohl, Michael 145, 146

Köhler, Horst 284, 289

Korte, Karl-Rudolf 336

Kossert, Andreas 59

Kossygin, Alexei 143

Krack, Erhard 216

Kraft, Hannelore 333

Kramp-Karrenbauer, Annegret 333, 338, 341, 343–5, 364

Krause, Günther 230, 289

Krawczyk, Stefan 194

Kreisky, Bruno 152, 153

Krenz, Egon 206–9, 212–14

Kretschmann, Winfried 312

Kroesen, Frederik 170

Krolikowsky, Werner 163

Kühnen, Michael 138

Külz, Wilhelm 23

Künast, Renate 286, 299

Kunert, Günter 132

Kunze, Reiner101, 132

Kurras, Karl-Heinz 139

Kurz, Sebastian 325

Lafontaine, Oskar 222, 233, 256, 262, 263, 291, 299, 354

Lambsdorff, Otto Graf 178, 189, 190

Langgässer, Elisabeth 131

Lappenküper, Ulrich 223

Laschet, Armin 344

Leisler Kiep, Walther 267

Lengfeld, Holger 329

Lenin, Wladimir 19, 91, 120

Lenk, Franz 218

Liebknecht, Karl 194

Ligachev, Igor 224

Limbach, Jutta 254

Loest, Erich 99

Lohse, Eckart 301

Lorenz, Peter 167

Loth, Wilfried 54

Löwenthal, Gerhard 130
Lubbers, Ruud 223
Lübcke, Walter 314
Lucke, Bernd 328
Luther, Martin 122, 183, 288, 293
Luxemburg, Rosa 194

Macron, Emmanuel 338–42, 364, 365
Mahler, Horst 260
Maleuda, Günther 213
Malik, Jakob 48
Mann, Heinrich 131
Mann, Thomas 131
Marcuse, Herbert 139
Marshall, George C. 39–41, 44, 53, 55, 56, 59, 160
Marx, Karl 193, 205, 213
Mastny Vojtech 76
Mazowiecki, Tadeusz 226
McCloy, John J. 31, 87
Maier, Reinhold 21
Meinhof, Ulrike 166, 167, 169, 261
Meins, Holger 169
Mende, Erich 148
Merkel, Angela 8, 248, 256, 269, 271, 281, 282, 284, 288–297, 299, 300, 302, 305–8, 310–12, 315–25, 328, 329, 331–6, 338–40, 342, 345, 358, 360–65
Merz, Friedrich 289, 290, 338, 344
Metz, Andreas 55
Mielke, Erich 203, 214, 218, 219
Milošević, Slobodan 30, 264
Mittag, Günther 163, 207
Mitterrand, François 184, 195, 223, 224, 365
Mock, Alois 201
Modrow, Hans 207, 208, 212–217, 219, 221, 224
Mohnhaupt, Brigitte 168, 170
Molotov, Vjatcheslav 40, 41, 261
Momper, Walter 216
Monnet, Jean 68, 126, 229
Morgenthau, Henry 59
Müller, Heiner 132
Müller, Helmut M. 163
Müller, Kerstin 262
Müller, Vincenz 77

Mueller, Wolfgang 41
Mundlos, Uwe 313
Münkler, Herfried 310, 319
Müntefering, Franz 281, 283, 284, 287, 291

Nagy, Imre 97
Németh, Miklós 201
Nixon, Richard 148
Nolte, Ernst 185
Norstad, Lauris 85

Obama, Barack 316, 360, 362
Ohnesorg, Benno 139
Ollenhauer, Erich 58, 65
Olmert, Ehud 296
Orbán, Viktor 318, 324
Özdemir, Cem 326

Pahlevi, Reza 130
Palaiologos, Manuel II 293
Palme, Olof 152, 153
Papen, Franz von 30
Petry, Frauke 328, 335, 336
Pfeiffer, Reiner 188, 190
Pieck, Wilhelm 21, 88, 89, 101, 121
Platzeck, Matthias 291, 292
Plenzdorf, Ulrich 132
Pleven, René 70
Poggenburg, André 336
Ponto, Jürgen 167, 168
Pöttering, Hans-Gert 294
Pudlat, Andreas 112
Putin, Vladimir 271, 285, 330, 360
Raab, Julius 114, 228
Ramelow, Bodo 311, 343, 344
Rapacki, Adam 113–15
Raspe, Jan-Carl 167, 169
Ratzinger, Josef 293
Rau, Johannes 254, 274, 289
Reagan, Ronald 181, 182, 184, 196
Regling, Klaus 308
Reichert, Karl 64
Reimann, Brigitte 132
Relotius, Claas 306
Renner, Karl 43
Reuter, Ernst 46, 49, 95